CONTRACTUAL ARRANGEMENTS, EMPLOYMENT, AND WAGES IN RURAL LABOR MARKETS IN ASIA

A Publication of the Economic Growth Center, Yale University

CONTRACTUAL ARRANGEMENTS, EMPLOYMENT, AND WAGES IN RURAL LABOR MARKETS IN ASIA

EDITED BY

HANS P. BINSWANGER AND MARK R. ROSENZWEIG

Yale University Press   New Haven and London

Set in Times Roman type by
Asco Trade Typesetting Limited, Hong Kong.
Printed in the United States of America by
The Alpine Press, Inc., Stoughton, Massachusetts.

Library of Congress Cataloging in Publication Data
Main entry under title:
Contractual arrangements, employment, and wages in rural
  labor markets in Asia.
  (Publication of the Economic Growth Center,
  Yale University)
  Bibliography: p.
  Includes index.
  1. Agricultural laborers—Asia—Addresses, essays,
lectures.   2. Asia—Rural conditions—Addresses, essays,
lectures.   I. Binswanger, Hans P.   II. Rosenzweig,
Mark Richard, 1947– . III. Series.
HD1536.8.C67   1983   331.7'63'095   83–5944
ISBN 0–300–03214–5

10 9 8 7 6 5 4 3 2 1

Contents

List of Figures

List of Tables

Foreword

This volume is one in a series of studies supported by the Economic Growth Center, an activity of the Yale Department of Economics since 1961. The Center is a research organization with worldwide activities and interests. Its purpose is to analyze, both theoretically and empirically, the process of economic growth and the economic relations between the developing and economically advanced countries. The research program emphasizes the search for regularities in the process of growth and changes in economic structure by means of cross sectional and intertemporal studies. Current projects include research on technology choice and transfer, household consumption, investment and demographic behavior, agricultural research and productivity growth, income distribution, labor markets, and international economic relations, including monetary and trade policies. The Center research staff hold professorial appointments, mainly in the Department of Economics, and accordingly have teaching as well as research responsibilities.

The Center administers, jointly with the Department of Economics, the Yale master's degree training program in International and Development Economics, primarily for economists in foreign central banks, finance ministries, and development agencies. It presents a regular series of workshops on development and trade and on microeconomics of labor and population and includes among its publications book-length studies, journal reprints by staff members, and discussion papers.

T. Paul Schultz, Director

Preface

Over the past forty years in most South and Southeast Asian countries the labor force has grown at an increasing rate. Moreover, the proportion of this labor force in agriculture has declined only modestly. In India it has actually remained constant at about 70 percent. At the same time, real rural wage rates have not risen rapidly, and in some regions they may have fallen.

Consumption studies, nutrition surveys, and micro and macro poverty studies have repeatedly drawn our attention to the tragic nature of the lives led by huge numbers of rural people whose major source of income is their labor power. Studying labor relations and the mechanisms that determine wages, employment, and earnings in rural areas is crucial to improving the welfare of the poor. Recognizing this fact, the Agricultural Development Council (A/D/C), the International Crops Research Institute for the Semi-Arid Tropics (ICRISAT), and the Ford Foundation sponsored a conference on "Adjustment Mechanisms in Rural Labor Markets in Developing Areas," which was held at the ICRISAT Research Center in Hyderabad, India, August 22–24, 1979.

Although improving the lot of poor people was a paramount concern of the conference, the authors of the papers included in this book as well as other conference participants were vitally concerned with the need for inclusion of empirically validated models of the rural labor market in all development theories in which agriculture plays a significant role. The track record of economists in developing these is not good. Conference discussions revealed not only that existing theories lack sufficient empirical testing but that researchers are clearly not in agreement as to the value of individual theories.

Development economists of the 1950s and 1960s were concerned with the rural work force primarily as a source of labor for nonagricultural sectors of the economy. Stylized facts of rural labor markets were built, as assumptions, into elaborate models of the intersectoral transfer process of labor without careful prior investigation of the empirical validity of such facts. Some of the theoretical models of the rural labor markets that were later built to justify these unvalidated facts are intellectual curiosities at best. With the availability of new and improved data, the 1970s have witnessed much more careful empirical work.

In organizing the conference, Hans Binswanger and Mark Rosenzweig hoped to contribute to the integration of theory and research in two ways. They hoped not only to integrate economic theory with empirical research but to bring about a rapprochement between economic theory and research and theory and empirical investigation in other social sciences. The conference papers and discussions demonstrated that some progress has indeed been made toward the first of these goals. However, the goal of integrating social with economic theories has yet to be achieved. Much remains to be done to attain a better understanding of both the causes of and the consequences for workers of social institutions and customs such as caste and sexual discrimination in labor.

A. M. WEISBLAT

Acknowledgments

We wish to thank A/D/C, ICRISAT, and the Ford Foundation for their generous support of the Hyderabad conference. In addition, we wish to express our gratitude to Abraham Weisblat (A/D/C), Leslie Swindale (ICRISAT), and Adrienne Germain (Ford) for their enthusiastic support of the project and to Mary Alice Price (A/D/C), N. V. N. Chari (ICRISAT), and the ICRISAT staff for carrying the major administrative burdens of the conference.

The papers selected for this volume are revised versions of some of those prepared for the Hyderabad conference. The only exception is the introductory essay, which was written after the conference. It incorporates the insights we gained from all the conference papers, the summaries prepared by discussion leaders, and the ensuing discussions, for which we would like to thank all the conference participants. We are also grateful for editorial assistance received from the ICRISAT editorial staff, Virginia Otis Locke, and Lois van de Velde.

HANS P. BINSWANGER AND MARK R. ROSENZWEIG

1

Contractual Arrangements, Employment, and Wages in Rural Labor Markets: A Critical Review

Hans P. Binswanger and Mark R. Rosenzweig

In recent years the economic development literature has shifted its focus to the rural sector of developing countries. Attention has turned from outlining the macro process of economic development to attempting to understand the role of institutions as well as the behavior of individuals and families in rural areas. In part this shift reflects the fact that the bulk of developing country populations live in the rural sector. In addition, the recent generation of an array of data sets—from intensive village studies to large-scale national surveys–along with advances in computer technology has facilitated more precise descriptions of these settings as well as provided the material that can be used to test assumptions, models, and hypotheses and thus to promote scientific progress.

The models and theories of the developing country rural economy that have evolved over the past thirty years have in general sought to do one of two things. Either they have tried to account for the existence of certain *stylized facts* that appeared to contradict the implications of competitive models, or they have attempted to provide the theoretical underpinnings for the assumptions that characterize the macro *surplus labor* models (Lewis 1954; Ranis and Fei 1961) that have dominated the development literature. Among the most popular stylized facts taken as data are (1) the coexistence of high unemployment and rigid wages, or discrepancies between the marginal product of labor and wage rates; (2) negative correlations between output per acre and farm size; and (3) the existence of share tenancy.

The papers presented at the A/D/C-ICRISAT Conference on Adjustment Mechanisms in Rural Labor Markets in Developing Areas, held in Hyderabad, India, in 1979, departed somewhat from the foregoing tradition.[1] These papers focused primarily on the determination of the earnings of

---

1. It has not been possible to include all contributions to the conference in this volume. But we will nevertheless refer to all papers presented, and those not included here are available from the authors. This chapter is based on a monograph of the same title (New York: Agricultural Development Council, 1981).

individuals in rural sectors of South and Southeast Asian societies, societies that share certain characteristics yet vary sufficiently to provide the contrasts that help illuminate the more fundamental regularities of rural labor markets. Although the papers' approaches and perspectives varied widely, one of their unifying themes was the characterization of the extent to which markets for the important factors of production in the agrarian setting operate, in particular labor markets, according to the principles of the supply-demand, competitive model. A second theme was the exploration of the nature of the sometimes unique institutional features of rural markets—sharecropping, other contractual arrangements, or even "institutional" wage rates. Do these features represent barriers to the efficient operation of markets? Are they optimal, albeit second-best, responses to exogenous, technically determined constraints on markets (market failure)? Or are they reflections of collusive or otherwise exploitive power relationships? By focusing on the underlying causes of institutional arrangements and the way such arrangements vary across different rural economic environments, the conference papers addressed an important policy question: How flexible is the response of institutional arrangements, as well as of labor market wages and earnings, when there are fundamental changes in the supply of or demand for the factors of production?

Much of the variation in rural wages and contract terms examined in the conference papers covered periods of five to fifteen years. General theories of development such as those of Arthur Lewis or Ranis and Fei, however, are concerned with trends of real rural wages over a much longer term. Such general models are silent as to the behavioral and institutional features of the rural sector. However, the wage determination and contractual choice theories of rural markets do not and cannot explain very long-term trends, because they treat the structure of technology and the sectoral composition of output as fixed. These theories also largely ignore the determinants of the reproductive processes and of the investments in human capital that underlie population growth and the growth and composition of the labor force. The conference specifically excluded from its agenda these very important issues—issues for which research must ultimately provide the linkage between the detailed, short-run models and evidence discussed here and a richer, more general theory of economic development.

Although the conference focused on the labor market, it is clear that employment and labor earnings are affected by characteristics of markets that do not directly involve labor. In a world of perfect markets for all factors of production (including credit and insurance), a person's annual income would simply represent the employment of his or her factor endowments valued at the market rate per unit. In such a world, the initial distribution of endowments among people—for given tastes and aggregate quantities of each factor—would uniquely determine the distribution of income among people.

Moreover, production—total output—would be not only maximal but unrelated to the distribution of factor ownership. Production techniques would be identical on all farms facing the same market environment and operating the same quality of land; for example, because output and employment per acre would be unrelated to farm size, barring scale economies, productive efficiency could not be improved by a rearrangement of factor uses or distributions. To explain labor earnings in a world of perfect markets with a given distribution of endowments requires that one explain the returns to each factor (wage rates, rent), a task for which the competitive supply-demand model has proved a powerful tool. The failure of one or more markets, however, would have serious implications for the distribution of earnings and productive efficiency and would probably mean that more complex models would be required for us to understand earnings determination. An important unresolved question is whether such models can outpredict the simpler competitive models when only some markets are imperfect or absent.

Attention to market failure, however, is important not only for understanding the determination of earnings and the achievement of productive efficiency. As we will discuss, and as many of the rural labor market conference papers suggested, it may also help us to understand the existence of and changes in the labor market's many and diverse institutional arrangements—different types of contracts and labor recruitment strategies and the interlinking of labor and one or more factors of production within one transaction.[2] Indeed, because of the general nonindependence, or interrelatedness, of all factor markets, market failures anywhere in the rural sector may have a significant effect on labor market earnings or arrangements even if the market for labor operates perfectly. In these circumstances, explaining earnings requires information beyond the determination of wages and labor supply.

This introduction presents a critical review of the existing literature on labor and other factor markets in rural areas. In particular, we look at the various models and theories of labor markets and tenancy and focus on the issues of absent markets, market failure, collusive power, and the interdependence of markets. A central theme arising from the review of these models and theories is that an understanding of institutional arrangements or imperfections in any one market (for example, the labor market) requires attention to the imperfections in or constraints on other markets (for example, the land or credit markets). We do not attempt an impartial treatment of all perspectives but emphasize the major lines of thought and recent empirical studies that are relevant to the concerns of the rural labor market conference. In addition, we discuss some important themes that we think the literature has neglected; in

2. Braverman and Srinivasan (chapter 3) define interlinked contracts as "transactions in more than one commodity or service made between the same pair of individuals and linked in an essential way" and add that "delinking the contracts would be infeasible or costly for at least one party."

concluding, we consider what, together, the conference papers and discussions suggest for future work on rural labor markets.

The theoretical and empirical literature that deals with the employment of labor and the determination of wage rates in rural areas of developing countries has been concerned with two major issues: How sensitive is aggregate agricultural output to the removal of agricultural laborers? Are there aspects of the rural labor market that bar the attainment of productive efficiency within agriculture? The first issue arises out of an essential assumption of some popular macro development models that, in the initial stages of industrialization, agricultural output will remain invariant in the face of the transfer of labor from agriculture to industry.[3] For the most part, the theoretical literature has posited rural labor market structures and/or models of peasant behavior that could make this surplus labor assumption true. Similarly, the empirical literature has been concerned with testing the validity either of this development model's assumption and implications or of those assumptions of the theoretical models of rural labor market behavior that were developed to rationalize the development model's assumptions.[4]

Two basic lines of thought characterize the surplus labor models of rural agriculture. According to the first, rural labor can be withdrawn from the agricultural labor market because there are large pools of unemployed or underemployed rural workers. The theoretical problem is to reconcile large-scale unemployment or underutilization of laborers with a nonzero wage for labor. Those who follow the second line of thought seek to explain the assumed insensitivity of agricultural output to the number of available laborers by distinguishing between that number and total labor supplied; this approach focuses on the labor supply behavior of the peasant household as well as on the labor market structure.

Nutrition and Efficiency Wages

The most influential surplus labor model that explains the coexistence of idleness and constant wages is the nutritionally based efficiency wage hypothesis elaborated first by Leibenstein (1957) and later by Mazumdar (1959), Mirrlees (1975), and Stiglitz (1976). This model assumes that at low levels of income there is a technically determined, positive relationship between nutri-

3. The literature on planning models and benefit-cost analysis of projects is also centrally concerned with the issue of the opportunity cost of withdrawing labor from agriculture.

4. See, for example, Jorgenson (1966, 1967), T. W. Schultz (1964), or Paglin (1975). In contrast to the empirical papers presented in this volume, most of the earlier work was carried out with data on macro-level aggregates.

tional level and labor effort per unit of time (or per laborer).[5] Direct empirical tests of this relationship are extremely rare. The most rigorous experimental study, of sugarcane workers laboring under actual field conditions in Guatemala, concludes: "Increased energy availability did not result in increased energy expenditure at work, or in increased supply of work units" (Immink and Viteri 1981, p. 251).

Given certain (weak) assumptions about the characteristics of the income-nutrition-effort relation, there is a unique wage—the *efficiency wage*—that minimizes the cost per unit of labor effort.[6] If farmers in surplus labor economies are to maximize their profits they must hire laborers until the marginal value product of total effort hired (expressed in efficiency units) is equal to the efficiency wage. In such a setting some workers will be left unemployed. They may be willing to work at a wage lower than the efficiency wage but, owing to the reduction in effort associated with lowered wages, it is not profitable for farmers to hire them no matter how much wages per unit of time are bid down. Given the goal of profit maximization, the large numbers of laborers relative to the amount of land, and the assumed (nonbehavioral) relation between level of nutrition and effort, it is clear that unemployment and positive—even high—wage rates will coexist. Moreover, removal of laborers from this system will affect neither output nor wages. Of course, if the marginal value product of the last laborer hired exceeds the efficiency wage and no more idle laborers are available, the wage rate will rise and the conventional supply-demand framework will pertain.

The problem with the profit-maximizing nutrition-wage version of the efficiency wage model is that in conditions of abject poverty, the unemployment equilibrium described cannot exist in the long run, for unemployed workers will have no means of survival. Three additional assumptions must thus be made to avoid a Malthusian result. Leibenstein (1957) assumes that because of social pressures, landlords will collude to lower wages, *sacrificing* profits and total output in order to support more people in the economy. He thus provides a rigorous definition of underemployment, if not a realistic model of the rural economy: those additional people who obtain wage work as a result of the collusive wage reduction below the profit-maximizing (efficiency wage) level are underemployed in the sense that their transfer out of agriculture will not lower output. Stiglitz (1976) achieves the same result by assuming that family farms have egalitarian concerns about the consumption of family members, but his model does not consider what happens to unemployed, landless workers.

5. As Bliss and Stern (1978) stress, a relationship that is not technical is almost impossible to test empirically.

6. The theory assumes that labor can be measured in efficiency units. As Binswanger (1978*b*, Appendix 5-1) has pointed out, this may not be possible when there are more than two factors of production.

In both versions of the nutrition-wage theory, because at any given time consumption determines the amount of labor effort supplied to work, utility maximization and profit maximization are incompatible. Equalizing consumption among workers (Leibenstein) or between workers and nonworkers in the family (Stiglitz) lowers effort and thus profits. Moreover, in both models the subtraction of laborers actually *increases* output since average consumption, and thus total effort, increases. As a result, the marginal product of labor is negative even though wages are positive.

Another way to deal with the issue of the possible starvation of unemployed, landless workers is to assume that the unemployed have a fallback option in self-employment activities—for example, hunting and gathering, or nonagricultural enterprises like mat weaving—that assure them survival at a lower utility than the agricultural wage. Such a model can indeed account for the coexistence of unemployment and a positive wage. However, because the marginal product of unemployed workers must be positive, they cannot be withdrawn to the industrial sector at zero cost. Furthermore, the supply of such workers will not be infinitely elastic at a wage equal to their marginal product in hunting and gathering: limits on the hunting and gathering grounds imply that withdrawal of some of the self-employed will lead to a higher marginal product, from self-employment, of the remaining workers.

The third way to "save" the nutritionally determined efficiency wage model is to assume that it holds seasonally (Rodgers 1975). At times of the year when labor demand is very low, the efficiency wage is the floor below which wage rates do not fall despite high (seasonal) unemployment. At other times, when labor demand is relatively high, the conventional supply demand framework holds. Based on a careful review of the nutrition literature, however, Bliss and Stern (1978) conclude that the relationship between nutritional intake and effort must be weak over short periods because the human body stores nutrients. It is unlikely, therefore, that a nutrition-effort association has any bearing on daily wage contracts. Furthermore, restricting the nutrition-wage theory to slack-season labor market phenomena clearly limits its empirical importance and, in the absence of estimates of the relationship between technical wages and the nutrition-effort ratio, makes detection of its relevance more difficult. Empirically, year-long open unemployment appears not to be a marked phenomenon in rural labor markets (Hansen 1969; Paglin 1965; Rosenzweig 1980). However, the absence of such open unemployment would seem consistent both with some versions of the efficiency wage model and with conventional competitive market theories.

Rodgers (1975) has attempted the most ambitious tests of the nutrition-wage framework, exploiting one of the theory's implications not emphasized by its advocates—namely, that employers will pay attention to workers' actual consumption. Thus, workers with dependents will need higher nutritionally based wages than unattached workers. Similarly, workers from landed households—households with rental income from land—would be better fed than landless workers and thus would supply the same effort as the latter but for a lower wage.[7] Rodgers finds that in one group of Bihar villages, average wage rates for the *area* are higher where households are primarily Muslim, that is, where women tend not to be workers. Although this evidence is consistent with the notion that employers pay higher wages to males who have more dependents, it is also predicted by the supply demand model in which male and female laborers are substitute factors in production. Rosenzweig's study of Indian district-level data based on a supply-demand framework (chapter 11) indicates that both male and female wage rates in agriculture are higher where Muslim households are prevalent. The hypothesis of *individual* heterogeneity in wages as a function of landownership or number of dependents is rejected in Rosenzweig (1980). The hypothesis is also inconsistent with the uniformity of wages for daily paid adult workers found (for a given sex and operation) by Bardhan and Rudra (1981) in West Bengal villages, by Binswanger et al. (chapter 8) in semiarid India, and by White and Makali (1979) in West Java villages.

Rodgers also points out that the nutrition-wage theory might account for labor-tying arrangements if effort is a function of sustained nutritional intake. But long term employment contracts (exceeding a few weeks) are not very common in the South and Southeast Asian countries (Bardhan and Rudra 1981; also chapter 8). When such contracts are entered into, they seem to be based on the demand for specialized skills on an assured basis—such as bullock driving or herding—and on workers' need for credit and problems of adequate collateral (Bardhan and Rudra 1981; Bhalla 1976; also chapter 8). Moreover, nutritional considerations cannot explain the absence of long-term contracts for female workers.[8] Given the generally lower wage rate for women, nutritional considerations should apply to them as well as to men.

Models of efficiency-wage relations, when based on other than nutritional grounds, have been applied primarily to the nonagricultural sector. Can such models be applied to agriculture as well? With workers of equal productivity, the efficiency-wage relation could be based on *morale* effects—

7. Bliss and Stern (1978), however, show that this prediction holds only for two regions with separate labor markets. In one such region all workers have land; in the other all workers are landless. If landless and landed workers coexist in the same region, the prediction is ambiguous. Furthermore, Bardhan (1979c) builds a model in which no nutrition-efficiency relation exists but in which monopsonistic employers face recruitment costs (which are themselves a positive function of the unemployment rate). If appropriate assumptions are made about recruitment cost differences among workers, Bardhan's model makes the same prediction about wage differences among workers as does nutrition theory. Thus the model is one example of the situation in which an efficiency-wage relation arises out of nonnutritional considerations.

8. Bhalla (1976) notes an exception in Haryana where, after the green revolution and the advent of substantial wage and income rises, women were also offered longer term contracts. But this finding clearly cannot be attributed to the wage-nutrition relation.

workers receiving higher absolute wages are assumed to put forth more effort. In such a model, survival of unemployed workers could be assured if employed workers from landless households shared their incomes with unemployed household members; in this case, however, the efficiency of the worker would not depend on his or her own nutritional intake. To our knowledge, the only efficiency wage model that can account for both the coexistence of unemployment and positive wages and a zero cost of withdrawing labor from agriculture is based on such a morale effect of absolute wage levels on effort. However, this model has not been subjected to careful theoretical or empirical analysis and may be untestable.

In particular, an absolute morale-wage relation has simply been postulated, rather than derived from theoretical reasoning or empirical observation. It might be equally "reasonable" to postulate morale relationships in which effort depends on relative wages among different classes of workers or among different seasons. Clearly, the implications of such theories would differ from those of the efficiency wage theory based on absolute wage levels. The fact that the precise way in which morale effects arise has a strong impact on model predictions and testability can be illustrated by two more nonagricultural models that lead to a relationship between wages and efficiency and thus to the coexistence of unemployment and positive wages. These models focus on *labor turnover* and *information constraints*. The labor turnover model (Stiglitz 1974*a*) is based on the notion that firms paying higher wages have lower labor turnover. Thus raising wages from a low level could initially reduce turnover sufficiently to reduce efficiency labor cost as well. However, in agriculture most labor is on a casual or daily basis (chapter 8; White and Makali 1979); for casual labor to be so important, the costs of labor turnover must necessarily be low. As a result, the turnover model would appear to have limited applicability in agricultural labor markets.

The second model of an efficiency-wage relation is based on the possible screening function of wages (Weiss 1980). If laborers are heterogeneous—that is, if they have different levels of inherent efficiency—high-quality workers should have high opportunity costs in some self-employment activities, whereas low-wage workers should have low opportunity costs. Thus at very low wages, the pool of applicants will consist of only the lowest quality workers. As wages rise to progressively higher levels, the pool will start to include workers of higher quality. If firms have no way of distinguishing between high- and low-quality workers and cannot pay them accordingly, they will draw at random from the applicant pool. Raising wages produces a work force of higher quality, which brings us back to the predictions of the efficiency wage theory. In a peasant agricultural setting, where labor is largely casual, the model is difficult to apply since information about the quality of laborers resident in the village accumulates over time and is widely shared. Moreover, information can be acquired at low cost: a worker can be hired for

FIGURE 1.1 Major Efficiency Wage Theories and Surplus Labor in Agriculture.

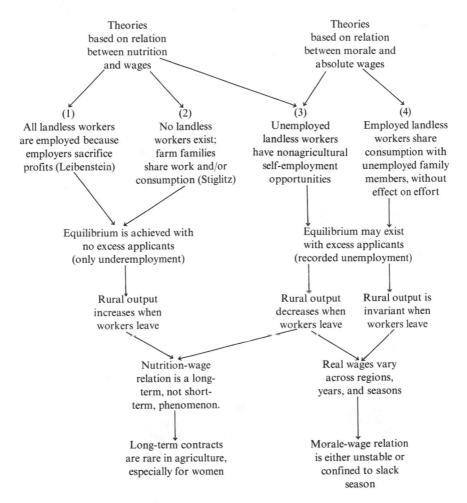

one day only. Note that in this model, unemployed (but self-employed) workers also have a positive marginal product and thus cannot be withdrawn from rural areas at zero cost. In the second major section of this introduction we will examine a similar model, that of Newbery and Stiglitz (1979), based on screening of potential tenants.

The assumptions and implications of the nutrition and morale versions of the efficiency wage hypothesis are summarized in figure 1.1. Note that because the turnover and screening versions are unlikely to apply in a peasant agricultural setting, they are not included in the figure. Variants 1 and 2 represent the nutrition-wage models of Leibenstein and Stiglitz, both of which rely on either landlord or worker altruism to achieve equilibrium. This equilibrium is characterized by underemployment rather than by open un-employment, and rural output increases as rural labor is withdrawn. When efficiency-wage relations are justified on nutritional grounds, an equilibrium with excess applicants can exist only if the landless unemployed have some nonagricultural self-employment opportunities in the rural areas that can prevent them from starving (see variant 3). If the efficiency-wage relation is based on morale effects, however, the landless unemployed can either rely on such self-employment or share in the consumption of their employed family members (see variant 4). The latter alternative is not possible in the nutrition-wage version without a loss in output.

Excess-applicant equilibrium is possible in variants 3 and 4 of the ef-ficiency wage hypothesis (see figure 1.1). However, it is only in the morale-wage model (where there is sharing and where morale effects depend on absolute wage levels—see variant 4) that rural output (agricultural and nonagricultural) is invariant despite the withdrawal of workers. Therefore, this is the only true surplus labor model.

No variant of the nutrition-wage model is likely to describe the behavior of rural wages or employment in Asia because nutritional intake is unlikely to affect effort appreciably in the short run and because short-term (daily) labor arrangements are the most common in Asian countries, particularly for female workers.

As we will see in the next section, incentives to greater effort can be provided to workers through a variety of sharing contracts rather than simply by means of an absolute wage. Furthermore, the wage-morale-effort relation is very difficult to detect. Since wages vary sharply across seasons, this relation either is not stable or applies only to the slack season. If the relation is unstable, the question becomes: What factors determine this relation at any specific time? Unless such factors have a stable impact on the relation, the theory is untestable and/or useless.

Our review suggests that major empirical facts are still not fully under-stood. By standard definitions, open unemployment is a reality in rural areas even though year-round unemployment rates appear to be low. However, seasonal unemployment rates are often much higher. Such rates also appear to vary substantially over the course of the year and to be inversely correlated with observed wage rates (Krishna 1975; also chapter 9). The partitioning of the effect of seasonal variation in labor demand into adjustments of wage rates and of unemployment rates cannot yet be explained by any of the theoretical frameworks proposed.

Labor Supply and Market Structure: The Duality Hypothesis

The alternative route to rationalizing the possibility that agricultural laborers will have a zero marginal product requires a distinction between labor time supplied and laborers. If the withdrawal of one family member (always or on average) leads other family members to increase their work to the extent that total work supplied equals that formerly supplied by the family, total output will remain constant. Thus the marginal product of labor time can be positive while the marginal product of an individual laborer is zero. Lewis (1972) evidently subscribes to this view. The theoretical issue then is: What model of the peasant *family* could account for this behavior? The empirical focus is on family labor supply determinants.

Following a long tradition of models of peasant farm families (Chayanov 1966), Sen (1966) proposes a model in which the family unit consists of workers and nonworkers who jointly maximize a family welfare function that contains, as arguments, each worker's leisure time and each family member's consumption. The family owns a fixed plot of land. Farm output and income are a function solely of total family labor time; family labor time cannot be sold in the market and labor time cannot be purchased. Assuming separability of the family utility function, Sen shows that when the number of workers is reduced, farm output remains invariant only if the marginal utilities of both consumption and leisure are constant within the relevant range so that the marginal rate of substitution between leisure and consumption is a constant.

Although the Sen conditions may or may not be plausible, it is important to note that they pertain to a farm household that is totally isolated from the labor market; indeed, the model assumes the absence of any rural labor market whatsoever. For households in which family members work for wages, however, the marginal rate of substitution between leisure and consumption is equal to the market wage rate; the latter varies independently of the individual household's behavior. Sen's condition that marginal utilities of leisure and consumption remain constant would thus lead to an indeterminate solution within the relevant range for a household with wage workers.

The inapplicability of the Sen conditions to households with wage earners—or in economies in which all households participate in the labor market—illustrates the importance of carefully choosing assumptions about the rural labor market in making predictions of peasant behavior, not the impossibility of completely compensating family labor supply behavior. Such compensation can arise in standard utility-maximizing household models. In a landless household that consists of identical workers with dependents (nonworkers), for example, a reduction in the number of family members (or the work time of one family member) will reduce the income (consumption) of every member but not the real value of time, which is the cost of leisure relative to the price of goods. In this case, the remaining workers will compensate according to the magnitude of the income effect on leisure, which is entirely an empirical issue. On the other hand, in a model with nonidentical wage workers (males and females, for example), it can easily be shown that the response of male (or female) work time to an exogenous change in female (or male) work time is equal to the ratio of the cross-compensated wage effect to the own-compensated wage effect; that is, the direction of response depends on whether male and female leisure times substitute for or complement one another in the family welfare function. Both United States labor supply studies (Schultz 1980) and Rosenzweig's Indian study (chapter 11) suggest that this cross wage effect on the labor supply is negative. Thus the creation of nonfarm employment will result in an increase in the agricultural work time of opposite-sex family members; some compensation takes place. However, neither these studies nor that of Barnum and Squire (1979), which assumes that family members are identical, indicates that family labor supply response will fully compensate for a reduction in the family labor force.

Sen's assumption of nonparticipation by households in the labor market, if valid, has at least two other important implications. First, among households with identical plots (size and quality) of land, the marginal product of labor will differ according to the households' preference orderings and to its demographic structure. In the absence of a well-developed market for land, these differential, "subjective" equilibriums will be inconsistent with the achievement of productive efficiency. Second, among households that cannot trade labor, increases in the price of output can lead to reductions in time worked (the dominance of the income effect) and thus in output supplied. This situation contrasts with that of the well-functioning market for all inputs (including labor), in which the price elasticity of output of individual farms must be positive.

If large-farm households can participate in the labor market while small family farms cannot, as long as the land rental market is also absent a *dualistic* agricultural economy results. This extreme dualistic assumption—that some farms maximize profits and utilize hired landless laborers whereas other, smaller farms use only family labor and do not participate in the agricultural labor market—is neither a necessary nor a sufficient condition for the existence of surplus labor. However, it is a popular explanation for the well-documented observation that small farms employ more labor per acre than large farms. (For a recent review of the literature on this last point, see Rudra and Sen 1980.) In this model, the cost of labor (wages) to large farms is likely to exceed the marginal rate of substitution between leisure and goods on isolated, small farms. As Sen points out, however, equilibrium in this "strong" version of labor market dualism requires the additional assumption that there be no transactions in land, since large landowners could increase their profits by leasing small plots of land to families, thus taking advantage of the families' low opportunity cost of labor. Given the failure of two markets, land and labor, a dualistic agricultural structure clearly is inefficient. The empirical evidence presented by Paglin (1965) for India and by Hansen (1969) for Egypt, which was confirmed by almost all the empirical studies reported on at the rural labor market conference, strongly suggests the impossibility of this extreme form of dualism in the Asian context. Members of small-farm households appear to participate substantially in the labor and land rental markets as both buyers and sellers.

Given the pervasive evidence on interfarm labor mobility within labor markets, more subtle hypotheses—which we will characterize as representing "weak" dualism—have been put forward to account for size differentials in output per acre in terms of labor cost discrepancies between large and small farms. The argument is that, given the uncertainty of agricultural production, employers of labor or sellers of labor from small farms (who may be the same persons) will be unwilling to make strong future labor commitments; there appears to be only a limited market for contingent labor contracts (Bardhan and Rudra, 1981). As a result, most labor is hired on a daily basis. Moreover, as Binswanger et al. (chapter 8) and White and Makali (1979) have shown, because of interfarm differences in the timing of operations, workers work for many employers during the year. Transaction costs associated with job search are thus quite high in the casual labor market, and there is substantial resorting of employers and employees each day. It is thus not surprising that the probability of finding employment or finding enough laborers on any given day is not equal to one. On small farms where people are primarily sellers of labor, days when workers cannot find market employment may be spent working on the land, up to the point where the marginal value of the utility of leisure, rather than the market wage, equals the marginal product of labor effort. On large farms, on days when not enough laborers can be found at the market wage rate, the marginal product of labor will exceed the market wage. Because of these frictions—or transaction costs—in the labor market, over the year the marginal product of labor can be lower on small farms than on large ones.

An important contribution made by the papers presented by Ryan and Ghodake (chapter 9) and P. K. Bardhan (chapter 12) at the Hyderabad conference is the computation of unemployment probabilities for wage labor. These researchers found that the proportion of working days on which sellers of daily agricultural labor reported they could not find wage work was 13–14 percent for male workers. (For female workers, included in the Ryan and Ghodake study, the figure was 21 percent.) P. K. Bardhan (1979b) also reports evidence that the probability of wage employment tends to influence the market participation behavior of women, not of men. Ryan and Ghodake have constructed a direct test of the "weak" duality hypothesis—that average opportunity costs of labor are greater on large farms than on small ones; this cost for the small-farm household is assumed to be the product of employment probability and wage. They find mixed results for male labor but confirmation for female labor because of the latter group's greater measured involuntary unemployment.

Frequent job matching and associated transaction costs constitute, of course, only one of the ways in which the rural labor market may depart from the perfectly competitive model. Others, consistent with the weak duality or *wage gap* assumption, are prejudices against wage employment—small farmers may "dislike" such employment, and there may be social pressures against it within certain groups or castes—and employer costs of supervising hired workers. The latter may be considered a scale diseconomy if one assumes that hired workers are used only if family labor time is insufficient to drive the marginal product down to the market wage. Again, however, the inefficiencies resulting from these labor market imperfections could be circumvented if the market for land were functioning perfectly. Indeed, as we will discuss in the next section, a major motivation for sharecropping is the problem of supervising hired labor (in the absence of a land *sales* market).

In summary, we note that strong dualism—that is, the absence of a rural labor market—is not necessary to achieve the labor surplus result of the Sen model. Maximizing models of the farm household in a perfectly competitive market setting can lead, theoretically, to fully compensatory labor supply behavior. The issue is entirely an empirical one, and the estimates by Rosenzweig (chapter 11) and by Barnum and Squire (1979) indicate less than full compensation. Thus neither strong nor weak dualism is either necessary or sufficient to yield the surplus labor result. Either assumption leads only to divergent opportunity costs of labor and therefore to differential factor use across farm sizes. Although there is little evidence to support strong dualism, both strong and weak dualism must assume that the land rental market has at least some imperfections. The tenancy literature that we discuss next addresses this topic.

TENANCY, SHARECROPPING, AND OTHER CONTRACTUAL ARRANGEMENTS

The literature that we have just reviewed, on the determination of wages and employment, takes the distribution of land as exogenously given—that is, it assumes that the sales or rental market for land is absent. In the rural economy, however, some labor is combined with land, not as a result of the temporary sale of labor services but as a result of the temporary acquisition of land. It is clear that the terms and arrangements associated with the market for land have a significant effect on the earnings of rural households and aggregate production. Four of the papers presented in this volume—two theoretical (chapters 2 and 3) and two empirical (chapters 4 and 5)—are part of a rapidly expanding literature on contracts that combine labor (and/or other factors of production) with land when certain factor markets are absent or incomplete. In general, the many theoretical models this literature proposes focus on two primary issues. First, what are the efficiency characteristics of a contract that provides laborers with a share of total agricultural output, an important contractual arrangement in the rural economy? Second, how do the welfare levels or earnings of such sharecroppers compare with those of laborers who work only for wages—that is, what determines the contract terms?

Recent Tenancy Models

If the sales market for land is absent or involves very high transaction costs, landowners can hire all cooperating factors of production, including bullocks and management, in quantities that are optimal for their own land. Landowners can then rent out any nonland factors owned that are in excess of these optimal quantities. Productive efficiency—equal factor ratios on all farms with land of equal quality—can still be achieved. Thus the absence of a sales market for land is not sufficient to force the use of tenancy. However, the institution of tenancy and the market for tenancies do substitute for the sales market. When there are no scale economies, at least one other factor market must be absent before the temporary rental of land becomes a necessary tool to achieve the most efficient factor ratios for all factors of production and all agents. The absent or incomplete markets (which require high risks or high transaction costs) may be those for insurance, family labor, bullocks, or managerial skills.

Economists beginning with Adam Smith have been occupied with the question of whether sharecropping, one form of tenancy, is a productively efficient system of cultivation as compared with either self-cultivation with the help of wage labor or fixed-rent tenancies. The classical economists, including Marx, understood sharecropping as an adjustment to the absence of markets or to market failure—in particular, the markets for credit and capital. Within a setting of imperfect markets, and on the premise that it is difficult to supervise labor, these economists viewed sharecropping as an improvement over wage labor because of its positive incentive effect. Because they share in the output, workers have an incentive to provide more labor than they might provide under a wage contract unless supervised very closely. The classical economists also recognized, however, that sharecropping provides the workers with less incentive to work than a fixed-rate tenant or an owner-cultivator would have. As discussed formally in Alfred Marshall's famous footnote in his *Principles of Economics*, on an exogenously given area of land and with a given share of output, the worker receives only a fraction of his marginal product, that fraction being equal to his or her share. (As Jaynes shows in chapter 2, Marshall's theory of sharecropping was a complete classical theory, and the footnote illustrates only the incentive problem.) The classical economists also understood that the same incentive problem applies to all other inputs and especially to long-term investments in land quality. As a result, they regarded long-term tenancy at a fixed rate as a superior system to sharecropping if a country's or region's level of development permitted it.

Cheung's (1968, 1969) work was the basis for the more recent sharecropping literature[9] because it established the major reasons for share tenancy and the major issues to be addressed. His work both attacked the negative efficiency (incentive) implication of sharecropping and broadened the scope of inquiry of the sharecropping literature to include discussion of the manner in which size of tenancy and share of crop are determined. Cheung and all subsequent writers on the subject have regarded both tenancy size and share level as endogenous to a particular model, while they have taken the wage rate as exogenously given. Contract terms, but not the wage rate, are thus determined by economic forces, and the equilibrium solution to the contract choice problem is maximization by both landlord and worker. The worker's equilibrium requires that "of the set of contracts available in the economy, there [exist] none which the individual worker prefers to the one which he has" (Stiglitz 1974*b*, p. 222). The landlord's equilibrium implies that "there exists no subset [of the available contracts] which the landlord prefers to the subset which he employs" (ibid.).

Cheung also assigned *risk* and *risk aversion* a much larger role in determining share tenancy than other economists have accorded them. He did not include them, however, in his formal model. Clearly, under a wage labor system all the risks of cultivation are borne by the owner-cultivator; owner-cultivator income is the residual after payment of production costs at fixed wages. Under a fixed-rate tenancy, tenants bear all the risk since their income is the residual after payment of a fixed rent. Under a share tenancy systems, however, the risk is divided between tenant and owner-cultivator in proportion to the crop share of each.

Jaynes shows, however, that Cheung's model achieves its efficiency outcome because it simply assumes away two problems—the negative incentives of sharing and the difficulty of monitoring effort. If these problems did not exist, we would not observe share tenancy. Thus Cheung must indeed introduce risk, risk aversion, and transaction costs in order to explain the existence of the contracts his formal model explores under conditions in which such sources of market imperfections do not exist.

With respect to the risk aversion motivation for sharecropping, Newbery (1975*a*) and Reid (1976) have shown that, with constant returns to scale, sharecropping provides no risk-sharing benefits that landlord and worker could not achieve by dividing a plot of land "into two subplots, one of which is

9. For other reviews of the literature discussed in this section, see Bell and Zusman (1979), Newbery and Stiglitz (1979), and P. K. Bardhan (1980).

rented out at a fixed rental R and the other is operated by the landlord who hires labor at a wage W" (Newbery and Stiglitz 1979, p. 314). Thus a model in the Cheungian tradition— without problems of worker incentives—does not explain the existence of share tenancy, even in the presence of production risk and risk aversion. Sharecropping can, however, be a means of risk avoidance under more complex characterizations of risk. Newbery and Stiglitz (1979) have demonstrated that with a second independent source of risk, such as wage rate risk in the labor market, share contracts are superior to a mixture of wage and fixed-rent contracts. If there are no incentive (monitoring) problems or economies of scale but there are multiple sources of risk, the sharecropping contract serves as the necessary instrument for the achievement of productive efficiency; it prevents rather than creates an inefficient allocation of resources.

Another class of tenancy models focuses on the costliness of labor supervision as a cause of sharecropping. One of Stiglitz's (1974*b*) models assumes costly supervision: the landlord sets the size of the tenancy just as he determines the size of the share, taking into account the impact of tenancy size on the tenant's input decision. The landlord can prevent the tenant from renting any other land or from working for wages, or he can include these restrictions in the contract and monitor and enforce them.[10] The landlord thus has an extra control instrument and can, by means of maximization, control the contract terms in such a way as to limit the tenant to his or her reservation utility level—that is, the wage rate. Of course, given the effort-monitoring problem, productive efficiency cannot be achieved in this model.

Braverman and Srinivasan (chapter 3) have extended the Stiglitz model of costly supervision to allow tenant and landlord to engage in a simultaneous share-*cum*-credit contract, the credit being used for the tenant's consumption. Such a tied contract becomes superior to an untied contract if the landlord has access to credit from third parties at lower rates of interest than the tenant can obtain. The landlord sets four contract terms: crop share, tenancy size, rate of interest to be charged the tenant, and the proportion of total credit that the tenant borrows from the landlord. Given that the landlord has two extra instruments available, the landlord can almost always hold the tenant to the utility level the latter would obtain as a wage laborer. As a result, policies like

---

10. Bardhan and Srinivasan (1971) developed a similar model, but they did not allow the landlord to control tenancy size. Newbery (1974) has pointed out that in their model, with incentive effects, full employment equilibrium could not exist since tenants would attempt to rent land until its marginal product was zero; that is, there would be excess demand for land. Braverman and Srinivasan (chapter 3) show that in Stiglitz's model, when landlords cannot control plot size there may in fact be an optimal share level that elicits the level of effort at which landlord profits are maximized but that gives sharecroppers a higher utility level than they would receive in the labor market. Just as in the efficiency wage models, therefore, an equilibrium with excess supply of tenants may exist.

tenancy reform or provision of credit to tenants at lower than market rates cannot improve the tenant's utility level. Nothing less than land redistribution, intervention in several markets, or rising alternative wage levels can improve the tenant's welfare.

In the models discussed here, costly supervision arises because of imperfect information. Information is asymmetrically distributed between landlord and tenant because only the tenant can know how much effort he or she will provide; the landlord cannot know this at sufficiently low cost. A central planner, who shares the landlord's lack of information, cannot improve on the existing allocation. Such improvement can be achieved only if the central planner has cheaper means of monitoring effort than the landlord, which, in agriculture, is not likely. Alternatively, the central planner will have to redistribute land to tenants in order to overcome their inability to buy land in the land market, which inability has led to their status as tenants. Such a policy, however, will also improve efficiency in a decentralized economy. As long as the underlying constraints on information or land transfer remain, the share tenancy equilibrium achieved is optimal with respect to these constraints; that is, it is a second-best optimum, relative to the set of informational constraints assumed in the model. This point is an important recurrent theme in the literature.

A problem that the models we have discussed so far fail to deal with specifically is the coexistence in the same region of all forms of contracts: owner-cultivator contracts, share contracts, and fixed-rent contracts. Moreover, *tenancy ladders* appear to be important in both developed and developing countries: workers become first sharecroppers, then fixed-rent tenants, and finally they acquire land of their own. (For a discussion of this phenomenon in the United States, see Reid 1979.)

There are three explanations for the coexistence of tenurial and contractual arrangements: (1) differences in risk aversion, (2) screening of workers of different quality, and (3) imperfect markets for inputs other than labor. Differential risk aversion alone cannot account for the tenancy ladder, since there is little reason to expect the same person to become completely risk-neutral as he or she becomes older, even if the person accumulates assets. (According to Binswanger 1980 and Sillers 1980, complete risk neutrality appears to be extremely rare among rural populations in developing countries.) It must be recognized, therefore, that workers differ in other respects such as ability, management skills, and capital endowments.

If productivity per hour of work differs among otherwise homogeneous workers but the productivity differences are known only to the workers and cannot be observed by the landlord without cost, landowners or workers face a screening cost.[11] Hallagan (1978) and, independently, Newbery and Stiglitz

---

11. This problem is similar to that found in screening models in the wage labor market. Here, however, the screening instrument is a contract with complex terms, not a wage rate.

(1979) have shown that the choice of contract conveys information about workers' perceptions of their abilities. "Individuals who believe they are most productive [as workers] will choose the rental contract; individuals who believe they are very unproductive will choose the wage contract and those in between will choose the share contract" (Newbery and Stiglitz 1979, p. 323). Each class of workers prefers its respective contract. Utility levels for the more able workers are higher than the levels they could achieve in a labor market without screening. Again, since information is asymmetrically distributed between landlord and workers, productive efficiency cannot be achieved. The implicit screening by means of contract choice again represents a second-best improvement in efficiency over the situation without tenancy contracts. This model leads to coexistence of contracts but not to a tenancy ladder unless workers move to higher efficiency classes as they grow older. (Note that the model considers only one type of efficiency—that of raw labor. Managerial efficiency is more likely to increase with age, however.)

Absent markets or imperfect markets for inputs other than labor are the surest guarantee of the existence of the tenancy ladder, the social differentiation of laborers, and the development of different types of tenants. Indivisibilities of inputs lead to economies of scale, and Newbery and Stiglitz (1979) point out that economies of scale can make sharecropping attractive in the absence of incentive effects, even if there are risks in production. Indivisibilities arise with regard to bullocks or capital equipment if rental markets are deficient. Bullock rental markets may be absent or poorly developed if there is lack of flexibility in the timing of operations in which bullocks are used, such as seeding.[12] Such inflexibility makes reliance on rented bullocks too risky. Indivisibilities may also arise with regard to management skills, as in the Bell–Zusman (1979) models (we consider their most recent 1980 model below), in which landlords can gain access to tenants' managerial skills only by renting land to them.

Credit market imperfections constitute the third major explanation for the coexistence of different contractual arrangements and are built into a capital rationing model without incentive effects by Jaynes (1982). In Jaynes's model, each contractual form (wage labor cultivation, sharecropping, or fixed-rent tenancy) requires a fixed amount of the landlord's supervisory time for each unit of land allocated by the contract in order to overcome incentive problems. Nevertheless, imperfect markets lead to the possibility of coexistence of all forms of contracts and, because tenants and landlords have

---

12. Bliss and Stern (1981) attribute the existence of sharecropping in the North Indian village they studied largely to imperfect bullock markets, and they show that bullock ownership is an essential requirement for renting land there. Jodha (chapter 4) confirms this hypothesis for semiarid India by showing that tenancy is closely associated with the equalization of bullock/land ratios across the farms studied. Bhalla (1976) shows that Haryana villages distinguish between tenancies and other long-term labor contracts paid by a crop share on the basis of whether the laborer or the landlord provides the bullocks.

varying factor endowments, to a differentiation of the terms of contracts among different tenant-landlord pairs. In sharp contrast to models where tenants are not differentiated by labor skills, untradable management skills, or capital endowments, the models with differentiated labor describe the welfare level of tenants as no longer being the exogenously given reservation utility level offered in the wage labor market. Different forms of contracts are available to different people because they allow them to make better use of their unique endowments, which (because of market imperfections) could otherwise be used only in a less efficient way. Thus contracts improve tenants' utility levels.

In their most recent theoretical model of bargaining, Bell and Zusman (1980a) consider risk, incentive effects, and four factors of production: (1) land that is tradable only through tenancy, not in a sales market; (2) labor that is freely mobile among share tenancy, fixed-rent tenancy, and the outside labor market; (3) fertilizers or other modern inputs, also freely tradable in a perfect fertilizer-*cum*-credit market; and (4) management capacity of the tenant, which can differ across tenants and is completely nontradable. As we have already noted, a landlord can gain access to the last factor only by renting land to tenants. Clearly, this fourth factor could instead stand for (or in addition include) other nontradable components of the tenant's endowment such as bullocks or even female family labor (as in Bangladesh; Cain, Khanam, and Nahar [1979] suggest that these female workers are permitted only very limited work outside their own farms). Output share, input share, fixed rental rate, and tenancy size are all determined in a bilateral, monopolistic bargaining process in which landlords and tenants each have some power whose extent is determined by their relative numbers and by the levels of their respective endowments. Thus Bell and Zusman's model can accommodate all levels of landlord power, from pure monopoly to large-number competition. In many parts of the world, tenants can deal with a large number of landlords. Equilibrium is reached when it is impossible to improve one's utility by signing other contracts (landlord) or by changing landlords (laborer). The inputs of labor, fertilizer, and management are tenants' discretionary variables. Clearly, the tenant's welfare in this model will be higher than the utility level he or she could achieve as a pure wage worker. The possession of management skills gives the tenant some bargaining power unless there is only one landlord and an infinitely elastic supply of tenants; in such a case, management capacity is no longer a scarce factor.

As summarized in figure 1.2, the theoretical literature on tenancy suggests that several alternative combinations of reasons explain the institution of sharecropping. In order to explain the existence of some form of tenancy, not only must the land sales market be riddled with imperfections or absent but a second market imperfection is also required (leading to conclusion *B*). When risks are present and crop insurance is absent, the mixing of fixed-rent

FIGURE 1.2. The Routes to Sharecropping.

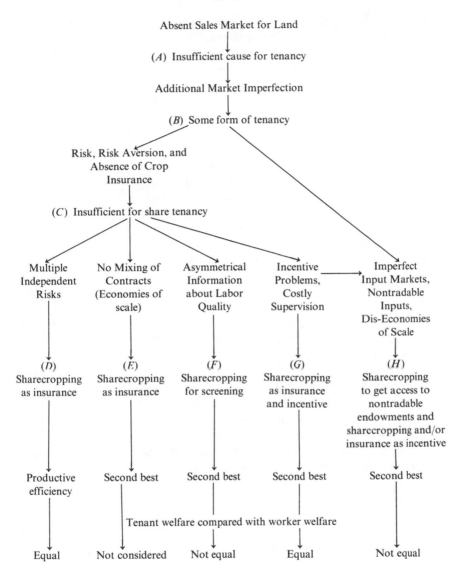

contracts with wage labor cultivation can substitute for the absent insurance market (conclusion *C*). When the mixing of contracts is impossible or uneconomical (because of economies of scale in cultivation), it becomes necessary to use the added instrument of sharecropping to substitute for the absent insurance market (conclusion *E*). The extra instrument of sharecropping is also required when mixing of contracts is feasible, but there are independent sources of risk (conclusion *D*). In this case, as long as incentive problems are absent, sharecropping is an instrument that leads to productive efficiency. Only second-best optima, however, can be reached if risk is combined with economies of scale, asymmetric information about labor quality, costly supervision, or imperfections in input markets (conclusions *E*, *F*, *G*, and *H*, respectively). Problems of risk and asymmetric information probably led to the input market imperfections in the first place. In these last four cases, though full efficiency cannot be achieved, sharecropping represents not a barrier to efficiency but an instrument that leads to improved efficiency in the face of market imperfections that would have resulted in even greater inefficiency in the absence of sharecropping.

With respect to welfare considerations, in all of these partial equilibrium models the tenant is at least as well off as a wage laborer for the simple reason that the tenant will not accept a contract if it does not offer him or her a gain over and above the utility level attainable by a wage laborer. In many models, however, the tenant cannot gain utility beyond the exogenously given wage laborers' level. In models that have no supervision costs and that reach productive efficiency, this result is attributable to tenant competition for tenancies and to the fact that landlords have the power to monitor and enforce all input levels. But it is not the institution of the share contract that prevents tenants from improving their welfare; rather, it is the assumed infinitely elastic supply of workers—and thus tenants—that forces this result. Only exogenous rises in wage levels—owing, for example, to more nonagricultural labor demand—can lead to improvement in workers' welfare.

The foregoing conclusion holds even when incentive effects are present and tenants are differentiated, as long as landlords have sufficient power to restrict tenants' choices, as in the Stiglitz (1974*b*) or the Braverman–Srinivasan (chapter 3) models. In both models, once tenants accept the contract terms, landlords can prevent them from working for other landlords or in the labor market. Clearly, landlords must be able to conspire among themselves in order to compel laborers to accept such conditions. It is not the share contract per se or the tying of share and credit contracts that enables landlords to squeeze tenants; landlords have some form of monopoly power. Binswanger et al. (chapter 8) show this clearly in an empirical study of tied labor-credit transactions, and Braverman and Stiglitz (1981) present a corresponding theoretical discussion.

Tenants' welfare can be better than that of wage laborers only if tenants have something to offer that landlords cannot get except through the tenancy contract and only if landlords cannot conspire over contract terms. In the Newbery–Stiglitz (1979) model, tenants offer labor skills; landlords cannot assess them without recourse to tenancy. In the Jaynes (1979) model, tenants offer untradable capital inputs; in the Bell–Zusman (1980*a*) model, they offer management skills. In all three models the tenant, as a simple laborer, cannot obtain the returns to these factors of production; that is, the tenant cannot easily rent out his or her extra labor skills, management skills, or capital endowments.

Changes in Contractual Arrangements

In this section we review recent empirical studies of contractual arrangements and terms. For the most part, the authors of empirical tenancy studies have not set such studies up to discriminate among precisely formulated models. Nevertheless, groups of models share some general implications that can be used to check each modeling approach for its fit with reality. Because these implications pertain to any contract involving labor, we will review all such contracts, not just share contracts.

According to the theories we have already reviewed, contracts allow individuals to make better use of their specific endowments in imperfect markets and to arrive at combinations of income, effort, and risk that reflect both their endowments and their tastes. As one would expect, in environments with heterogeneous labor (see section on "Neglected Themes") and market imperfections, many different types of contracts coexist in small regions, and contract terms vary among people, across regions, and over time. According to several empirical studies (Bardhan and Rudra 1981; Bhalla 1976; Clay 1976; and chapter 8), one can find, within the same village, a number of different types of labor contracts—daily time wage; daily piece wage; daily harvest share payment; contractual group payment, based on piece rates to resident or migrant groups of laborers; and sometimes a bewildering variety of longer term contracts. The same sources document even wider varieties of contracts across villages and regions. Moreover, the coexistence of share and fixed-rate tenancies is widespread.

Sharecropping terms are generally assumed to be fixed, most often at 50 percent of harvest gross output. But although the 50/50 split is common, (in many areas, it is the dominant arrangement), many different types of arrangements are found within small geographic areas or even within villages (Bardhan and Rudra 1980; Mangahas 1975; and chapter 5). Furthermore, even a formal 50/50 split may hide many variations. Crop by-products (often up to 15 percent of crop value) may accrue entirely to either owner or tenant; nonlabor inputs may be shared differently from output or from labor; and output may be divided either before or after costs of seed, fertilizer, and harvest labor are deducted. If output is divided after harvest costs are deducted, for example, tenants can increase their share by participating in the harvest. Thus as Bell (1977) points out, the 50/50 split of the main product hides many complexities and may lead to substantially different splits in value added, depending on the full set of sharing rules.

Virtually all models of tenancy suggest that contract terms militate against tenants as wages fall. Roumasset (chapter 4) cites scattered evidence for Indonesia and Bangladesh and presents cross-sectional regressions for selected crops in the Philippines that are consistent with this hypothesis. Kikuchi et al. (1974) cite Philippine sources that indicate that when Central Luzon haciendas were opened for cultivation early in this century, land with zero or low fixed rentals was given to tenants in exchange for land clearing. As population density grew, however, share payments became more prevalent and share levels increased.

Changes in wage rates should be reflected in changes in the terms or in the mix of labor contracts available. A decline in wages, for example, should be reflected in contract terms or mixes that imply either lower income, increased effort, increased risk, or a combination of all three. Three studies, focus on this issue: those of Clay (1976); Bhalla (1976); and Kikuchi, Hafid, and Hayami (chapter 6). Clay documents a declining real wage situation in Bangladesh in which shifts occurred in the contract mix from the fairly common use of harvest share payments to the more frequent use of cash payments and of harvesting contracts with gangs of migrant workers. These shifts implied reduced real wages. Clay reports the existence of statistically significant relationships between the bewildering variety of harvest shares paid in the same year and in the same sets of villages and three independent variables (yield, labor requirement, and output price): shares were lower the higher the yield of the plot, the higher the labor requirement (the length of time worked and the earnings), and the higher the price (or quality) of the grain harvested. Clay also notes, however, that these variables explain only a small part of the observed variance.

Bhalla's (1976) study of green revolution areas in Haryana that had rising real wages stresses shifts in the contractual mix toward longer term contracts for men and, to a lesser extent, for women. These shifts were associated with higher incomes and reduced risks. Bhalla attributes this trend to increased labor demand, increased demand for timeliness of operations, and attempts by employers to subvert the increased bargaining power of laborers as a group by fostering more one-to-one relationships, cemented by credit and other side benefits.

P. K. Bardhan (1981), Bardhan and Rudra (1981), and Binswanger et al. (chapter 8) explain a number of the variations in the incidence and nature of long-term labor contracts observed cross-sectionally by (1) relative demand for securing timely labor, which differs across areas and according to technology used; (2) labor demand relative to labor supply in local areas; (3) credit requirements of landless laborerers, who lack suitable collateral to obtain credit from formal lenders or traditional moneylenders; and (4) alternative employment and borrowing opportunities that arise in the slack season in rural works programs or as a result of temporary migration. Bardhan (1981) builds a model along these lines and offers a statistical analysis of 1956–57 Agricultural Labor Enquiry data for thirty-eight zones of India. The multiple regression analysis used cannot be considered a causal model, but its results are consistent with the view that the securing of timely peak-season labor in tight labor markets may be the most important determinant of the use of long-term contracts.

Kikuchi et al. (chapter 6) document declining real wage payments in Javanese villages characterized by technological stagnation and increasing labor supply. Real wages were reduced by two factors. First, harvest shares underwent an initial modest reduction. Second, and more important, although at the beginning the harvesting operation was open to all who wanted to join, access to it was then restricted to villagers and, finally, to people who were directly invited to join. Moreover, weeding and other labor became requirements for joining the harvest; thus for a given harvest share and given risk, the worker had to contribute increased working time and/or effort. Note, too, that this arrangement amounted to the worker providing the farmer with credit in the form of the labor cost of weeding.

Tenancy models that rely on credit constraints for both landlord and tenant predict that changes in technologies that have the effect of raising purchased-input requirements should lead to more cost sharing. C. Hanumantha Rao (1975) cites a number of cross-sectional studies that confirm this prediction, and Bhalla's (1976) rare time series study also offers supportive evidence. In addition, Bardhan and Rudra (1980) show that in eastern India, where technical change has been occurring much more slowly than in other parts of the country, the higher tenants' shares in input costs are, the higher their output shares are. Roumasset (chapter 4) also reports this finding.

Technological and risk considerations involved in the cultivation of certain crops should also influence the choice between share and fixed-rent tenancy. C. Hanumantha Rao (1975), in a cross-sectional study of Andhra Pradesh, shows that fixed rents predominated for the highly profitable crops—tobacco, chilies, and sugarcane—that require a high degree of skill and large amounts of purchased inputs and whose markets are risky.[13] Rice, on the other hand, was cultivated primarily under share tenancy. C. Hanumantha Rao attributes this difference to the scope for entrepreneurial

13. C. Hanumantha Rao's findings are confirmed by an analysis of more aggregative data (Singh 1981). Note also that rents fixed in terms of produce predominate for trade (plantation) crops such as tea or coconut, where price risks are especially high relative to yield risks.

decision-making permitted by the first set of crops and to tenants' desire to appropriate the full returns of their management input. As the preceding section of this chapter suggests, capital constraints on owners may favor the leasing of lands for crops with high purchased-input requirements to larger tenants with good access to capital. Such a phenomenon would be consistent with C. Hanumantha Rao's finding of larger farms among fixed-rent tenants.

Finally, a prediction suggested by many recent tenancy models is that landlord shares should be higher on higher quality land because such land commands a higher implicit land rent. Roumasset (chapter 4) confirms this prediction for the Philippines, and Jodha (chapter 5) presents some evidence for semiarid India. Roumasset also finds that shares vary systematically with the crop: the more profitable and less labor-intensive crops command a higher landlord share.

Empirical Studies of the Efficiency of Sharecropping

A major question raised by the tenancy models reviewed here is the extent to which incentive problems arising in share contracts can be overcome by agreements about or control of labor and other inputs. Empirical inquiry into this issue is directed not to finding out whether incentive problems exist— because they certainly do—but to discovering (1) the means by which such problems can be overcome and (2) the extent to which they can be overcome, as indicated by the presence or absence of differences in input and output intensities between sharecropped and owned farms and/or plots.

Castillo (1975) and Singh (1981) surveyed a number of studies of these issues conducted in the Philippines and in South Asia, respectively. Both researchers found that there is widespread supervision by landlords of harvests and of the sharing of the harvest to ensure adherence to contract terms. Moreover, many landlords seem to participate significantly in cultivation and input decisions. Such participation gives rise to opportunities for both determining and supervising the use of nonlabor inputs and for checking labor inputs more closely. The sharing of fertilizer and other purchased inputs is another means of reducing incentive problems and/or controlling input levels.

None of the studies reviewed here report either direct agreements between landlords and tenants on labor input or direct supervision of labor input. Most important, controlling labor input indirectly by manipulating the size of the plot given to the tenant is not common; in most regions, tenants typically rent land from more than one landlord, and members of tenant households work for wages. Thus it seems unlikely that an individual landlord would be able to manipulate plot size by restricting a tenant family to working exclusively on the landlord's plot. (For the most careful investigation of this issue, see Bardhan and Rudra 1980.) These findings contrast with the assumptions of the Stiglitz (1974*b*) and Braverman and Srinivasan (chapter 3) models discussed earlier.

A large number of studies have attempted to document differences in input and output intensities between sharecropped and owned farms and/or plots. At best, when farm size effects are controlled for, most studies find only very minor differences; that is, they suggest that incentive problems are largely overcome. However, Chakravarty and Rudra (1973) and Chattopadhyay (1979) found that on very small farms in West Bengal, Andhra Pradesh, and Punjab, input and output levels were somewhat lower under sharecropping than under owner occupancy. Moreover, small sample studies in Bihar (Bell 1977), Haryana (Bagi 1979), and Bangladesh (Hossain 1977) have shown that value of output on owned plots is somewhat higher than it is on the same farmers' tenanted plots. In Bihar this effect was primarily the result of higher cropping intensities and the planting of higher valued crops on owned land. This finding is consistent with Singh's (1981) investigation of a 1970–71 national probability sample from rural India in which differences between owned and tenanted plots were found to occur only in West Bengal, Bihar, and Orissa.

Sharecropping and Innovation

It has long been alleged that sharecropping, alone or in combination with linked credit transactions, acts as a barrier to innovation because landlord and tenant each receive only a portion of output and thus neither may be willing to carry the costs. Our theoretical discussions cast serious doubts on such a view. If contractual arrangements are by and large efficiency enhancing in a static context with several market imperfections, one should expect that when innovations promise new income streams—that is, increase utility possibilities for the population as a whole—new or revised institutional arrangements will emerge to overcome barriers that prevent the realization of such new streams. The view that sharecropping (or tenancy, more generally) retards innovation may stem from the observation that small farmers are usually later adopters. It is true that tenants are often (though not always) small farmers, and as our discussions suggested, they may be severely capital constrained. These conditions, which cause adoption lags, may often be confused with the conditions surrounding sharecropping.

The most extreme version of the view that sharecropping may retard innovation is found in Bhaduri's (1973) model of tied sharecropping and credit transactions, which gained popularity and influence long before it was subjected to a rigorous empirical test. In Bhaduri's model, referred to as a model of *semifeudal production relations*, a number of variables either are exogenously given or are entirely under the control of monopolistic or collusive landlords. These variables are crop share, tenancy size, rate of interest the landlord charges the tenant, amount of effort the tenant expends on the land, and technology of production used by the tenant. The tenant's only discretionary variable is the amount he or she must borrow from the landlord for consumption. The tenant's consumption level is assumed to be an exogenous subsistence level determined by an alternative wage. There is no risk, and incentive effects of the share contract are not considered.

This model argues that landlords may wish to withhold profitable innovations; innovations that increase output will increase both the landlord's rental income and the tenant's income from cultivation. At the same time, since there is only consumption credit, tenants' increased income will enable them to reduce their indebtedness to the landlord, and the landlord's income from moneylending will be reduced. The model does not consider the fact that most agricultural innovation increases the demand for purchased inputs and, as a result, the demand for credit.

The major theoretical criticism of Bhaduri's model has come from Newbery (1975b), who points out that if some of the contract terms are not exogenous but are rather under the landlord's control, the landlord has the power—by resorting to other means—to extract from the tenant all the surplus generated by the innovation; thus the landlord would be better off to do so, rather than to withhold the innovation. "The basic point is that if the landlord has sufficient monopoly power to exploit the peasant and to withhold the innovation then he ought to have sufficient power to extract the extra profits generated by the innovation" (Newbery 1975b, p. 270).[14] The Braverman–Srinivasan model (chapter 3) reinforces this point, showing that in a much more complex world in which landlords have extensive power over share contract and credit terms, they need only one instrument of control, namely, the plot size, to extract all rents from tenants.[15]

On the empirical side, not a single study of the adoption of high-yielding varieties that adjusts for farm size effects has shown serious adoption lags on

14. We will return to monopolistic power in a subsequent section of this chapter. In order to support the hypothesis that landlords will choose to withhold innovation rather than to extract rents by other means, one must show empirically that is easier to collude to ban an innovation and to enforce such a collusive agreement than it is to enforce other contract terms.

15. Under certain theoretical conditions, it is obviously possible that an innovation's net effect on landlord's income will be negative (the usual technological treadmill problem). This point is elaborated in Braverman and Stiglitz's (1981) recent theoretical investigation of utility-based models that are more general than the Bhaduri model. These researchers find that, first, even if innovations increase utility possibilities for landlords and tenants, the competitive market equilibrium existing after the introduction of an innovation may leave landlords worse off. In this case, it may be to their advantage to conspire to withhold the innovation, unless they can appropriate the surplus generated by the innovation in some other way. Second, Braverman and Stiglitz find that technological change may alter labor productivity in such a way that it may pay even individual landlords to withhold an innovation because their optimal contract under the new technology would lead to reduced tenant effort and decreased landlord shares. These researchers also show that innovations, depending on their risk-return characteristics, may lead to either an increase or a decrease in the tenant's demand for consumer credit. Thus Bhaduri's conclusions are not as totally implausible as Srinivasan (1979) has argued.

tenanted or sharecropped farms or plots (Castillo 1975; Singh 1981). Moreover, Bardhan and Rudra's (1980) extensive survey of villages in eastern
India—the very region Bhaduri had in mind when he constructed his model—
provides data that contradict the major assumptions and conclusions of
Bhaduri-type models. Similar inconsistencies were found in a survey conducted in Bangladesh (Rahman 1979) and in a study of semiarid tropical
agriculture (see chapter 5).

NEGLECTED THEMES

The preoccupation with surplus labor, labor market dualism, and the
rationalization of contractual arrangements that is evident in the literature
has led to the neglect of a number of important features of and issues
concerning the rural labor market. Among these topics—many of which were
addressed in the papers presented at the Hyderabad conference—are (1) the
dynamics, or flexibility, of labor market characteristics, institutions, and
arrangements; (2) the heterogeneity of labor, particularly as evidenced by sex
differences in employment; (3) the geographical dispersion of wages and the
mobility of laborers; (4) the power of monopoly and its sources; (5) the impact
of risk and credit market imperfections on labor relations; and (6) the applicability of the conventional supply-demand or competitive models of labor
markets to the low-income rural economy.

Dynamics

The development literature is centrally concerned with the evolution of real
agricultural wage rates over time, since such changes not only are an important reflection of the progress of economic development but provide evidence
in support of or against surplus labor, macro development models. Evidently,
because in many areas of the less developed countries and ever since the
eighteenth century real wages have fluctuated around a basically stagnant
trend (Bhattacharya and Roy 1976), the view that wages and contract terms
are institutionally fixed has pervaded thinking about the process of development. This view has diverted attention from the analysis of the causes of
variation, across space and over time in wages and contract terms.

Geographical variations in nominal wages, real wages, and contract
terms are pervasive in South and Southeast Asia. In themselves, such variations are not inconsistent with the view that wages and contract terms are
fixed by custom or by culturally determined subsistence norms. If pressed
hard, most holders of this view would probably also allow that institutional
wage and contract norms at least partially reflect the very long-term economic
forces that affect a particular region. They would probably also argue, however, that institutional rigidities are very strong—that changes in economic

conditions could have only very long-run effects on such norms. According to this view, norms adjust so slowly that for practical planning, modeling, and development policy purposes, one might as well ignore changes in them. Moreover, partial explanation of cross-sectional variations in terms of regional supply and demand forces, even if successful, would still be quite irrelevant.

Since geographical differences are consistent with flexible as well as rigid wages, the question becomes whether changes in supply and demand forces are reflected in changes in wages and contract terms within relatively brief periods. This question can be answered only by conducting longitudinal investigations. A finding that wages and contractual arrangements change rapidly would undermine explanations of wage and earnings determination that rely on institutional or cultural rigidities. Of course, culture and institutions may still be important determinants of wages, since these factors can affect the supply of or demand for labor.

From *Agricultural Wages in India, 1970–71* (Directorate of Economics and Statistics 1976) and other, more scattered (but possibly more carefully collected) data sources we know that, for a day of standard length and in monetary terms, agricultural wages vary substantially, not only regionally but annually and seasonally. Monetary wages are not real wages, and the controversies over what exactly has happened to real wages continue (Bardhan and Srinivasan 1974; Griffin 1974; Jose 1974; Lal, 1976a).[16] At any rate, it is clear that real wages are not constant. They have risen sharply and rapidly in the Punjab and in other areas where the green revolution has led to increases in labor demand. On the other hand, in Bangladesh they fluctuated widely around a falling trend in the twenty-seven years prior to 1975. In that year, owing to the disturbances of partition and a series of natural calamities, they were roughly 30 percent or more below the level of the late 1960s (Ahmed 1981; Clay 1976). These data for what is possibly the poorest country of the world thus sharply contradict efficiency wage theories, whose major implication is the fixity of a wage floor. White and Makali (1979) have presented the first (albeit still scanty) evidence, based on Indonesian data, that at the village level real wages vary considerably both seasonally and annually, in ways that are largely consistent with supply and demand interpretations.

The foregoing are only a few examples of variations observed over time

---

16. The reasons for the weak statistical evidence and the continued controversies over real wages are twofold. First, in most countries there has been no sustained secular trend in real rural wages that is easy to document, and fluctuations in real wages are interpreted differently, depending on the cost-of-living deflators used. Second, three factors make constructing one or more rural wage series difficult: labor is heterogeneous; contracts offered to a single broad group of laborers are heterogeneous; and simultaneous payments in cash, kind, and food result in severe valuation problems. Of these factors, probably the heterogeneity of contracts has led to the most severe conceptual difficulties.

that are inconsistent with institutional views. Also inconsistent with these views are the sharp seasonal variations in wage rates that are well known from many aggregative studies and that have been further documented by Ryan and Ghodake in chapter 9, and by White and Makali (1979). In the section on "Changes in Contractual Arrangements," we reviewed four studies that indicate that contractual arrangements for wage payments tend to respond rather rapidly to changes in economic forces: Bhalla 1976; Clay 1976; Kikuchi, Hafid, and Hayami (chapter 6); and Kikuchi et al. (1980).

Clearly, a great deal of work is required to reach an understanding of the causes of wage and contractual changes. It is not known why, for example, in certain areas adjustments typically take the form of changes in contract terms, whereas elsewhere terms remain unaltered but there are shifts in the relative importance of different types of contracts. More generally, because economic development is inherently a dynamic process, to predict its consequences and/or to attempt to understand how to foster development clearly requires the study of change.

Heterogeneity of Labor

Both the theoretical and the empirical literature on rural labor markets have tended to ignore the heterogeneity of labor. Theoretical discussions focus on "the" rural wage, and empirical studies often average male and female wage rates to create one wage (see, for example, P. K. Bardhan 1979b; Barnum and Squire 1979; Rodgers 1975). However, four dimensions of the heterogeneity of rural laborers appear important: (1) hired versus family field-workers, (2) manager-entrepreneur versus field-worker, (3) age differences, and (4) sex. As we have already noted, it may be important to distinguish between hired and family labor in determining the demand for land and productive efficiency. Family members should have fewer incentives to shirk than hired laborers—if not because of their altruism, then because of their participation in farm profits. This is one reason why (1) small farms, which employ primarily family labor, can be more efficient than large farms, which must hire and supervise nonfamily workers (sharecroppers); and (2) sharecropping is so prevalent.

The fact that managerial skill is a distinct input in agriculture is also relevant to the issue of the relative efficiency of large and small farms. Although Paglin (1965) finds that the market for field labor functions well, his data indicate that large farms employ fewer inputs per acre than small farms. Paglin explains this finding by suggesting that families with large landholdings and/or high incomes have less "motivation" to be efficient. This hypothesis implicitly assumes, however, that there is neither a market for managers and managerial skills nor a rental or sales market for land. The assumption of the absence of a managerial market is puzzling because, although there may be problems (costs) associated with determining the marginal contribution of an individual field-worker, the performance of a farm manager can be readily evaluated; the "bottom line" for managers is farm profitability. Because the assumed absence of a market for managerial skills may play an important role in tenancy (Bell and Zusman 1976), this segment of the rural labor market clearly needs more attention.[17]

A little-studied topic related to the distinction between managers and field laborers is occupational mobility over the life cycle. In particular, little is known about the typical earnings and occupations profile over the life cycle of a person in the rural labor market or about the probability that a landless worker will become a manager and/or own land. The existence of such a tenancy ladder suggests that there may be substantial life-cycle mobility in some rural labor markets, as does the finding of Binswanger et al. (chapter 8) that labor contractual arrangements are typically different for the young and for the mature worker. Binswanger et al.'s village-level evidence and Rosen-zweig's (chapter 11) data also suggest, however, that age is not importantly related to wage rates among casual field laborers; any life-cycle advancement in earnings is thus likely to be a function of the acquisition of specialized skills, access to or ownership of land or other assets, or changes in sectoral location.

The role of children in the rural labor market, found to be quantitatively important by Hansen (1969) in Egypt and by Cain (1977) in Bangladesh, has also received little attention. India district-level data studied by Rosenzweig and Evenson (1977) and by Rosenzweig (chapter 11) indicate that both the supply of and the demand for child labor are quite sensitive to levels of adult, sex-specific wages as well as to the level of child wages. Moreover, Rosen-zweig and Evenson found that both children's schooling and parental fertility varied significantly with the relative market values placed on the labor serv-ices of adults and children. Labor market arrangements and patterns, as they pertain to age-groups, thus have an important effect on the long-run quantity and quality of the labor force as well as on the contemporaneous distribution of earnings.

To date, the role of women in the rural labor market has also been given little attention. Two of the papers presented at the Hyderabad conference—those of Cain, Khanam, and Nahar (1979) and K. Bardhan (chapter 10)—included an intensive examination of the question of why female patterns of employment and wage rates, in terms of specific work tasks or occupations, differ so markedly from male patterns and wage rates in the rural labor market. Binswanger et al. (chapter 8) and Ryan and Ghodake (chapter 9) document these evident differentials, and Rosenzweig (chapter 11) and P. K. Bardhan (chapter 12) examine the separate labor supply behavior of women and men. All these studies suggest that in developing as in developed coun-

17. Castillo (1975) reports Philippine census results that indicate that only 0.1 percent of farm operators are hired managers, covering less than 5 percent of the operated area.

tries, rural labor markets exhibit differential patterns of male and female employment and earnings. Female wages are generally lower and female unemployment rates are higher (see chapters 9 and 10), and women are absent from certain segments of the labor market. Indeed, in Bangladesh (Cain, Khanam, and Nahar 1979), women seem not to participate in field labor at all, apparently because of social restrictions legitimized on religious grounds. (But note that in Indonesia, Muslim women do a lot of fieldwork; religion alone evidently is not a sufficient explanation of the lack of participation by Bangladesh women.)

In many areas of India (see chapter 10), the fact that higher class women do not perform field labor is traceable to caste-related taboos. In semiarid India, men but not women are hired according to long-term field labor contracts,[18] and in general women have access to contract work paid on a piece-rate basis or to temporary migration only through male members of their families (see chapters 7 and 8). These patterns cannot easily be explained either by the division of labor associated with childbearing and household production or by market productivity differentials. Moreover, the evidently more restricted occupational and farm-to-farm mobility of women as compared with men has implications for production efficiency and makes welfare evaluations of rural labor market mechanisms more difficult.

Mobility and Geographical Dispersion of Wages

One of the most important but neglected features of rural labor markets is the geographical dispersion of wage rates within sex and skill categories (Hansen 1969; Rodgers 1975; Rosenzweig 1978). Although the evidence suggests that, at least for males, mobility between farms and tasks within geographical areas is high (that is, dualism is absent), these geographical wage disparities suggest limited geographical mobility of labor. In addition to impediments to geographic information flows associated with high transportation and communication costs, two causes appear important: asymmetrical information and the virtual absence of a sales market for land. With respect to the first cause, the problem of shirking (with concomitant supervisory costs) makes landowners reluctant to contract with wage workers or tenants who are complete strangers; asymmetrical information thus contributes to geographical immobility by reducing the private returns to migration. An imperfect sales market for land, however, increases the private costs of any permanent, long-distance move that involves an entire household, since such a move may entail a significant capital loss. Immobility here does not imply absence of choice; instead, it may reflect a second-best adjustment to the informational and land

18. This practice may occur generally throughout the subcontinent. Bardhan and Rudra (1981), for example, did not interview women who were regular field-workers.

market problems. This is another example of how the characteristics of one market (land) affect the attributes of another market (labor).

Determining how responsive labor flows across geographical areas are to wage disparities is as important as understanding the sources and causes of immobility. Breman (chapter 7) cites an example in which the incentives related to seasonal disparities in geographical wage rates lead to the temporary migration of laborers. We believe that Breman's example is particularly interesting, although we differ with his interpretation. The moves Breman describes are organized by middlemen who also help to solve the asymmetrical information problem and provide credit to groups who seem to have difficulties obtaining it through other channels. Although the misery and the poor working conditions described by Breman are appalling, this institutionalized migration clearly augments both participating workers' income and total agricultural output under the constraints of production seasonality and high ratios of workers to land.

Most studies of migration in developing countries have focused on the implications of rural–urban flows for urban or rural development (Lipson 1980; Sabot 1981). Dhar (chapter 14) was one of the first to study nonseasonal (permanent) migration, by males, to and among rural areas in India. Dhar has found that although interstate mobility is not high, interdistrict mobility is considerable; people migrate to areas where there are better opportunities, as measured by wages and unemployment. Rosenzweig (chapter 11), studying wage determination, treats each district as a distinct labor market and reports micro data that show that men from households owning land and women from all households tend to be less geographically mobile than men from landless households. But the study of the importance of geographical mobility with regard to both earnings inequality and production is just beginning.

Sources of Market Power

Competitive market outcomes can result in extremely low wages and/or in adverse contract terms if the labor supply is large relative to demand. Thus even extremely low wage levels do not necessarily indicate either market failure or the prevalence of monopolistic or monopsonistic exploitation. In addition, as we have discussed, the linking of contracts is not necessarily a source or an indicator of market power. However, the assumption that imbalances in market power are a basic cause of poverty in rural areas underlies much thinking about rural labor markets. Even so, only a few studies have been concerned with identifying and quantifying the gains appropriated by different social groups arising out of monopolistic power. And a more careful theoretical characterization of differences in competitive and monopolistic equilibrium in a world with contracts has only just begun (Braverman and Stiglitz 1981).

The spatial distribution of agriculture and the high travel or migration costs (in terms of money, time, and/or capital losses) discussed earlier make the exercise, by landlords, of local monopolistic power a distinct possibility. This possibility is particularly strong where one or a few large owners confront many workers or potential tenants in a small geographic area. In most South and Southeast Asian countries, landholdings vary greatly in size. Unlike South America or the postbellum United States South, however, these countries have very few large ownership holdings of, say, 100 hectares (ha) or more. Except for the tea, rubber, and sugar plantations operated with permanent hired labor forces, such extensive ownership holdings are confined largely to Pakistan and some areas of Bihar. It is in these areas that one ought to look for monopolistic power of owners and for constraints imposed by owners on tenancy size and outside labor market involvement. In areas with smaller holdings it makes more sense to look at the oligopolistic or oligopsonistic power of a few owners and at the resulting wage-setting or contract-setting behavior (Bardhan and Rudra 1981). The monopolistic power relationship of large owner over small tenant is also undermined by the possibly increasing phenomenon of *reverse tenancy* documented in many studies, in which small owners rent land to larger landowners.

Studies of informal collusion by employers or landlords to fix wages or contract terms are very rare. The common assumption that contract terms are fixed by custom may have diverted the attention of many researchers from this topic, or perhaps monopolistic collusion has simply been taken for granted (Griffin 1974). In five of the six villages they studied, Binswanger et al. (chapter 8) observed attempts to fix either daily or regular farm servants' wages. However, these researchers also report a widespread recognition, by employers and workers, that *daily* wages are virtually not controllable by collusion. Clay (1976), Bardhan and Rudra (1981), Kikuchi et al. (1980), and Kikuchi, Hafid, and Hayami (chapter 6) studied the process by which daily wages or contract terms are altered and did not find much indication of collusive behavior. Thus there is little evidence, in the market for daily labor, of important departures from competitive behavior.[19] Moreover, as we have

19. In one of their six villages, Binswanger et al. did find evidence of employers' highly successful collusive behavior in setting contract terms of *annual farm servants*. This collusion was facilitated by the unusual isolation of the village from outside temporary or permanent labor opportunities and by the village community's disparagement of the caste group primarily involved in the contracts. Bardhan and Rudra (1981) also found what appears to be Stackleberg-type leadership behavior in a number of daily wage markets in West Bengal: employers apparently follow a single leader in their wage revisions.

A somewhat different issue is extraeconomic coercion to extract unpaid labor commitments from debtors or tenants. Bardhan and Rudra (1980, 1981) show that in eastern India, such unpaid labor commitments are rare. Also, very little is known about the use of individual violence or threats thereof to enforce contract terms such as labor commitments or debt repayments. In some of the villages studied by Binswanger et al., employers, moneylenders, and village officials used to beat workers or debtors with impunity, but such practices have become very rare.

discussed, there is virtually no evidence of the landowner's capacity to control tenants' involvement with other landlords, other employers, or other lenders—the crucial monopolistic power instruments for the Stiglitz (1976), Braverman and Srinivasan (chapter 3), and Bhaduri (1973) models.

Workers' organizing into unions represents, in part, their attempt to increase their collective power vis-à-vis employers. In India, however, efforts to organize rural labor unions (which are often affiliated with political parties) have been confined to Kerala, Tamil Nadu, and West Bengal. And it is only in limited areas of Kerala that unions have enjoyed stability and growth over an extended period (Alexander 1978; Beteille 1972; Jose 1976). More widespread is sporadic, unorganized agitation by workers (Bardhan and Rudra 1981; Bhalla 1976), and there is evidence that landowner organization is particularly important in areas where labor movements have been strong (Alexander 1978; Beteille 1972). Throughout South and Southeast Asia, however, rural labor movements appear weak and unimportant in comparison with labor unions in industrial sectors. Moreover, although the history of these limited rural labor movements has been fairly well documented, little is known about their effectiveness in raising earnings—the product of employment and wages.

The lack of evidence of the conditions that are required for monopolistic power or that indicate successful collusion does not, of course, deny that wage and contract terms reflect the relative bargaining strengths of (1) entire social groups, whose strengths arise out of relative demand and supply; or (2) individuals, whose strengths arise out of comparatively unique characteristics and endowments that are tradable only in imperfect markets for factors of production. Systematic investigation of these issues has only just begun.

Risk, the Credit Market, and Labor Relations

A number of the studies we have cited present fairly detailed data on the prevalence of different types of labor transactions that are linked to credit. These studies also suggest that lenders' collateral requirements and certain borrowers' lack of suitable collateral both play important roles in determining the kinds of labor or tenancy contracts in which such borrowers can engage. Although the evidence in this area is still scanty, it suggests not only that bullock requirements are important in determining access to tenancy contracts, as discussed earlier, but that capital and bullock market imperfections are much more important determinants of contract terms than any but the latest formal models have assumed. But capital market imperfections are themselves very poorly understood, although they must be closely related to the structure of production and to the market risks faced by farmers and hence by lenders. Our ignorance is caused partly by the great difficulty of collecting accurate data on the terms and collateral requirements of informal credit transactions.

Where transactions are linked with credit, little is known about the relation between the amount and terms of credit, on the one hand, and the additional terms of labor or tenancy contracts, on the other. In 86 out of 110 villages in West Bengal studied by Bardhan and Rudra (1981), loans could be taken for future labor commitments: "In 58 of these villages the number of days in which the loan is repaid by the laborer is calculated at a wage rate which is below the market wage rate prevailing at the time of repayment" (p. 93). Repayment at slightly lower than the market wage rate was also found by Rahman (1979) in Bangladesh. And in a regression analysis of the wages of regular farm servants in one of their villages, Binswanger et al. (chapter 8) found some evidence that workers receiving loans at lower than the usual interest rate also received higher wages—that is, within an individual contract, a person's relative bargaining strength appears to be reflected in both wage payments and credit terms. Jodha (chapter 5) found some link between the giving of loans *by tenants to owners* and owners' higher input shares. Both the classical economists and the most recent tenancy models have attached great importance to credit market imperfections as a source of tenancy arrangements, and the link between credit and longer term labor contracts is clearly empirically important. More research effort is urgently required here.

Testing the Supply-Demand Framework

Given the data problems inevitably encountered in the study of low-income countries, it is not surprising that the literature records almost no attempts to estimate and test the most developed of the alternative models of the rural labor market—the supply-demand model. The data requirements are formidable, as one important implication of this model is that the employment level of each factor of production depends on the prices of all other factors. Three of the papers in this volume—by Rosenzweig (chapter 11), P. K. Bardhan (chapter 12), and Evenson and Binswanger (chapter 13)—represent some of the first attempts to estimate the components of the supply-demand model using rural labor market data from a low-income country; see also Barnum and Squire (1979) for a formal approach and Lal (1976*b*) and K. Bardhan (1973) for informal applications.

The Evenson–Binswanger study uses modern duality theory to parameterize and estimate the demand, in India, for labor as well as for some other major factors of agricultural production—land, bullocks, and fertilizer. Because they derive their specifications from an underlying model of profit maximization, these researchers are able to obtain estimates of the responsiveness of labor demand to changes in wage rates, output price, and other factor prices and to test the behavioral restrictions associated with profit maximization. Rosenzweig focuses on labor supply behavior and also bases his specifications on an optimizing model, which permits him to test implied behavioral restrictions. Both P. K. Bardhan and Rosenzweig estimate the supply and demand functions for labor jointly (in a simultaneous equation, general equilibrium system), treating the distribution of land as exogenously given but treating wages and employment as endogenous variables.

All three of these papers call into question the basic assumptions of the surplus labor models, suggesting that reductions in labor supplied will significantly increase agricultural wages and that the variability in wage rates over time and across space is explained to a considerable degree by variations in demand for and supply of labor. The three studies also suggest that household and farm behavior in developing countries is not markedly different from that observed in high-income countries and that the competitive model of the labor market cannot readily be rejected, even though all the studies indicate (and rely on) a significant degree of geographical immobility. In addition, Rosenzweig's study suggests that male and female wage differentials in rural agriculture are greatly affected by sex differences in demand and supply as conditioned by both economic and cultural factors.

These three econometric studies of employment and wages ignore the institutional labor market complexities that were the focus of many of the other papers presented at the Hyderabad conference; in particular, the three studies abstract from issues of tenancy. Future work within the supply-demand framework is thus likely to be concerned with two tasks: integrating more fully the land, credit, and labor markets; and testing, for the importance of additional modeling of greater institutional detail, nonwage contract terms, and conditions pertaining to the employment of labor.

CONCLUSIONS

The literature on rural labor markets in low-income countries appears to be characterized by two major inconsistencies—the first between theory and fact, the second among models that describe different aspects of the rural economy. With respect to the former, the pervasive regional, annual, and seasonal variations of wages revealed in almost all empirical studies contrast with both the obsessive preoccupation of wage determination models with justifying fixed wages and the assumptions imposed by theoretical models of contractual choice. The contractual choice models and the special surplus labor and dualistic models have been formulated in part because of the presumed inability of market-oriented supply-demand models to provide an adequate means of determining employment, wages, and earnings in rural areas. But from such areas we have no convincing evidence to contradict the implications of this basic approach to rural wages and employment, whether in the most rudimentary form or in the form of a more complex econometric model.[20]

20. Supply and demand frameworks appear to have substantial power to explain the direction of changes in wages, earnings, and contractual rewards. However, it is difficult to say

It is important to recognize, however, that labor contracts have welfare dimensions other than that of the implicit or explicit wage. Such contracts may serve as insurance devices or they may allow people to make better use of their unique capabilities or endowments in otherwise inadequate markets. Supply and demand frameworks are neither designed nor able to predict how contract terms or the mix of contracts available will change as labor demand, supply, and technology change. Thus they cannot predict the full welfare consequences of such changes; that is, their likely effects (for groups of people who have endowments that are not easily tradable) on effort, risk, and capital gains or losses.

In a longer run perspective, economic development is accompanied by improvements in transportation and communication. These improvements in turn remove some of the underlying risk and credit market imperfections and create new markets. The supply and demand framework, which takes markets as given, cannot predict the sequence in which such markets will emerge or their distributional consequences. Since the construction of the transportation and communication infrastructure often involves the public sector, better models are indeed required by those who shape policy so that the patterns of emerging markets can be influenced in an informed way.

Progress toward a richer, more integrated theoretical framework that can deal with the complexities resulting from or inducing market failures as well as the determination of wages and other contract terms has been hampered by the evolution of theory along two mutually inconsistent paths. The rural wage determination models developed so far assume the complete absence of a land rental or sales market; they take land distribution as exogenously given.[21] The contractual choice models, on the other hand, treat the wage rate as exogenously given, while concentrating on land and credit market transactions; thus they have little to say about the determination of earnings or employment. The strength of the contractual choice models lies in their clarification of the efficiency and equity implications of contracts and in their identification of the underlying causes of the market imperfections that have led to the contracts. These models also suggest the difficulties of policy intervention in single-tenancy or credit markets that is aimed at curing symptoms or apparent deficiencies in such arrangements. Without this integration of all the major interrelated markets—land, labor, credit—into a single, coherent rural model, however, social scientists will be severely hand-

how well they predict the magnitudes of changes because we lack a criterion for the meaning of "well." We do not yet have in empirically testable form—which would allow us to compare different models' predictive powers—alternative theories of wage/earnings determination that take the contractual realities into account.

21. P. K. Bardhan's (1979*a*) two-season model is an exception. But it determines only peak-season wages. Slack-season unemployment and the crop share are exogenously given. The fixity of the crop share in particular is inconsistent with the assumed strong monopoly power of landlords in the tenancy markets.

icapped in attempting to predict the consequences of economic development in the rural sector.

We have been arguing for more modeling work when apparently there is already a confusing overabundance of models. But many of these models are not helpful in increasing an understanding of the rural economy or in predicting its behavior because some of their crucial assumptions are clearly contradicted by simple observation of rural realities. At best, such models can sharpen intuitions by forcing us to work out the logical implications of counterfactual assumptions. Models must certainly make simplifying assumptions that are at variance with the complexities of the real world. However, this should not be taken as an excuse for making assumptions that crucially determine the conclusions of the models but that are specifically and pervasively rejected by empirical studies, at least those of conditions in South and Southeast Asia.

In part, the proliferation of models and the lack of attention to testability stems from the lack of good data. Such data are now becoming more prevalent, however; thus attention can be turned to winnowing out models that are counterfactual or that perform badly as predictors. The studies we have reviewed show what can be done with patience and persistence. The successful prediction of change over time is the sharpest test of a model or theory, particularly a theory of economic development. More attention should be focused on generating good panel data or resurveying old samples in order to accelerate the transformation of models into knowledge.

We conclude with the reminder that the models or frameworks that are reviewed here and that formed the bases for the analyses reported in the papers presented at the rural labor market conference are models of institutions and behavior in existing rural markets, not models of economic development. Explanations of the long-term changes that accompany development must be found, ultimately, in models that explicitly treat the reproductive and technological behavior that leads to the long-term evolution of supply and demand. Attention has recently turned to the study of decisions that have long-term consequences—decisions about human capital investment, fertility, health, technological change, and agricultural intensification (see, for example, Behrman and Wolfe 1980; Binswanger and Ruttan 1978; Boserup 1965; Darity 1980; Harris 1971; Rosenzweig and Evenson, 1977; Rosenzweig and Schultz 1982). Such decisions, however, are themselves conditioned by the outcomes and institutional arrangements in rural factor markets. The integration of market and household behavioral models within a specific dynamic framework is yet to come.

I

TENURIAL ARRANGEMENTS:
THEORY AND EVIDENCE

2

Economic Theory and Land Tenure

Gerald David Jaynes

The economic aspects of land tenure systems have recently attracted the interest of a growing number of economists. The resulting contributions to our understanding of various land tenure relationships have come from an unusually diverse set of individuals drawn to the subject for a variety of reasons.[1] Among these reasons we may include a growing reemergence of the belief that agriculture has a primary role to play in the development process of contemporary economics; a closely related realization that land tenure institutions must be understood if past agricultural societies are to be put in historical perspective; and, finally, the recognition that tenurial organization is connected to the problems that have given rise to the theory of information, uncertainty, and incentives. Land tenure organizational systems have been associated with the problem of agricultural productivity and growth and have been a main focus of attention since at least the time of Adam Smith. However, one of the points I shall discuss in this paper is that recent contributions to the literature have uncovered the previously neglected fact that rural labor market structure itself is connected to the organization of land tenure.

In this paper I view the existing literature from the perspective of two important and intricately related questions:

1. What, if any, are the differences in the productive and distributional resource allocation effects of various tenurial arrangements?
2. What determines the choice of tenancy?

Of these two fundamental questions, the first takes precedence. In actuality, the second cannot be answered independently of the first. I shall establish that this fact has been an important source of confusion for some writers.

---

1. The list grows longer by the month. See the extensive bibliography at the end of this book.

43

There have been two general answers to these questions. The first, which I shall unimaginatively term the *classical doctrine*, has had a long, but largely misunderstood, history. This position was shared by such classical economists as Adam Smith and Karl Marx with the neoclassicist Alfred Marshall. Marshall's position, we shall see, has been completely misinterpreted by modern writers. The second general answer to our questions has been extant for only a short time. The first known expositor of the *private rights doctrine* was Steven Cheung. I shall argue that his attempt to dichotomize the two primary questions caused his analysis serious trouble, making his entire conceptual framework logically unacceptable.

These two positions will be introduced and discussed in the first section of the paper. This will give us insight into some important properties of rural labor markets and bring to light some crucial aspects pertinent to agrarian reform. In the second section these issues are discussed with reference to some recent literature on the economics of land tenure, the primary focus being the relationship between land tenure organization, rural labor market structure, and the efficacy of agrarian reform.

APPROACHES TO THE ECONOMICS OF LAND TENURE

The Classical Doctrine

The classical position is that the appearance and adoption of various land tenure systems is a historical-evolutionary process that has been conditioned by the development of *monetized market capitalism* and affected by efficiency-improving changes in the organization of agricultural production. Basic to this position is the idea that there are four primary modes of tenancy:

1. Rent in the form of labor
2. Share-rents
3. Fixed rents in the form of produce
4. Fixed rents in the form of money

They can be ranked from bottom to top with respect to productive efficiency but are ranked top to bottom with respect to evolutionary precedence.

This position has been expounded, more or less explicitly, by a list of writers that includes A. Turgot, Adam Smith, Richard Jones, J. S. Mill, Karl Marx, and Alfred Marshall. The most complete statement of the historical-evolutionary basis of the position, from which all subsequent writers on the subject drew, was enunciated by Richard Jones. According to this position the mode of tenancy is dictated by the development of institutions and market conditions required for the support of various tenurial forms. In Jones's words (*Peasant Rents*, p. 8), an attempt to understand land rents must be accompanied by the realization that "in the actual progress of human society, rent has usually originated in the appropriation of the soil, at a time when the bulk of the people must cultivate it on such terms as they can obtain or starve." From the perspective of the classical doctrine, the existence of a large class of money-rent-paying tenants was no more possible in nineteenth-century rural China than it was in thirteenth-century England. As Jones puts it in his lectures and tracts (p. 434):

> The rent of land may be paid in money, in produce, or in services. Payments in money are rare: they suppose an advance in the organization of society, which is found in few spots on the globe. There must be both markets to supply specie, and a tenantry capable of risking the variations of such markets, and able to contract on their own responsibility for money rents with a reasonable probability of their being able to perform such contracts.

This short statement is indicative of the classical approach. A well-developed system of money rent payment requires not only a well-organized credit market but also a class of tenant-cultivators wealthy enough either to self-insure or to obtain market insurance on their income streams. According to the classical doctrine, the choice of tenure will be dictated by the most efficient available arrangements that are compatible with the state of economic development and *existing* market institutions.

The Private Rights Doctrine

The private rights doctrine was introduced by Steven Cheung, whose analysis was based on the growing economics and private property rights literature. One rather simplistic interpretation of this literature is that given well-defined property rights and rational agents, economic allocations must be efficient. Cheung's interpretation of the property rights doctrine goes no deeper than this, and consequently he not only misuses its conceptual framework but lays a false trail toward the understanding of land tenure development. According to Cheung (1968, p. 1121), "if economic efficiency is viewed as a condition of market equilibrium logically deduced from the theory of choice under private property rights, devoid of welfare implications, one wonders why the inefficiency argument of share contracts has prevailed for so long." This statement indicates why it is not surprising that Cheung concluded that given well-defined property rights, resource allocation must be Pareto-efficient, independent of the choice of land tenure.

Many factors have been suggested as being influential in determining the choice of tenure. The four most common have been:

1. Share tenancy as an incentive system
2. Share tenancy as a credit system

3. Share tenancy as a method of spreading and sharing risk
4. Share tenancy as a means of avoiding transaction costs

Note that most of these factors place an emphasis on explaining the existence of share tenancy. We shall see that the classical writers stressed the first two, whereas some contemporary economists, following the lead of Cheung, have emphasized the second two.

As stated earlier, the historical-evolutionary aspect of the classical doctrine was stated in a comprehensive form by Richard Jones. However, we shall start with Adam Smith, from whom Jones clearly drew inspiration. Smith, in his typically thorough and insightful manner, not only addressed both of our primary questions but discussed them in the logical order. He clearly endorsed the incentive argument as a major economic determinant of the choice of tenure. In *Wealth of Nations* (p. 366) he argued that European *métayers* (share tenants) succeeded landed slaves (serfs) as the primary tenants in Europe: "Such tenants, being free men, are capable of acquiring property, and having a certain proportion of the produce of the land, they have a plain interest that the whole produce should be as great as possible.... A slave, on the contrary, who can acquire nothing but his maintenance, consults his own ease."

Smith proceeded with his evolutionary argument (p. 368) by explaining that métayers were succeeded by "farmers properly so called, who cultivated the land with their own stock, paying a rent certain to the landlord." Why this transition from métayage, or "steel-bow tenants" as Smith referred to them, to fixed renting? Smith again used the incentive argument in his well-known indictment of share tenancy (p. 366): "It could never, however, be the interest even of this last species of cultivators to lay out, in the further improvement of the land, any part of the little stock which they might save ... because the lord, who laid out nothing, was to get one-half of whatever it produced."

Smith viewed métayage as inefficient but pointed out that the source of inefficiency differs from that of slavery or labor rents. The slave shirks his labor supply, while the share tenant has an incentive to work hard but not to invest his own stock. This distinction is important, because most modern critics of the classical writers have discussed this problem in the context of undersupply of labor, ignoring capital in their formal arguments. In his *Lectures* (p. 101), Smith had made this evolutionary incentive argument even clearer by anticipating the concept of a Pareto-improving exchange: "After this custom [métayage] had continued for a long time the tenants picked up so much as enabled them to make a bargain with the landlord to give him a certain sum for a lease of so many years; ... this is plainly an advantage to the landlord; the ground every year is better cultivated, he is at no expense, and the half of the product was better to the tenants than any sum they would give." This last assertion was interpreted by the editor, Edwin Cannan, to mean "the half of the product which the tenants used to hand over to the landlord, and now kept for themselves in addition to the other half, was of more value to them than any money rent they were likely to pay instead of it." Since Smith uses an incentive-efficiency argument to explain the transition to fixed renting, it is fair to ask why the system did not change directly from labor rents to fixed rents. Smith's answer (*Wealth of Nations*, p. 367) was that "a villain enfranchised, ... having no stock of his own, could cultivate it only by means of what the landlord advanced to him, and must, therefore, have been what the French call a métayer." So he is essentially arguing that the transitional stage of share tenancy is necessitated by the tenant's lack of capital and, presumably, of credit.

Smith clearly viewed the tenancy issue as a historical-evolutionary process. Cheung, in his survey (1969, p. 33), attacks this point of view. He argues:

> Although the meaning of economic efficiency was not clarified until much later, Smith's idea of analyzing the development of land tenure systems on grounds of more gainful resource use is certainly an important one; however, the approach he used is not deep enough to yield fruitful results. Once property laws define a specific set of constraints on competition, there may exist several forms of contractual arrangements which imply the same resource use. ... When these property laws are altered, the contractual arrangements may change. It follows that the appropriate approach in analyzing land tenure development is to trace the alterations in property laws; and not, as Smith did, to interpret (or advocate) the change in laws by tracing what might appear to be defective leasing arrangements.

Cheung also makes the interesting remark that Smith's noting of the rarity of sharecropping in England might be a result of the freehold lease which legally enforced lifelong tenant leases. Such long-term leases would deprive landlords of the right to evict undesirable tenants. Both Cheung and D. Gale Johnson (1950) considered short-term leases and the possibility of eviction to be important controls by which landlords could ensure that share tenants worked hard. In the passage just quoted, a primary aspect of the difference between the classical and private rights approaches is revealed. The issue is best formulated as a simple Marxian-Hegelian contraposition. Do the material conditions of production dictate the form of the legal structure (property rights), or do the existent property laws ultimately dictate the material form of production? In this passage, Cheung clearly indicates that the latter causal relation receives his endorsement. Smith could hardly have anticipated the emergence of a controversy some 200 years later, yet he defended his position admirably well. Regarding the point that métayage may have disappeared because of the freehold system, it seems fairly clear that Smith was definitely arguing that fixed renting replaced métayage and was followed by enactment of the freehold laws:

> When such farmers (renters) have a lease for a term of years, they may sometimes find it for their interest to lay out part of their capital for the further improvement of the farm; because they may sometimes expect to recover it, . . . before the expiration of the lease. The possession even of such farmers, however, was long extremely precarious, . . . they could before the expiration of their term be legally outed of their lease, by a new purchaser. (*Wealth of Nations*, p. 368)

He then discussed the introduction of the freehold system and extolled the virtues of long leases that grant tenants the property rights to any long-term capital investments they might make in the land.

Regarding this second, more comprehensive point, it is difficult to imagine that anyone seriously believes that the development of economic institutions is dictated by legislators who pursue theoretical discussions in isolation from the material conditions impinging upon them and their constituencies. On this point Cheung is even in disagreement with the private property rights approach. Harold Demsetz (1967), a major contributor to the literature, states that "property rights develop to internalize externalities when the gains of internalization become larger than the cost of internalization. Increased internalization, in the main, results from the development of new technology and the opening of new markets, changes to which old property rights are poorly attuned." Indeed, Smith, and the classical approach in general, is much more aligned with the private property rights approach than is Cheung.

We see that Adam Smith presented a logically consistent theoretical analysis of the development and allocational effects of land tenure systems. His theoretical analysis was based upon the different incentives provided by various tenure forms and the different wealth and capital endowments of tenants. Not only did Smith not base his indictment of share renting on an undersupply of labor, as implied by modern writers, but he explicitly recognized the positive labor supply effects of share tenancy. Smith's criticism of métayage was a dynamic one based upon inappropriate capital investment incentives.

Reference to Anne Robert Jacques Turgot's best-known work on matters of political economy, *Reflections on the Formation and the Distribution of Riches*, shows that his efficiency ranking of the forms of land tenure agrees completely with the ranking I have associated with the classical doctrine. This work does not give enough details to explain the reasoning that led Turgot to this conclusion. To find evidence of this reasoning one must consult a memoir written in 1766, while Turgot was a minister of agriculture. At that time Turgot was concerned with evaluating the legitimacy of complaints by inhabitants of poor rural provinces such as Limoges that the imposition of the *taille* (tax) was unfairly burdensome upon them. To assess this problem Turgot believed that it was absolutely necessary to understand the fundamental differences between *la grande culture* as practiced in wealthy provinces and *la petite culture* as practiced in poor provinces ("*à la culture par métayers*"). Turgot apparently undertook an extensive empirical survey of the state of agriculture in France. His conclusions clearly anticipate some of the more cogent points made by later classical writers. To Turgot the fundamental difference between the two systems was that landlords in the prospering districts were able to find tenants wealthy enough to pay a fixed money rent for land upon lease for a *given number of years*. Such tenants were also wealthy enough to obtain credit for, or to finance out of their own savings, all the expenses of farming. These money rent tenants Turgot called true entrepreneurs producing cash crops for the markets in nearby wealthy towns: "Ce qui distingue véritablement et essentiellement les pays de grande culture de ceux de petite culture, c'est que, dans les premiers, les propriétaires trouvent des fermiers qui leur donnent un revenu constant de leur terre et qui achètent d'eux le droit de la cultiver pendant un certain nombre d'années. Ces fermiers se chargent de toutes les dépenses de la culture." [2]

The use of métayers was forced, in la petite culture, because the available tenants did not possess either personal wealth or access to credit. Turgot argued that this condition forced landlords to make credit advances to tenants; thus the landlord's income was derived from his land rent, interest, and return on capital advances. Turgot went on to describe conditions that later writers commenting upon different regions and times have called "debt peonage." However, a close reading of Turgot shows that he considered poverty a cause of métayage and not vice versa. This is an issue confused by many writers, including Arthur Young in his famous *Travels in France*. Turgot perceived métayage as existing because "les pays de petite culture, ... sont ceux où il n'existe point d'entrepreneurs de culture; où un propriétaire qui veut faire valoir sa terre ne trouve pour la cultiver que des malheureux paysans qui n'ont que leurs bras; où il est obligé de faire à ses frais toutes les avances de la culture, ... d'avancer même à son métayer de quoi se nourrir jusqu'à la première récolte." [3] Finally, he explicitly recognized that credit

2. "Mémoire sur la surcharge ...," in *Oeuvres de Turgot*, 1: 543–44: "That which truly and essentially distinguishes the regions of large farms from those of small farms is that, in the former, landlords find tenants who pay them a fixed revenue for their land and buy the right to farm during a certain number of years. These tenants pay all the expenses of farming themselves."

3. "The regions of small farming are those where there exists no class of entrepreneurial farmers; where a landlord who wants a return from his land can find only farmers who are poor peasants, possessing only their arms [labor]; where the landlord is obliged to make all the advances for farming, ... even to advance subsistence consumption to his métayer until the first harvest" (ibid., p. 545).

markets were not available to these tenants: "Mais les métayers de la petite culture ne sont pas exposés à une pareille tentation [to borrow as wealthy farmers were because of falling interest rates]; les bas intérêt de l'argent ne peut conserver à l'agriculture des capitaux qui n'existent point: ces cultivateurs ne possèdent même pas assez pour pouvoir emprunter."[4] Turgot also discussed the evolution of money rent tenancy from métayage in parts of France, making it clear that fixed tenure and long leases were important because they enabled the tenant to capture savings from his own investments.

The incentive argument for métayage can also be found in Turgot's *Reflections*. He explicitly argued, without analysis, that the métayer had a greater incentive to exert his labor than either the slave or the wage worker.

John Stuart Mill undertook a fairly extensive discussion of the allocational effects of various land tenures. For his valuable practical discussion of the conditions of métayage in France and Italy, he drew from the theoretical work of Adam 'Smith and Richard Jones.[5] Mill recognized and attached value to the incentive argument for métayage as well as the benefits of long leases and security of tenure: "The metayer has less motive to exertion than the peasant proprietor, since only half the fruits of his industry ... are his own. But he has a much stronger motive than the day laborer, who has no other interest in the result than not to be dismissed" (p. 304). Note that Mill is comparing the labor exertion of a wage worker with that of a métayer, finding métayage an improvement. With respect to capital investment he quotes Adam Smith's remarks about the tenant's disincentive to invest his own stock, calling it the "characteristic disadvantage" of the system. Perhaps the most illuminating aspect of Mill's work is found in the last section of his chapter "Of Metayers." In this section he ranks money rent tenancy as more efficient, noting that "the metayer tenure is not one which we should be anxious to introduce where the exigencies of society had not naturally given birth to it; but neither ought we to be eager to abolish it on a mere a priori view of its disadvantages" (p. 316). Following this passage Mill discusses with great intuitional acumen the problems of predicting the allocative and welfare effects of a market change from métayage to money renting in the context of market and institutional imperfections. The nature of the market imperfections and social conditions impairing the market change—the tenant's lack of wealth and credit—is described in his conclusions.

If this transformation [from métayage to money rents] were effected and no other change made in the metayer's condition; if preserving all the

4. "But metayers with small farms were not exposed to a similar temptation [to borrow money as wealthy farmers were because of falling interest rates]; the low interest on money cannot enable farmers to save on nonexistent capital: these tenants owned too little even to borrow" (ibid., p. 549).

5. Mill borrowed from Jones the tenure classification system used in Mill's *Principles of Political Economy* (1976).

other rights which usage insures to him, he merely got rid of the land-lord's claim to half the produce, paying in lieu of it a moderate fixed rent; he would be so far in a better position than at present, as the whole, instead of only half the fruits of any improvement he made, would now belong to himself, but even so, the benefit would not be without alloy; for a metayer, though not himself a capitalist, has a capitalist for his partner, and has the use ... of a considerable capital; ... and it is not probable that the landowners would any longer consent to peril their moveàble property on the hazards of agricultural enterprise, when assured of a fixed money income without it." (p. 320)

Mill was perhaps the only classical writer explicitly to recognize that a comparison of the efficiency properties of share renting and fixed money renting was a comparison of two systems in the presence of very imperfect and perhaps incomplete markets. *Given these conditions*, he recognized that it was not clear at all which system was superior. This accounts, I believe, for what some writers have considered a kind of hedging on his part as to the merits of the two tenures.

The fact that the historical-evolutionary doctrine of land tenure develop-ment of the classical economists was adopted by Karl Marx should come as no surprise. In his discussion of the "Genesis of Capitalist Ground-Rent," Marx adopts completely the classification system introduced by Richard Jones. It is clear that Marx considers tenancy by money rent payment the only pure form of the capitalist mode of production, as the final and most efficient form of tenure on Jones's list.

The transformation of rent in kind into money-rent, ... presupposes a considerable development of commerce, of urban industry, of commod-ity-production in general, and thereby of money circulation. ... How unfeasible it can be without a certain development of social labor pro-ductivity is proved by various unsuccessful attempts to carry it through under the Roman Empire, and by relapses into rent in kind.... The same transitional difficulties are evidenced, e.g., in prerevolutionary France when money-rent was combined with and adulterated by, survivals of its earlier forms. (*Das Kapital* 3:803)

These remarks should be compared with those of Turgot and Mill. As for métayage, Marx devotes only one paragraph to that form of tenancy.

As a transitory form from the original form of rent [labor rent] to capitalist rent, we may consider the metayer system, or sharecropping, under which the manager (farmer) furnishes labour (his own or another's), and also a portion of working capital, and the landlord furnishes ... another portion of working capital. On the one hand, the farmer here lacks sufficient capital required for complete capitalist management. On the other hand, the share here appropriated by the landlord does not bear the pure form of rent. On the one hand, the sharecropper ... is to lay claim to a portion of the product ... as possessor of part of the instruments of labour, as his own capitalist. On the other hand, the landlord claims his share not exclusively on the basis of his land-ownership, but also as lender of capital. (ibid.)

For the first time the sharecropper is explicitly considered a capitalist, although a credit-rationed one. In this short passage Marx summarizes each of the key points made by his predecessors about the choice of tenancy. The major emphasis is placed upon share tenancy as a credit system and the income distributional implications. In the next section we shall see how the neoclassical economist Alfred Marshall extended the classical analysis he inherited.

To summarize, we have found that the classical economists all argued that the efficiency attributes of various tenancies differ and that these tenancies can be ranked. They believed the type of tenancy chosen would be the most efficient mode available, subject to the constraints of available institutions and markets and the circumstances of prospective tenants. The two determinants of the choice of share renting they stressed most were the need for credit by tenants unable to obtain it in a specialized credit market and the incentive that the receipt of a share of the crop gives the tenant to work hard, thus lessening the supervision costs (transaction costs) of the landlord.

Perhaps the most misunderstood of all writers on the question of land tenure was Alfred Marshall. Marshall is considered by Cheung and Johnson to have held the simple view that share renting is inefficient because the marginal conditions necessary for static production efficiency cannot be satisfied under a system where the cultivator receives only a percentage of the output. I shall show that this view of Marshall's analysis is completely erroneous.

Marshall did not sanction what has become known as the Marshallian, neoclassical, or tax-equivalent approach. What he did was to give a clear presentation of the argument. The source of the erroneous belief has been a general preoccupation with a footnote that a close reading of his entire text reveals to be merely secondary to the main argument.

This plan [share renting] enables a man who has next to no capital of his own to obtain the use of it at a lower charge than he could in any other way, and to have more freedom and responsibility than he would as a hired laborer; and thus the plan has many of the advantages of the three modern systems of cooperation, profit sharing, and payment by piece-work. But though the metayer has more freedom than the hired laborer, he has less than the English farmer. His landlord has to spend much time and trouble, either of his own or of a paid agent, in keeping the tenant to his work; and he must charge for these a large sum, which, though going by another name, is really earnings of management. (1961, p. 644)

These words are a clear statement of what Marshall considers to be the advantages of and motivation for share tenancy. The tenant receives capital through the landlord at lower credit terms than he could elsewhere. This statement implies that the credit market is not textbook-perfect. The allusion to the modern advantages of cooperation, profit sharing, and a piecework payment system is certainly a ratification of the incentive argument for share tenancy. However, Marshall also notes that these advantages have their costs in terms of the landlord's need to spend much time supervising the tenant. The reason for this is given in the sentence following the preceding quotation.

For, when the cultivator has to give to his landlord half of the returns to each dose of capital and labor that he applies to the land, it will not be to his interest to apply any doses the total return to which is less than twice enough to reward him. *If*, then he is free to cultivate as he chooses, he will cultivate far less intensively than on the English plan ... his landlord will get a smaller share even of those returns than he would have on the plan of a fixed payment.

It is precisely at this point that Marshall indicates a reference to the famous footnote that begins, "This can be most clearly seen by aid of diagrams" and continues with a geometrical version of the excise tax analogy. I see no reasonable way that this footnote can be interpreted as the central part of Marshall's argument. The footnote is merely an alternative way of demonstrating what would occur *if* the tenant were unsupervised and allowed to pursue his own interest only. That the argument in the text and not the footnote is more important to Marshall is absolutely clear. The footnote only shows why the landlord must supervise and incur heavy transaction costs.

Marshall continues his analysis, referring to what he calls the "plasticity" of métayage. He then states the credit argument: "The landlord can deliberately and freely arrange the amount of capital and labour supplied by the tenant and the amount of capital supplied by himself to suit the exigencies of each special case." In another comparison of fixed versus share tenancy, he claims that "there is no other business [fixed-rent farming] in which a man can borrow what capital he wants at so low a rate, or can often borrow so large a part of his capital at any rate at all. The metayer indeed may be said to borrow an even larger share, but at a much higher rate." Thus Marshall notes that not only can borrowers be credit-rationed, but interest rates may differ between borrowers. His system recognizes and includes the transaction costs of enforcing contracts and therefore prefigures a complete theory of income distribution under share tenancy. Indeed as we shall presently see, Marshall includes the elements considered by Cheung with the addition of capital and credit and integrates all the elements in one complete analysis.

The major problem with share tenancy, as perceived by Marshall and the classical economists, must be construed as improper incentives for capital investment over time. Each writer considered in this paper devotes considerable space to this problem. All recognize that even under fixed renting, proper investment incentives require long leases and secure tenancies—in short, well-defined and properly formulated private property rights.

Cheung stated the purpose of his initial published work (1968), on the problem of resource allocation and land tenancy, as follows: "It will be shown here that ... the implied resource allocation under private property rights is the same whether the landlord cultivates the land himself, hires farmhands, ... leases, ... on a fixed rent basis, or shares the active yield with his tenant." His intent was to construct a model capable of demonstrating that with well-defined private property rights and free markets, resource allocation must be efficient, regardless of the choice of tenancy. This he managed to do by setting up a maximization problem where the landlord chooses all contractual parameters, subject to the constraint that the tenant's income (or more generally, utility, as pointed out by D. M. G. Newbery [1974]) equals what the tenant might achieve in a perfectly competitive wage labor market. It is fair to say that Cheung maximized subject to the constraint that the outcome be efficient. Given the independently derived efficiency argument, Cheung's private property rights approach finds itself in a logical contradiction from which (it shall be shown) it cannot extricate itself. If all forms of tenure lead to the same allocation of resources—that implied by a Pareto-efficient competitive equilibrium—what determines the choice of tenure?

Cheung broaches this question in a separate work (1969). His well-known answer is that different transaction costs for alternative tenure systems and agents' risk aversion in the presence of uncertainty lead to the choice of multiple tenurial arrangements. Under transaction costs he lists negotiation and enforcement costs of contracts. He argues that these combined costs are greater under share than under wage or rental contracts, because share contracts require both negotiation and enforcement. Evidently he assumes that wage and rental contracts have no negotiation costs. Given his assumption, it is evident that no pair of agents would choose share contracts. To circumvent this problem he argues that in the presence of uncertain agricultural returns, risk-averse agents would, other things being equal, strictly prefer share contracts, which allow some sharing and spreading of risk. Therefore, the choice of contract depends upon a balancing of different transaction costs and risk-sharing benefits. Different agents at various times and locations might choose many arrangements. It has since been shown that given Cheung's assumptions, share contracts offer no improvement in the allocation of risk bearing beyond that achievable with a mixture of rental and wage contracts.[6] Therefore, upon these grounds alone Cheung's analysis fails to provide an answer to our second fundamental question: What determines the choice of tenancy?

The case against Cheung's approach is actually much more damaging at a deeper level. The very suggestion that share contracts are introduced to improve the allocation of risk bearing is a suggestion that some market is either nonexistent or imperfect. In this case there cannot exist a complete set of markets for the trading of Arrow–Debreu securities. There is no perfect insurance market. We have seen that the entire point of Cheung's analysis has been to show that given well-defined private property rights, the allocation of resources will be Pareto-efficient in a *first best* sense. Therefore, he carefully avoids any mention of market imperfections. But the very existence of transaction costs may imply that some markets are incomplete. Cheung (1969) himself argues that transaction costs lead to the incompleteness of insurance markets.

Furthermore, in the presence of transaction costs there is absolutely no reason to expect underlying production-exchange relationships to exhibit the convexity properties required by the marginal analysis with which Cheung attempts to discuss Pareto efficiency. All the rigorous work concerning market equilibrium with transaction costs and incomplete markets since the mid-1960s convincingly tells us that first-best efficiency is just not possible in general. Indeed, in the presence of incomplete Arrow–Debreu security markets, not only may a competive equilibrium not be first-best efficient, but the introduction of additional markets may actually make some agents worse off.[7] Recall the quotation from J. S. Mill and the remarks by Marx. The entire point of all this is that once Cheung refers to the existence of transaction costs and incomplete markets, he has descended into the world of second best and this completely vitiates his entire original analysis of first-best efficiency based upon his private property rights doctrine. There is simply no justification for Cheung's unsubstantiated assertion that "economic theory implies a tendency toward the same set of marginal equalities of resource use even if transactions costs exist" (1969, p. 86).

Let me recapitulate this section. Cheung begins by arguing that, under well-defined private property rights and free markets, resource allocation is efficient and is invariant with regard to the choice of land tenure. This implies

---

6. This proposition has been demonstrated by Reid (1976), Stiglitz (1974*a*, *b*), Newbery (1977), and Hammond (1977).

7. See Radner (1970), Hahn (1971), Green and Sheshinski (1975), and Hart (1975). Much of this literature postdates Cheung's work, but many basic ideas were known before. Arrow's well-known 1963 paper addresses many of these problems.

that there is no reason for any agent, landlord or tenant, to prefer any form over another. To show that the choice of tenure is determined by more than mere chance, he introduces a separate analysis. However, his second analysis relies upon premises, transaction costs, and incomplete markets for risk bearing, which strongly imply that market equilibriums will not be efficient. The second half of Cheung's dichotomy destroys the first half. This inconsistency in the analysis is a direct consequence of his approach, which completely ignores the overwhelming evidence that the determination of the choice of tenure is founded on the existence of underlying fundamental market imperfections.[8] Cheung's own analysis implicitly, and apparently without his comprehension, rests upon this very proposition.

RURAL LABOR MARKET STRUCTURE AND AGRARIAN REFORM

The approaches to the economics of land tenure previously discussed provide a useful framework from which to begin systematic evaluation of the need for and impact of structural reform in agrarian markets.

Suppose we begin by assuming that there exists a complete set of Arrow–Debreu markets, that is, there is insurance for all risks and a competitive price for every good or service any agent desires to trade. If, in addition, all necessary convexity assumptions regarding preferences and production-exchange relationships are satisfied, it is well known that a competitive equilibrium will be a full, Pareto-efficient allocation. In this case no intervention in the market can result in an unambiguous welfare improvement. By definition, any improvement in one agent's welfare must decrease another agent's well-being. Therefore, market intervention can only be concerned with value judgments about the distribution of income and presumably can offer no gains in productive efficiency. This fact should make us very dubious of using a theoretical framework that admittedly seeks to impose Pareto efficiency as a condition of market equilibrium in order to evaluate the efficacy of agrarian reform. Analysis has shown not only that equilibriums in rural markets may not be efficient but that any attempt to explain the use of share contracts in agriculture must be based upon the existence of a market imperfection. The important question is: What types of imperfections in and impediments to a complete set of markets are likely to exist in an agricultural setting?

Transaction Costs

In his works Cheung (1968, 1969) listed under transaction costs both the enforcement and negotiation costs of contractural arrangements. He believed

8. This proposition has been independently stressed by Newbery (1977), Stiglitz (1974*a*, *b*), and Jaynes (1979).

that share contracts have higher costs, because they require both negotiation and enforcement. A close analysis indicates that there is no a priori basis for this presumption. The assumption that wage and rental contracts involve no negotiation costs includes an implicit assumption that markets for those contracts are costlessly auctioneered. In reality these contracts entail considerable negotiation costs, for agreement must be reached on numerous questions, such as: What is the duration of the contract? What are the specific duties and rights of the wage hand? Precisely what is the tenant allowed to do with rented land and the property on that land?

On a strict a priori basis, I suggest that the negotiation costs of contracts be considered equal. This leaves enforcement costs and opens the way for the incentives argument. It is interesting to note here that although Cheung discusses enforcement costs, he never mentions the possibility that share contracts may provide workers with extra incentives to work hard. The reason for this is that once work incentives are considered, it is obvious that resulting allocations will not generally be first-best efficient. The incentive argument is predicated upon the economic fact that if a worker's remuneration for any effort is less than the full marginal product of that effort, he has a personal motive to supply less effort than his employer would desire. Under a rental contract the full marginal product belongs to the renter, whereas a wage system provides practically no incentives. Furthermore, if there is uncertainty in production, the rental contract forces all the risk upon the tenant. Since the landlord is likely to be more able and therefore more willing to bear risk, the straight rental contract will often be inefficient. Consequently, the share contract is offered as a method of making the tenant's remuneration depend positively upon his effort. In this analysis a share contract is best viewed from the landlord's perspective as a means of trading off expected profit (because the tenant receives a share) and what may be very heavy costs of supervision. When the fact that capital and other variable inputs are needed in the production process is considered, the importance of the incentive argument becomes even clearer. In many share contracts all the variable inputs except labor are initially supplied by the landlord, with the tenant's contractual share of costs subtracted from his share of output after harvest. In many of these cases the landlord supplies the tenant with subsistence at credit terms. The sharing of risk is then very asymmetrical. In the words of Turgot: "Le propriétaire, qui fait les avances, court tous les risques des accidents de récoltes."[9]

These points are related to another important one. The preceding remarks show that incentives and risk sharing are related. The incentive problem can be eliminated by choosing a rental contract that may load too

---

9. Turgot (1844), p. 545: "The landlord, who makes the advances, bears all the risks of uncertain harvests."

much risk on the tenant. The share contract is sometimes argued to be a compromise between these two conflicting conditions. But this problem has been well analyzed in the principal-agency literature for the two-input case of effort and land. If the principal (landlord) has any useful information about the state of the world, the optimal contract will generally not be a simple linear share contract, but a nonlinear sharing rule that can be interpreted as a rental contract with a second-best optimal insurance policy. Expressed more simply, the landlord will remit a portion of the tenant's rental payment when the tenant can satisfy the landlord that the poor performance was beyond the tenant's control and not a result of moral hazard.[10]

Does the fact that we find linear share contracts in abundance indicate that the special conditions necessary for their optimality approximate reality? I doubt this strongly. The fact that both parties must ultimately share in the cost of capital inputs is a more likely answer. Given that costs are shared, each party, being something of a capitalist, will desire that the return to his capital investment be systematically related to the marginal product of his capital.

Imperfect Capital Markets and Entrepreneurial Decisions

The recognition that farming requires many more inputs than simply land and labor is a major step toward understanding the use of different forms of land tenancy. During the growing season, a large number of important decisions must be made by the cultivators of the land. What crop mix should be chosen? What seed varieties and fertilization methods should be used? These are simple examples of the selection of different production techniques. When a landlord hires wage labor to work his land, there is no question who makes these entrepreneurial decisions. This same claim is often made with regard to fixed cash renting, but the claim is not strictly true. The cash renter's choice of crop mix will in all likelihood have to conform to the landlord's crop rotation plans for his land. The choices of techniques available to the renter are likely to be restricted to those the landlord considers, if not beneficial, at least not detrimental to prudent soil conservation requirements. The negotiation costs of rental contracts will not be negligible. This indicates that the cash renter will not have complete entrepreneurial authority but will be able to exercise his own discretion within the bounds of his rental contract.

With share contracts we have not only these difficulties, but also a problem in deciding how landlord and tenant can ajudicate the final decisions, even within the bounds of proper conservation methods dictated by the landlord. If there exists no price or production uncertainty, there is no problem. If both landlord and tenant are profit maximizers, each will want

10. The principal-agency literature is burgeoning. See the bibliography.

to apply inputs to the land until the marginal revenue product of the input equals the marginal cost of the input to himself. Therefore, if each has the same share of input costs as his share of output, they will agree upon total input use. It is often pointed out that this result still holds if there is only multiplicative production uncertainty. Let output in state θ be $Y(\theta)$ and let X_i be the ith input. Under multiplicative uncertainty, output may be written

$$Y(\theta) = g(\theta)F(X_1, \ldots, X_N),$$

where $F(\ldots)$ is the production function and g is a scaling factor depending upon an exogenous factor like the weather. We consider a two-period world with a growing and a harvest-consumption season. Assume that the tenant and landlord have additively separable utilities. The tenant has an income y in the first period. He consumes a subsistence

$$C = y - \sum_{i-1}^{N-1} \alpha^i p^i \cdot X_i - S$$

with savings S and α^i his share of input costs $p^i X_i$. If the tenant supplies $L = X_N$ units of labor to the rented land, he will desire to

$$\max_{X_i, S} V(C, L) + EU[\alpha Y(\theta) + rS],$$

where r is the gross interest on savings. The first-order conditions are:

$$-V_C \alpha^i p^i + EU' \alpha F_i g = 0, \qquad i = 1, \ldots, N$$

and

$$-V_C + EU'r = 0.$$

Assume that $\alpha^i = \alpha$ for all i. Then these equations reduce to

$$F_i = \frac{rp^i \cdot EU'}{EU'g}.$$

A similar condition will hold for the landlord who faces an interest rate ρ_i:

$$F_i = \frac{\rho_i p_i EU'}{EU'g}.$$

Even if landlord and tenant agree about the expected value of g and have identical preferences, they will agree about the amount of input to use only if they face the same rate of interest. This is very likely not going to be true, particularly if the landlord is the tenant's creditor, as he often is. Then any transaction costs will cause a divergence between borrowing and lending rates, and even if there is agreement about prospective outcomes, the tenant will desire to use fewer inputs than the landlord. If the landlord is the lender, it is probably reasonable to assume that in negotiation his

views about input choices take better-than-equal precedence. But costs will
be incurred in making sure that the tenant, who supplies the direct labor,
does indeed use all the inputs supplied by the landlord and does not resell
them to supplement his first-period subsistence. More generally, any lender
to a tenant, whether a share or a fixed-rent tenant, must expend some effort
in ensuring that the tenant chooses a profitable technique. If there is a
possibility of bankruptcy resulting from crop failure and/or low prices, not
only must borrowing and lending rates differ (in the absence of perfect
insurance markets) but the different objectives of borrower and lender may
cause the lender to ration credit to each borrower. Since the landlord must
monitor the terms of his contract with the tenant anyway, it will often be
advantageous for him also to be either the tenant's direct creditor or an
intermediary between the tenant and a credit specialist. Note that agreement
about the choice of inputs also requires that the landlord know exactly how
much labor the tenant actually supplies to the land. Otherwise, there will
still be a divergence of opinion. If for some reason all of these assumptions
are satisfied, there is still little reason to expect agreement. The assumption
of multiplicative risk is very strong. If risk is not multiplicative, it is not
enough that agents agree only upon the expected value of $g(\theta)$.

Elsewhere (1982) I have argued that these conditions have a substantial
impact upon the nature of the market for tenancies and wage labor. Given
the need for a substantial financial fund to carry out a farming operation,
many landlords, large and small, may find themselves short of capital. In
the presence of an imperfect capital market, many sources of credit may be
sought. The landowner who finds a tenant with a plow and possibly his own
team of bullocks may find that offering a share tenancy to this agent is a
cheaper way of obtaining this capital than having to risk some portion of
his own property as collateral for a loan that would allow him to lease or
purchase all the necessary capital inputs himself and to hire wage labor.
Given the cost of capital, the possibility of credit rationing, and the differing
supervision costs of various tenancies, each landlord must choose the mix
of contracts that best allocates his capital, land, and supervisory time to
profit. Let $C^i = [C_1^i, \ldots, C_K^i]$ be the ith contract offered by the landowner.
The jth component C_j^i represents some input level or share of cost or output.
Suppose that there are constant returns in production and that the profit
to be earned from contract C^i in state θ is $\pi(C^i, \theta)$. Then if n^i is the number
of type i contracts offered by the landowner and $R = [R_1, \ldots, R_N]$ is his
endowment of resources such as land, capital, and financial wealth, we have
the nonlinear programming problem:

$$\max_{n^i} EU \left[\sum_i \pi(C^i, \theta)n^i, \sum C_K^i n^i \right] \quad \text{S.T.} \quad \sum_i C_j^i \le R_j, \quad j = 1, \ldots, N$$

$$(C_K^i = \text{supervisory labor of landlord})$$

and the constraint that each offered contract is acceptable to some agent. In equilibrium, the demand by tenants for each offered contract is greater than or equal to its supply. If demand is strictly greater for any contract, the prospective tenants desiring that contract must be receiving a bare subsistence income and/or a reservation utility below which they withdraw from the legal market, perhaps by migrating. The first important point to note is that not every agent can fulfill the conditions of each contract. A landless worker with little property and therefore no collateral is unlikely to have access to enough credit to stock a farm. He therefore cannot give a reasonable guarantee that a rental contract he signs will be fulfilled. Knowing this, landlords will not offer contracts to agents who do not have the resources to fulfill them. Agents with different endowments of resources will be offered and must accept different labor-tenancy contracts. This result is a direct consequence of incomplete and nontextbook-perfect markets and is, in my opinion, fundamental to the understanding of rural labor markets.

By applying simple duality theory to the first-order conditions of a simpler landowner's allocation problem, I have shown that the income accruing to landlord and tenant pursuant to a given contract will depend directly upon the marginal product of all inputs provided by each in the contract. That an individual's earned income is a function of the marginal product of his resources is, of course, hardly surprising. The point here is that this total income is all tied up in one source, the tenancy. In a complete market setting, the labor income of agents could be divorced from their nonhuman capital income. In the present setting, any agent who invested his capital in the imperfect market and then sought a separate return for his human capital in the labor market would find his contractual opportunities very limited. His labor opportunities are tied to his capital resources. As has been pointed out by others, this is even true for the poor propertyless laborer. His employment contract will often include some consumption credit as well as a wage and labor requirement.[11]

Theory tells us that the income accruing to the parties of a tenancy contract will depend upon the marginal product of resources and the share of the resources provided by each. But in practice we have no means of making a precise imputation. The landlord must be imputed income for his labor spent in supervision, for example. Where does this income show up in the final division of profit? I suggest that one of the places is in the interest rates charged tenants. These interest rates include not only a risk premium but a premium for the considerable transaction costs of extending small agricultural loans.

11. These are precisely the points that were made by P. K. Bardhan (chap. 12), Braverman and Srinivasan (chap. 3), and Mitra (1982) in their discussions of interlinked contracts in rural markets during this conference. The issues were also stressed by the classical economists and follow from their assumption of nonperfect capital markets.

What characteristics does the allocation in such an economy have? The allocation of resources will not be Pareto-efficient. The marginal product of inputs will differ across farms, and marginal rates of substitution will differ between individuals. Determination of whether the allocation is efficient, given all the market imperfections, is a complicated second-best problem whose significance has only recently begun to be appreciated by modern economists. The implications for agricultural policy in underdeveloped areas are very important. Agrarian reform cannot be accomplished by a simple substitution of share tenancies for money rent tenancy by legislative fiat. This point was clearly recognized by many of the classical economists. In particular, John Stuart Mill and Karl Marx recognized that the problem of agrarian reform is what modern economists term a problem of the second best. Our general knowledge of second-best problems informs us that piecemeal policy changes are generally not desirable. The paper presented by Braverman and Srinivasan at this conference (chapter 3) reveals the ineffectiveness of piecemeal policy. Agrarian reform must be concerned not just with the types of contracts in use, but with the institutional features that cause the use of those contractual relations. Alternatively, the fact that share contracts serve a useful purpose does not mean that agrarian reform is unnecessary and will be ineffectual, as has been argued by Cheung. For we have seen that the use of share contracts must be understood as an imperfect response to incomplete and imperfect markets caused by fundamental imperfections of information and the resulting transaction costs.

The research needed on this topic seems to me to be not only considerable in amount but of great importance, and I hope that more pens are set upon the issues in the near future.

3

Agrarian Reforms in Developing Rural Economies Characterized by Interlinked Credit and Tenancy Markets

Avishay Braverman and T. N. Srinivasan

It is often claimed that because the rural economies of developing countries are characterized by a noncompetitive market structure, policy analysis of such economies will differ significantly from a similar analysis of a competitive world. We discuss here the possible impact of policies such as land reform, as well as alternative tenancy and credit reforms in a rural economy characterized by interlinked land, labor, and credit markets. One of the many contributors to the literature on interlinking states: "It is misleading when talking about individual operators to hypothesize that each producer confronts technical data and market prices in an impersonal environment and all are equally free to take behaviour in any one single market without knowing how the markets are interlinked by price and non-price relations, for the fields of *feasible* choices in the different markets are not, as assumed under competition, definable *a priori* independently of each other."[1] While this statement is suggestive, it is by no means a complete definition of interlinking. After all, the typical consumer's choice problem, as usually formulated in microeconomic theory, implies that the consumer's actions in the market, with regard to each of the set of goods, are interlinked by his budget constraint. Similarly, in a typical producer's choice problem, profit maximization links his choice of inputs and his choice of outputs given his technology. In any case, at the economy-wide level, general equilibrium implies simultaneous equilibrium in *all* markets, with the supply and demand in each market being dependent on *all* relevant prices.

A possible definition of interlinked contracts could be the following: *contracts made between the same pair of individuals concerning exchanges*

The views and conclusions presented in this paper are the sole responsibility of its authors and should not be attributed to the World Bank. We would like to thank Deepak Lal, Pradeep Mitra, and Joseph Stiglitz for helpful discussions and Vivianne Lake for editorial assistance. For a more detailed technical exposition of the views presented here see Braverman and Srinivasan (1981).

1. See Bharadwaj (1974*b*).

of more than one commodity or service, the contracts being linked in an essential way—in other words, contracts between a pair of individuals in two or more commodities that are linked by coincidence. Contracts that could as well have been concluded without change at different points in time and not necessarily between the same individuals are not interlinked in this sense. This definition is not meant to exclude intertemporal linking of contracts. On the contrary, a very important aspect of interlinking is the linkage of present and future transactions.

In the present paper we concentrate on one form of linkage between land, labor, and credit contracts in the context of sharecropping. In this context, the following conditions lead to interlinking: (1) there is an incentive problem because of the cost of monitoring and supervising effort; (2) the tenant has no accumulated savings; so he must borrow at the beginning of the production period; and (3) there are imperfections in the capital market in the form of differing costs of capital to the landlord and to the tenant.

One major result of this paper is valid both in the context of interlinked credit and tenancy contracts and in the context of sharecropping contracts alone. It is that as long as the landlord can vary the size of the plot given to a tenant and there are enough potential tenants, the equilibrium will be characterized by "utility equivalent" contracts even if the landlord does not control any other term of the contract, such as crop share or interest rate on credit. This means that in equilibrium, a tenant's utility obtained through sharecropping will be the same as that which he could have obtained as a full-time wage laborer. Newbery and Stiglitz (1979) assert, without providing a satisfactory proof, the same result in the context of sharecropping alone, and a similar, though not identical, conclusion has been obtained in a different setting by Cheung (1969). Our proof follows from our result that, *ceteris paribus, the tenant's optimal effort per hectare is a decreasing function of the size of the plot he cultivates.*

The utility equivalence result has the fundamental implication that policies other than land reform (that is, reform that confers ownership on the tenant of the piece of land he is cultivating) will leave the welfare of each potential tenant unaltered while affecting the level of output, the extent of tenancy, and the welfare of the landlord. Given the possibility of linking tenancy and credit contracts, it is shown that the landlord will resort to linking only in a situation where it will *lower* the cost of credit to the tenant. If the government offers the tenant subsidized credit at a cost lower than the landlord's opportunity cost of funds, the landlord will move out of the tenant's credit market and allow the tenant to borrow from the government. The increase in surplus as a result of government subsidization of tenant's credit will fully accrue to the landlord as a consequence of the utility equivalence result. Hence, *government subsidization of tenants' credit results only in the subsidization of landlords.* Other partial reforms by the government, however, may force the landlord to link credit and tenancy contracts even if the government provides the cheapest source of credit; this linkage leaves the tenant's utility unaltered at its prereform level while affecting total output and the extent of tenancy.

Our model is also able to provide a theoretical underpinning for two almost opposite phenomena that are sometimes observed: low-interest consumption loans from landlord to tenant and the opposite—high-interest, low-volume loans.

We begin with an extended discussion of the various possible forms of interlinked contracts and the circumstances in which they are likely to arise. In the next two sections we present the model, which is followed by a characterization of the equilibrium. We then discuss policies of tenancy, credit, and land reform as well as the impact of taxation and technological progress. Finally, in the last section we briefly summarize our conclusions and relate them to the literature on sharecropping and on interlinked credit and tenancy contracts.

TYPES OF INTERLINKED CONTRACTS

As stated at the beginning of this paper, interlinked contracts may be defined as transactions in more than one commodity or service made between the same pair of individuals and linked in an essential way. An example will perhaps make the concept of interlinking clearer. Suppose a landlord and a tenant enter into a contract in which the tenant rents a piece of land at a stipulated rent, and at the same time the landlord extends the tenant credit, again on specified terms. If the contract in land (credit) could have taken place *independently* of that in credit (land) with no additional cost to either party, the two contracts are not interlinked. An essential feature of this definition, therefore, is that delinking the contracts would be infeasible or costly for at least one party. If it is infeasible, the two parties either transact in all the relevant goods and services or do not transact in any of them. If it is costly, linking rather than not linking will benefit at least one party.

The infeasibility of delinking for both parties can arise from the nonexistence of certain markets (for example, the market for bullocks' services); however, interlinking covers a much wider range of contracts than those simply created to circumvent the absence of certain markets. Quite often the linking of contracts occurs when there is a moral hazard problem, which results in an "inappropriable" externality.[2] Moral hazard arises in a

---

2. In the broader sense, even this class of contracts can be defined as arising due to nonexistence of markets where the missing markets are themselves defined as the markets for the externalities.

risk-sharing contract when one party, often called the agent (tenant, insuree), can affect the probability distribution of the outcome (output, accident) through his action (effort, driving habits), which the other party, often called the principal (landlord, insurer) cannot effectively or cheaply monitor. In such a situation, the agent has an incentive to change the probability distribution of the outcome in his favor, once the parties have agreed on the terms of the contract. Since both parties know this, the form of contract as well as its terms will often include provisions that cover the moral hazard problem, such as the deductible feature of an insurance contract. Consider the case of sharecropping. The tenant's effort, which cannot be perfectly monitored or inferred by the landlord through observation, is affected by his capital endowment. If the tenant lacks capital he will try to borrow some. The borrowing affects his effort and, consequently, output and the landlord's profits. Since the landlord can neither perfectly monitor the tenant nor force the tenant to exert a certain level of effort (it is too costly), there is an inherent externality from the credit market into the production process. Since the landlord is aware of this externality he can internalize it (address the moral hazard problem) by linking the credit and tenancy contracts, thus promoting greater efficiency in production and increasing his own profits.

This linking may constitute a Pareto-superior move as opposed to a delinked situation, since the increase in total surplus allows for an improvement in the welfare of at least one party, without making the other party worse off. Such linking is clearly *voluntary*. Linking, however, may not necessarily constitute a Pareto-improving move if one party, who possesses more market power, decreases the other party's welfare through interlinking of contracts. Such linking could be termed *forced linking*. The weaker party would prefer delinking if that option were open to him; however, since this option is not allowed by the more powerful party, the weaker party chooses to accept the "tie-in" package rather than not to transact at all.

There are two more classes of interlinked contracts. One class arises from voluntary linking and results from *lowering transaction costs* for both parties. Many examples of linking often found in developed countries— such as tie-in sales, extension of supplier's credit, and shopping for unrelated items in a large store—result, to some degree, from lowered transaction costs. A second class constitutes a screening device necessitated by imperfect information regarding the attributes of a heterogenous population. In a world where some attributes, such as tenant's managerial skills, are unobservable, interlinked credit and tenancy contracts may serve as a screening device for landlords to identify more able tenants.

The equilibrium, in all of the preceding cases, is achieved in the context of an incomplete set of markets, imperfect markets, or both. Hence, welfare propositions relating to such equilibriums are often of the "second-best" kind. In an environment characterized by market distortions, for example, a move toward eliminating a subset of distortions does not necessarily imply an improvement of welfare. Therefore, policy intervention, either by creating some, but not all, of the previously nonexistent markets or by eliminating market power through reform, will not necessarily lead to a more *efficient* allocation of resources compared with the preintervention equilibrium. Clearly, equity or the distributional aspects of such intervention will depend very much on the prior structure.

Nonexistence of markets is the rule rather than the exception, particularly in less developed countries. Landless rural households endowed with the labor of women and children who do not work either because there is no market for their labor or because social taboos prevent them from working for others often lease in land. The leased-in land is farmed mostly by nonmarketable family labor, while those members of the household who can work as wage laborers outside the household farm do so, to a significant extent. In this case, transactions in land and family labor become linked. There are several other examples of linkage of a similar nature, arising from the nonexistence of markets for draft power and for tenants' managerial input.

Intertemporal linking is quite prominent, especially in the labor market. If the availability or cost of wage labor in peak agricultural seasons is uncertain, a landlord may wish to employ a permanent or attached farm laborer whose services are available to him throughout the year. In this case, the linking occurs in an attached labor contract, which is an agreement to buy and sell labor in *both* peak and off-peak seasons. The unlinked alternative is to hire wage labor in each season separately.[3]

THE MODEL

The Tenant

The form of rental contract discussed here is sharecropping. If *only* incentive problems exist (the landlord can neither force the worker to contribute a specified level of effort nor can he monitor it), the fixed-rent contract will be best suited to remedy them; it will, in fact, dominate a fixed-wage or a sharecropping contract. The tenant obtains all the fruits of his effort after paying the fixed rent. Fixed rents, however, imply that the tenant must bear all risk resulting from output uncertainty resulting from exogenous conditions (weather, illness). If the tenant is risk-averse, a fixed-rent contract will be inefficient, in which case a sharecropping contract will dominate it.

It follows that risk-sharing effects seem to be necessary to explain the

3. For more examples, see P. K. Bardhan (1980).

phenomena of sharecropping, unless there are absent markets (see, chapter 2). Incentive problems arising from the cost of supervision are also necessary, since any risk sharing obtained through a share contract can also be obtained by a linear combination of wage and fixed-rent contracts (Stiglitz 1974, Newbery 1977). However, we shall not consider risk elements here; we focus instead on the relations between incentive effects and the tenant's lack of funds.

We assume that all workers are identical, in that they face two employment alternatives; they may work either as tenants on the landlords' land or as wage laborers outside the farm. Each tenant is offered a plot of land of size H hectares for cultivation, in return for which he agrees to pay the landlord a share $(1 - \alpha)$ of the harvest. None of the workers possess any savings at the beginning of the production year. Wage workers are paid wages, W, during the production period and therefore have no need to borrow for consumption. The tenant, however, borrows at the beginning of each season his entire consumption needs for the coming season and repays his loan with interest at the end of the season, after harvest. He does not store any grain from one season to the next nor does he have any investment opportunity.

The tenant obtains a proportion v of his borrowings (either as a voluntary or as a tie-in package with a tenancy contract—see the next subsection) from his landlord at an interest rate r_T per season. He obtains the remaining proportion of his borrowings $(1 - v)$ from an alternative source (local moneylender, cooperative, government credit) at an interest rate r_A. He treats r_T and r_A as parameters over which he has no influence. We assume that he cannot default, (1) in order to simplify the argumentation, and (2) because in many areas landlords virtually hold the harvested crop as collateral. Clearly, if the tenant can borrow all the present value of his consumption at either r_T or r_A, he will choose to borrow the entire sum from the cheapest source. However, since our discussion focuses on linking, we start by assuming that the tenant takes v as given, so that $v > 0$ will represent linking over which he has no influence.

Labor provided by the tenant for cultivation (including all operations, from land preparation to harvesting) is denoted by eL, where L denotes the number of man-days per season and e denotes the effort per *man-day of labor*. Thus, eL represents labor in efficiency units. Output Q is a concave function exhibiting constant returns to scale in land H and eL.[4] Thus:

$$Q = F(H, eL). \tag{3.1}$$

4. Bell and Braverman (1980) show that landlords will prefer cultivation with wage labor to sharecropping, if the production function is one of constant returns to scale and there is no uncertainty. Since we do not allow the landlord the option of self-cultivation with wage labor, the Bell–Braverman result does not apply to our analysis for this and other reasons having to do with the modeling of tenant's effort and behavior.

Assuming the number of man-days, L (labor in natural units), to be exogenously fixed, we can set (without loss of generality) $L = 1$. Thus we can rewrite equation (3.1) as:

$$Q = \frac{1}{x}F(1, ex) \equiv \frac{f(ex)}{x}, \tag{3.2}$$

where x is man-days of labor per hectare of land. Given that $L = 1$, x represents the reciprocal of the size of the plot tenant is allotted. The function f represents the average product per hectare of land. By assumption, f' is positive and f'' is negative where the primes (single and double) denote the first and second derivatives of f, respectively. The tenant's share of the harvest Q is α and his income is therefore αQ.

From our assumption that the tenant borrows his entire consumption needs at the beginning of the season and has no carry-over stock or investment opportunities, it follows that its consumption c in any season equals his income αQ at the end of the season, discounted by $(1 + i)$ where i is the effective interest rate on his borrowing. Of course, i equals $vr_T + (1 - v)r_A$. Thus:

$$c - \frac{\alpha Q}{1 + vr_T + (1 - v)r_A} \equiv \beta Q \tag{3.3}$$

where

$$\beta = \frac{\alpha}{1 + vr_T + (1 - v)r_A} \tag{3.4}$$

is the discounted share of the tenant.

We assume that the tenant's utility function $U(c, e)$ is strictly quasi-concave in consumption and in leisure, where leisure is defined as $\tilde{e} \equiv -e$. Further, both consumption and leisure are assumed to be normal goods.

The potential tenant's choice or control variable is e. He will not choose to work as a tenant unless $U(c, e)$ is at least as large as $\bar{U}$, the utility he could assure himself by working as a wage laborer. The supply of tenants is assumed to be infinitely elastic at $\bar{U}$, that is, $\bar{U}$ is exogenous. Thus, we can solve the potential tenant's choice problem in two steps. First, let the tenant maximize:

$$\max_e U[c(e), e] \quad \text{S.T.} \quad \text{(3.2) and (3.3).} \tag{3.5}$$

Let the maximized value of U be U^*. Second, let the tenant compare U^* with $\bar{U}$. If $U^* \geq \bar{U}$, he works as a tenant; otherwise, he works as a wage laborer.

It is immediately apparent from equations (3.2)–(3.5) that the parameters α, v, r_T, and r_A enter the tenant's constraint set and utility function

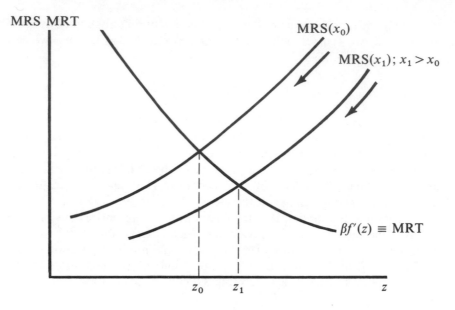

FIGURE 3.1. Tenant's Optimal Effort per Hectare.

only through their effect on his discounted share β. By substituting equations (3.2), (3.3), and (3.4) in equation (3.5), maximizing with respect to e, we get the first-order condition[5]

$$\beta f'(ex)U_1 + U_2 = 0, \tag{3.6}$$

that is, at the margin, the change in the tenant's utility of consumption caused by a change in effort must compensate for the change in his disutility caused by the same change in effort.

Now, define effort per hectare as $z \equiv ex$ and rewrite equation (3.6), to obtain

$$\beta f'(z) = -\frac{U_2}{U_1}. \tag{3.7}$$

On the left-hand side of equation (3.7) we have the marginal rate of transformation between consumption and leisure through production (MRT), and on the right-hand side of equation (3.7) we have the marginal rate of substitution between consumption and leisure through consumption (MRS). Whereas MRT is a function of β and z, MRS is a function of β, z, and x. The relation in equation (3.7) is crucial to an understanding of the utility equivalence result and of the impact of land reform on output. We present the relation graphically in figure 3.1. The MRT curve, given β,

5. It can be shown that the second-order condition is satisfied from our strict quasi-concavity assumption concerning U and the strict concavity of f.

is downward sloping in effort per hectare, z, due to diminishing marginal productivity (that is, $f'' < 0$). The MRS, given β and x, is an increasing function because of the normality of both consumption and leisure (see Braverman and Srinivasan 1981 for a proof of this and all other propositions discussed in the remainder of this paper).

Now consider the impact of a ceteris paribus reduction in plot size (an increase in x) on tenant's welfare, effort e, and effort per hectare, z. Clearly, his welfare declines. The impact on e cannot be determined unambiguously since it depends on the relative absolute magnitudes of the income and substitution effects, which are opposite in sign. However, there is no ambiguity in the impact on z. Consider figure 3.1: a change in the plot size *does not affect* the MRT curve. A reduction in plot size, however, shifts the MRS curve outside and downward since, ceteris paribus, such a reduction results in a decline in the tenant's income (which is identical to the tenant's consumption), thereby increasing the marginal utility of consumption vis-à-vis leisure and calling for increased effort per hectare to restore equality between MRS and MRT. This reduction leads, therefore, to the following proposition:

PROPOSITION 1. *The tenant's effort per hectare increases with a reduction in the size of his plot. This holds even if the tenant's effort declines with such a reduction in plot size.*

Remark. The instrument other than plot size, namely, β, shifts both curves; thus, in order to derive the impact of policies that change β (for example, land reform), we need to specify the relative movements of the two curves.

The Landlord

With an infinitely elastic supply of identical tenants and constant returns to scale in production, maximizing profits is equivalent to maximizing profits per hectare. Hence, our model yields the same results whether different landlords possess different amounts of land or not. Therefore, without loss of generality, we can assume that all landlords are identical and possess one hectare of land each, which they divide into plots of size $1/x$ to give to each of x tenants. As stated earlier, the landlord may require that each of his tenants get a proportion v of his borrowings from him at an interest rate r_T. Assuming that an alternative use of funds would have earned the landlord an interest of r_L per season (probably from deposits in the city's bank), his income g can be shown as:

$$g = \frac{f(z)}{x}\{1 - \beta[1 + vr_L + (1 - v)r_A]\}.$$

Multiplying g by the number of tenants, x, we get the landlord's income G:

$$G = \{1 - \beta[1 + vr_L + (1 - v)r_A]f(z)\}. \qquad (3.8)$$

The interest rate, r_T, charged by the landlord on his loans to his tenant is seen from equation (3.8) to affect his income *only* through its effect on β, the tenant's discounted share.

The landlord maximizes G with respect to his choice variables given the tenant's effort function $e(ex, \beta)$. The choice variables include the plot size $1/x$ and may include the tenant's crop share α, v (if there are no laws against the landlord providing credit) and r_T, the rate of interest charged.

UTILITY EQUIVALENCE

For the moment, let us focus on the choice of x (the number of tenants or, equivalently, the plot size per tenant). The landlord's income, G, is an increasing function of output per hectare, f, and f is an increasing function of its argument, effort per hectare, z—(see equation [3.8]). Furthermore, proposition 1 states that z is an increasing function of x. Therefore, the landlord's income *increases* with x; a decrease in each tenant's plot size, with a corresponding increase in the number of tenants, increases the landlord's income. On the other hand, a tenant's welfare clearly *decreases* as x increases. Thus, if at any value of x the tenant's utility U^* exceeds his utility $\bar{U}$ in an alternative use of his labor (so that he chooses to be a tenant), the landlord, by reducing plot size (increasing x), can increase his income while pushing the tenant toward $\bar{U}$. As long as there are enough potential tenants, the landlord's choice, x, will be to push the tenant to a utility level equaling $\bar{U}$.[6] Thus sharecropping will be utility equivalent to the best alternative use of the tenant's labor. Hence, we have proposition 2:

PROPOSITION 2. *The equilibrium in the land-labor market will be characterized by utility equivalent contracts.*

It should be noted that this proposition does not depend for its validity on the presence or absence of any linkage between tenancy and credit transactions. The landlord's use of plot size as his *sole* instrument variable is sufficient to result in a utility equivalent contract equilibrium, an outcome obtained by Cheung (1969) in a different model. Our model is that of Stiglitz (1974), subsequently utilized by Newbery and Stiglitz (1979). Assuming the tenants' utility function to be separable into consumption and leisure, these researchers claimed that competition between landlords will drive the

---

6. It can also be argued that if at an initial x, U^* is less than $\bar{U}$, the potential tenant will not choose sharecropping. In order to obtain someone to cultivate his land, the landlord will then have to increase the plot size, that is, reduce x. We are ignoring the fact that a tenant is "indivisible" whereas land is divisible.

inequality $U^* > \bar{U}$ to equality, thereby achieving utility equivalence. We have already shown that the utility equivalence outcome results from profit maximization by landlords and not from competition. That there is an infinitely elastic supply of potential tenants at $\bar{U}$ does not render the proposition insignificant, since the possibility of an excess applicants equilibrium at $U^* > \bar{U}$ can occur if the output share, instead of the plot size, is the only control variable of the landlord. A well-known case of excess applicants equilibrium arose as a result of applying the efficiency wage hypothesis (see Leibenstein 1957, Mirrlees 1975, Stiglitz 1976, and Bliss and Stern 1978, primarily because the landlord is not allowed to use an instrument completely orthogonal to effort to reduce U^* to $\bar{U}$ without affecting effort. In our model, the use of the power to vary the plot size, although nonorthogonal to effort, guarantees the utility equivalent contract result since the tenant's effort per hectare increases with a reduction in his plot size. Additional instruments such as crop share and interest rate are not needed for this purpose.

Of the two assumptions used in deriving our result, namely, that both consumption and leisure are normal goods, and that the tenant is prohibited, as part of his contract, from working as a part-time laborer outside the farm, the latter is perhaps more controversial. Its actuality is primarily an empirical issue. It is true that tenants work as part-time laborers in many villages, but the extent of such work is often limited. There is also some evidence to suggest that landlords believe that a tenant will put greater effort into cultivation, the smaller his plot size.

From utility equivalence $U[c(x, \beta), e(x, \beta)] = \bar{U}$, x can be solved as a function of the tenant's discounted share β. It is easily shown that $x'(\beta) > 0$, that is, in order to maintain the tenant on his isoutility curve, the landlord must increase the tenant's discounted share if he reduces the plot size. Thus, when analyzing changes in β, unless other changes are specified, we assume that the landlord changes x along the curve $x(\beta)$ so as to maintain the tenant at a welfare level of $\bar{U}$.

Consider the impact of change in β both on effort per hectare, z, and total effort, e. It can be shown that effort per hectare *increases* with an increase in β. *Total effort*, however, will increase (decrease) with an increase in β if the elasticity of substitution between effective labor and land, σ, is larger (smaller) than one. Formally, it can be shown that

$$\frac{de}{d\beta} = A \cdot \frac{(1 - \sigma)}{\sigma} \tag{3.9}$$

where $A < 0$.

The results derived so far do not utilize the credit aspects of the model. We know the landlord's credit instruments (v, r_T) and crop share x, so we can write his income G as

$$G = (1 - \beta\theta)f(ex), \tag{3.10}$$

where $\theta = 1 + vr_L + (1 - v)r_A$. It is seen that (α, v, r_T) enter G only through their effect on β and θ, since e and x are functions of β. Now it is clear from equation (3.10) that G is decreasing in θ for given β. Hence an income-maximizing landlord will, first, choose his optimal θ to be θ^*, the minimum feasible θ for any given β; then he will choose β to maximize $(1 - \beta\theta^*)f(ex)$. Since θ depends only on v, which lies between 0 and 1, if the given value of β does not restrict the choices of 0 and 1 for v, then:

$$\theta^* = (1 + r_L) \text{ and } v^* = 1 \text{ if } r_L < r_A;$$
$$= (1 + r_A) \text{ and } v^* = 0 \text{ if } r_L > r_A. \tag{3.11}$$

Recalling that v is the proportion of borrowing by the tenant from the landlord, we can state equation (3.11) as the following proposition:

PROPOSITION 3. *The landlord, with no restriction on his choice of crop shares, will ensure that the tenant gets credit from the cheapest source. He does this by linking credit to tenancy if he is the cheaper source ($r_L \leq r_A$) and by not offering any credit if he is not.*

Remark When $r_L \leq r_A$, that is, where linking is optimal, it remains optimal even if there is an institutionally imposed floor on the tenant's crop share, α. The reason is that with full linking, any given $\beta \equiv \alpha/(1 + r_T)$ (and a fortiori the optimal β) can be achieved with an infinite set consisting of pairs (α, r_T), of which an infinite subset will meet the required floor.

   Proposition 3 is consistent with empirical observations (Bardhan and Rudra 1978) that landlords often offer interest-free loans to their tenants. When the landlord is the cheapest credit source, for example, and hence, there is linking ($r_L \leq r_A$), the interest rate r_T charged by the landlord is essentially arbitrary and could well be zero. In this instance, linking is essentially voluntary. However, this will not be true, as we will show later, if the environment faced by the parties is subject to certain constraints such as government regulations.

   Returning to the case where there is no floor on α, it can be derived and shown that

$$\beta^*\theta^* \gtreqless S \text{ according as } \sigma \gtreqless 1, \tag{3.12}$$

where $S \equiv (exf')/f$ is the imputed share of labor in output. When $r_L \leq r_A$, $\theta^* = (1 + r_L)$ and $\beta^* = \alpha^*/(1 + r_T)$; whereas when $r_L > r_A$, $\theta^* = (1 + r_A)$ and $\beta^* = \alpha/(1 + r_A)$. Since in the first case, r_T can be chosen to be r_L, $\beta^*\theta^*$ becomes the crop share α^* in either case. Using equation (3.12) we can thus state proposition 4:

PROPOSITION 4. *If there is no restriction on the landlord's choice of instruments* (α, v, r_T), *his optimal strategy is to offer his tenant a crop share* α^* *such that* $\alpha^* \gtreqless S$, *according as* $\sigma \gtreqless 1$.

Remark. When $r_L \leq r_A$, since $\beta^* \theta^* = [\alpha^*(1 + r_L)]/(1 + r_T)$, the landlord can offer an α^* that is less (greater) than S, even if σ is greater (less) than unity by choosing (α^*, r_T) with r_T sufficiently less (greater) than r_L.

Newbery and Stiglitz (1979) established proposition 4 without incorporating credit or its linkage to tenancy. The preceding remark extends their result to a situation where it is optimal for the tenant to borrow from his landlord. It also implies that it is possible to observe crop shares that are less than the imputed share of labor even for a production function with an elasticity of substitution larger than one.

POLICY ANALYSIS

Tenancy Reforms

Consider a reform that imposes a floor, α_F, on the tenant's share α of the harvest. This is a common feature of many agrarian reform laws in India. When $r_L \leq r_A$, if in an equilibrium $(\alpha^*, 1, r_T^*)$ prior to the promulgation of the reform law $\alpha^* < \alpha_F$, the landlord will respond to the reform by raising the crop share to α_F and simultaneously raising the interest rate to r_T^{**} so that in the new equilibrium $(\alpha_F, 1, r_T^{**})$, $\alpha_F/(1 + r_T^{**}) = \alpha^*/(1 + r_T^*) = \beta^*$. Since output depends only on β^*, it is unaffected by reform. Given utility equivalence, the tenant's welfare is unaffected anyway.

Consider now the following two alternatives: (1) an initial equilibrium in which the landlord is not the cheapest source of credit, that is, $r_L > r_A$ so that $v^* = 0$, $\beta^* = \alpha^*/(1 + r_A)$ with $\alpha^* < \alpha_F$; or (2) initially $r_L \leq r_A$ and $v^* = 1$, $\beta^* = \alpha^*/(1 + r_T)$ with $\alpha^* < \alpha_F$, but as part of a tenancy reform, the interest rate on the tenant's alternative source of credit is brought below r_L. In other words, the imposition of a floor, α_F, coincides with a change in r_A that brings r_A below r_L. This joint reform of tenancy and credit can be viewed as two consecutive reforms: first, a credit reform with no tenancy reform, so that the landlord switches from a one-asterisk to a two-asterisk equilibrium; and second, a tenancy reform imposing a floor. Then we need discuss only the first tenancy reform where $r_L > r_A$. In this case, it can be shown that the landlord can partially nullify the tenancy reform by *forcedly* linking the credit and tenancy contracts. In Braverman and Srinivasan (1981) we demonstrated that although there is no *optimal* policy for the landlord after reform, policies exist that will give him an income as close as he wishes to his income prior to reform. By forcing the tenant to take small loans (v is small) with a high interest rate r_T,[7] the landlord ensures that on the whole the tenant will both use the cheapest source of credit, r_A, and the landlord will collect from him γr_T, which increases the income of the landlord. (γr_T, however, is not an orthogonal lump-sum levy on the tenant.)

The preceding discussion implies that, if linking is permitted, the landlord can reduce the tenancy and credit reform to insignificance. Suppose now that the government bans linking, along with tenancy and credit reforms. Clearly, the landlord's income will decline, but the tenant's welfare will remain at the level he could have achieved while working as a wage laborer. What will be the effect on output? Since the landlord no longer has the instrument by which he can maintain the prereform discounted share, β^*, of the tenant, the reform will raise β. We know from proposition 1 that $dz/d\beta > 0$, so we can assert that output $f(z)$ will increase.[8] Thus we can state proposition 5:

PROPOSITION 5. *A tenancy reform that imposes a floor on the tenant's share of the crop with or without credit reform (to make credit available to the tenant at a rate lower than the landlord's opportunity cost of capital) will have no effect on output. If it is coupled with a ban on the linking of credit and tenancy transactions, it will raise output, reduce the tenant's plot size, and increase the number of tenants.*

Now consider only a ban on linking of credit and tenancy. Such a ban is, of course, meaningless when the landlord is not the cheapest source of credit, since no linking will be observed anyway. Suppose the ban is imposed when there is linking—when $r_L \leq r_A$ and $v^* = 1$. Obviously, this immediately raises the cost of extending credit to the tenant to r_A. In the landlord's income maximization problem, fixing v at zero (preventing linking) fixes θ at $(1 + r_A)$, that is, raises θ from its optimal value of $1 + r_L$ prior to the ban to $(1 + r_A)$. Since G is a monotonic decreasing function of θ, at *any value* of β, G is lower than before. Even with the optimal value of β, G is lower. This means that landlord's income definitely decreases. What about output? As long as $f(z)$ as a function of β is concave, optimal β for any specified θ is a decreasing function of θ. Hence, as θ is increased from $(1 + r_L)$ to $(1 + r_A)$, optimal β decreases. This means that, first, the optimal plot size increases, thereby reducing the number of tenants, and second, output decreases since $f(z)$ is an increasing function of β.

7. This is perhaps a rationale for empirical observations of tenants being charged high interest for rather small loans.

8. Recall the interpretation of this result. An increase in β raises the number of efficiency units of labor per hectare, (that is, *ex* supplied by *each* tenant) and increases the *number* of tenants as a result of a reduction in plot size. If the elasticity of substitution is less than unity, effort per tenant will decrease, so that output per tenant will also decline. But the increase in the number of tenants more than offsets this decline.

Finally, consider a credit reform alone where $r_L < r_A$. With this reform, the government-subsidized credit becomes the cheapest source of credit, that is, $r_A < r_L$. Before the reform the landlord lends to his tenants, but afterward, the landlord withdraws from the tenants' credit market. Yet, by the utility equivalence result, the landlord extracts all the surplus created by the government's cheap credit. Therefore, the government subsidization of tenants' credit results only in the *subsidization of landlords*.

Land Reform

Suppose that starting from an initial equilibrium (α^*, v^*, r_T^*) and $x(\beta^*)$, each tenant is given the ownership of the plot he cultivates and has to forgo the opportunity to borrow from one landlord. Clearly, the tenant's welfare improves, for if $r_L > r_A$, $v^* = 0$ and $\beta^* = \alpha^*/(1 + r_A)$. With reform, α becomes unity, r_A remains unchanged so that the tenant's (now a landowning peasant's) discounted share β increases, while the size of the plot remains the same. Thus, without changing his effort e (and its disutility), the tenant will gain in consumption and, hence, total utility. By optimally adjusting his effort to the changed β, he can increase his utility even further.

Now if $r_L \leq r_A$, initially $v^* = 1$. Since the landlord is indifferent in this case as to alternative combinations of (α, r_T) that result in his optimal β^*, we can view the land reform as if it first changed the interest rate charged by the landlord to r_A with a corresponding change in α to maintain the same β^*, and then raised the tenant's crop share to unity. The two effects together imply that the tenant's postreform discounted share is higher. From this point, the argument is the same as in the previous case.

What is the effect of land reform on output? Land reform increases the discounted share β while keeping the plot size fixed. Thus output is $f[e(\beta)x]$ where x is fixed. Hence, output will increase if tenant's effort increases. In Braverman and Srinivasan (1981) we provided the following condition:

$$\frac{\partial e}{\partial \beta} \gtreqless 0 \quad \text{according as} \quad -c\left(\frac{U_{11}}{U_1} - \frac{U_{21}}{U_2}\right) \lesseqgtr 1. \tag{3.13}$$

This leads to the following proposition:

PROPOSITION 6. *A land reform that confers ownership to the plot of land that a tenant used to cultivate under a sharecropping contract with a landlord will increase, not decrease output, according as* $-c\left(\dfrac{U_{11}}{U_1} - \dfrac{U_{21}}{U_2}\right) \lesseqgtr 1.$

To interpret equation (3.13) we can again utilize figure 3.1. Since the plot size is fixed, an increase (decrease) in effort implies an increase (decrease) in effort per hectare. The term on the right-hand side of equation (3.13) is the elasticity of the MRT with respect to β for given x *and* e *; the term* *on the left-hand side is the elasticity of the* MRS *with respect to β, which equals the elasticity of the marginal rate of substitution with respect to consumption. A reform that increases β shifts the curves in figure 3.1 in opposite direction. The dominant effect is obtained by a comparison of the two elasticies.*

Consider the case of a separable utility function, $U(c, e) = u(c) - v(e)$. Then equation (3.13) becomes

$$\frac{\partial e}{\partial \beta} \gtreqless 0 \quad \text{according as} \quad -\frac{u''c}{u'} \lesseqgtr 1. \tag{3.14}$$

The negative of the elasticity of marginal utility $[(u''c)/u']$ is defined by Arrow (1971) as the measure of relative risk aversion. The intuitive explanation for the value of this elasticity that is of relevance to our case, even though there is no uncertainty, is as follows. On the one hand, an increase in β increases tenant's income; hence, the marginal utility of income declines relative to the marginal disutility of effort, and, ceteris paribus, the new landowner will want to reduce his effort. On the other hand, his share in the marginal productivity of effort increases, with increasing β, thus creating an incentive for more effort. Whether the income effect or the marginal productivity effect is the dominant force depends solely on the elasticity of the marginal utility.

When land reform distributes the land to more owners than the original cultivators, it may increase total output even if $-c[(U_{11}/U_1) - (U_{21}/U_2)] > 1$ since, ceteris paribus, output per hectare increases with reductions in plot size.

Note that the preceding discussion also applies to analyses of sharecropping contracts if α is substituted for β. This holds for the remaining policy analysis as well.

Taxation and Technological Progress

Suppose the government imposes a proportional output tax at rate t on tenants and landlords (the rural community) in order to increase the amount of food for the urban workers. Since, for any β, this tax is equivalent to a reduction in the discounted share of the tenant from β to $\mu \equiv \beta(1 - t)$, the tenant's decision function $e(x, \beta)$ becomes $e(x, \mu)$. It is also easily seen that the landlord's choice set $x(\beta)$ becomes $x(\mu)$.

It can be shown (Braverman and Srinivasan 1981) that $d\mu/dt < 0$ and $df[z(\mu)]/dt = f'(dz/d\mu \cdot d\mu/dt) < 0$, that is, output declines due to the imposition of a proportional tax. The implied decline in the aftertax share, μ, necessitates an increase in the tenant's plot size in order to maintain the tenant on his reservation utility $\bar{U}$. The increase in plot size implies both a reduction in the number of tenants, x, and a decline in output. We thus obtain the following proposition:

PROPOSITION 7. *The imposition of a proportional output tax on landlords and tenants will cut the aftertax share of the tenant, increase the plot size per tenants, and reduce the number of tenants as well as total output.*

Modeling a Hicks neutral technical change is equivalent to modeling a proportional output tax; a Hicks neutral technical change is a shift in A where the production function is $Af(z)$. The only difference is the direction of the impact. Considering a Hick neutral technical change and applying proposition 7, we obtain proposition 8:

PROPOSITION 8. *A Hicks neutral technical change will increase the aftertax discounted share of the tenants, decrease the plot size per tenant, and increase the number of tenants as well as total output.*

Now, consider the case of a Cobb–Douglas production function. Given the unit elasticity of substitution, the tenant's effort is independent of $\mu \equiv \beta(1 - t)$—see equation (3.9)—that is, the decline in the aftertax share is totally compensated for by the increase in plot size, so as to leave the tenant's effort unaltered. Furthermore, it is easily seen, applying equation (3.12) that the optimal β is unaffected by the tax or technical changes. For the Cobb–Douglas case, all factor-augmenting technical changes can be viewed as Hicks neutral changes. Thus, considering irrigation as a land-augmenting technical change and applying proposition 8, we obtain:

PROPOSITION 9. *If the production function is of the Cobb–Douglas type, introducing irrigation will leave the discounted share contract unaltered, decrease the tenant's plot size, and increase the number of tenants as well as total output.*

Increase in the Tenant's Utility Level in an Alternative Occupation

Suppose that through an increase in the nonagricultural wage rate, the utility ($\overline{U}$) that the tenant could obtain in an alternative occupation increases. Assuming once again a Cobb–Douglas production function so that the tentant's effort is independent of β, it is clear that the landlord can meet the higher $\overline{U}$ only by increasing the plot size, therefore reducing the number of tenants and the output. Equilibrium β is unchanged. Hence, we have proposition 10:

PROPOSITION 10. *If the production function is of the Cobb–Douglas type, any increase in the utility that the tenant could obtain in an alternative occupation will increase the equilibrium plot size and reduce the number of tenants and the output, while leaving the discounted crop share unaltered.*

CONCLUSIONS

We can now summarize our results and relate them to the literature.[9] Our main result is that in a world in which (1) production takes place under constant returns to scale in land and labor in efficiency units, (2) a landlord can subdivide his land into as many plots as he choose, and (3) a tenant chooses his effort so as to maximize his utility, equilibrium will be characterized by utility equivalent contracts. In other words, even if a landlord has no power over crop shares or terms of credit, by choosing the plot size appropriately, he will force the tenant to a utility level equal to that which the tenant could have obtained in an alternative occupation as long as there are enough potential tenants. The landlord is able to do this not only because there is a perfectly elastic supply of tenants at this reservation utility level, but also because the *tenant's effort per hectare increases with a reduction in his plot size.*

This result is similar to that obtained by Cheung's (1969) model, where the tenant's effort per unit of raw labor is invariant. Cheung shows that landlords will provide each tenant a plot of land on which the tenant can earn no more than he could have earned in an alternative occupation. Whereas forcing the tenant's labor input is necessary in a Cheungian world, constraint takes a different from in our model: it ensures that the tenant does not split his working time between sharecropping and an alternative occupation.

In this world of utility equivalent contracts, it will be in the interest of the landlord to ensure that the tenant gets his credit from the cheapest source. If the landlord's opportunity cost of capital is lower than that charged by the local moneylender, the landlord will ensure that the tenant gets credit at the cheapest interest cost by offering a linked tenancy-*cum*-credit contract. In our models, unlike the models of Bhaduri (1973, 1977, 1979), linking credit with tenancy is not an instrument that extracts a surplus that would otherwise have accrued to the tenant. Linking, where optimal, increases output and the landlord's income (compared with nonlinking) by reducing the plot size per tenant, and therefore it increases the number of tenants, while leaving the utility of each tenant unchanged. Each tenant thus cultivates a smaller plot of land and devotes less effort per unit of his labor. Ipso facto, a ban on linking, when it is optimal, will reduce the landlord's income and output. In the debate between Srinivasan (1979) and Bhaduri, the issue was the alleged lack of incentive for the landlord to introduce

---

9. Sharecropping contracts have also been analyzed in relation to the postbellum South. Discussion of pure sharecropping was initiated by Reid (1973), and the interlinkage of credit and tenancy arrangements by the country store was subsequently discussed by Ransom and Sutch (1978). We do not elaborate on these or other works on the postbellum South since they are not directly applicable to our model.

yield-raising innovation, given linked tenancy-*cum*-credit contracts. Using the Bhaduri model, Srinivasan showed that as long as borrowing was not considered an "inferior" good by the tenant (which it was not in the Bhaduri model), there was no such disincentive.[10] In our model, borrowing is, by definition, noninferior since it equals the tenant's discounted income; linking is chosen, not imposed, only if it is optimal. The tenant is pushed down to his alternative utility level, not by the credit instrument but by plot size variations.

Finally, in our model, utility equivalence implies that nothing short of land reform will affect the tenant's welfare, as long as he is a tenant. Indeed, other reforms such as setting a floor on the tenant's share of the crop, making credit available to the tenant at a cost below the opportunity cost of capital to the landlord, or banning credit and tenancy linkage either have no effect on the equilibrium at all or have an effect on the number of tenants, the output, and the landlord's income. Empirically, our model provides a theoretical underpinning for two almost opposite phenomena that are sometimes observed: low-interest consumption loans from landlord to tenant (Bardhan and Rudra 1978) and the opposite—high-interest, low-volume loans.

Our model does not include production credit. Braverman and Guasch (1984) discuss production credit in situations where interlinked credit and tenancy contracts are used as a screening device by landlords to distinguish more able tenants. Bell and Zusman (1980b), Mitra (1982), and Braverman and Stiglitz (1982) discuss interlinked credit and tenancy contracts in the presence of uncertainty and unequally distributed information.

---

10. However, when uncertainty is incorporated into the analysis, this may not be true (see Braverman and Stiglitz 1981).

4

Explaining Patterns in Landowner Shares:
Rice, Corn, Coconut, and Abaca in the Philippines

James Roumasset

The growing concern about "institutional constraints" in the agricultural development literature recently—see, for example, Asian Development Bank (1977)—suggests a need to learn more about the facts of rural institutions and about their causes and consequences. Focusing on the institution of share tenancy, Roumasset and James (1979) have documented and explained certain "stylized facts" about the relationship of landowner shares and other variables using data pertaining to Philippine rice farms.

The present work was undertaken to investigate these and similar patterns in selected areas of the Philippines in coconut, corn, and abaca. First I review the results obtained for rice by Roumasset and James (1979). In the next two Sections I discuss patterns for other crops and make cross-crop comparisons. The last section includes a summary and methodological inferences.

EXPLAINING PATTERNS IN LANDOWNER SHARES: RICE

Land Quality and Landowner Shares

Cheung (1969), Roumasset and James (1979), Rudra (1975*b*), Geertz (1965), and others have documented the positive association between land quality and the percentage of the gross harvest received by the landowner as his share. The explanation of this finding is based on the competitive theory of share contracts developed by Cheung (1969), Reid (1976), and Roumasset (1979). According to this theory, if property rights are properly defined and easily enforced, contracting costs are zero, and the number of competing

The data used for abaca, corn, and coconut were collected by Eutiquio Lumayag (see Lumayag 1979), Apolonia Matias (see Matias 1979), and Emma Escover, respectively. These studies were part of the New Institutional Economics and Agricultural Organization project sponsored by the Agricultural Development Council, Inc. I would like to thank Marilou Uy for helpful comments on a previous draft and the National Science Foundation for research support under grant no. SOC 76-83845, administered by the University of Hawaii.

agents is sufficient to make bargaining power small, then contracts tend to act as perfect substitutes for markets. How this principle relates to less abstract theories is discussed at the end of this paper.

In order to apply this first best theory of contracts to share contracts where land is heterogeneous, we assume that land can be classified into types such that if $i < j$, then $f_i'(\ell) > f_j'(\ell)$, where $f_i(\ell)$ is output per hectare as a function of labor per hectare on land type i; and $\ell_i \leq \ell_j$, where ℓ_i is defined as the greatest ℓ_i such that $f_i'(\ell_i) = 0$. If $i < j$, it is natural to say that land type i is of better quality than land type j. In other words, better quality land yields a higher marginal product of labor for the same labor intensity; moreover, the marginal product of labor on better quality land does not become zero at a higher labor intensity than the marginal product of labor on inferior land.

From these assumptions, it follows that equilibrium labor intensity on better quality land, ℓ_i^*, will be greater than ℓ_j^*. Furthermore, rent per worker, $R/L \equiv r/\ell$, is higher for better quality land (Roumasset 1976; Roumasset and James 1979). The following notation is used. Rent, R, is equal to rent per hectare, r, times the number of hectares, H. Total labor, L, is ℓH. Therefore, rent per worker R/L can be written as r/ℓ. The higher rent per worker condition implies in turn that the landowner's percentage share is also higher on better quality land. These results are illustrated in figure 4.1. H_1, H_2, and H_3 stand for the best medium, and worst types of land, respectively.

For convenience, figure 4.1 embodies the assumption that total labor per farm is constant at $\overline{L}$. Farm size is thus determined by the equilibrium condition that the marginal product of labor must be equal to the wage on all types of land. Assuming that family size is independent of land quality, the higher labor intensity on better quality farms implies that better quality land will be divided into small farm units. This helps explain the commonly reported inverse relationship between farm size and yield per hectare, a point that is developed in more detail elsewhere (Roumasset 1976, chapter 4).

Landowner's Share and Labor Quantity

There is limited evidence that a rough correlation exists between landowner's share and physiological population density across countries.[1] In the Philippines, landowner shares of less than 30 percent or more than 50 percent have been uncommon (Mangahas, Miralao, and De Los Reyes 1976). In Bangladesh and Central Java, Indonesia, however, share contracts provide landowners with shares ranging from 50 to 67 percent (Bangladesh Rice Research Institute 1977; Geertz 1965). Since Bangladesh and Central Java are more densely populated than the Philippines, these observations

---

1. Physiological density is defined as population in a particular area divided by the area of arable land.

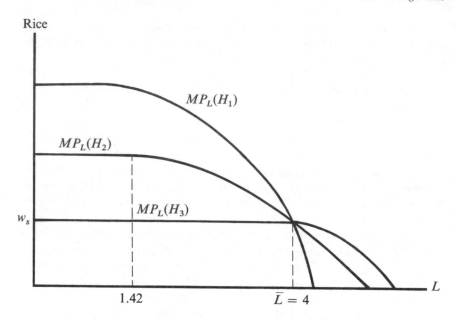

FIGURE 4.1. Marginal Product of Labor Curves for Three Different Land Qualities and Equilibrium Farm Sizes.

are consistent with the hypothesis that landowner shares are directly related to physiological density.

Even within the Philippines, landowner shares adjust to regional disparities in labor supply relative to land. In densely settled, low-wage areas, landowner shares are higher than in areas of low physiological density and relatively higher wages. In sparsely settled Isabela province, for example, landowners usually receive 30 percent compared with the 50 percent that was typical in densely settled Ilocos Norte prior to the 1960s, even though both provinces are in the northern, Ilocano-speaking part of the Philippines, and average land quality in Isabela is slightly higher. As permanent and seasonal migration to Isabela has reduced wages relative to those paid in Ilocos Norte, tenant shares have also been reduced.[2] Similarly, landowner shares in Palawan, a province with a low population density and relatively high wages, range from 10 to $33\frac{1}{3}$ percent,[3] even on good-quality land.

---

2. Lewis (1971) reports a 3 percent decrease in tenant shares from 1963 to 1970. More recent researchers have found further decrease (James 1979).

3. Eder (1974). Part of the explanation for rents as low as 10 or 20 percent also lies in the fact that the rice farms studied are upland and average yield per hectare (1,400 kg) is slightly lower than that obtained under typical lowland conditions. On lowland farms James (1979) has found share rents of 30 and $33\frac{1}{3}$ percent to be typical in recently settled areas. Wages for tasks such as transplanting, harvesting, and threshing are significantly higher in Palawan than in areas of out-migration, such as Ilocos Norte.

The same relationship has also been observed over time. In Bangladesh, especially in the vicinity of Dacca, the shares of some tenants have been reduced from one-half to one-third as population pressure has reduced real wages (Ali 1979). In Java, patron-client relations have been gradually changing in favor of owners since about 1928, when land prices began to rise relative to rents. Between 1868 and 1928, in contrast, when land expansion relative to population growth was still favorable and economic growth was rapid, changes in landowner-tenant relations generally favored tenants (Ruttan 1978, p. 336, citing evidence from White 1974).

To explain the relationship between low real wages, high physiological density, and high landowner shares, we postulate that production of rice can be represented by the CES production function:

$$Q = A[\delta H^{-\rho} + (1 - \delta)L^{-\rho}]^{.-1/\rho}$$

Following available empirical evidence, we further postulate that $\rho > 0$ even in the long run, that is, the elasticity of substitution, σ, is less than one.[4]

Since according to our hypothesis, factors are paid their marginal products, the landowner's share can be written as

$$\frac{H}{Q}\frac{\partial Q}{\partial H} = \frac{\delta}{A^\rho}\left(\frac{Q}{H}\right)^\rho.$$

A higher physiological density will tend to be reflected (via factor prices) in a higher labor intensity per hectare of rice land, which, in turn, implies a higher output per hectare, Q/H, and therefore, a higher landowner's share.[5] This explains the association between physiological density, factor prices, and landowner shares.

Figure 4.2 illustrates the relationship between factor prices and landowner shares. The marginal products of labor for two quantities of type 1 land are drawn so as to be consistent with figure 4.1. H_{12} is equal to 1 unit. H_{11} is fixed so that labor intensity with 4 units of labor is just sufficient to yield a marginal product of $2w$. Thus, H_{11} is the equilibrium farm size for a wage equal to $2w$, and H_{12} is the equilibrium farm size for a wage of w. We can now interpret the increasing labor intensity associated with the shift from H_{11} to H_{12} as the equilibrium response of a halving of the real wage. Inspection of the figure reveals that the landowner's share has increased (roughly from one-fourth to three-fifths).

4. Yotopoulos, Lau, and Somel (1970), for example, using the Indian farm management data for 1957–62, estimate ρ to be equal to 0.349, that is, $\sigma = 0.74$. Yotopoulos and Nugent (1876) cite evidence suggesting that with the advent of the high-yielding varieties, the elasticity of substitution in agriculture is presently lower than during the 1957–1962 period. See also Ranade (1977) for supporting evidence concerning rice production in the Philippines.

5. Since we are implicitly using "land" here as a synonym for "nonlabor inputs," the prediction of a higher output per hectare should be interpreted as a higher output per unit of nonlabor input or as a lower output per worker.

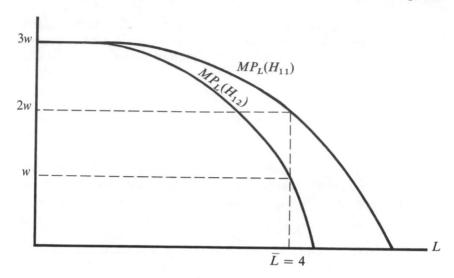

FIGURE 4.2. Effect of a Wage Decrease on Landowner's Share.

As a preliminary test of both the land quality and labor quantity hypotheses, the landowner's share (Y) was regressed on average rice yield per
hectare (X_1) and physiological density (X_2). The data used were the provincial
averages for the 31 primary rice-growing provinces, based on the 1971
census.[6] Physiological density (X_2) was approximated by the ratio of total
farm population to total cultivated area for each province. The resulting
ordinary least squares equation is

$$\hat{Y} = 0.25 + 0.0026x_1 + 0.0387x_2.$$
$$(3.19) \qquad (4.90) \qquad R^2 = 0.54$$

The coefficients of both x_1 and x_2 are significant at the 1 percent level
(t values are in parentheses).

Other Patterns

Another pattern that has been documented for share contracts on rice farms
is that the landowner's share varies directly with his contribution of inputs
(Lewis 1971, Vyas 1970, Cañete 1971, Rudra 1975b, Takahashi 1969, and
Roumasset and James 1979). The higher the percentage of fixed and variable
capital inputs (equipment for land preparation and harvesting, chemicals,

6. The provinces selected were those where the proportion of share-tenanted farms to
the total number of farms growing primarily rice was greater than or equal to one-half, but less
than or equal to one. This allowed the inclusion of most major rice-producing provinces while
excluding provinces where sharecropping was unimportant or primarily used for nonrice crops.

TABLE 4.1. Landowner's Share in Total Cost and Explanatory Variables for Relatively Homogeneous Groups: Abaca

Province	Landowner's Share (percent)	Number of Respondents	Land Quality Index 1 (LQI$_1$)	Land Quality Index 2 (LQI$_2$)	Wage Index (WI)	Percentage of Cost Contributed by Landowner (C)
Davao						
	10	4	409	0.511	9.06	0.0
	20	6	768	0.924	8.79	0.0
Catanduanes						
	33	11	147	−0.713	6.40	4.5
	50	1	147	−0.460	6.40	12.5
Leyte						
	25	6	257	−0.702	6.71	12.5
	50	6	237	−0.692	6.29	31.2
Albay, Sorsogon						
	50	15	630	0.658	6.39	14.3
	60	1	120	−0.541	5.37	12.5

Notes:
LQI_1 = yield per hectare in kilograms,
LQI_2 = a standardized combination of weighted average annual yield and land value per hectare,
WI = mean of the daily wage rates of various farm operations,
C = percentage of production costs contributed by landowner.

and seeds) provided by the landlord, the higher will be his output share. This is a direct implication of the first best principle, which requires that all factors be paid the value of their marginal products. The payment to the landowner must therefore be the sum of the marginal product of land times the amount of land and the marginal product of capital times the amount of capital contributed by the landowner. All other things being equal, the greater the amount of capital contributed by the landowner, the greater will be his share.

Landowner shares in rice production have tended to decline over time in the Philippines despite population pressure and more or less stable wages. This appears to be the result of a combination of land reform and land-saving technological change (Roumasset and James 1979).

LANDOWNER'S SHARE, LAND QUALITY, AND WAGES FOR OTHER CROPS

Abaca

In order to see if the same patterns are found in abaca production, farmers were interviewed in two villages in each of five Philippine provinces. The breakdown of landowner shares is given in table 4.1. The corresponding mean values of the land quality index (*LQI*), the wage index (*WI*), and the landowner's percentage contribution to production cost (*C*) are also given in the table. These observations closely conform to the expected patterns. Taking 50 percent as the standard of comparison, landowner shares are low in Catanduanes, apparently because of the low land quality, and even lower in Davao because of the relatively high wages and the low contribution by landowners.

Regression estimates documenting the relationships of landowner shares to land quality and to wage level (a proxy for the scarcity of labor relative to land), and landowner's contribution to production costs and to management are shown in table 4.2. As expected, the wage variable is negative and significant in all three areas. The land quality variable is positive and significant in both Bicol and Davao, but not in Leyte. Landowner's contribution to costs was highly significant in Leyte but not in Davao and Bicol. (A management index was used in Davao in place of landowner's contribution to production costs because we did not have enough observations recorded for this variable.)

Coconut

Table 4.3 shows the distribution of landowner shares for coconut farms in five provinces in the Philippines. To explain the table it is convenient to begin with the largest group of contracts—the eleven Bicol tenants with shares of one-third (landowner shares of 67 percent). Average yield per hectare for these farms is just under 4,000 nuts, and wages are slightly over 6 pesos a day. In contrast, the most common landowner's share in Catanduanes is 50 percent. This is explained by the substantially lower yields in Catanduanes, since the wage levels are about the same. The same explanation holds for the 50 percent landowner's share observed in Luisiana, Laguna. In Sariaya, Quezon, the landowner's share, as in Bicol, is 67 percent. In this case, the higher yield per hectare appears to be offset by the higher wage. However, in San Pablo, Laguna, where productivity is much higher and wages are only slightly higher, landowner shares are at the maximum at 86 percent.

Further documentation of these patterns is given by the regression estimates in table 4.4, which also includes management index (*MI*) and kinship (*K*) variables. For both regressions, the land quality and landowner contribution variables are significant, with the correct sign. The estimated coefficient of the wage variable is small and insignificant.

Corn

Table 4.5 shows the breakdown of landowner output shares for corn in four Philippine provinces. There is a heavy concentration of shares at the

TABLE 4.2. Landowner's Share Regression Estimates for Abaca

Variable	Pooled Data	Leyte	Davao	Bicol 1	Bicol 2*
Intercept	0.99	0.99	0.62	0.73	0.75
	(13.60)	(3.29)	(2.23)	(4.74)	(11.13)
LQI	0.060	0.058	0.110	0.056	0.026
	(5.33)	(0.62)	(3.25)	(4.01)	(2.70)
WI	−0.098	−0.110	−0.067	−0.047	0.046
	(−9.89)	(−2.38)	(−2.14)	(−1.93)	(−5.31)
C	0.440	0.700			0.166
	(4.99)	(3.89)			(1.66)
MI			0.045		
			(1.56)		
R^2	0.78	0.71	0.64	0.40	0.74

Notes:
LQI = land quality index (standardized weighted average of productivity and land value),
WI = wage index,
C = percentage of production costs contributed by landowner,
MI = management index (measure extent of management contribution by landowner).
(t values are in parentheses.)

*Includes Albay, Sorsogon, and Catanduanes.

TABLE 4.3. Landowner's Share in Total Cost and Explanatory Variables for Relatively Homogeneous Groups: Coconut

Province	Landowner's Share (percent)	Number of Respondents	Land Quality Index 1 (LQI$_1$)	Land Quality Index 2 (LQI$_2$)	Wage Index (WI)	Percentage of Cost Contributed by Landowner (C)
Laguna						
San Pablo	86	7	13,694	4,556	7.86	4.66
Luisiana	50	3	2,697	1,899	5.44	9.68
Quezon						
Sariaya	67	10	8,292	2,820	6.45	2.40
Lucban	60	4	3,222	1,253	9.92	5.75
Camarines Sur, Albay						
	70	4	6,820	2,350	6.93	3.00
	67	11	3,896	1,187	6.79	4.70
	50	2	2,261	217	5.28	1.35
Catanduanes						
	67	5	1,590	623	5.30	0.0
	60	2	1,993	758	6.54	0.0
	50	7	1,312	354	6.17	0.0

Notes:
LQI$_1$ = number of nuts per hectare,
LQI$_2$ = implicit rent per hectare,
WI = weighted average of daily wages in various coconut farm operations,
C = percentage of production costs contributed by landowner.

TABLE 4.4. Landowner's Share Regression Estimates for Coconut

Variable	Run 1	Run 2	Run 3
Intercept	56.21	57.87	58.36
	(19.91)	(18.22)	(18.04)
LQI_1	0.001	0.0008	
	(4.31)	(2.51)	
LQI_2			0.002
			(2.14)
WI	−0.045	−0.070	−0.140
	(−0.81)	(−0.29)	(−0.56)
C		0.180	0.197
		(2.55)	(2.72)
MI		0.540	0.970
		(0.76)	(1.38)
K		−2.99	−2.77
		(−1.21)	(−1.09)
R^2	0.29	0.41	0.39

Notes:
LQI_1 = land quality index 1,
LQI_2 = land quality index 2,
WI = wage index,
C = percentage of production costs contributed by landowner,
MI = management index (measures extent of management contribution by landowner),
K = dummy variable for kinship.
(t values are in parentheses.)

TABLE 4.5. Landowner's Share in Total Cost and Explanatory Variables for Relatively Homogeneous Groups: Corn

Province	Landowner's Share (percent)	Number of Respondents	Land Quality Index 1 (LQI_1)	Land Quality Index 2 (LQI_2)	Wage Index (WI)	Percentage of Cost Contributed by Landowner (C)
Isabela, Cagayan	33	10	31.7	14,285	11.2	6.07
	30	19	30.1	11,716	10.6	2.69
	25	4	27.2	7,612	9.1	0.0
Cebu	33*	21	13.4	2,228	5.97	10.71
	33†	2	28.8	760	5.0	11.50
Batangas	50	5	38.3	13,783	11.0	50.00
	33	4	34.0	8,281	11.2	16.50
	25	5	24.1	9,499	10.7	0.0
	20	3	23.7	8,697	10.4	0.0

Notes:
LQI_1 = yield per hectare,
LQI_2 = implicit rent per hectare,
WI = weighted average of daily wages in various corn farm operations,
C = percentage of production costs contributed by landowner.

*Landowner paid for transportation costs,
†Tenants paid for transportation costs.

33 percent and 30 percent levels. This is largely a result of the offsetting forces of land quality and wage. In Cebu, where both land quality and wages are low, all landowners receive 33 percent. Since land quality is higher in Cagayan and Isabela, we would expect higher landowner shares, but this force is offset by the higher wages in those provinces. Where equal (50–50) sharing does occur (in Batangas), it tends to be on higher quality land than in Cagayan and Isabela, but without higher wages. The incidence of 25 percent shares for landowners is partly attributable to the effects of land reform. Nonetheless, these farms tend to be on lower quality land, suggesting that ceilings on landowner shares are easier to enforce on relatively poor-quality land. The existence of 20 percent landowner shares suggests the possibility that land reform, which sets the lease payment equal to 25 percent of the average value of a harvest, may leave the tenant worse off.[7] For the farms in Cagayan and Isabela, the difference between landowner shares of 30 percent and 33 percent is explained by responsibility for transportation of the corn. In those contracts where the landowner's share was 33 percent, the landowner was responsible for transportation costs. In the 30 percent contracts, the tenants generally were responsible for transporting the corn to the landowner's house.

The regression results for corn are shown in table 4.6. With neither landowner's contribution to production cost (C) nor management index (MI) included as variables, R^2 is rather low, although the coefficients of the land quality and wage variables are of the right sign and almost significant. The reason for the low R^2 is presumably that since wage and land quality tend to be offsetting variables in this particular sample, the variation in landowner shares is small, with most values being at or close to one-third. The small variations that do occur may be caused by other factors. In runs 1 and 2, where management index and landowner's contribution, respectively, are added as regressors, the R^2 values increase substantially, the coefficients for the land quality and wage variables remain of the correct sign, and for run 1 the land quality variable becomes significant.

Cross-Crop Comparisons

Despite the substantial variation of landowner shares from one crop to another, there is for each crop a striking consistency in the proportion claimed as the landowner's share. The landowner share in corn and abaca production, for example, tend to be substantially less than 50 percent, and corresponding shares in coconut production tend to be substantially greater than 50 percent. For corn and abaca, we hypothesize that the lower shares

---

7. Some observers note that owner of poor-quality rice land have in fact enlisted bogus tenants in order to quality for a lease fixed by the government at 25 percent of the average value of a harvest.

TABLE 4.6. Landowner's Share Regression Estimates for Corn

Variable	Run 1	Run 2	Run 3	Run 4
Intercept	33.73	28.06	34.95	35.37
	(8.26)	(7.96)	(7.86)	
LQI_1	0.580			
	(2.30)			
LQI_2		0.00014	0.0002	0.00069
		(1.58)	(1.60)	(2.95)
WI	−0.69	−0.38	−0.69	−0.90
	(1.52)	(−1.02)	(−1.41)	(−1.40)
C		0.46		0.51
		(7.33)		(8.31)
MI	61.91			
	(6.32)			
B^*				4.59
				(−1.32)
R^2	0.36	0.45	0.04	0.50

Source: Matias (1979).

Notes: Runs 1–4 are regression estimates with actual landowner's share (S_1) as the dependent variable. Run 5 uses adjusted landowner's share (S_2) as the dependent variable. (S_2 = Actual landowner's share adjusted to landowner's cost contribution over his net income per share.)

LQI_1 = land quality index 1,
LQI_2 = land quality index 2,
  WI = wage index,
   C = percentage of production costs contributed by landowner,
  MI = management index (measures extent of management contribution by landowner).
   B = 1 if cebu; 0, otherwise.
(t values are in parentheses.)

*B is a dummy variable to control for geographical distribution of respondents.

result primarily from the lower quality land on which these crops are grown. It is well known that corn and abaca yield substantially lower rents than rice does. Corn tends to be planted in areas where there is insufficient water for rice crops. Abaca is often planted in rolling hills where the terracing and irrigation required to produce rice would be extremely costly. The higher landowner shares in coconut production presumably represent a return not only on the land but also on the fixed capital investment—the trees themselves.

The laborer's share in coconut production, as measured by the quantity of labor times the shadow price of labor divided by the value of production, also tends to be lower for coconut than for other crops because the major labor requirement is only for harvesting.[8] Thus, our hypothesis is that

8. Alternatively, we can view the value of trees as equal to the value of the labor utilized in the planting operation (plus the capitalized value of the nut planted). In this case, since the landowner owns the trees, the landowner can be viewed as contributing the labor for the planting operation. This view again leads us to the prediction that landowner shares will be higher for coconut than for most other crops.

variations in landowner shares across crops are explained by land quality and by the landowner's contribution to inputs. If wages also differ across regions that are dominated by different crops, then wages may also help account for differences in landowner shares.

Regressions Using Pooled Data

The following regression equations are based on the pooled data for all three crops (t values are in parentheses):[9]

$$S = 62.04 + 2.18LQI_1 - 31.79DC - 61.93DA - 1.27WI$$
$$(51.69) \quad (3.30) \quad\quad (-20.91) \quad (-37.12) \quad (-1.92) \quad\quad R^2 = 0.89$$

$$S = 61.93 + 1.89LQI_2 - 29.29DC - 61.72DA - 0.75WI$$
$$(50.80) \quad (2.89) \quad\quad (-15.68) \quad (-36.48) \quad (-1.14) \quad\quad R^2 = 0.89$$

where DC and DA are dummy variables for corn and abaca. For both regressions, land quality is positive and significant, and the dummy variables for corn and abaca are negative and significant as expected. The wage index is significant at 10 percent in the presence of LQI_1 but is not significant in the presence of LQI_2.

SUMMARY AND FINAL REMARKS

Substantial variations in the landowner's share have been found to exist in the Philippines for rice, abaca, coconut, and (to a lesser extent) corn. These variations tend to be positively related to land quality and the landowner's contribution of nonland inputs, and negatively related to wage.

Both the land quality and the wage patterns are explained by combining the competitive theory of contracts with additional restrictive, but reasonable, postulates. To explain the land quality pattern, we assumed that types of land can be classified from best to worst according to conditions determined by the marginal productivities of land and labor. For the wage or factor price explanation, we assumed that the elasticity of substitution between land and labor is less than one. These assumptions, plus the assumption that factors of production are paid their marginal products, lead directly to the prediction that the landowner's share is positively related to land quality and negatively related to wages relative to land rents.

---

9. Except for the land quality index, all the other data for the cross-crop regressions are unadjusted. The earlier derived land quality indexes for each crop were standardized, based on the formula

$$z_i = \frac{\text{Value of variable } x_i - \text{Mean } (x_i)}{\text{Standard deviation of } x_i},$$

where x_i is the land quality index.

The Methodology of the New Institutional Economics

In an earlier paper (Roumasset 1974), I argued that the economic function of institutions is to minimize excess burden in the face of unavoidable transaction costs and that the theory of institutions therefore has much to gain from the economics of the second best. In most of the preceding analysis, however, I have abstracted from transaction costs. Lest this appear to be backsliding, it is appropriate to indicate how the present study fits into the larger scope of the new institutional economics (Williamson 1975; Roumasset 1978; Ben-Porath 1980).

In explaining institutions and institutional change, it is useful to allow for more than one level of abstraction. The present study and related empirical work done in the Philippines and Java (Roumasset and James 1979; Hayami and Kikuchi 1981) suggest that it may prove useful to abstract from transaction costs in order to explain the terms of contractual arrangements. With zero contracting costs, competition, and superadditivity in production, contracts serve as perfect substitutes for markets (Roumasset 1979). Under these conditions, the negotiated terms of contracts will be identical to those predicted by supply and demand analysis. This may be called the "first efficiency principle."

The "second efficiency principle" suggests that excluding asymmetries in bargaining costs, voluntary contracts tend to minimize excess burden. This principle has been used to explain employment patterns in sugar production (Roumasset and Uy 1980). Thus we have explained, for example, why piece rates tend to be chosen in high-wage areas and time rates tend to be chosen in low-wage areas. Piece rates have been used in high-wage areas because the shirking that would result from using time rates would be prohibitively expensive. Piece rates have also been favored on large farms. Large farms tend to have less information about worker quality and can achieve economies of scale in gathering information about appropriate piece rates.

In summary, the following preliminary rules of thumb can be advanced. In a competitive environment favorable to voluntary contracting, one can explain the terms of contractual arrangements in abstraction from transaction costs, that is, with marginal product pricing. One can explain the form of contracts by applying the principle that contracts minimize excess burden. For other cases, one may invoke principles of political economy, especially government-imposed restrictions on free contracting and biases in the exercise of bargaining power.[10]

10. For a more complete explanation of the new institutional economics, see Roumasset (1978), which also includes a brief discussion of how to incorporate political economy considerations into the analysis.

Using Positive Explanations for Policy Conclusions: A Final Note

Just as using the postulate of rationality to explain individual behavior does not prove that individuals are rational, using the postulate of efficiency to explain certain institutions does not prove that those institutions are efficient. Indeed, we have not tried to determine to what extent agricultural institutions are efficient. However, the framework used to explain patterns in agricultural contracts could also facilitate such a test. To the extent that one can find patterns in agricultural institutions that cannot be explained by the efficiency principles but that can be explained by other considerations (such as monopoly power), one has established a prima facie case for inefficiency.[11] However, the success of the efficiency principles in explaining certain observed patterns does invalidate any a priori conclusions about the inefficiency of particular contracts, such as share tenancy, and similarly tends to invalidate the theory that assumes that such institutions necessarily act as constraints to development.

11. This still does not imply that government intervention is warranted, however. To prove that, one must weigh the benefits of reduced inefficiency resulting from the government intervention against the cost of the government intervention itself.

5

Agricultural Tenancy in Semiarid Tropical India

N. S. Jodha

The temporary transfer of land via tenancy is one of the oldest of the institutional devices that have evolved to facilitate adjustments in agricultural factor markets. However, one of the side effects of the adjustment process, resulting mainly from the unequal position of landlords and tenants, has been the possible exploitation of tenants. Consequently, as in India prior to independence, tenancy has largely been viewed as an instrument of exploitation of the weak. For this reason, regulation of tenancy became a key objective in postindependence India. The regulatory measures, along with the fast-declining land/man ratio and the technological improvements in agriculture, have considerably transformed the objective circumstances under which tenancy now operates in that country.[1]

Tenancy seems to have acquired new reasons for existence and varied forms. This has drawn attention to the need for a fresh and closer look at agricultural tenancy, especially as a means of adjustment, and at interlinked operations in agricultural factor markets (P. K. Bardhan 1978a; Srinivasan 1978). However, despite the strong desire of scholars to document the extent and forms of tenancy and despite the availability of theoretical models that attempt to establish the rationale for agricultural tenancy, efforts directed to the study of tenancy per se usually do not succeed. Because of the great

Early drafts of this paper were prepared while the author was an economist at the International Crops Research Institute for the Semi-Arid Tropics (ICRISAT), whose assistance is gratefully acknowledged. The author is also grateful to Hans P. Binswanger, Dayanatha Jha, and James G. Ryan for their valuable suggestions during the preparation of the paper. He wishes to thank M. J. Bhende, S. S. Badhe, K. G. Kshirsagar, V. Bhaskar Rao, and T. Balaramaiah, the economic investigators who helped in conducting this study.

Submitted as conference paper no. 2 by the International Crops Research Institute for the Semi-Arid Tropics.

1. For documentation and analysis of tenancy in India in recent years, see Vyas (1970), Khusro (1973), Rao (1972), Rao (1975), Joshi (1975), P. K. Bardhan (1976b), Sanyal (1978), Bardhan and Rudra (1978).

capacity of farmers to hide it, agricultural tenancy simply disappears once researchers start investigating it in the usual one- or two-round surveys. Because of its very sensitive nature, the subject calls for greater emphasis on participant observation over a longer period.

In this paper I discuss some dimensions of agricultural tenancy in three agroclimatic zones in semiarid tropical India. The paper is based on fairly continuous observation of and intensive interaction with rural households for a period of three to four years. The details presented here complement the information presented by two accompanying papers in this volume, those by Binswanger et al. (chapter 8) and by Ryan and Ghodake (chapter 9), which discuss different facets of the agricultural labor market in the same areas and which are also based on the same ICRISAT village-level studies (VLS).

THE ICRISAT VILLAGE-LEVEL STUDIES

All three papers focus on six villages in three areas: Aurepalle and Dokur in the Mahbubnagar district of Andhra Pradesh, Shirapur and Kalman in the Sholapur district of Maharashtra, and Kanzara and Kinkheda in the Akola district of Maharashtra. The three districts represent distinct climatological, agronomic, and social and economic zones of the semiarid tropics of India.

As part of the ongoing VLS, data have been collected from a randomly selected panel of 240 households at intervals of 20 to 40 days since May 1975. The panels in each village consist of 30 farm households and 10 labor households. (The latter include land operators with less than 0.2 hectares of operated area.) Data have been collected on a broad spectrum of socioeconomic and agrobiological characteristics by resident investigators who have a rural background and a master's degree in agricultural economics and who belong to the same linguistic group as the farmers. Data collection is supervised by economists of ICRISAT center.

The agroclimatic characteristics of the regions and the villages are summarized in table 5.1. Mahbubnagar is a region of medium to shallow Alfisols (red soils with relatively high aluminum and ferric content) with an average medium to low annual rainfall of 710 mm, which is fairly erratic. The present Mahbubnagar district was part of the dominions of the nizam of Hyderabad from the later seventeenth century, when the dynasty of this feudal ruler was established in this part of south central India, to 1949, when Hyderabad State was absorbed by independent India.[2] Although dry, the district has long supported a considerable amount of rice cultivation, based on irrigation from numerous runoff collection reservoirs, or tanks, and from

2. Historical articles on the following regions can be found in the *Imperial Gazetteer of India*, 1907–09: Akola district (vol. 5), Akola town (vol. 5), Berar (vol. 7), Hyderabad State (vol. 13), Mahbubnagar district (vol. 12), Murtizapur *Taluk* (vol. 18), Sholapur district (vol. 22), and Sholapur town (vol. 22).

TABLE 5.1. Agroclimatic Characteristics of Six Indian Villages

| Village | District | State | Rainfall | | Soil Type | Irrigation (percent)* | Farm-size Groups† | | |
			Annual Average (mm)	Variability CV (percent)			Small (ha)	Medium (ha)	Large (ha)
Kanzara	Akola	Maharashtra	820	27	Medium-deep Vertisols	4.9	0.21–2.25	2.26–5.60	>5.60
Kinkheda	Akola	Maharashtra	820	27	Medium-deep Vertisols	3.8	0.21–3.00	3.01–5.60	>5.60
Kalman	Sholapur	Maharashtra	690	29	Deep and medium-deep Vertisols	10.4	0.21–6.00	6.01–10.75	>10.75
Shirapur	Sholapur	Maharashtra	690	29	Deep Vertisols	13.3	0.21–2.50	2.51–6.00	>6.00
Aurepalle	Mahbubnagar	Andhra Pradesh	710	28	Shallow and medium-deep Alfisols	21.0	0.21–2.50	2.51–5.25	>5.25
Dokur	Mahbubnagar	Andhra Pradesh	710	28	Shallow and medium-deep Alfisols	60.1	0.21–1.00	1.01–3.00	>3.00

Note: ICRISAT has been conducting studies in these six villages since May 1975 (Jodha et al. 1977).

* Gross irrigated area as proportion of gross cropped area (average of three years).
† On the basis of operational landholding.

wells. Tank building, as a means to assure a water supply for rice cultivation, has for centuries been an important activity of kings and other rulers in the upland, semiarid granitic areas of what are now western Andhra Pradesh and western Tamil Nadu.

Sholapur has a mixture of deep Vertisols (black cotton soils) with very high moisture retention capacity; the annual average rainfall is 690 mm. While the amount of rainfall is similar to that in Mahbubnagar, the rainfall is much more erratic in Sholapur, especially within each year (not reflected in the coefficient of variation of annual rainfall), so Sholapur is agriculturally the least prosperous of the three districts.

The area forming most of the present Sholapur district was captured from the nizam by the Marathas in 1795. Between 1818 and 1848, the British gradually wrested control from the Marathas. A British collectorate was established in 1838. Under the British, Sholapur city was developed as a cotton milling center. In 1903–04 there were three cotton mills in the city, employing a total of 5,239 people. The population of Sholapur city was 61,281 in 1881; by 1901 it had risen to 75,288. The population of the district as a whole was 720,977 in 1901. This area has experienced drought and scarcity for most of its history; periodic famines and public works projects to relieve them were reported well before the study period. During periods of drought in the late nineteenth century, large numbers were reported as employed in relief works: 95,617 in January 1877 and 156,000 in April 1900. In 1900 most land in Sholapur was freehold.

The Akola district is agriculturally the most prosperous area with a higher and more assured rainfall (820 mm/year) than the other two districts. It has primarily medium to deep Vertisols. The present Akola district formed part of Berar in the nizam's dominions in 1853, when it was assigned to the British in payment for a loan. In 1900 most land was freehold. The district had been heavily cultivated and had been famous for its cotton for a long time before that. During the second half of the nineteenth century, demand for Indian cotton increased following the reduction in the amount supplied by the United State during the Civil War. Between 1867 and 1881 and after the installation of a railway, the cultivated area in Akola increased 50 percent and revenue increased 42 percent. In 1901 Murtizapur, the *taluk* or sub-district headquarters near the study villages of Kanzara and Kinkheda, had seven cotton presses and ten ginning factories.

Other aspects of the selected villages and households are discussed in Jodha, Asokan, and Ryan (1977) and Binswanger et al. (1977). Here we note that Mahbubnagar and Sholapur are high-risk areas because of their shallow soils (Mahbubnagar) and very unreliable rainfall (Sholapur). Akola is an assured rainfall zone where farmers face much lower yield risks.

Detailed information on tenancy did not begin to be collected until 1977, two years after fieldwork began in the villages (May 1975), and it pertained to the ownership status of each plot. The initial concealment of tenancy plots disappeared over time. Collection of input-output data that were later cross-checked with data on household transactions and bullock and labor utilization included in schedules further helped to reveal not only tenancy transactions but also their terms and conditions.

All plots resulting from land transfers between households via tenancy agreements as well as from sale, purchase, gift donation, or succession during the first four years of the VLS (with the exception of Kalman and Kinkheda, where only three years of data were used) were first listed. Separate interviews to collect additional data about those plots were conducted in the third and fourth years of fieldwork. Information from both parties to the land transfer was collected even if one of the parties was not a panel respondent of the VLS. The data relate to their resource endowments and the terms, conditions, and background of the transaction. The quantitative information was supplemented by investigators' personal observations and the author's own field notes.

RESULTS AND DISCUSSION

I first examine the importance of tenancy transactions in the total land transfer. The rest of the discussion is devoted to tenancy only: the partners in tenancy transactions; terms and conditions of leases (including period of lease); the reasons given by farmers for lease transactions; resource adjustment; and interlinking of factor markets. Finally, the reasons for leasing are verified by comparison with other data.

The Tenancy-dominated Land Market

Table 5.2 presents the new land transfers occurring during the four years via leasing in, leasing out, return of land because of termination of earlier leases, sale, purchase, gift donation, succession, or property division in which at least one party was a VLS panel respondent.

In these villages every year, 14 to 46 percent of the operated area of the sample households was temporarily or permanently changing hands through new land transfers of the different types. Furthermore, 77 to 97 percent of new land transfers were tenancy transactions only. This confirms the fact that in Indian villages the land market operates largely through tenancy rather than through outright sale or purchase (Bardhan and Rudra 1978).[3]

3. Ownership of land is one of the biggest sources of security in the villages. No one wants to sell land unless forced to. During periodic crises such as droughts and floods, farmers prefer to mortgage or lease out the land in the hope of getting it back at some future time. If they fail to regain the land, the leased or mortgaged land is sold or purchased (Jodha 1978; see also Rao 1972).

TABLE 5.2. Percentage Distribution of Total (New) Land Transfers by Type of Transaction in Six Indian Villages, 1975–76 and 1978–79

Village	Transferred Area (ha)*	Type of Transaction		
		Tenancy[†]	Sale/Purchase	Other[‡]
Kanzara	117.6 (16)	92	0	8
Kinkheda	87.7 (15)	96	2	2
Kalman	257.9 (36)	97	1	2
Shirapur	416.0 (46)	90	6	4
Aurepalle	64.3 (14)	89	10	1
Dokur	80.5 (20)	77	20	3

Notes: Based on the data from 240 panel households and their partners in land transactions in the six villages. Data for Kalman and Kinkheda are for first three years only.

*Includes all land transactions in which at least one of the parties was a panel household. Figures in parentheses indicate the transferred land (area transferred/operated area per year) as percentage of total operated area of sample households.

[†] Includes all land transfers resulting from leasing in and leasing out of land and termination of previous leases. Leased-in and leased-out lands for which lease arrangements already existed at the beginning of fieldwork have been excluded.

[‡] Includes all land transfers resulting from gift donation, succession, and enactment of land reform laws.

Thus it is appropriate to study the land market and its functioning largely in terms of tenancy.

The intervillage differences in the extent of land transfers were largely a result of differences in the extent of tenancy. The larger area under tenancy in the Sholapur villages was caused by the delayed impact of a prolonged drought of 1971–72 and 1973–74, during which the majority of farmers lost their bullocks and other assets and failed to recoup them in subsequent years (Jodha 1978, Jodha, Asokan, and Ryan 1977). In the highly irrigated village of Dokur (Mahbubnagar), the practice of leasing land on a seasonal basis (twice a year) was responsible for the high extent of tenancy relative to the other village (Aurepalle) in the same district.[4] Both irrigation and drought seem to necessitate periodic resource adjustments, which are partly achieved through tenancy.

4. One of the reasons for the low extent of tenancy and therefore of total land transfers in Aurepalle was the extent of absentee landlordism; the lease period in most cases exceeded 2–3 years, and no new land transfers resulting from termination of leases could be recorded.

Partners in Land Tenancy

The following discussion concerns different aspects of all the land transactions resulting from tenancy—those existing at the beginning of the fieldwork as well as those taking place during three or four years of fieldwork. The land transfers resulting from termination of previous leases are excluded in the remainder of the analysis.

Table 5.3 presents the shares of different farm-size groups[5] in the total land leased in and leased out. Contrary to the conventional belief that a tenant is invariably a small farmer or a landless laborer being exploited by a landlord with a large holding, table 5.3 reveals that large farmers also leased in and small farmers also leased out substantial areas of land. In four out of six villages, the large farmers got the largest share (from 42 to 69 percent) of total area leased in. Only in one village (Kinkheda) did small farmers receive the largest share of leased-in land. On the other hand, of the total land leased out, large farmers contributed the largest share only in two villages; the bulk of the land leased out belonged to small and medium farmers. The implications of this for policy planning are discussed in the last section.[6]

Concentration of Land

The data about partnership in land leasing are presented in a different form in table 5.4.[7] There was considerable transfer of land within the same farm-size groups. Between approximately 30 and 60 percent of land transfers fell into this category (sum of columns 1 and 2). In two out of six villages the largest share of area leased was transacted among the large farmers them-

5. For the definition of farm-size groups, see table 5.1.

6. The large-scale emergence of the large farmer as a tenant seems to be a rather recent phenomenon in India and appears to have developed as an adjustment to land reform laws that attempt to reduce and restrict the growth of ownership holdings but not of operational holdings that include leased land. In some areas, technology based on high-yielding varieties (Vyas 1970) and rapid tractorization (Jodha 1974) have also induced large farmers to lease in land in place of leasing out, as they did in the past. No extensive data on this dynamic aspect of tenancy could be collected in the study villages. However, some relevant details were gathered from (1) a small number of households that have been traditionally leasing in or leasing out land; and (2) village *patwaris* and other revenue officials at higher levels, most of whom had been witnesses to the changing agrarian situation in their areas. The data provided in these discussions (especially data from the *patwari* records) clearly confirm the recent trend toward land leasing by large farmers.

7. For the purpose of table 5.4, relative landholding positions of partners were considered. Accordingly, the land transfer from small farmer to medium farmer and the land transfer from medium or small farmer to large farmer were put in the same category. Similarly, land transferred from small farmer to landless laborer and from large farmer to medium farmer or to small farmer were put in the same category. Hence the "smaller" and "larger" categories of table 5.4 are different from the farm-size categories of table 5.1.

TABLE 5.3. Percentage Share of Different Farm-size Groups in Tenanted Land Areas in Six Indian Villages, 1975–76 and 1978–79

	Area Leased in by:			Area Leased Out by:		
Village	Small Farms	Medium Farms	Large Farms	Small Farms	Medium Farms	Large Farms
Kanzara	34	16	50	22	34	44
Kinkheda	56	30	14	31	27	42
Kalman	39	48	13	59	30	11
Shirapur	26*	17	57	19	41	40
Aurepalle	27	4	69	42	16	42
Dokur	17*	41	42	22	59	19

Notes: Based on data from the 240 panel households and their partners in tenancy transactions in the six villages. Data for Kalman and Kinkheda are for first three years only. Table includes all cases of leased-in and leased-out land of panel respondents that existed at the beginning of the fieldwork as well as new transactions that took place during the four years of fieldwork. This and subsequent tables in this chapter exclude the land transfers resulting from termination of leases. For definitions of farm-size groups, see table 5.1. Labor households that participated in tenancy transactions are included with small farmers.

*Includes some initially landless labor households.

TABLE 5.4. Percentage Distribution of Leased-Out Land by Groups of Tenancy Partners in Six Indian Villages, 1975–76 and 1978–79

Village	Share of	Leased within the Same Farm-size Groups		Leased from Smaller to Larger Farmers	Leased from Larger to Smaller Farmers
		Large Farms	Others		
Kanzara	Area	29	17	24	30
	Transactions	(20)	(27)	(25)	(28)
Kinkheda	Area	12	33	8	47
	Transactions	(8)	(37)	(13)	(42)
Kalman	Area	0	33	43	24
	Transactions	(0)	(39)	(46)	(15)
Shirapur	Area	26	18	30	26
	Transactions	(10)	(31)	(37)	(22)
Aurepalle	Area	42	24	27	7
	Transactions	(20)	(53)	(13)	(14)
Dokur	Area	6	24	31	28
	Transactions	(6)	(28)	(55)	(11)

Notes: Based on data from the 240 panel households and their partners in tenancy transactions in the six villages. Data for Kalman and Kinkheda are for first three years only. Table includes all cases of leased-in and leased-out land of panel respondents that existed at the beginning of the fieldwork as well as new transactions that took place during the four years of fieldwork. Figures in parentheses are percentages of transactions covered by the respective categories; other figures are percentages of area covered. For definitions of farm-size groups, see table 5.1. Labor households that participated in tenancy transactions are included with small farmers.

selves. In four out of six villages, the proportion of land transfers from relatively smaller to relatively larger farmers was greater than vice versa whether one considers area or number of transactions. In other words, land was transferred from smaller operators to larger operators, which implies a modest tendency toward concentration of operational holdings.

Detailed discussions with farmers revealed that many small farmers prefer to lease out land to large farmers, who have a relatively better resource position and management capacity to ensure a higher rate of production and therefore a greater absolute share to the landowner of the gross production. The possibility of advance payments in cash or in kind to be adjusted against the crop share also induces smaller farmers to lease out the land to relatively larger ones. Also, when small landowners find it difficult to supplement their landholdings through leased land, they may decide to lease out their own land.

Furthermore, especially in Aurepalle, where absentee landlords are numerous, large farmers usually transact land within their own group because of increased political and legal awakening among the rural poor, who may take advantage of tenancy laws, thus creating problems for their landlords.

Period of Lease

Tenancy laws usually confer the ownership right to the actual tiller of leased-in land after he cultivates it for a specific period. Apprehension created by these laws was quite widespread and was not confined to large farmers. This was partly confirmed by the short period of lease of most of the transactions. To guard against the loss of land through long-term lease of land, landowners either tried to change tenants every year or tried to lease out the land to the same tenant on an annual basis. Table 5.5 shows that except for Aurepalle, 70 to 98 percent of the area (or 66 to 96 percent of the transactions) was leased out for one year or less. In the highly irrigated village of Dokur, the leases were mostly on a one-season basis. In Aurepalle, the pattern was different because of a greater proportion of absentee landlords (to be discussed in the next subsection). Close examination of the tenancy transactions based on a lease period of three years and more revealed that 52 percent of such transactions in all villages combined involved landowners who were absentee landlords. Another 37 percent of these transactions involved landowners who were relatively small farmers and had to lease out their land due to indebtedness to the tenant. (Alternatively, they worked as informally attached laborers to the tenant.) The remaining transactions based on long-term leases involved landowners who leased out land because of old age, disabilities, or kinship ties with tenants. Furthermore, most long-term tenancy transactions established a fixed rental payment as against crop-sharing

TABLE 5.5. Percentage Distribution of Leased-Out Land by Period of Lease in Six Indian Villages, 1975–76 and 1978–79

Period of Lease	Share of	Kanzara	Kinkheda	Kalman	Shirapur	Aurepalle	Dokur
1 year or	Area	74	95	70	98	18	79
less	Transactions	(83)	(96)	(66)	(95)	(40)	(78)
2 years	Area	19	Negligible	16	Negligible	72	6
	Transactions	(8)		(20)		(33)	(12)
3–5 years	Area	4	Negligible	6	Negligible	10	7
	Transactions	(3)		(8)		(26)	(2)
>5 years	Area	Negligible	Negligible	8	Negligible	Negligible	8
	Transactions			(6)			(8)

Notes: Based on data from the 240 panel households and their partners in tenancy transactions in the six villages. Data for Kalman and Kinkheda are for first three years only. Table includes all cases of leased-in and leased-out land of panel respondents that existed at the beginning of the fieldwork as well as new transactions that took place during the four years of fieldwork. Figures in parentheses are percentages of transactions covered by the respective categories; other figures are percentages of area covered.

arrangements. This is quite understandable in view of the type of partners who conclude long-term leases.

Terms and Conditions of Leases

Other terms and conditions of the lease arrangements also showed considerable similarities among villages. Except in Aurepalle, and to only some extent in Kanzara, the proportion of land area under fixed rental agreements was not important. In Aurepalle more than 76 percent of the leased area had fixed rental arrangements, chiefly because of the large number of absentee landlords. (This was 73 percent of all lease transactions.) The phenomenon of absentee landlordism in Aurepalle can probably be attributed to (1) nearness of the village to the city of Hyderabad, to which most of these landowners, both small and large, have migrated, leaving land to reliable caretaker tenants who pay only nominal rent; and (2) the unique social structure of the village, which has given more power over all village transactions to large farmers than any other of the six villages (see also chapter 8).

Sharing of output by landowner and tenant was found to be the most common arrangement in all villages except Aurepalle. Between 77 and 99 percent of transactions were in this category. Table 5.6 presents the proportions of leased land as well as the proportions of lease transactions according to the share of tenant in input and output. In practically all the output-sharing cases, the tenant received 50 to 75 percent of gross output. However, the arrangements concerning sharing of inputs were not as clear-cut. Important variations occured even within each agroclimatic zone. In Kinkheda,

TABLE 5.6. Percentage Distribution of Tenancy Land by Terms and Conditions in Six Indian Villages, 1975–76 and 1978–79

Village	Share of	Fixed Rental	Tenant's Share in Input (I)/Output (O)			Total
			I = 100 percent O = 50–75 percent	I = 50 percent O = 50 percent	I = 50–75 percent O = 50–75 percent	
Kanzara	Area	17	42	32	9	100
	Transactions	(23)	(33)	(31)	(13)	(100)
Kinkheda	Area	2	96	0	2	100
	Transactions	(4)	(92)		(4)	(100)
Kalman	Area	4	4	90	2	100
	Transactions	(7)	(6)	(81)	(6)	(100)
Shirapur	Area	1	96	1	2	100
	Transactions	(1)	(96)	(1)	(2)	(100)
Aurepalle	Area	76	19	0	5	100
	Transactions	(73)	(24)		(3)	(100)
Dokur	Area	3	0	94	3	100
	Transactions	(3)		(93)	(4)	(100)

Notes: Based on data from the 240 panel households and their partners in tenancy transactions in the six villages. Data for Kalman and Kinkheda are for first three years only. Table includes all cases of leased-in and leased-out land of panel respondents that existed at the beginning of the fieldwork as well as new transactions that took place during the four years of fieldwork. Figures in parentheses are the percentages of transactions covered by the respective categories; other figures are percentages of area covered.

for 96 percent of the leased area, the tenant carried all input costs, while in Kanzara this was true for only 42 percent of the leased area. There was a complete reversal in the Sholapur district; in Kalman 50 percent input sharing was practiced in 90 percent of the area, while in Shirapur this type of input sharing occurred only in 1 percent of the cases.

Detailed questioning of farmers, backed by actual observation, revealed the following. Under normal circumstances the tenant's share was 50 percent of both input and output. The tenant's share could rise to 75 percent or more if the leased-in land had soil problems and crop production entailed considerable risk. The tenant's share in output also increased above 50 percent if the landowner, especially if he was a small farmer, failed to provide the inputs (such as labor) agreed on in the lease. Such contingencies arose when small landowners out-migrated due to midseason drought; when other weather conditions compelled the landowners to concentrate first on self-cultivated plots—for example, on weeding at a critical time; or when unforeseen circumstances such as sickness or death of family workers or bullocks affected the landowner's resource position.

Thus the midseason contingencies requiring increased costs of cultivation for the tenant usually entitled him to a higher share in output according to an informal and flexible pattern. These observations at the micro level are consistent with those of Roumasset (1979) at the macro level, across crops, in the Philippines.

The tenant's input share could exceed 50 percent if he had not compensated the landowner in other ways at the beginning of the deal. As observed particularly in the Sholapur villages (and in some of the Akola villages), some *tenants* (who were often larger landowners) provided advances or loans to the poorer *landowners* as a part of the tenancy transaction. The amount was adjusted against the landowner's share in the output at harvest time. If the full amount was not adjusted in one year because of a poor crop, the lease was renewed for the next year. The tenants who did not give such advances to the owners usually had to bear a higher proportion of the input costs.[8]

If the tenant decided to raise crops requiring costly inputs such as fertilizer or pesticides, the tenant's share in input as well as output increased accordingly. Owing to such input- or output-sharing arrangements, tenancy did not discourage the adoption of improved technology. It was observed that crop choice was largely left to the tenant. However, where tenants (small landowners) depended on landowners for provision of input supplies and credit, crop choice was usually dictated by the landowner. A very limited number of such cases were observed in Kanzara, where farmers planted hybrid cotton in some plots and the sharing arrangements for different inputs differed.[9]

In the preceding paragraphs I have broadly described the normal pattern of input- and output-sharing arrangements in the six villages. The exceptions existed only where tenants were highly dependent on landowners and vice versa for different inputs and other provisions.

An analysis of the terms and conditions of tenancy in relation to farm size of tenants and landowners did not reveal any clear-cut differences that could be attributed to the unequal position of landowners and tenants, defined in terms of the pretenancy size of their operational holding.

Relative to the opportunities for factor ratio adjustments or for gains from interlinked transactions discussed below, formal terms and conditions or problems raised by them were not often mentioned as reasons for or against tenancy.[10]

8. Such advances, however, were not paid if lease transactions concerned problem soils that presented a greater risk in crop production.

9. For an analysis of sharing arrangements for plots requiring fertilizer use, see Jha (1979).

10. This is partly suggested by the fact that we could detect very few cases where the formal terms and conditions (lease period, share in output and input) constituted the reason for the breakup or reformation of tenant-landowner teams in the six villages. Out of a total of forty-six cases where tenancy partnerships changed due to mutual differences, only three resulted from disputes over the formal terms and conditions.

TABLE 5.7. Percentage Distribution of Tenancy Transactions by Landowners' Reasons in Six Indian Villages, 1975–76 and 1978–79

Reason	Farm-size Group	Kanzara	Kinkheda	Kalman	Shirapur	Aurepalle	Dokur
Resource	Small	71	40	40	62	10	50
adjustment	Medium	57	57	30	43	60	37
	Large	31	29	33	28	33	44
	Total	55	41	38	54	29	39
Interlocking of	Small	8	20	17	13	20	11
factor markets	Medium	7	0	40	8	0	13
	Large	0	0	34	11	34	22
	Total	6	8	21	15	7	12
Alternative earning	Small	12	10	3	10	7	33
opportunities	Medium	0	0	0	6	20	33
	Large	0	0	0	11	0	11
	Total	3	4	2	11	7	32
Traditional absentee	Small	0	10	3	3	30	0
landlordism	Medium	0	14	0	0	0	6
	Large	54	43	33	22	33	11
	Total	18	25	9	6	36	5
Other	Small	9	20	37	12	33	6
	Medium	36	29	30	35	20	6
	Large	15	28	13	28	0	22
	Total	18	22	30	14	21	15

Note: Based on details from the 240 sample households and their partners in tenancy transactions in the six villages. Data for Kalman and Kinkheda are for first three years only.

Reasons for Leasing Land

Farmers revealed more than thirty specific reasons for leasing their land. For purposes of analysis, these reasons have been grouped in the following categories: (1) resource adjustments; (2) interlocking of factor markets; (3) alternative earning opportunities (a reason given by small landowners who leased out land); (4) traditional absentee landlordism; (5) miscellaneous reasons, including physical considerations such as distance of plots from the village and plots with problem soils that presented management and risk problems; and (6) social and kinship ties.

The percentage distribution of tenancy transactions and of the land area transacted were tabulated separately for tenants and for landowners. As there was no difference in the substantive conclusions suggested by the two tabulations, table 5.7 classifies transactions only by reason for leasing. Furthermore, the table gives the distribution of tenancy transactions by landowner's reasons only. Differences observed when the same transactions were analyzed according to tenants' reasons will be indicated below.

Except in Aurepalle, resource adjustment was the principal reason for the tenancy transactions, as I have stated, especially for small landowners.

If the availability of alternative earning opportunities is also viewed as a resource adjustment, the role of resource adjustments in tenancy transactions becomes even more significant.[11] If the miscellaneous category of reasons is disregarded, the next most important reason for owners to lease out land is that they are absentee landlords. This was, understandably, more important for large farmers. For small landowners, interlocking of factor markets was more important.

When the same data were analyzed according to the reasons for tenancy given by tenants, temporary out-migration and absentee landlordism evidently disappeared as reasons; the roles of resource adjustments and interlocking of factor markets were thus further strengthened.

Resource Adjustment through Tenancy

To achieve optimum or fuller utilization of available resources such as family labor or bullocks, the farmer tries to hire different resources in or out. The extent to which this adjustment has been achieved through leasing of land is revealed by table 5.8, which presents the availability of land area per family laborer and per owned bullock both before and after the tenancy transaction for landowners and tenants. Only those cases are considered where resource adjustment was the main reason for tenancy. In four out of the six villages, tenancy did not tend to equalize the land/family labor ratios; on the contrary, it further widened the differences in the ratios in these villages.[12] This implies that tenancy transactions are not entered into primarily to adjust land availability with family labor availability. On the other hand, except for Aurepalle, land tenancy tended to equalize land/bullock ratios in these villages. If the fallow land is excluded from the analysis (figures in parentheses in table 5.8), the tendency toward equalization of land/bullock ratios between landowners and tenants is further strengthened. This supports the earlier findings reported by Bliss (1976). The fact that it is primarily the land/bullock ratios that are equalized and not the land/labor ratios suggests that the labor-hiring market operates more smoothly than the bullock-hiring market.[13]

11. With regard to the role of alternative earning opportunities in inducing particularly the small landholders to lease out their lands, it must be noted that in most cases these alternative opportunities are offered by rural work programs such as the Employment Guarantee Scheme. This is yet another example of the impact of public intervention on the operations of agricultural factor markets. For other examples; see chapter 8 and Jodha (1978).

12. An important limitation of table 5.9 is that it does not give any weight to irrigated land, which needs greater input of human and bullock labor. Of course, irrigated plots were important only in Dokur, but there, both tenant and landowner had irrigated lands prior to and after the lease transactions.

13. For more detail concerning the impact of factor markets on factor proportions, see Ryan and Rathore (1978).

TABLE 5.8. Resource Adjustments through Land Tenancy in Six Indian Villages, 1975–76 and 1978–79 (in hectares)

Partner in Tenancy	Land Available per Family Worker		Land Available per Bullock	
	Before Transaction	After Transaction	Before Transaction	After Transaction*
Kanzara				
Landowner	2.6	1.9	9.5	7.2 (5.8)
Tenant	1.5	1.9	3.4	5.1
Kinkheda				
Landowner	3.3	2.1	7.7	5.0 (4.5)
Tenant	1.1	1.7	1.9	4.0
Kalman				
Landowner	1.7	0.9	18.3	5.5
Tenant	2.2	3.8	3.4	7.2 (5.8)
Shirapur				
Landowner	1.7	0.4	30.9	5.8
Tenant	1.0	1.9	4.4	8.2 (7.4)
Aurepalle				
Landowner	1.1	0.9	2.6	2.1
Tenant	3.1	3.9	3.7	9.8 (8.7)
Dokur				
Landowner	0.5	0.2	3.8	1.5
Tenant	0.6	0.8	1.2	1.6

Notes: Based on data from the 240 panel households and their partners in tenancy transactions in the six villages. Data for Kalman and Kinkheda are for first three years only. Table includes all cases of leased-in and leased-out land of panel respondents that existed at the beginning of the fieldwork, as well as new transactions that took place during the four years of fieldwork. It also includes details of all those landowners and tenants whose main reason for tenancy transaction was resource adjustment.

*Figures in parentheses indicate the situation existing when fallow land is excluded from land availability per bullock.

Interlinking of Factor Markets

Interlinking of factor markets in Indian agriculture is discussed by Bharadwaj (1974*a*), Bardhan and Rudra (1978), and others. In the present study the concentrated effort to determine interlinked transactions by analyzing different VLS schedules and conducting follow-up investigations led to the finding that between 6 and 21 percent of tenancy transactions can be regarded as "interlinked factor market operations." The definition of interlinked factor market operations was fairly broad and included all factor, product, and service market transactions between tenancy partners where tenancy was a direct or an indirect cause or effect of the transaction. The first row of table 5.9 repeats information on interlinking from table 5.7 and shows that interlinked transactions with tenancy were fairly important in the Sholapur district, followed by the Mahbubnagar district, but were negligible in the

TABLE 5.9. Percentage Distribution of Interlinked Transactions among the Partners in Tenancy in Six Indian Villages, 1975–76 and 1978–79

	Akola District		Sholapur District		Mahbubnagar District	
	Kanzara	*Kinkheda*	*Kalman*	*Shirapur*	*Aurepalle*	*Dokur*
Interlinked transactions as proportion of all tenancy transactions	6	8	21	15	7	12
Proportion of interlinked transactions involving						
Land lease + credit	6	5	43	31	8	5
Land lease + labor	18	11	13	9	18	21
Land lease + credit + labor	6	17	15	27	10	30
Land lease + credit + marketing	47	40	8	10	16	7
Land lease + other	23	27	21	23	48	37
Proportion of all tenancy transactions involving labor commitments	1.5	2	6	6	2	6

Note: Based on data from the 240 panel households and their partners in tenancy transactions in the six villages. Data for Kalman and Kinkheda are for first three years only.

Akola district. The importance of different interlinked transactions differed from zone to zone. In Sholapur villages, for example, the land lease and the credit transactions were primarily linked. In these villages, contrary to the conventional pattern, the tenants gave loans to the landowners to get the land on lease. However, where old debts existed, the reverse was true, and in such cases lease of land, credit, and labor supply, through tied or untied labor, was sometimes simultaneously involved. In the Akola villages, the few interlinked transactions concerned primarily land lease, credit, and marketing. One of the reasons for this pattern was the public intervention in the form of the monopoly purchase of cotton by the Cotton Marketing Federation in Maharashtra, which, during the early years of our fieldwork, deferred payments and had other rigidities of operation. Small farmers with a limited holding capacity sometimes had to use large farmers as informal intermediaries to do their cotton marketing, a practice that led to interlinked tenancy credit and market transactions. In Mahbubnagar, land transactions were linked with a variety of miscellaneous transactions. Most of them concerned off-farm activities, procurement of inputs of scarce supplies, and distribution of irrigation water.

Links between land lease and labor do occur but are not very common. From the first row and the third and fourth rows of table 5.9, one can compute the proportion of all tenancy transactions linked with any labor commitments. These figures appear in the last row and indicate that labor commitments are involved in 6 percent or less of the transactions.

CONCLUSIONS

This study is based on farm-level data over three to four years, collected by the ongoing village-level studies of ICRISAT. The very high proportion (77 to 97 percent) of total land transfers that are land transfers via tenancy confirms that in India the land market is largely a tenancy market. The relatively higher extent of tenancy in those villages that are subject to drought or that have substantial irrigation suggests that both these factors tend to necessitate greater periodic resource adjustments, which are facilitated by tenancy.

The recent emergence of large farmers as tenants and small farmers as landowners contradicts the conventional presumption that the tenant is usually a poor, small land operator whereas the landlord is invariably a large farmer. In the study villages, 13 to 69 percent of total leased-out land was acquired by large farmers, and 56 to 89 percent of total leased-out land belonged to small and medium farmers. This has several policy implications. First, the heterogeneity of the tenant class further complicates tenurial policies. Tenancy policies cannot be considered as oriented exclusively to benefit the poor, since the large tenants can also benefit. Second, the heterogeneity of tenants may adversely affect the small tenant because he now has new competitors who are in a superior resource position and are competing for limited land resources. Competition has sometimes induced small landowners to lease out their land instead of supplementing it by leasing in land. Third, tenancy allows large farmers to circumvent land ceiling laws that apply only to owned land, not to leased-in land.

Output sharing rather than fixed rental was found to be the most common pattern in all villages except Aurepalle. Terms of tenancy were very flexible and adjusted substantially to (1) land productivity, (2) availability of capital from landowner and tenant, and (3) midseason contingencies affecting either of the parties. This was true both across and within villages. Because of the practice of direct linking of output share to input share and because crop choice was largely left to the tenant, tenancy did not appear to discourage adoption of (high cost) new technology by tenants.

Resource adjustment was the principal reason for leasing of land in five out of six villages. In the sixth village (Aurepalle), the traditional type of absentee landlordism dominated the tenancy situation. In all villages except Aurepalle, tenancy clearly tended to reduce the large gap between landowner and tenant in availability of land per bullock. However, tenancy did not tend to equalize the land/family labor ratios. This is quite plausible, as there are several alternative means to handle oversupply or undersupply of family labor in relation to owned land.

Interlocking of factor markets or factor product markets, indicated by interlinked transactions where tenancy was either cause or effect, was found to be the next most important reason for tenancy in some villages. Land lease and credit were often interlinked in Sholapur villages, where, contrary to the conventional pattern, tenants extended credit to landowners to get land on lease. In Akola villages, land lease, credit, and cotton marketing were most frequently interlinked. Interlinked transactions in Mahbubnagar were more complex and varied. They concerned supply of scarce inputs, urban–rural links, sharing of water facilities, and so on.

Thus, tenancy is primarily an outgrowth of bullock power adjustments and credit market imperfections (which leads to linked transactions with credit). The human labor market seems to be functioning sufficiently well and few households seem to lease land particularly for reasons of oversupply or undersupply of family labor in relation to owned land or because of difficulties in hiring daily labor.

Terms of tenancy are very flexible and greatly responsive to the resource positions of tenant and landowner and to midseason contingencies affecting either of the parties.

II

Dynamics and Rigidity in Labor Markets:
Contractual Arrangements, Wage Adjustments,
and Segmentation

6

Changes in Rice Harvesting Contracts and Wages in Java

Masao Kikuchi, Anwar Hafid, and Yujiro Hayami

Harvesting is the last stage in the rice production process. It is at this stage that a major portion of the income from rice production is distributed among resource contributors. Typically, various production costs, such as loan repayments for the purchase of fertilizer and other inputs, are deducted from the output, and the residual is divided between landlord and tenant. Harvesting workers receive a significant share, since harvesting and threshing costs are usually the largest of the paid-out costs in rice production.

The wages from harvesting work are the major source of income for landless agricultural workers, who are at the bottom of the social structure of the rural community. Therefore, these wages are a critical parameter for the determination of the income levels and living standards of the rural poor. This parameter depends on contractual arrangements as well as on the technology for harvesting rice.

Recent changes in rice harvesting systems in Asia have been identified as dramatic evidence of the major changes in village-community institutions that have been induced by the forces of modernization such as commercialization and new technology, with serious consequences for income distribution. In Bangladesh a shift from the traditional output-sharing contracts among villagers to the fixed daily wage contracts with migrant workers has been reported in a number of villages (Clay 1976).[1] In Central Java the traditional *bawon* system, which allowed a wide sharing of output, has been replaced by the new *tebasan* system, in which farmers sell standing crops to middlemen who employ only contract workers for harvesting and thus reduce

The research on which this paper is based was supported jointly by the Agro-Economic Survey in Indonesia and by the International Rice Research Institute. Partial financial support was provided by the Agricultural Development Council, the Ford Foundation, and the International Development Center of Japan. We are indebted to Chaerul Saleh and Sri Hartoyo for fieldwork. More detailed results of our study are presented in Y. Hayami and M. Kikuchi (1981, chaps. 7 and 8).

1. Clay argued at the conference that some of these shifts may have been temporary.

the harvesters' share (Collier, Wiradi, and Soentoro 1973; Collier et al. 1976; Utami and Ihalauw 1973). In the Philippines the traditional *hunusan* system (same as the *bawon* system in Java) has been replaced by the *gama* system, in which only those workers who weeded the field without receiving wages are allowed to participate in harvesting (Hayami and Kikuchi 1981, chaps. 4 and 5).

In all these cases, the real wage rates were reduced by the changes in contractual arrangements. It became necessary to adjust agricultural wages to the rapid changes in the labor supply caused by population pressure that outpaced the changes in the demand for labor, and these examples suggest that the wage adjustments were made through changes in village institutions in the form of changes in contractual arrangements.

In this paper we investigate one such process of agricultural wage adjustments made through institutional changes in the harvesting system of one of the regions of Java. We first attempt to delineate the changes in rice harvesting systems in a large number of villages throughout Java and then analyze one village system in greater detail.

CEBLOKAN AND TEBASAN SYSTEMS IN JAVANESE VILLAGES

Geographical Distribution

Figure 6.1 shows the geographical distribution of various types of rice harvesting systems in Java. The data were collected as part of an extensive survey of forty-eight villages in Central and West Java conducted in August and December 1978 (Hayami and Hafid 1979).

It is important to recognize that the traditional "purely open" *bawon* system, where everyone can participate in harvesting, has increasingly been restricted in scope and is rarely practiced today. The system nearest to the traditional concept of *bawon* harvesting as a communal activity is one in which harvesting is essentially open only to people of the same village, with a limited number of outsiders being allowed to participate. A second system does not limit participation to the inhabitants of the same village but sets a limit to the total number of participants. Those who arrive at the harvesting site after the prescribed number has been reached are rejected. The third system imposes a more severe restriction: participation is confined solely to those who have received specific invitations from farmers (mostly relatives and neighbors). A fourth system limits the harvesters to those who have performed extra services such as transplanting and weeding without pay; this system is called *ceblokan* (alternatively called *kedokan* and *ngepak-ngedok*).

According to our survey the *tebasan* system, in which the farmer sells his standing crop to middlemen, was practiced in eighteen out of our forty-eight sample villages. In all these villages, the *tebasan* system coexisted with

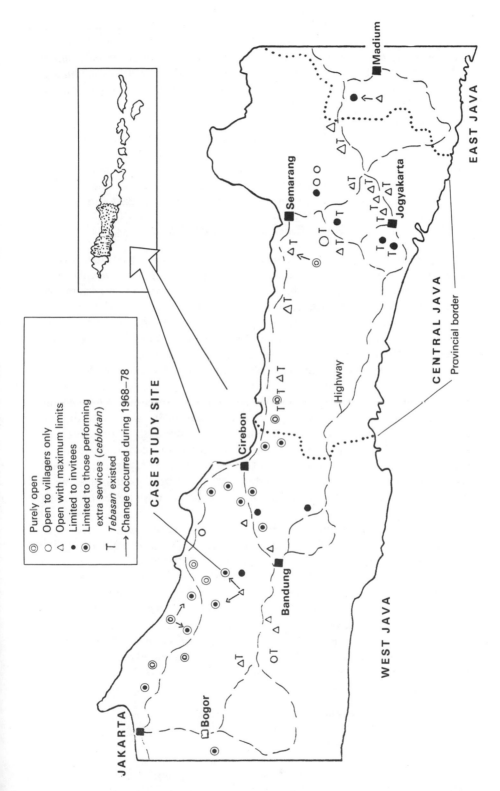

FIGURE 6.1. Geographical Distribution of Rice Harvesting Systems in Java.

the *bawon* system. If, for the sake of brevity, we refer to them as "*tebasan* villages," it must be understood that they are mixed *tebasan-bawon* villages. Figure 6.1 and table 6.1 show that the *tebasan* system is strongly concentrated in the Central Java sample, sixteen out of eighteen *tebasan* villages being located in Central Java.

It appears that the distribution of *tebasan* is inversely correlated with that of *ceblokan*. In our sample all the *ceblokan* cases were located in West Java; in none of these villages was *tebasan* reported. We found that *ceblokan* was most widespread in the eastern border area of West Java. The *ceblokan* system seems to have been spreading from this area to the east and north.

Roles of *Tebasan* and *Ceblokan*

The "purely open" *bawon* system, most commonly found coexisting with *tebasan*, was practiced by more than 90 percent of the *tebasan* villages in Central Java. We found that in these villages the purely open system had been traditional. As growing population pressure resulted in demands for participation from too many harvesters, farmers developed the practice of rejecting harvesters after a certain level had been reached. However, it was difficult for them to limit the number of harvesters to an optimum level because the traditional community obligation demanded a wide sharing of income and working opportunities. The *tebasan* system was crucial here, because the middlemen who bought the standing crops and managed the harvesting were free from the traditional obligation (Collier, Wiradi, and Soentoro 1973). Likewise, the middlemen could more easily reduce the harvesters' share when the supply of labor increased more quickly than the demand. Thus, the shift from *bawon* to *tebasan* may be regarded as a shift from a personalized employment system within village communities, based on the principles of mutual help and income sharing, to an impersonal market system.

Ceblokan was another way to limit the participation of workers in harvesting and to reduce their wage rates. The adoption of *ceblokan*, unlike the adoption of *tebasan*, does not represent a shift from the personalized nonmarket system to the impersonal market system.[2] Rather, the personal tie between employers and employees is strengthened because one farmer patronizes a smaller number of workers, employing them for various farm tasks in a patron-client type of relationship. However, *ceblokan* reduces the wage rate in the same way as does the *tebasan* system. The traditional output share for harvesters may be maintained but the same share is paid for a larger amount of labor, including obligatory work in addition to harvesting work.

2. "Market" in the present context refers to the concepts conventionally used in the texts of neoclassical economics, such as Walrasian auction markets.

TABLE 6.1. Distribution of Sample Villages by Type of Harvesting System, 1978

Harvesting System	West Java			Central Java			Total		
	Total	Tebasan Villages		Total	Tebasan Villages		Total	Tebasan Villages	
	No. (1)	No. (2)	Percent (2)/(1)	No. (3)	No. (4)	Percent (4)/(3)	No. (5)	No. (6)	Percent (6)/(5)
Purely open	4	0	0	2	2	100	6	2	33
Open to villagers only	2	1	50	3	1	33	5	2	40
Open to all with maximum limits	5	1	20	11	10	91	16	11	69
Limited to invitees	3	0	0	5	3	60	8	3	38
Limited to those performing extra services (ceblokan)	13	0	0	0	0	—	13	0	0
Total	27	2	7	21	16	76	48	18	38

TABLE 6.2. Changes in Average Shares of Harvesters in Sample Villages, 1968–78
(percent)

Village/system	1968 (1)	1978 (2)	(1) − (2)
Mixed *bawon-tebasan* villages			
Under *bawon**	11.2	10.0	1.2
Bawon to *tebasan*†	11.2	8.2	3.0
Bawon villages			
Ceblokan	18.2	16.2	2.0
Non-ceblokan	13.3	11.8	1.5

*Assuming that all farmers stayed with the *bawon* system.
†Assuming that all farmers shifted from *bawon* to *tebasan* in mixed *bawon-tebasan* villages in the period 1968–78.

Table 6.2 compares the changes in the harvesters' share in the sample villages under different harvesting systems. The comparison demonstrates the significant effect of *tebasan* in reducing the harvesters' share. It should be noted that the output shares of the harvesters remained much higher in the *bawon* villages, especially those employing the *ceblokan* system, than in the *tebasan* (mixed *bawon-tebasan*) villages. Of course, this does not mean that wage rates were higher under the *ceblokan* system but that *ceblokan* workers received higher wages in kind for the increased amount of work they did. How efficiently the wage rate can adjust to changing demand and supply as a result of nonmarket institutional adjustments such as the shift from *bawon* to *ceblokan* is the problem investigated by the intensive case study described in the next section.

CEBLOKAN IN A WEST JAVA VILLAGE

A village in West Java was selected for our case study of the wage adjustment process brought about by the shift from the *bawon* to the *ceblokan* system (indicated as the case study site in Figure 6.1). A complete enumeration survey of one *kampung* (hamlet) in the *desa* (village) was conducted in January 1979 (for details, see Kikuchi et al. 1980).

Village Characteristics

The hamlet under study is characterized by complete rice monoculture except for some home gardening of fruits and vegetables. Most areas are unirrigated rice fields (*sawah*) where double-cropping of rice is practiced. There has been virtually no expansion of the area cultivated and no significant improvement in irrigation systems for the past few decades. Technology has been largely stagnant. A government program (BIMAS) was instituted to introduce modern high-yielding varieties, but because those varieties

TABLE 6.3. Size Distributions of *Sawah* Landownership and Operational Land-holdings in a West Java Village, 1979

| | Ownership Holdings | | | | Operational Holdings | | | |
| | Owners | | Area | | Households | | Area | |
Size (ha)	No.	%	ha	%	No.	%	ha	%
1.00 and over	5	4	6.21	25	4	4	4.72	19
0.60–0.99	4	4	3.23	13	4	4	3.30	13
0.30–0.59	14	13	6.23	25	17	15	7.44	30
0.10–0.29	41	37	7.85	32	41	37	8.17	33
0.01–0.10	21	19	1.34	5	17	15	1.10	5
0	25	23	0	0	27	25	0	0
Total	110	100	24.86	100	110	100	24.73	100

Average area per household (ha)	0.23		0.22
Gini coefficient	0.58		0.54

were found to be highly susceptible to insects and pests, most farmers who tried them have changed back to traditional varieties.

The man/land ratio is highly unfavorable. At the time of this survey, the total population of 419 persons in 113 households depended for their livelihood on only 29 hectares (ha) of land, of which 88 percent was *sawah*, 10 percent was garden, and 2 percent was fishpond. The average farm size was extremely small and yet the size distribution was highly skewed (table 6.3). Most farmers were owner-operators, although the incidence of tenancy was increasing.

Population growth decelerated during the past three decades due to the use of birth-control methods (such as forms of abortion) that were not based on modern medical science, but the labor force continued to increase until recently.

The population pressure on the land is reflected in the decline in the real wage rate. The real daily wage rate for hand hoeing, for example, measured in terms of paddy, declined from 9.5 kg in 1968–71 to 8.5 kg in 1978. With the decline in the cost of manual labor, animal (cattle or carabao) plowing was increasingly replaced by hand hoeing.

Diffusion of *Ceblokan*

Concomitant with the growing population pressure and the decreasing return to additional labor applied to a limited land area, there was a change in the type of harvesting contract used, from the traditional *bawon* system to the *ceblokan* system. The *ceblokan* system was first adopted in 1964 by seven farmers. It very rapidly replaced the *bawon* system and, by 1978, more than 95 percent of the farmers had adopted *ceblokan* (table 6.4). However, even before the introduction of *ceblokan*, not all the farmers had

TABLE 6.4. Changes in the Rice Harvesting System in a West Java Village (percent of farmer adopters)

Year	Bawon*				Ceblokan†				
	PO	OV	OM	LI	1/6(T)	1/7(T)	1/7(T + W)	1/7(H + T)	1/7(H + T + W)
1978				4		72	19	1	4
1976–77				4	7	67	18	2	2
1974–75				7	15	67	10	1	
1972–73				8	17	67	8		
1970–71			2	10	33	51	4		
1968–69	1	4	6	19	44	24	2		
1966–67	3	10	8	27	52				
1964–65	9	16	16	32	27				
1962–63	16	34	33	17					
1960–61	29	31	21	19					
1950s	35	29	18	18					

Bawon system: PO = purely open; OV = open for villagers only; OM = open with maximum limit; LI = limited to invitees.

†*Ceblokan* system: 1/6, 1/7 = harvesters' share; T, W, H = obligatory work to establish the harvesting right (T = transplanting, W = weeding, H = harrowing).

practiced "purely open" (PO) *bawon* because not everyone was allowed to participate in harvesting. The system closest to the traditional PO *bawon*, in which harvesting was a communal activity, was one where harvesting was open only to inhabitants of the same village (OV). A second system limited the maximum number allowed to participate (OM). A more severe restriction was imposed by the third system—participation was limited to those who had received specific invitations from farmers (LI). The data in table 6.4 indicate that the farmers gradually shifted from the more open *bawon* system to the more restricted *bawon* system, until *ceblokan* was introduced.

The *ceblokan* system also includes a spectrum of arrangements concerning the harvesters' share and obligatory work. Originally, *ceblokan* harvesters received a traditional share of one-sixth for harvesting if they had transplanted rice without receiving payment. (Usually meals were served even though cash wages were not paid.) Later, their share was reduced to one-seventh, and weeding and harrowing were added to the list of obligatory work required of them before they could participate in harvesting. The harvesting systems in this village show successive changes, from more open and generous arrangements to more restrictive and less generous ones (table 6.4).

By 1978 the shift from *bawon* to *ceblokan* was almost complete. The number of laborers employed and the wages earned under the *ceblokan* system now constituted the major share of the total hired work froce and wage income of laborers. Of all households whose family members were

TABLE 6.5. Average Hired Labor Time and Wage Earnings per Household Employed in Rice Production in a West Java Village, 1978 Dry Season

	Labor Hours Employed		Wages Earned*	
	Hours	*%*	*Rp*	*%*
Land preparation				
Daily wage[†]	89.3	(35)	6,542	(44)
Ceblokan	2.9	(1)	86	(1)
Total	92.2	(36)	6,628	(45)
Transplanting				
Ceblokan	31.7	(13)	670	(4)
Weeding				
Daily wage	12.7	(5)	650	(4)
Ceblokan	23.1	(9)	566	(4)
Total	35.8	(14)	1,216	(8)
Harvesting and threshing				
Ceblokan	89.2	(35)	6,260	(42)
Bawon	1.5	(1)	83	(0)
Total	90.7	(36)	6,343	(42)
Other				
Daily wage	2.6	(1)	104	(1)
Total				
Daily wage	104.6	(41)	7,296	(49)
Ceblokan	146.9	(58)	7,582	(51)
Bawon	1.5	(1)	83	(0.5)
Total	253.0	(100)	14,961	(100)

Note: Averages for 54 small farmer households and 23 landless worker households.

*Includes meals.
†Includes wage payments according to area-rate contracts.

hired for rice production during the 1978 dry season, the total average hours worked by those employed under the *ceblokan* system was about 60 percent of the total hired labor time, and the total average income earned from *ceblokan* work was about 50 percent of total wages earned (table 6.5).

Employer-Employee Relations

In the shift from more open and generous arrangements to less open and less generous ones, large farmers usually took the lead and small farmers followed. As shown in the first part of table 6.6, a clear tendency developed: the larger the farmers, the less generous were their arrangements in the employment of harvesters. The second part of table 6.6 shows that as employees, the landless and near-landless workers (less than 0.1 ha) tended to be employed under somewhat less generous conditions than workers from medium-scale and large-scale farmer households.

TABLE 6.6. Distribution of Employers and Employees in Rice Harvesting by Type of Contract and by Size of Operational Holding in a West Java Village, 1978 Dry Season

			Ceblokan			
Farm-size Class (*ha*)	*Family Only**	*Bawon* ($\frac{1}{7}$)	$(\frac{1}{7})(T)$	$\frac{1}{7}(T + W)$ *or* $\frac{1}{7}(T + H)$	$\frac{1}{7}(T + W + H)$	*Total*
Employer						
Less than 0.1 (No.)	6		11			17
(%)	(35)		(65)			(100)
0.1–0.29 (No.)	1	2	34	4		41
(%)	(2)	(5)	(83)	(10)		(100)
0.3–0.59 (No.)			10	6	1	17
(%)			(59)	(35)	(6)	(100)
0.6 and over (No.)			1	6	1	8
(%)			(13)	(74)	(13)	(100)
Employee						
0 (No.)			7	18		25
(%)			(28)	(72)		(100)
0.01–0.1 (No.)			6	10	1	17
(%)			(35)	(59)	(6)	(100)
0.1–0.29 (No.)		1	22	9	4	36
(%)		(3)	(61)	(25)	(11)	(100)
0.3–0.59 (No.)			10	1		11
(%)			(91)	(9)		(100)

Note: 1/7 = harvesters' share; T, W, H = obligatory work to establish the harvesting right (T = transplanting, W = weeding, H = harrowing).

*Harvesting done by family labor alone.

Such data suggest that the rich (large farmers) employed the poor (landless workers and near-landless workers), whereas the middle-class people (medium-scale farmers) employed each other. These relations are confirmed by a matrix that relates employers to employees for the different farm-size classes (table 6.7). The matrix shows that landless workers and near-landless farmers with landholdings of less than 0.1 ha depended most heavily on large farms of 0.6 ha and over for their employment opportunities. Medium-scale farmers in the size brackets of 0.1–0.29 ha and 0.3–0.59 ha found the most numerous employment opportunities on farms whose size was comparable to their own farm-size classes. Therefore, employment relations among medium-scale farmers were, by nature, equivalent to labor exchange. In contrast, the employment of landless workers by large farmers was equivalent to a patron-client relation.

The shift from *bawon* to *ceblokan* can be considered a shift from a mutual help and income-sharing system within a whole village community to a system of patron-client and labor-exchange relations in smaller groups.

TABLE 6.7. Matrix of Employer-Employee Relations in Rice Harvesting in Terms of Paddy Area (ha) Contracted in a West Java Village, 1978 Dry Season.

Employee Employer	0 ha (landless)	0.01–0.1 ha	0.1–0.29 ha	0.30–0.59 ha	Outside kampung
Less than 0.1 ha	0.13 (2)	0.71 (14)	0.24 (3)	0.02 (18)	0 (0)
0.1–0.29 ha	1.31 (20)	1.41 (28)	3.26 (37)	0.62 (31)	0.35 (23)
0.3–0.59 ha	1.56 (24)	1.13 (24)	2.50 (29)	0.88 (43)	0.72 (46)
0.6 ha and over	2.96 (46)	1.54 (31)	2.15 (25)	0.36 (18)	0.48 (31)
Outside kampung	0.52 (8)	0.13 (3)	0.52 (6)	0.14 (7)	—
Total	6.48 (100)	4.97 (100)	8.67 (100)	2.02 (100)	1.55 (100)

Note: Figures in parentheses are percentages.

However, this shift does not mean that some members of the community were excluded from employment opportunities. All members were part of the employment matrix within the community, although the employer-employee relations were distinctly different among the various classes— the labor-exchange type was prevalent among medium-class farmers and the patron-client type prevailed between large farmers and landless/near-landless people.

Even the disadvantaged members were not excluded. Two large farmers who had adopted the least generous arrangements of *ceblokan*, where transplanting, weeding, and harrowing were obligatory, exempted widows and their families from harrowing work, because land preparation was considered man's work. This example suggests that the community's traditional value system of mutual help and income sharing has not entirely disappeared and that contravention of this system can prove to be a costly experience.

Wage Adjustments under *Ceblokan*

It is our basic hypothesis that the *ceblokan* system represents an institutional instrument to reduce the harvesters' share of output and so to bring it in line with the market wage rate of the region. As a test, an imputation was made of the wage rates for alternative harvesting arrangements. In the calculation, meals given for obligatory work, such as transplanting and weeding, were valued at one-half of the market wage rate per day. (Meals were not given for harvesting work.) The results show that the harvesters' share under the *bawon* system with the one-seventh share was 40 percent higher than the market wage rate. As a result of the shift to the *ceblokan* system with the sole obligation of transplanting, the gap between the harvesters' share and the market wage rate was reduced to 20 percent. The addition of weeding to the obligation made the harvesters' share equal to the market wage rate (table 6.8). Such results are highly consistent with our hypothesis. Similar results were reported for the *gama* system in the Philippines (Hayami and Kikuchi 1981, chaps. 4 and 5; Kikuchi et al. 1980).

CONCLUSION

A general overview of the geographical distribution of various rice harvesting systems in Java reveals two types of institutional changes that have occurred in response to growing population pressure on land: the shift from the traditional *bawon* system to the *tebasan* system in Central Java, and the shift from the *bawon* system to the *ceblokan* system in West Java. The former seems to represent a change from a communal employment system to an impersonal capitalistic market system; the latter is a shift to a personalized

TABLE 6.8. Imputation of Wage Rates for Harvesting Works

Number of working hours of *ceblokan* labor (hr/ha)		
(1) Harvesting and threshing		324
(2) Transplanting		111
(3) Weeding		147
Actual share of *ceblokan* harvester		
Quantity of paddy (kg/ha)		421
(4) Imputed value of paddy (Rp/ha)*		27,365
Imputed wage rate (Rp/hr)		
(A) *Bawon* $\frac{1}{7}$	(4)/(1)	84
(B) *Ceblokan* $\frac{1}{2}$(T)	$(4)/[(1) + 0.5(2)]^{\dagger}$	72
(C) *Ceblokan* $\frac{1}{2}$(T + W)	$(4)/[(1) + 0.5(2) + 0.5(3)]^{\dagger}$	60
Market wage rate (Rp/hr)		60

* Use Rp 65/kg for the market price of paddy.

† Assume that the cost of meals served for transplanting and harvesting was one-half of the market wage rate per day for those tasks.

employment relation under the guise of the mutual help and income-sharing principles of traditional communities. Although the *tebasan* and *ceblokan* systems were organized under entirely different principles, both were designed to limit the number of harvesting workers employed for the benefit of management and to reduce the real wage rate to a level consistent with the decreasing marginal productivity of labor.

Our case study of a village in West Java indicated that the *ceblokan* system, which was organized as a highly personalized relation entirely different from the impersonal market relation, was effective in reducing the wage rates implicit in the harvesters' share to the level of market wage rates. This result suggests the hypothesis that the institutional process of wage adjustment within the framework of a traditional community system is equally efficient as the market adjustment mechanism.

It is beyond the scope of this paper to discuss why *ceblokan* was adopted in West Java and *tebasan* was adopted in Central Java. The major question is why, of all the available alternatives, the *ceblokan* system was adopted to limit participation in harvesting and to reduce wage rates. Why did they not replace the *bawon* system with the labor of daily wage workers, for example? Most likely any such change that deviated from the long-established system in the village community would have entailed significant cost in various forms (malicious gossip and noncompliance or even secret retaliation by the poor, who might attempt to damage crops and other properties). Cases of this nature were reported in the Philippines (Hayami and Kikuchi 1981).

Another way to reduce the wage rate was to reduce the harvesters' share in the *bawon* system. This change was easier to implement and was, in fact, effected. However, reduction of the share rate was not quite so consistent with the basic traditional village value system of mutual help and income sharing. In terms of the patron-client relations common in those village communities where there were multifaceted ties, less social friction would have resulted if some extra obligations had been added while maintaining the same share rate.

Compared with daily wage contracts, the *ceblokan* system may also have an advantage in motivating labor because output sharing builds in an incentive for employees to be more conscientious in their obligatory tasks. Workers may also prefer this system because future employment and income are more secure.

It is true that *ceblokan* facilitated the reduction in the wage rate and resulted in a decline in the welfare of poorer members of the rural communities. However, if *ceblokan* had not been adopted, the system would have changed to a capitalistic market system with the same distributional consequence and with a sharper class conflict. The basic economic factor underlying the growing misery of the poor is the decreasing return to labor owing to growing population pressure on land. Consequently, the challenge of rural poverty is best met by intensified efforts to counteract the decreasing return to labor applied per unit of land in the form of improved irrigation and the development of land-saving and labor-using technology.

7

Seasonal Migration and Cooperative Capitalism: The Crushing of Cane and Labor by the Sugar Factories of Bardoli, South Gujarat

Jan C. Breman

After the construction of a new system of canal irrigation in South Gujarat, a rapid change took place in the agricultural patterns of the Surat district. The land under sugarcane in the Bardoli area, the location of my fieldwork, leaped from a mere 583 acres in 1958–59 to 5,945 acres in 1965–66, 9,675 acres in 1969–70, and 15,645 acres in 1974–75. The proportion of sugarcane is continually increasing, and by 1979 more than two-thirds of all the irrigated land in this *taluka* (subdistrict) was under sugarcane. The new crop became the foundation of agroindustries in the region. At the time of my visit in 1977 there were five sugarcane factories in operation in South Gujarat, four in the Surat district and one in the Valsad district. Although I collected some data on all these enterprises, my most detailed fieldwork was confined to a region around Bardoli in which three factories are situated not more than 15 to 20 km from each other. The largest and oldest factory was established in 1956–57; the other two were founded in 1964 but only went into production in the 1968–69 season. I shall refer to these establishments as *X*, *Y*, and *Z*, respectively.

THE RECRUITMENT AREA

In view of the abundant supply of local labor in South Gujarat, it is remarkable that for the harvest, all the sugar factories make exclusive use of seasonal migrants who are recruited in huge numbers in West Maharashtra. In fact, however, the preference for migrant labor appears to be a general feature of this industry. In Maharashtra also, temporary workers brought in from distant regions have for many years formed a substantial part of the labor force during the harvest season. When, some twenty or so years ago, the first factory was set up in Bardoli, recruitment of workers who were already familiar with cane cutting and the organization of the work in general was naturally an attractive prospect. By appointing a manager who came from Maharashtra and who was experienced in handling seasonal migrants, the same practice could be followed in South Gujarat. The factories set up later have copied this example, with the result that the annual movement of labor out of Maharashtra to the coastal plain has continued on an ever-expanding scale.

All the factories of South Gujarat have their own offices in the town of Dhulia, where the required number of workers are recruited from over a wide area. Khandesh, in the northwest of Maharashtra (the districts of Dhulia and Jalgaon and part of Nasik), is the most important recruitment area, and the migrants are therefore referred to in Gujarat by the collective term *khandeshi*. However, from the data I gathered during my research it appears that a substantial minority of the cane cutters are from the even more distant district of Aurangabad, which forms a part of the Marathwada region.

The migrant workers belong to an area situated in the rain shadow of Maharashtra; much of the land in this dry agricultural zone is of very poor quality. Cultivation is mainly limited to coarse grains, such as millet and sorghum. The rural population consists for the most part of small landholders and landless peasants for whom, after the harvest of the crops at the end of the rainy season, there are hardly any possibilities for earning a living. Their poverty forces them to hire out their labor elsewhere for a large part of the year. The Maharashtra and Gujarat sugar factories can therefore draw from a sizable reservoir of cheap labor that, particularly in times of serious and sustained drought (as occurs once every three or four years on average), is virtually inexhaustible. As has already been said, the cane cutters are mainly small landholders and landless laborers, and as such they belong to the lowest castes in the district from which they come. Apart from upper-caste Marathas and Dhangars, and a few members of service and artisan castes (Barbers and Tailors), my respondents include Mahars (neo-Buddhists) and other Harijans (lower castes) and many who are chiefly from tribal groups (Bhils, Banjaras, and Gamits).

THE CONTRACT BETWEEN FACTORY AND BROKER

The first point in the agreement drawn up between the factory and the *mukadam* (jobber) stipulates the number of *koytas* the brokers will supply. *Koyta* is the name of a cutting knife, but the term is also used to refer to a unit consisting of three laborers—the cutter and two helpers, who clean the cane, bind it, and help the cutter load it.

The *mukadams* fall into two categories: those who hire out these work teams with a bullock cart and those who hire them out without. The *gadivalas* (carters) are employed as cutters in the fields and also take the cane to the factory in their bullock carts. The *koytavalas* are solely concerned with cutting and loading the cane alongside the roads; lorries transport it from

TABLE 7.1. Work Teams Contracted by Factory Z in the 1976–77 Season

Team Composition	Mukadams *of* Koytavalas	*Number of* Teams	Mukadams *of* Gadivalas	*Number of* Teams
0–5	—	—	27	111
6–10	5	45	42	320
11–15	118	1,513	13	161
16–20	82	1,539	11	189
21–25	41	925	2	46
>25	18	624	3	90
Total	264	4,646	98	917

Note: The 264 labor brokers of *koytavalas* plus the 98 brokers of *gadivalas* had a combined total of 5,563 cutting teams under them that together included 20,111 members, according to factory data. This implies an average of 3.62 persons per *koyta*; older children are included in the number. In addition, an estimated 5,000 migrants were not involved in the harvesting—chiefly the very young children—and therefore, they were not registered by the factory.

there to the factory. During the year of my visit, the three factories (X, Y, and Z) had a total of 802 labor brokers in their service, of whom 270 were in charge of teams consisting of cutters-*cum*-carters, and 532 (nearly double that number) headed teams restricted to carrying out the actual cutting work in the fields. Table 7.1 reports the composition and number of work teams contracted by factory Z in the 1976–77 season.

In July each factory sends a few recruiting agents to Dhulia to open up the office and make contact with labor brokers who have supplied *koytas* in previous years. The *mukadams* get a letter inviting them to meet the factory's agent in a nearby place on a particular date to estimate the number of work teams they can supply and to furnish workers' names and places of residence. Brokers are inclined to overestimate the number of *koytas* they have under them, in an attempt to get the maximum advance payment. The recruitment area is split up into various zones; an additional number of agents go around the villages to check whether the brokers in each zone can in fact supply the stated number of *koytas*.

On the basis of this information and the *mukadam*'s service record—the number of years he has worked for the factory, his reliability, and his thoroughness—the number of teams he may recruit is finally determined. A written contract is signed by him and by the factory representative. New jobbers are also selected at this point, on the recommendation of other trustworthy *mukadams*. Information is then gathered on their standing in the village—the creditworthiness of these aspirants, their qualities of leadership, and so on. Most factory recruiting agents themselves began as *mukadams*, have maintained close contacts with their district of origin, and have a personal interest in bringing particular candidates to the fore. In their first years the newcomers are on trial and may recruit only a limited number of *koytas* to make up a gang. In this way they gradually build up their credit as a *mukadam*.

The factory pays an advance, which is then used for setting the seal on the bond of work teams to the jobbers for the coming year. This cash handout is made in two or three separate installments: the first after the signing of the contract (during September, at the *Dasara* festival) and the final one or ones a few days before the start of the migrants' journey. For the whole year, the factory pays out a total amount of Rs 25–40 for the *koytavalas* and a much higher sum—about Rs 300–350—for the *gadivalas*. This amount is not fixed; it fluctuates from year to year and also between *mukadams*. Hard bargaining takes place over it. The jobbers want as large an advance as possible and the factories want to keep payments as low as they can; sometimes they manage to. In 1971–72, I asked at one of the other sugar factories (not *X*, *Y*, or *Z*) why the average advance to carters that year was not more than Rs 150. I was told that because of the drought prevailing in Khandesh, the rural poor were nearly dying from hunger, and migrants were therefore having to make do with much less. It was added— without cynicism—that such circumstances work out to the advantage of the factory.

The factory agents keep themselves informed throughout the monsoon about the progress of the recruitment drive—especially of the payments being made to the heads of *koytas* out of their advance—to avoid unwelcome surprises. If many of the work teams are missing when the time comes to migrate, the whole harvest campaign can be jeopardized. In practice things appear to work well enough: of the 350 *mukadams* whom factory *X* contracts annually during the monsoon, for example, an average of only about 10 default with their whole gang of *koytas*. By using various formal sanction mechanisms, the factories are able to cover themselves to a large extent against the risk of nonfulfillment. The jobber has to give his property (land, house) as security for the discharge of his obligations. Should he not succeed in recruiting the agreed number of teams, he has to return the excess of the advance made. If a *koyta* who has received cash fails to turn up at the last moment, the resulting liability falls on the jobber. If many teams do not show up at time of departure, the *mukadam* as the leader of the gang may well see fit to stay away from the factory himself. The factory is then perfectly within its rights to take immediate legal action but usually does not. The agents are too busy organizing the mass departure to hunt up absent gangs at this point. *Mukadams* who fall short generally get the chance to supply their *koytas* the next season or are given time to repay the advance already made.

More effective than the formal sanctions, however, is the informal peer pressure on the labor broker. The factory requires two or three jobbers to be one another's guarantors, and they must sign an agreement to that effect. Informal checks and balances are thus made among the jobbers to guarantee that all is going well. Should one *mukadam* have difficulties in recruiting, his guarantors come to his aid in their own testified interest. Finally, the *mukadam* is well aware that noncompliance with the agreement will automatically lead to expulsion. Profitable and trusted positions, built up with much difficulty, are not lightly put at stake. Furthermore, a *mukadam* is not a free agent. He remains bound to the factory for which he has previously worked and may only offer his services to another factory with written permission.

Although each South Gujarat factory has its own office in Dhulia, there is in fact little visible competition among them during the mass recruitment of seasonal migrants. On the contrary, they put their mutual interest first. By limiting the freedom of movement of the labor brokers, the factories prevent the brokers from imposing their own conditions upon the factories. Answering my question on this point, the employers confirmed their mutual understanding and indicated that because labor is plentiful they do not need to cross one another. This collaboration is further evidenced by the uniform labor conditions they have established and by their efforts to standardize the size of the advance given to *mukadams* for distribution among their *koytas*. New factories are the only ones with recruitment troubles because they do not have command of any permanent force of *mukadams*. However, assistance from neighboring enterprises can be counted upon. The expansion of crushing capacity in South Gujarat has taken place on the assumption that for the time being a sufficient number of workers can be mobilized, and this prospect helps to soften the competition among the factories.

The *mukadam* system results in controlled seasonal migration, which assures the sugar factories of sufficient labor at the right time, for the least cost, and without the risks usually attached to the recruitment process. In short, it is a cheap, reliable, efficient, and workable system for making extensive use of temporary labor.

RECUITMENT OF WORKERS BY THE LABOR BROKER

The move out of Khandesh to the sugar factories is a necessary evil for the landless peasants and small landholders. Several members from almost every household in the village where the recruitment takes place—most of the able-bodied in fact—are absent for the better part of the year. The seasonal migrants are taken on exclusively in *koytas*, and the three workers who make up this team usually belong to the same household: husband, wife, children old enough to work, or any other combination of members from a family unit. The *mukadam* only contracts complete *koytas*; the agreement made is only with the head, who is the cutter. This individual is then responsible for bringing the other two who will work with him. If a *koyta* cannot be formed from his own family or household, the cutter will himself hire an extra hand or hands who will receive an agreed-upon payment of Rs 100–150 at the end as well as food during the time.

The contract with the *koyta* is for one season. Unlike the jobbers, the laborers are not obliged to give their services in the cane harvest every year. There is an avowed preference for remaining in the village when the rainy season is over, and large households try to rotate the work among their able-bodied members over the years.

The degree of poverty and the lack of any reserves to tide them over the unemployment during the slack season, however, make it impossible for most of the laborers (especially the members of smaller households) to free themselves from the yearly necessity to migrate. The earnings from cane cutting are so low that a large section of the rural population is more or less condemned to migrate at the end of every rainy season.

Whereas the labor brokers are bound to one factory and able to switch only with written permission, the workers are free in their choice of where to go though many of them have no real preference. In principle, the migrant workers can offer their services to different *mukadams* and then accept the most attractive offer. However, in practice the broker operates as far as possible in a familiar area and prefers to take on workers who are already known to him. Some of these workers will be relatives, neighbors, members of his own caste, and others from his own village or at least from the immediate area.

The workers also prefer to go with a *mukadam* who is known to them; in strange surroundings they are wholly dependent upon him, both for their sustenance during the harvest and for the payment made at the end of it. It is therefore advisable for them to go with a *mukadam* who will provide good protection and on whom demands of a more personal nature can be made on the basis of a multifaceted relationship. The idea of free choice is thus lost under the pressure of circumstances compelling them to take a safe course. This explains why the cane cutters usually reacted rather awkwardly and with some perplexity to my question about what area they liked best. Their choice is determined by the extent of their trust in the *mukadam*, the reputation of the factory for which he works, and their acquaintance with other *koytas* who go with the same broker. Most gangs consist of a number of cutting teams that worked under that particular *mukadam* the previous year, in addition to new koytas who have been contracted for the first time. The turnover is such that I recorded a number of cases where the work gang was completely different from that of the previous season; there was not one gang of *koytas* whose membership was unchanged from the year before.

The labor contract, which is binding for the whole harvest season, is closed by the first cash payment made to the head of the cutting team. The broker has to negotiate with the workers the amount of cash to be distributed; this is not a set amount and varies among *koytas*. It makes a great difference, however, whether the money is going to *koytavalas* (cutters) or to *gadivalas* (cutters with their own bullock carts). As was mentioned earlier, the former get much less money than the latter, but for both categories the amount is considerably more than that which has been given by the factory. This credit can rise to 100 rupees or more for a *koytavala*; for a *gadivala* it can be as much as ten times that amount. The broker must make up the difference between the advance he gets from the factory and the credit he makes to the migrants he contracts. This can often amount to a large sum, and if he cannot pay it from his own pocket he must take out a loan from a local moneylender. The rate of interest is fixed per month or per quarter, and over the period of the loan—from about September to the end of May—it amounts to 60–75 percent. This usury is, of course, passed on and ultimately has to be borne by the cutter himself.

Apart from the recruitment risk, the *mukadam* must also be able to rely on those he contracts to perform adequately in the harvesting. In making up his gang he will therefore prefer to take on teams he already knows—people from his own neighborhood on whom he can keep a direct or indirect check. The factory officials speak of a bond of trust they suppose to exist between the *mukadam* and his *koytas*, but this is an altogether too idyllic picture of the way in which the former exerts his authority. The pressure he brings to bear is chiefly of a noncontractual nature and is mostly or wholly ineffective if a personal relationship is lacking. Brokers are therefore very wary of recruiting for their cutting teams people who are outside their circle of personal influence or who are not related to other members of their gangs on whom they do have a hold. Another excellent way to safeguard against nonfulfillment is to make the *koytas* liable. The migrant workers are therefore made to stand as a guarantee, for each other or for their close relatives, for the cash advanced to them. In this way the *mukadams* are following the example of the sugar factory, which covers itself against this sort of risk in the same way.

The labor brokers, most of whom can read and write, administer their own affairs. With a few exceptions, however, the workers are illiterate and have to acknowledge receipt of the money with a thumbprint. Such a situation offers every possibility for malpractice—for example, noting down an amount higher than is actually paid out. What seems to happen more often, though, is that the brokers promise higher advances at the beginning than they actually pay in the end. The brokers defend themselves against such accusations by saying that the factory has not made good what it initially promised.

Although the paying out of advances can be fixed in many ways that are to the disadvantage of the workers, their repayment is zealously supervised. For the *gadivalas*, who are selected on the basis of their creditworthiness, this is seldom a problem. If they do prove to be a bad investment—do not show up or repay the advance made them—they are forced to do so by various sanctions, which may mean that they lose their bullocks, their other cattle, or even their houses.

Recovering the money in case of default from the *koytavalas*, who possess next to nothing, is more difficult. Their poverty explains the higher percentage of absenteeism in this category. I doubt, however, that absenteeism at the time of departure is indeed as high as 20 percent, as some of my informants among the *koytavala* brokers would have me believe. For this would negate the effectiveness of the arsenal of sanctions by which the seasonal migrants can be called to book and which are applied with the brutality customary in a social climate that systematically prefers the strong. It is considered wholly in order, even by their victims, that the *mukadams* should demand and eventually enforce their rights. The factories discharge the recruitment risks to the labor brokers, who consequently shift them to the actual workers. The cane cutters have no means of defending themselves against unjust or unreasonable claims and either resign themselves to their fate or protest weakly against it.

Like the factories, the *mukadams* have hardly any need to compete with each other. There is no question of a floating pool of labor. Both labor brokers and cane cutters prefer to come to an agreement with persons known to them, and in fact, owing to debts going back to the previous season, they are certain that the required number of workers will be available. Acceptance into the *mukadam* corps has come about through the advocacy of others who have already attained this trusted position, and such recommendation will obviously have been made for relatives and persons of close social acquaintance. In other words, many ties exist among the brokers themselves, and together they form a network of intermediaries between factory and workers that sees more salvation in mutual assistance than in competition. The existence of uniform labor conditions is a help to them. Certainly, brokers differ in the speed and ease with which they can assemble their cutting teams. Apart from a *mukadam*'s personal reliability and honesty and the reputation of the factory for which he is recruiting, ease of recruitment is determined to a great extent by the size of the advance he is prepared to make. Here there is a certain amount of competition, but it is not the supply of labor but the solvency of the brokers that is the deciding factor.

Do all those who seek work as a seasonal migrant in fact succeed in obtaining it? This question can only be answered by doing research on the spot. However, most of the *mukadams* among my informants claimed that there are generally more than enough applicants. If enrollment ever seems to lag, this can be altered by increasing the amount of the advances.

THE JOURNEY

The yearly exodus at the end of November demands much organization and is carried out in the manner of a military operation. The actual time of departure is laid down well in advance by the factories. The mass transfer must be achieved in a very short time, and to prevent chaos during the journey and a delay in the start of the harvest it is imperative that everyone stick to the tightly constructed timetable. The recruiting office informs the brokers of the date of departure and the place to report to. No deviation is allowed; uncooperative workers are threatened with immediate discharge or the calling in of the advance paid.

The *koytavalas* are transported by train. They have to make their way to the nearest station on the Tapti line (Surat–Bhusaval). To ensure that they do, a number of young matriculates are temporarily employed to collect the *mukadams* and their workers at their villages and to take them, by buses or carts hired for the occasion, to the station. Checklists of names are drawn up by the factory to make sure that the gangs are complete and that the brokers take neither too many nor too few *koytas* along.

The departure of the bullock carts is also organized with great exactitude. Dhulia is the collecting point for the *gadivalas*. The *mukadams* receive orders to report to the recruiting office on a certain day. They are welcomed by the factory agents and also by the manager, who inquires after their health and well-being—a display of bonhomie that has the ulterior purpose of cementing ties and demonstrating what store the factory sets by maintaining a good understanding with these intermediaries. The journey time to the harvest area is approximately eight days from Aurangabad, six from Jalgaon. In Dhulia each carter is given, through his *mukadam*, Rs 15 for expenses for the five-day journey to the factories in South Gujarat. This is insufficient even for the barest needs of both men and animals. The *gadivalas* can therefore undertake the journey only if they bring their own grain with them.

At the factory, each gang is given a *koyta*, or cutting knife, and three mats plaited from leaves of the *khajuri* palm plus bamboo poles for building a shelter. On arrival the migrants are vaccinated, supplied with their equipment and a ration of grain for the first fifteen days (30 kg per *koyta*) and then sent straight off with a member of the field staff to the fields where they will be cutting cane for the coming period. Within a few days all the groups have been distributed over the whole area.

THE FIELD ORGANIZATION OF CANE CUTTING

The area of operation of factory X comprises approximately 7,000 hectares. It includes sugarcane fields in about 170 villages spread over four *talukas*.

To follow the tight schedule of harvesting over such an extensive area, a well-run field organization is imperative. The estate manager is in overall charge; under him are agricultural officers, mostly graduates, who head the four sections into which the acreage to be harvested is divided. Each is responsible for his own section and reports every day on the flow of production and on any problems. Each section is divided in turn into four zones and field supervisors are appointed at this level to oversee the harvesting.

Together with his staff members, the estate manager draws up the timetable for the harvest—determined by the regularly measured sucrose content of the cane. Every day cutting takes place simultaneously in an average of 80 villages. Planning is such that the work is done, as far as possible, in blocks of adjacent fields, several teams being assigned there under their *mukadams*. The farmers of these plots are told to stop irrigating a month before the harvesting begins so that the fields will be accessible to the cutters and the ground will be dry enough for transporting the cane away. The laborers are allotted a piece of waste land near the fields where they are stationed for the time being, on which they improvise their shelters with the materials from the factory. As soon as the fields in the immediate vicinity have been worked over, the laborers move these shelters to a new camp near the next plot to be harvested.

The lowest link in the field organization is the slip boy, so called because of the note or slip on which he records the details of each load that leaves the field (date, field location, name of owner, name of *mukadam*). The original is for the factory administration, the first copy is given to the landowner, and the second copy goes to the *mukadam* concerned. The load gets weighed on arrival at the factory. Both the final bill of payment for the farmers and the periodic payment of wages to the *mukadams* are computed on the basis of this system. The slip boy, who is in daily contact with the *mukadams* of the gangs working in the fields, checks that the cutting is done according to the regulations and that the cane stalks are properly cleaned and transported without delay. He has strict instructions to warn his superiors immediately should any problems arise. The estate manager inspects the cutting sites every morning to check on the progress of the harvest. In the afternoons, he is available in his office to receive farmers, *mukadams*, and anyone else who may wish to meet him.

Transporting of the cane by bullock carts takes place within a radius of 8–10 km from the factory; at greater distances, only lorries are used. The oxcarts' share in the transportation of the cane has fallen sharply in the last 10 years—from 58 percent in 1966–67 to 20 percent in 1976. Although the carts are inexpensive and the same teams handle both cutting and transport, the enormous expansion in milling has made the use of lorries imperative for the sake of speed and efficiency. The number of bullock carts has increased from 500 in 1965–66 to 917 in 1976–77; the number of lorries has increased more rapidly, from 16 to 150 over the same period. Although factory X is clearly the front-runner in this increase, the shift in favor of lorries also applies to the other sugar factories in South Gujarat.

This trend has brought about structural changes in the composition of the labor force. The proportion of *koytavalas* to *gadivalas* has greatly increased, meaning that more and more of the seasonal migrants belong to the category of landless peasants and small landholders. The decreasing need for *gadivalas*—landholders who are accustomed to working as independent producers and who possess more agrarian capital, bullocks, and carts than the *koytavalas*—signifies progressive proletarization of the cane-cutting labor.

The campaign is based on the cutting and transporting of a fixed tonnage per day. It is assumed that one cutting team can cut about 1 tonne a day and that the maximum load of an oxcart and of a lorry is 1 tonne and 10 tonnes, respectively. It is further estimated that each lorry will be delivering 25–30 tonnes on each of three runs a day. Thus a total of about 30 teams (*koytavalas*) must work for one lorry. Few gangs have as many cutting teams as this and two or more smaller gangs are usually put to together to make up the required number; they work together supplying the same lorry every day throughout the harvest. Cutting wages are paid according to the weight. The *mukadams* must ensure that there is always enough cane cut and ready to load on the lorry immediately. The *koytavalas* must load the lorries. Cutting takes place only in the daytime, but transport is not restricted to any set hours.

The *gadivalas* transport the cane they have cut to the factory in their own carts. The gangs of carters who are stationed within a radius of about 5 km of the factory can sometimes manage to cut and deliver two loads in a 24-hour period. Supervision of these gangs is a privilege given to old trusted *mukadams*. Encampment close to the factory brings in more earnings and is therefore greatly coveted by the *gadivalas*. Each gang of *gadivalas* is given a specific time (during the day, evening, or night) for reporting with their load at the weighbridge in the factory compound. At almost every hour, there is a long line, however; carts waiting their turn to be weighed are invariably made to give way to the lorries. Because of the necessity to handle the daily production in a steady flow, the bullock carts are in fact used as buffer stock in the delivery, an arrangement that is highly disadvantageous to the *gadivalas*, who are not paid any compensation for the waiting time. The difference in dispatch time can be noted from the following table, taken from the administration of factory Z, pertaining to an arbitrarily chosen day during the campaign:

Vehicles Waiting in the Factory Compound on 2/3/1977

Time	Lorries	Carts
At the beginning of the 1st shift (0400 hrs)	30	54
At the beginning of the 2nd shift (1200 hrs)	32	280
At the beginning of the 3rd shift (2000 hrs)	23	280

Once begun, the harvesting goes on continuously for an average of a little over five months. The factory itself stays in operation round the clock; there is a few hours' pause in the deliveries only in the early morning. The rhythm of work is regulated purely according to the milling capacity of the factory. There is absolutely no question of free time or days off. This continuous production process is brought to a standstill only in order to clean the factory one day every fortnight and no work is done that day for that reason alone.

As already explained, the harvest is performed according to a tightly written scenario. The job of the work gangs is to see that there is always enough cane cut and ready for transporting; however, it must be carted off within a few hours of being cut to avoid an excessive drop in the sucrose content. Nevertheless, the process frequently comes to a standstill because of the congestion in deliveries at the factory, electricity cuts, breakdown of machinery or lorries, and other unforeseen but regularly occurring mishaps. These setbacks demand a great capacity for improvisation among the field staff, but it is the workers who actually suffer from this enforced flexibility. All the risks involved in the cutting and transporting are passed on to be borne by them. Whenever production is delayed or the production line broken, cutting is at once halted. The labor contract made with the *mukadams* includes a clause stating that the factory accepts no liability whatsoever for loss of wages resulting from these interruptions in the daily work. The factory not only allows generous margins in the utilization of the cane-cutting work force without paying any extra, but so regulates the harvest that losses arising out of work stoppage fall on the workers alone. The interest of the factory is set above the interests of all others and implies an unlimited subservience on the part of the labor force.

8

Common Features and Contrasts in Labor Relations in the Semiarid Tropics of India

*Hans P. Binswanger, Victor S. Doherty, T. Balaramaiah,
M. J. Bhende, K. G. Kshirsagar, V. B. Rao, and P. S. S. Raju*

The main objectives of this paper are (1) to document and explain labor market arrangements in different agroclimatic and socioeconomic zones on the basis of intensive survey data; (2) to explore linkages of transactions in labor markets with transactions in other markets such as those for credit, draft power, and outputs, as well as linkages between caste status and type of labor performed; and (3) to characterize, as far as possible, the changes, if any, in labor relations over time.

The paper complements the papers by Jodha (chapter 5) and by Ryan and Ghodake (chapter 9) also presented in this volume. The villages and the regions, as well as the data gathering processes, are described in Jodha's paper, which focuses on tenancy relations. The Ryan–Ghodake paper is a quantitative assessment of wages, opportunity cost of labor, and working hours of individuals who participate in the daily labor market. In this paper the focus is on the institutional mechanisms in the daily market and on the market for regular farm servants (RFSs).[1] In the first section we discuss common features of the labor markets studied. The second section focuses on differences in labor demand and income in the three study areas; the third is concerned with differences in markets for RFSs and contract workers. In the last section we interpret the evidence and put forth further hypotheses regarding monopsony labor demand, intercaste competition, market segmentation, and interlinked transactions.

Useful comments on an early draft were made by Pranab Bardhan, Mark R. Rosenzweig, and Benjamin White; the improvements made since this early version owe much to them. The assistance of the International Crops Research Institute for the Semi-Arid Tropics (ICRISAT) in carrying out the work on which this paper is based is gratefully acknowledged.

Submitted as conference paper no. 94 by the International Crops Research Institute for the Semi-Arid Tropics.

1. We use the term "regular farm servant" (RFS) for any laborer whose labor contract exceeds three months.

The paper is based on several different types of data from the ICRISAT village-level studies as (VLS), as explained in table 8.1 (for details of the regions and villages, see chapter 5). The basic sample is the penel of 240 households that have been interviewed monthly as part of the VLS of the ICRISAT since May 1975. Panel interviews focusing on labor relations were conducted from May to August 1979 with members of all farm-size groups, but emphasis was given to collection of information from RFSs. In addition, special informants were selected by four of the authors of this paper, who had resided in these villages for more than two years as investigators. The special informants were primarily asked questions about changes in labor relations over time. Even this information was insufficient to help us understand the rather special features of the Aurepalle labor market discussed in this paper. Therefore, in January and February of 1980 a three-caste census was carried out, from which a further random sample was chosen for the collection of information on wages and other data. We will refer to these data sources as necessary.

COMMON FEATURES OF THE LABOR MARKETS

The labor markets in these six villages consist of several submarkets, as shown in figure 8.1. The irregular market is divided into a market for daily rated labor, where payment is made every day for a fixed number of hours worked; and a market for contract jobs, where farmers or a government agency (directly, or via contractors or labor brokers) give out work—usually on a piece-rate basis. Daily incomes from contract jobs are generally higher than from daily rated jobs, although contract jobs often require longer hours and/or more strenuous work. As opportunities arise, individuals change from the contract job market to the daily rated markets and vice versa.

Access to contract jobs is gained via personal networks that may be caste related in some of the villages. Groups for harvesting work or earthwork, or groups of temporary migrants are organized by male leaders who sometimes have formed fairly stable groups with other households. The females recruited into these groups are most often wives or other family members. Groups for hand weeding and paddy transplanting are most often organized by female leaders.

From the interviews with the panel members and with the special informants, it was clear that male-female differences play an important role in access to contract jobs almost everywhere. Caste appeared to play a minor role in the Akola region and the Sholapur region, whereas caste was frequently mentioned as a basis of group formation in the Mahbubnagar area, especially in Aurepalle. This was one of the reasons for organizing the three-caste census and the random sample there. In the process of collecting that information we recognized how difficult it is to understand

TABLE 8.1. Structure of the Data Set

Source	Sample Size	Location	Selection Criteria
Panel	240 households	All villages	Random sample selected in 1975
Panel interviews	More than half	All villages	All households with an RFS, May–August 1979
Special informants	Roughly 20 individuals	All villages	Elderly, articulate community members, May–August 1979
Three-caste census	108 households	Aurepalle only	All Madigas, Malas, and Kurmas of main settlement of Aurepalle, January–February 1980
Three-caste random sample	25 households	Aurepalle only	Random sample from above, February–March 1980

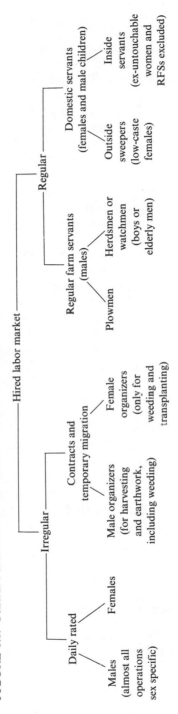

FIGURE 8.1. General Features and Submarkets of the Market for Hired Labor.

the impact of caste on access to labor opportunities, both because informants are not always conscious of it and because they do not like to mention it. Many other features of the villages indicate that our first impression concerning the lesser importance of caste in access to contract jobs in the Maharashtra regions is correct, but a follow-up inquiry of the type made in Aurepalle is currently being carried out in order to trace even subtle influences that might still be present.

In contrast to the contract labor market, the most striking characteristic of the daily rated market for farm work is its essentially impersonal nature. In the evening employers and their RFSs or the wives of the RFSs will go to the workers' houses and invite them for work.[2] Although they may have preferences for certain workers, especially for jobs requiring certain skills, employers are willing to hire anyone capable of doing the job in this market, regardless of caste or other socioeconomic relationship, if a preferred worker is not available. Similarly, workers are willing to work for any employer. One effect of this is that workers work for a large number of employers in the course of the year.[3] (Answers to a question on this point range from twenty employers per year to much higher numbers.) The daily rated market, although less attractive than the market for contract jobs, at least appears to give everyone a chance to participate on nearly equal terms.

A second characteristics, which may stem from the impersonality of relationships in this market, is that a daily rated worker cannot under any circumstances get a loan or an advance from an employer on the basis of a promise that he will work for him in a peak period whenever needed. This is in contrast to findings of Bardhan and Rudra (1978) in eastern India. Without collateral, workers can only obtain loans (interest-bearing debt) or advances (noninterest-bearing debt) from employers by entering into a RSF relationship for a minimum of three months in Akola or for a minimum of one year in all other areas. In all these areas, it is nearly impossible for landless laborers to obtain loans from farmers or moneylenders[4] without other collateral such as sheep and goats, gold, and utensils, or regular

2. Workers generally do not go and ask farmers for work. Only in Sholapur do some of them do so when very few work opportunities are available. It seems that asking for work puts one in a very poor bargaining position.

3. Obviously, it is possible for both farmers and laborers to avoid partners whom they consider inappropriate because of relative caste status; high-caste workers are not usually expected to work for very low-caste landholders.

4. They can occasionally get small loans in the neighborhood of Rs 5–10 from shopkeepers, farmers, or friends. But any amount in excess of roughly Rs 20–50 requires collateral in the form of long-term labor, or assets, or regular income. Also, in Sholapur some farmers will occasionally accept repayment of a small loan in the form of work if the borrower cannot repay in cash and if the farmer requires labor. But such an agreement is never made when the loan is given.

income from activities such as toddy tapping. The consequence of this, as we shall see, is that a primary motive for entering an RFS arrangement is the possibility of salary advance or loans.

Third, we did not observe tenants or their family members providing labor to their landlord's farm on a preferential basis, in either the regular or the irregular market. Jodha (chapter 5), however, found a few poor landlords working regularly for wages for their tenants in Sholapur as part of the terms of the contract.

Fourth, with the exception of harvesting, agricultural daily rated tasks are sex specific. Males do plowing, female do transplanting and weeding. Even in harvesting and threshing, many operations (such as winnowing) are often done by members of one sex only. However, there are some regional variations in the sexual division of labor. The regular submarket is clearly divided between males and females. In the whole inquiry we found (in the three-caste census) only one female working as an RFS, watching fields. Among the RFSs the plowmen are mostly adults between sixteen and thirty years of age. Herdsmen are usually young boys of ten years or older. Watchmen may be elderly men who are not strong enough for other work; they may also be boys. Domestic servants are females or young boys. Outside sweeping is a one- or two-hour job performed daily by females, usually drawn from any low caste. Women and RFSs from ex-untouchable castes are still excluded from jobs inside the home.

In the regular labor market, linkages with the employer other than via debt are unusual. Of the ninety-eight RFS contracts signed by households in the panel, only three contracts were noted that stipulated that employers should provide bullocks to the RFS to work on the land of the RFS, and in all three contracts the bullock rental rate was to be deducted from the wages of the RFS. With a few exceptions (in Aurepalle), RFS relationships do not constitute long-term or complex patron-client relationships.[5] They are usually confined to the labor and credit/advance contract, are often of short duration, and usually do not involve other family members. As can be seen from columns 3 and 4 of tables 8.2 and 8.3, families in all areas tend to put only one of their members in this relationship at a time. The number of panel members currently serving as an RFS exceeds the number of families having

5. We did observe a single very long-term relationship in Shirapur in which a son worked as an RFS for thirty-four years, for the same farmer for whom his father had previously worked for a total of more than thirty years. This worker family belonged to the caste of Mahars (ex-untouchables, common in Maharashtra where many of them have become Buddhists) whose occupation has traditionally been characterized by such long-term relationships. This Mahar RFS clearly enjoyed higher wages and superior status relative to other RFSs in the same village; the exceptionally favorable circumstances were presumably what induced him to remain in this relationship.

TABLE 8.2. Participation in the Wage Employment Market and Current and Past Involvement in the Regular Farm Servant Market: Mahbubnagar District

Household Group	Present Employment Status (June 1979)				Past Involvement in Permanent Servant Market					
	Number of Respondent Households (1)	Number of Households Where Someone Works for Wages (2)	Number of Households Where Someone Is an RFS (3)	Number of RFSs Involved (4)	Number of Households Where Someone Was Ever an RFS (5)	Number of Individuals Involved (6)	Number of Marriage Loans (Households) (7)	Cases without Loans (Households) (8)	Average Years of Total Service (9)	Average Years of Service per Employer (10)
Dokur (Mahbubnagar) Panel										
Landless	9	9	4	5	6	8	1	1	8.8	3.7
Small	10	10	1	1	5	6	2	2	7.2	2.4
Medium	10	10	1	1	2	3		1	3.3	2.5
Large	10	8	2	2	4	7		3	3.6	2.5
Total	39	37	8	9	17	24	3	7	6.2	2.9
Aurepalle (Mahbubnagar) Panel										
Landless	10	10	6	9	7	12	4	1	5.6	5.2
Small	10	10	2	2	2	3	3		6.7	4
Medium	9	5								
Large	10									
Total	39	25	8	11	9	15	7	1	5.8	4.8

Aurepalle (Mahbubnagar)

Caste	Three-Caste Census				Present Status of Three-Caste Random Sample					
Kurma	27	26	3	5	3	5	3	0	5.4	3.9
Mala	16	18	6	7	6	7	4	1	4.0	4.0
Madiga	63	59	34	45	11	15	4	9	3.8	3.8
Total	106	103	43	57	20	27	11	10	4.1	3.9

TABLE 8.3. Participation in the Wage Employment Market and Current and Past Involvement in the Regular Farm Servant Market: Sholapur and Akola Districts

Household Group	Present Employment Status (June 1979)				Past Involvement in Permanent Servant Market					
	Number of Respondent Households (1)	Number of Households Where Someone Works for Wages (2)	Number of Households Where Someone is an RFS (3)	Number of RFSs Involved (4)	Number of Households Where Someone Was Ever an RFS (5)	Number of Individuals Involved (6)	Number of Marriage Loans (Individuals) (7)	Productive Capital Loan (8)	Average Years of Total Service (9)	Average Years of Service per Employer (10)
Shirapur and Kalman (Sholapur)										
Landless	20	20	6	7	10	13	5		12.7*	5.6*
Small	20	20	2	2	9	10	3	1	6.9	3.4
Medium	18	16	1	1	6	10	1	3	3.1	1.8
Large	17	12			2	2			—	—
Total	75	68	9	10	27	35	9	4	7.5*	3.8*
Kanzara and Kinkheda (Akola)										
Landless	17	17	8‡	9‡	—	—	4	—	—†	—
Small	19	19	8	11	—	—	5	—	—	—
Medium	20	19	4	4	—	—		—	—	—
Large	20	6			—	—		—	—	—
Total	76	61	20	24	—	—	9			

Note: Dash (—) indicates not applicable or not available.

*Based on those individuals for whom data on both years and number of employers are available.

†We observed only four cases in which a person was involved in a relationship that extended over more than one year. One person was a tractor driver, one was working for relatives, and one was an unskilled RFS.

‡These contracts cover only three to four months.

such members by only 20 percent for all villages combined. Furthermore, we did not uncover a single case in the panel where one family sends two or more of its members as an RFS to the same farmer. This appears to be a sensible arrangement if the possibility of obtaining loans or advances is indeed a primary motivation; a family would presumably wish to multiply rather than to limit its number of potentially useful relationships if seeking access to loans or advances in this way.

Male children and elderly men usually work as herdsmen or watchmen; here the credit motivation may not be as overriding. Also, a few RFSs believe that this kind of work is physically less demanding than the work available in the irregular market.

The regular market has very few full-time opportunities for women; such opportunities are restricted to domestic work in wealthy households. Women from ex-untouchable groups are excluded from this opportunity as well. A large number of usually low-caste women do part-time work as outside sweepers.

Since the RFS opportunities are restricted to males, women without personal assets such as land, jewels, or gold cannot usually raise any loans that exceed trivial amounts. The fact that women are excluded from the RFS market and often have access to contract jobs only via their male family members may also explain the very large wage differences and differences in probabilities of employment between males and females observed in these villages by Ryan and Ghodake (chapter 9).

The last common feature is that attempts by farmers to collude to fix wages are common. Farmers in Dokur, Kanzara, and Kinkheda have tried to fix daily wages several times but have failed each time. Laborers are generally unconcerned about possible success of such attempts. The large yield or quality reductions caused by delays in agricultural operations such as seeding, weeding, and harvesting appear to result in competitive pressures on the labor demand side that make collusion unsuccessful.

In Shirapur farmers have tried to fix a (fairly wide) range of cash payments to RFSs. These ranges seem to respond to market conditions and often are not adhered to by farmers. In contrast to this is the impressively successful fixing of salaries and conditions of RFSs in Aurepalle discussed in detail below.

DIFFERENCES IN OVERALL LABOR DEMAND AND INCOME

This section is a brief discussion of differences in labor demand. Quantitative reflections of these differences are given in chapter 9.

Per family with labor income (column 2, table 8.2), Aurepalle has the lowest labor income—only Rs 603 (table 8.4). The demand for agricultural labor has very large seasonal variations. On the Alfisols only one crop per

TABLE 8.4. Monthly Salary Arrangements for Plowmen and Hired Labor Incomes (cash figures in rupees)

Village	Range of Kind Payments* (1)	Range of Cash Payments* (2)	Cash Equivalent of Total Wages* (3)	Interest on Loans Given to RFSs (percent) (4)	Ryan–Ghodake Monthly Wage Equivalent, 1975–76† (5)	Income from Hired Labor Participating per Family, 1976–77 (6)
Mahbubnagar District						
Aurepalle	44.5 kg paddy/month (Rs 0.86/kg) + one pair of sandals/year + pinch of tobacco/day	0	43.0/month (panel) 42.5/month (three-caste random sample)	18	53.10	603
Dokur	1 blanket every two years @ Rs 100		73 121	18	59.10	963
Sholapur District						
Shirapur	27.5 kg of sorghum/month (Rs 1.40/kg)	41.50 62.60	77 98	0	54.00	985
Kalman	Food	75 105	75 105	0	75.00	
Akola District						
Kanzara	Negligible	120 120	120 150	May take form of salary reduction	61.50	1,416
Kinkheda	Negligible	120‡ 150	120‡ 150	Negligible	75.60	

* Adjusted to 1975–76 prices.
† Calculated on the assumption that a permanent servant is willing to work for wages 300 days per year, but subject to the village average unemployment probability. See Ryan and Ghodake, table 9.1.
‡ In this village we found an instance of an RFS being paid Rs 90 per month on a full-year contract, which is extremely rare.

year can be grown and irrigation facilities are limited to 12 percent of the total cropped area. Soils and rainfall patterns in Aurepalle and Dokur are similar, but the extent of irrigation in Dokur is much greater (32 percent of total cropped area) and a substantial proportion of irrigated area is double-cropped, so that agricultural labor demand is both greater and more evenly distributed in Dokur than in Aurepalle. Labor incomes per participating panel family are 50 percent higher in Dokur than in Aurepalle. Neither of the two villages has other nearby sources of labor demand, such as an industrial center or government projects. Some families in Aurepalle send members as rickshaw pullers to Hyderabad (80 km away), but otherwise demand from Hyderabad for unskilled labor does not appear to reach this village. Dokur, which is farther away, is even less affected by urban labor demand. From Dokur many unskilled laborers migrate temporarily over long distances to government projects, but there is no such migration from Aurepalle. This contrast will be discussed again in the following section.

In the Sholapur district agricultural labor demand probably has as much seasonal variation as in Aurepalle. On the most fertile soils only one crop is grown, in the postmonsoon season with residual moisture, and irrigation amounts to only 9 percent of total cropped area. But nonagricultural demand for unskilled or semiskilled labor comes from the city of Sholapur, which is a center of the textile industry. In addition, the Maharashtra government operates several government projects within walking distance of the villages. The construction of percolation tanks meant to increase groundwater and initiated as a relief measure during the severe drought of the early 1970s belongs to a longstanding tradition of publicly operated relief projects. More recently, construction of a canal was begun that draws labor from Shirapur. Labor incomes per participating panel family are therefore as high in Shirapur as in Dokur.

The Akola region is an assured rainfall zone that requires little irrigation. It is a highly commercialized area that has been growing cotton as a major cash crop for centuries. Cotton requires large amounts of labor over a fairly extended harvesting period that begins after the major food crop, sorghum, has been harvested. Nonagricultural demand for unskilled labor comes almost exclusively from nearby government-operated land improvement or irrigation projects, which have been intensified since the mid-1960s. More recently, the Employment Guarantee Program of Maharashtra State makes work available in a systematic way during the period between the cotton harvest and the onset of the subsequent monsoon. For all these reasons labor demand is most steady in the Akola region and this demand is reflected in labor incomes of Rs 1,416 per participating household—more than double the household labor incomes in Aurepalle.

DIFFERENCES IN MARKETS FOR REGULAR FARM SERVANTS AND CONTRACT WORKERS

The differences in the extent and regularity of labor demand appear to have a major impact on the nature and length of contracts entered into in the market for RFSs and on the market for contract jobs.

Akola District

In Akola virtually all wages for hired labor are paid in cash. Because of the high and steady labor demand, RFS contracts are for period of three to five months between the onset of the monsoon and the beginning of the cotton harvest, at which time workers prefer to leave regular employment for harvesting work. The RFS contract period is the leanest season and also coincides with the high-demand period for plowmen. Of the twenty-four RFSs observed in this region, only four had relationships that extended more than one year. One was a tractor driver, another was an RFS with a yearly contract, and the other two worked for periods of three to five months in several successive years.

Table 8.4 compares wages paid to RFSs with what we call the Ryan-Ghodake monthly wage equivalent (see chapter 9). This is the average annual daily wage in the irregular market multiplied by the probability of employment. The table reveals that the RFS wages in Akola exceed the monthly daily wage equivalent by up to 100 percent. Of the twenty-four RFSs, only nine were indebted to their employers. Of the nine cases of indebtedness, five were not loans but advances on wages given without interest. Obviously, interest on advances may be hidden in other terms of the contract. The interest rates charged on two of the loans were comparable to those a moneylender would charge, namely, somewhere between one-quarter and one-half of the principal over a four- to five-month period. One of the advances appeared to include an even higher hidden or implicit interest rate, since the wage rate used for paying back the loans was roughly one-half of the normal monthly wage. Needless to say, at the end of the payment period the worker left his job. All nine loans or advances were taken for marriage purposes. Interlinking of labor and credit transactions therefore seems to be limited in these villages to cases in which laborers or small farmers work off a marriage loan (or advance on salary) over a period of roughly three to five months, during which they are fed by the remaining members of their family.

The smaller of the two Akola villages, Kinkheda, appears to be fairly self-sufficient in terms of labor and neither imports nor exports substantial amounts of if daily. The larger village, Kanzara, has a labor surplus in all seasons except the harvesting season. Since the mid-1960s, when government projects started to become an important source of employment for the laborers and small farmers of Kanzara, one man of the Mahar caste has become an important organizer of contract labor gangs for these projects. He organizes large gangs of laborers, preferably from his own village but also from other villages if necessary. For one project in 1978, he drew together 900 laborers with the help of organizers from other villages. Of the 900 laborers, 400 came from Kanzara.

On government projects families tend to work as a group and are paid on a piecework basis averaging out to Rs 7.00 or 8.00 per day. This implies that in this area, at least, females do not engage in such work on their own, but only as part of their families. In addition, workers on government projects can purchase highly subsidized food grains as a result of the Food for Work Program.

The *mukadam*, as the labor organizer is called, supervises the work alone or, if there are large groups of laborers, with the help of additional supervisors. He is paid roughly twice a laborer's daily wages for supplying a group of thirty to fifty laborers and supervising them. He may also certify to shopkeepers that some people are working on a government program, after which the workers can take small loans of Rs 10–20 from shopkeepers. It is assumed that he gets some money from the shopkeeper for that service as well. Two women, as well as the *mukadam*, organize large gangs of female workers for weeding during the monsoon season. They only negotiate the wages with the landlords and organize up to fifty women to work in a particular farmer's fields. They take twice a female worker's wages from the farmer for their service. This is the only area in which we found a man organizing gangs of women laborers for a female-specific agricultural operation.

The *mukadam* is well liked by the workers; he was elected to the village *panchayat* in the last two elections and was a member of the *taluka*-level *panchayat* for a two-year term. He seems also to be well liked by the farmers, although small farmers who require only small groups of laborers dislike the fact that they have more trouble getting those workers because of his activities.

A striking feature of the area is that no consumption loans are made at the beginning of the monsoon period to small farmers and landless laborers. At the most, some shopkeepers may advance Rs 10–20 worth of supplies, usually on an interest-free basis and to be repaid very quickly.[6] It is our impression that the three- to five-month labor contracts that cover the lean season are operating as a substitute for consumption loans. This impression is strengthened by the fact that the monthly wages are often not paid at the end of the month but are given in small amounts of Rs 10–20 every few days, with accounts kept of the amounts paid. Part of these wages

---

6. Interest may (or may not), of course, be hidden in the price in such circumstances.

is often given in kind but we have heard no complaint that the accounting price of whatever was given in kind was valued above the current market price.

We did not note any caste-based patron-client arrangements. Such a system probably existed in the past. Also, our observations may have been biased, as the Akola sample includes only two families from the lowest castes. But the failure to observe such relationships is to be expected because of the generally open and unlinked nature of labor market transactions in Akola and the free way, for example, in which lowest caste people sit and converse with higher caste individuals.

Sholapur District

In Sholapur the majority of wage payments are in the form of cash. The RFS contracts are annual contracts (table 8.3). Individuals who ever were an RFS did this kind of work for an average of 7.5 years but usually split this period among several employers. Currently there are fewer RFSs in the Sholapur sample than in Akola, or in Aurepalle and Dokur combined.

In Shirapur in the late 1930s, an RFS could earn Rs 40/year in cash and three bags (a total of 330 kg) per year of sorghum. The rate in 1962 for one respondent was Rs 400 plus three bags of sorghum. In 1979 the range was Rs 500–750/year, plus the same three bags of sorghum. In the 1930s there was an optional system, in which payment could be taken exclusively in cash. One respondent earned a flat rate of Rs 100/year and worked for seven years until he was married; the money went to his father, who used it for family needs including the marriage of the respondent's brother. In 1979 there also exists the option of working for cash wages but this is rarely taken.

The basic ration of sorghum (330 kg/year or 28.5 kg/month) can provide an important part of the food needs of an average family. We observed two or three cases where RFSs receive meals for themselves instead of grain, but such cases are rare in Shirapur. However, they are more frequent in Kalman, in the same district. Wages in kind are less important there and are often provided in the form of meals rather than grain.

Shirapur, as already noted, is an exceedingly drought-prone village. The importance of receiving wages in kind is evident. It is not surprising, then, that the basic food grain component of the RFS wage has remained essentially constant over at least the last forty years while the cash component has been driven up by inflation. Workers demand basic security in return for their contract, but employers are unwilling, in a scarcity zone, to assume risks beyond those represented by this level of kind payments.

Several respondents noted that during the drought period beginning in 1972, many RFSs were laid off; the claim of RFSs on their employers evidently does not extend to being carried through periods of prolonged scarcity. It is an open question whether this readiness to dismiss RFSs during period of great stress is increased by the existence of the drought relief projects discussed in the last section. Most respondents reported that the number of RFSs has declined substantially relative to the pre-1972 period; they ascribe this to the continued availability of employment opportunities from government projects.

The possibility of obtaining the cash portion of the wage as an *interest-free* advance continues to be a major motivation for entering the RFS relationships, and many of these advances are taken for marriage purposes. Usually the cash portion of the wage is given in two or three installments but the advances can be up to the full year's cash portion. Some respondents reported that before 1972 it was possible for an RFS to obtain more than one year's cash portion in advance but such transactions are no longer observed.

The cash equivalent of total wages varies from Rs 75 to 105 and, as in Akola, exceeds the Ryan–Ghodake monthly wage equivalent by a substantial margin.

Contract jobs are given only for harvesting. Labor supply for other agricultural operations—once they are started—is assured by another region-specific feature. If laborers are hired on the first day of a given operation (hand weeding, for example), they will work for several days for the same farmer until completion of the operation, unless sickness or work on their own farms prevents them from doing so. Farmers will stop the work only if forced to do so by weather conditions or lack of funds. During the entire operation, daily wages set on the first day are not renegotiated, regardless of what happens to market wages elsewhere in the village. This system enables farmers to estimate costs at the beginning of an operation nearly as accurately as if they were using contracts.

Groups for government contract jobs are much smaller in Shirapur than in Kanzara and are less formally organized. Although, as elsewhere, they are always organized by males, the groups do include females who are not related to the male members and are hired as required. The network that do operate in these situations may be relatively unstructured, or they may be influenced by such phenomena as caste.

Mahbubnagar District: Aurepalle

The hired labor market in Aurepalle has a number of unique characteristics, many of which are linked to the caste system. Virtually all wages are paid in kind. The data on labor market participation (table 8.5) indicate that none of the members of the first two caste ranks in this village participates in the market for hired labor, whereas in Dokur (in the same district), members from all caste ranks participate. The RFSs are almost exclusively

TABLE 8.5. Caste Rank and Labor Market Participation, 1976–77

Village	Caste Rank*							Total
	7	6	5	4	3	2	1	
Aurepalle	6(6)†	9(9)	2(2)	8(10)	0(2)	1(2)	0(9)	26(40)
Dokur	6(6)	2(2)	4(4)	12(12)	5(5)	2(2)	6(9)	37(40)
Shirapur	4(4)	1(1)	9(9)	1(1)	1(1)	2(2)	22(22)	40(40)
Kalman	2(2)	1(1)	8(8)	2(2)	2(3)	2(2)	18(21)	35(39)
Kanzara	1(1)	8(8)	3(3)	1(1)	2(2)	14(17)	6(8)	35(40)
Kinkheda	1(1)	3(3)	2(4)	8(8)	8(9)	0(2)	12(13)	34(40)

Note: To derive these ranks the authors, who were resident for a time in each village, ranked the castes appearing among their regular VLS respondents on the basis of general (social) status. The ranks for each caste were then reassigned, assuming for convenience a possibility of only 7 distinct ranks in any village. The number of castes actually encountered in each sample ranged from 8 to 12.

*7 is the lowest rank, 1 is the highest.

† The first figure in each pair is the number of households in a given caste rank that reported any amount of paid or exchange labor participation by any family member during the year 1976–77. The figure in parentheses is the total number of households of that rank in the sample.

recruited from the two lowest caste groups, which is not true in the other regions.

That caste is indeed a major factor in controlling males' access to labor opportunities (except for the daily rated market) is confirmed by the three-caste census data and the random sample from it. Females' access to all labor opportunities except daily rated agricultural labor is influenced by caste.

Members of three castes were interviewed particularly intensively in Aurepalle regarding their labor market participation. Kurmas are shepherds by traditional occupation and are Hindus of low caste rank. Malas are ex-untouchables whose traditional occupation is agricultural labor. Madigas are leatherworkers by traditional occupation, and therefore are also ex-untouchables. Their traditional trade has declined due to availability of industrially produced leather goods or substitutes for leather goods.

Among working males the frequency of participation in the irregular market and the frequency of self-employment (other than as a shepherd) are about the same for the Mala and Kurma castes combined, compared with the Madigas. Only Kurmas work as shepherds; the RFSs come primarily from the Madiga caste—41 percent of all Madiga males currently work as RFSs.

Table 8.6A shows the kinds of work done by those males in the three-caste random sample who do not work as RFSs. Clearly, the Kurmas and Malas have much better access than the Madigas to higher paid contract jobs (primarily well digging or well deepening for farmers—no government

TABLE 8.6A. Days Worked on Different Jobs by Other Than RFSs in Three-Caste Random Sample during Seventeen Days of Observation in February 1980

	Contract Work		Daily Rated Jobs		Average Daily Wages Received			
Caste	Alone	As a Group	Agricultural Operation	Tree Cutting or Drainage Clearing	Males	Number of Males Involved	Females	Number of Females Involved
Mala + Kurma	7	51	4	33	4.91*	10	2.39**	17
Madiga	0	4	9	8	3.76*	5	1.89**	12

*Difference between Madigas and Malas + Kurmas is statistically significant at 5 percent level.
**Difference between Madigas and Malas + Kurmas is statistically significant at 10 percent level.

TABLE 8.6B. Primary Occupation of Males by Caste in Three-Caste Census of Aurepalle

Number of Families	Number of Families with an RFS	Number of Working Males	Number of RFSs	Number of Shepherds	Number of Irregular Workers	Number of Self-employed (Including Migrants* but Excluding Shepherds)
Mala	18	30	7	0	9	14
Kurma	27	38	5	12	9	12
Mala + Kurma	45	68	12	12	18	26
			(18)		(26)	(38)
Madiga	63	111	45	0	28	38
			(41)		(25)	(34)

Note: Figures in brackets are percentages of males.
*Migrants work as self-employed rickshaw pullers in Hyderabad.

contracts are involved). The average number of hours worked per day in all types of jobs is nearly the same (although work intensity may differ). The better access to contract jobs results in substantially higher average daily wages for the Malas and Kurmas compared with the Madigas, which is statistically significant. Note that for females, the wage rate differences are much smaller but are still significantly different. The wage difference may be attributed in part to the better access to contract jobs for Mala and Kurma women via their male family members.

The main settlement of Aurepalle presently (January–March 1980) has four groups of contract workers, all engaged in digging wells. The core membership of these groups is stable but additional workers are hired as necessary. Three of the groups have mixed caste membership—Malas, Kurmas, Bogama (dancers), Mangali (barbers), Chakali (washermen) or Telaga (cultivators)—but they do not include a single Madiga member. The fourth group comprises exclusively Madiga members.

From the interviews with panel members and special informants, we found that Madigas are socially quite low in this village, where they are known as weak, lazy, and untrustworthy. This reputation is backed up by stories that are gross exaggerations. Twenty Madiga households received forty milk buffalo from government programs with credit provided two years ago, for example. Several informants claimed that all these buffalo were sold and the funds used for consumption purposes. However, of the twenty families, seventeen still have one buffalo and one family has two. Interestingly, the Madigas occasionally described themselves in the same terms and showed signs of insecurity during the interviews. Given this alleged lack of reliability, it is most astonishing to find them concentrated in the RFS jobs, which require regular work attendance and skills in handling of the bullocks. Furthermore, these relationships are based on trust in that they involve debt and present opportunities to steal crop outputs and other things from employers. Malas are also ex-untouchables but are reputed to be trustworthy and hardworking; a certain self-confidence was clearly reflected in their behavior during interviews. Their social status is much more comparable to that of the Kurmas and other poor-caste groups than to that of the Madigas. In the first round of interviews with panel members and special informants, the Malas and high-caste respondents told us that Malas virtually never work as RFSs and that they do virtually all of the physically hard contract work. Only the three-caste census revealed the distortion of reality in these statements (see table 8.6B). But they clearly indicate an ideology that appears to be useful both to the high-caste groups in fixing wages for RFSs and to the Malas and other caste groups in the competition for contract work.

Unlike the situation in all other villages, the RFS relationship in Aurepalle sometimes extends to the wife or another female member of the

RFS household, who performs the duty of outside sweeper and/or calls the female daily rated laborers for the husband's employer, for whom she therefore works whenever the farmer has work at the same rate received by other female laborers. For the calling of laborers and the outside sweeping she gets the equivalent of Rs 24–36/year in the form of various crop outputs and sometimes a sari. Whether or not the female member of the family does perform these duties appears to depend on mutual convenience—no special value is attached to these opportunities.

Even more than in the other regions, RFSs in Aurepalle enter this relationship because of their need for loans. In the panel only one family that ever had a permanent servant had not taken a loan from the employer. A large part of the loan demand arises from ceremonial expenses related to marriage, although consumption loans and medically related loans are also common. Male Madigas at the present time typically spend Rs 1,000 for their marriages, much of it raised as loans from their employers. They normally pay 18 percent interest to their employers for these loans, which is deducted from their wages.

Table 8.4 shows the other normal wage conditions. Wages in Aurepalle are completely paid in kind and the total monthly cash equivalent of these wages is currently Rs 43 per month for the panel (valued at 1975–76 prices), the lowest of any village. It takes the RFSs on average 5.8 years to pay back the debts, at which time these laborers enter the daily wage market again. (They will usually not return to the RFS status unless compelled to by the need for a loan or by physical weakness—and then they become watchmen.) Most of this time is spent with the same employer, although it is possible to change employers if the second employer is willing to buy off the loan from the first. Farmers can refinance these loans by borrowing from moneylenders at 18 percent interest.

Regression equations were fitted to the twenty-seven observations of RFS wages using the following variables: INTRATE = interest rate on loans; AGE = age in years; YRSASRFS = years of experience as regular farm servant; COWHERD = cowherd dummy; KURMALA = dummy variable for Kurmas and Malas. (An *F* test indicated that separate dummy variables for Kurmas and Malas are not required, which is consistent with their otherwise nearly equal social standing.) The following three variables were also tried but were eliminated after an *F* test showed that jointly they did not add to the explanatory power of the regression: age squared, amount of loan outstanding, and a dummy variable indicating whether a female member of the household of the RFS was working as outside sweeper for the employer of the RFS. The final regression is as follows (standard errors are in parentheses and * and ** indicate statistical significance at the 10 percent and 5 percent levels, respectively):

$$\text{WAGE/MONTH} = 52.0 - 0.88 \text{ INTRATE*} + 0.19 \text{ AGE}$$
$$(.43) \qquad\qquad (.16)$$

$$-0.11 \text{ YRSASRFS} - 22.54 \text{ COWHERD**}$$
$$(.41) \qquad\qquad (2.82)$$

$$+ 4.31 \text{ KURMALA*},$$
$$(2.37)$$

$$\bar{R}^2 = .81, \qquad \text{d.f.} = 21, \qquad F = 23.7.$$

The regression equation indicates that personal characteristics such as age and experience have little influence on the wage received and that the most massive wage differences are associated with the type of job done (cowherd or plowmen). The regression further shows that Kurmas and Malas are slightly favored over the Madigas in wage payments, which is consistent with the findings in table 8.6A, although the percentage difference in RFS wages is small compared with that in daily wages. The interest rate variable shows that the few favored individuals who pay low interest rates also enjoy other wage benefits. Over 80 percent of the variation in wage conditions is explained by this regression. Although nothing in it clearly supports or contradicts the effectiveness of wage fixing, the fact that personal characteristics have little to do with the wage received is consistent with it.

Although there are individual variations in wage conditions, the wage fixing is perceived by both farmers and laborers as effective. For fifteen years prior to 1977 the agreed-upon wage was fixed at roughly 36 kg of paddy with 24 percent interest on loans. A one-day strike in 1977 organized by the Madigas enabled them to push the base condition to close to 45 kg and 18 percent interests on loans, but a second strike in 1978 was ineffective. The fixity of the wage in kind for RFSs over many years is in sharp contrast to the fluctuations in the wages each year in the irregular labor market (see table 9.1).

The fixity of the wage in kind for permanent servants obviously shifts all the price risk of the labor contrast to the farmer. Given the low wages, laborers are probably quite interested in shifting all the price risk to the farmer and farmers are probably able to carry that risk relatively easily. At the present time, workers are grumbling that they would prefer cash wages because paddy prices are low. However, at the beginning of the VLS in 1975, we understood that workers preferred wage in kind when paddy prices were high.

Table 8.4 shows that in Aurepalle, unlike the other villages, RFS wages are substantially below the Ryan–Ghodake monthly wage equivalent. We will return to this point in the last section, after discussing Dokur.

Mahbubnagar District: Dokur

The main differences between Aurepalle and Dokur are as follows. (1) Labor demand and incomes are much higher in Dokur, as already discussed. (2) All caste groups participate in the hired labor markets, and only the two highest caste groups have never had any RFSs among their family members. (3) The large majority of panel members who were ever RFSs started as herdsmen between the ages of ten and fifteen years, and among those currently serving as RFSs there are only a few plowmen. (Indeed, to collect the wage information for plowmen in table 8.4, we had to go outside the panel households.)

We attribute the low number of plowmen to the superior earnings opportunities available as a result of temporary migration, which apparently has begun since the early 1950s. There is an extensive network of labor subcontractors in the Dokur area that recruits labor for these projects by advancing amounts of from Rs 200 to a maximum of Rs 1,000 to individuals or to units, each made up of a man and his wife, who agree to work for the subcontractor on large government projects for five to eight months. Subcontractors are usually family members of large and medium farmers from Dokur and surrounding villages, and they sometimes gather up to seventy laborers at one time. The advances are financed partly out of the subcontractors' own funds, but most of the money is obtained from the contractors who deal with the government. The projects are often quite far from Dokur; the most distant one we encountered was a railway project in Madhya Pradesh. Wages for both males and females working on these projects range from Rs 75 to Rs 100/month, plus two meals per day plus shelter at the work site. The monthly cash wage is applied against the advance, although workers can further borrow small amounts of Rs 10–50 from the subcontractor while on the job. Medical costs, if provided, are adjusted in full against the worker's salary.

It is clear from our investigation and from the consistent statements of the workers themselves that the demand for advances is the primary motive for participation in this system. Table 8.7 shows that the households that provide RFSs are virtually the same as those which send out temporary migrants. It thus appears that the typical history of an individual in these families it first to work as a herdsman between the ages of ten and fifteen, serving up to the age of sixteen or eighteen, and then to begin daily farm labor supplemented by temporary migration to obtain project work during the dry season. The availability of advances from project work obviates the need for marriage loans from employers of the RFSs; in table 8.2, column 7, there are only three such cases out of twenty-four. Furthermore, in seven out of twenty-four cases, RFSs in Dokur did not take any loans from their employers.

TABLE 8.7. Temporary Migrants in Dokur

| | 1979 Status | | Past Involvement in Temporary Migration | | |
| | Households with Temporary Migrants (1) | Individuals Involved (2) | Households with Temporary Migrants (3) | Individuals Involved (4) | Households That Have Both Temporary Migration and Permanent Servant History (5) |
Landholding Class					
Landless	3	—	6	13	5 of 6
Small	1	2	3	6	3 of 3
Medium	1	3	1	3	1 of 1
Large	3	6	5	15	4 of 5
Total	8	—	15	37	13 of 15

It is not clear whether Dokur ever had as poor conditions for RFSs as were observed in Aurepalle, but the similarities of the social structure and the agroclimate, as well as the proximity of the villages to each other, suggest that the situations may have been the same. The additional flexibility and opportunity to work and to take advances made possible by temporary migration appear to have transformed labor relations to a degree in Dokur, in favor of the laborers. Large farmers and high-caste farmers have also responded to the improved labor market opportunities by participating much more actively than their Aurepalle colleagues.

INTERPRETATION AND HYPOTHESES

In this section we interpret the evidence presented in this paper, placing special emphasis on the observed differences in the contract and RFS submarkets. Clearly, since we have only six villages, many of our inter-pretations cannot be verified statistically, and since they are based upon many exogenous variables, alternative interpretations are possible. How-ever, our interpretations have to be evaluated in conjunction with the many pieces of evidence presented in this paper as well as in the two companion papers on the same villages included in this volume (see chapter 5 and 9).

Importance of the Amount and Alternative Sources of Labor Demand

The presence or absence of substantial labor demand influences conditions in all submarkets. In Akola steady agricultural labor demand and demand from nearby government projects combine to put laborers in a superior bargaining position that is reflected in high wages and high incomes in all submarkets. Annual contracts have given way to shorter contracts, which enable laborers to shift to the submarket with the most attractive terms in the course of the year. Furthermore, we believe that this steady demand has led to substantial erosion of the role of caste in controlling access to labor opportunities, although sexual differentiation has been fully maintained here as elsewhere. We think that the operating factor here has been the growth of an agroeconomic environment in which there is steady demand for labor from a variety of alternative sources. Moreover, we feel that the Maharashtra State government's Guaranteed Employment Program has been instrumental in the consolidation of these gains in the conditions of rural labor, providing an important addition to the labor demand that began at least a hundred years ago to grow with the greatly increasing importance of cotton in the area.

In the Sholapur district, alternative labor opportunities have existed for a long time, as we noted earlier in our discussion of the growth of Sholapur city as a mill town and of the long history of drought relief works in that area. Even though they are less well off than their Akola counterparts, laborers in Sholapur still enjoy fairly favorable conditions. Also, the recent intensification of government projects seems to have led to a decrease in the importance of RFS relationships and to have made them looser.

Although Dokur has neither nearby government projects nor an urban labor demand, the strong labor demand coming from irrigation, in combination with the opportunities to migrate, results in fairly substantial labor incomes. The migration opportunities provide an alternative source of loans and employment to the RFS relationship and this employment has virtually replaced RFS work for adult males. Such beneficial effect on the labor market where migrants originate must be kept in mind when interpreting the bleak conditions that the temporary migrants may face at their locations of work and that are so well documented in Breman's paper (chapter 7). In important ways both the migrants and those whom they have left behind are better off.

Monopsony and Caste Competition in Aurepalle

Laborers in Aurepalle are penalized in all submarkets for the low level of labor demand from local agriculture and the absence of other opportunities. It is this absence of other local or more distant opportunities combined with the strong traditional caste system that appears to enable farmers to exercise monopsony control in at least the market for plowmen. This is the only village in which payments to plowmen fall substantially short of the Ryan–Ghodake monthly wage equivalent, and this shortfall may be interpreted as a monopsony rent.

For the monopsony hypothesis to hold, it is quite immaterial whether workers respond to the low wages offered in the submarket for plowmen by selecting themselves into these positions if they find them attractive relative to other opportunities. The RFSs may indeed be the physically weaker members of the labor force although the skill requirements are probably higher for these positions than for the more lucrative earth-digging contract jobs. (This statement is consistent with the higher wages received by plowmen in other areas relative to the Ryan–Ghodake monthly wage equivalent.) Selection is simply a response on the labor supply side to the conditions offered on the demand side, and whether these offers are low because of collusion or for other reasons is quite immaterial for the interpretation of these supply-related phenomena.

Furthermore, we believe that self-selection alone could not account for the very low wages of plowmen in Aurepalle. Personal characteristics such as age and experience fail to have a statistically significant effect on plowmen's wages whereas caste does. Access to the more lucrative contract work opportunities is also caste related.

In further support of the monopsony hypothesis one needs to take into account the caste-related ideological superstructure used to justify the low wages. Since the majority of RFSs come from the allegedly weak, lazy, and unreliable Madiga group their "low productivity justifies the low wages" in the eyes of the villagers. Ideology seems to be used as a means to support farmer's control over this group of laborers although, as mentioned before, the ideology is at best a massive exaggeration.

But why do RFSs from the Madiga and other low-caste groups go into so much debt for marriage when they have such a hard time paying it back and clearly dislike the RFS status? (They usually do not return to it unless forced to by misfortune.) The most likely reason is the necessity—frequently stressed by respondents when pressed on this issue—to validate themselves relative to their own caste group. Since access to many labor opportunities is indeed influenced substantially by caste, and since other economic opportunities are also caste related,[7] expenditures on marriage for validation purposes may well be a rational investment decision, apart from the social benefits of being a well-respected member of one's caste.

In Aurepalle intercaste competition for contract jobs also seems to exist and suggests an interest on the part of the Malas as well as on the part of the high castes in supporting the local ideology of the inferior Madiga. This could be so despite the fact that Malas suffer from the same untouchability restrictions as Madigas. These restrictions still prevent them from taking water from wells of caste Hindus, continue to force them to stand in their presence and to give high-caste members other marks of respect, and prevent them from performing RFS duties that require inside work.

Labor Market Segmentation

Throughout this paper we have avoided using the term "labor market segmentation." An operationally meaningful definition of segmentation must imply that (1) the segments of the market include distinctly different groups of individuals differentiated by such characteristics as caste, sex, age, wealth, or education, *and* (2) the individuals can move from one segment to another only with substantial difficulty. If individuals are not essentially immobile between the submarkets that form the different segments, wages in the submarkets will vary to compensate for differences in employment conditions such as hours of work, intensity of work, or skill requirements. Furthermore, if the groups in the segments are not identifiable by clear-cut characteristics or are mobile between submarkets, segmentation may hurt some individuals relative to others, but it will not penalize or benefit entire socioeconomic groups (and possibly, as a result, this will call for policy intervention on behalf of the specific groups).

7. Madigas, for example, have been exclusive beneficiaries of a government housing scheme and a buffalo distribution scheme in Aurepalle.

Defined in this way, segmentation is virtually absent in the male sub-markets in all villages except possibly Aurepalle. Participation in all sub-markets is too broad-based and mobility among them is too high to consider them segments. Even in Aurepalle one may not want to use the term "market segment" to refer to the male RFS submarket and the market for contract jobs. The RFS submarket includes primarily poor young males, but virtually all of them leave that submarket before they reach the age of thirty, although often with great difficulty. Madigas predominate in this submarket, but other caste groups also participate in it, so it cannot be termed a caste-based segment in any case. The market for contract jobs is accessible by members of all castes, although Madigas may have more difficulty in entering it. But it is clearly not a segment since there is substantial mobility between this submarket and the daily rated submarket.

On the other hand, one can clearly see distinct male and female segments in the markets in all villages. The male segments are generally not accessible to the females with very few exceptions, such as some of the harvesting operations and some of the earth-digging contract jobs. Even in these earth-digging jobs the women generally do different tasks than the men; in all villages (with the exception of Shirapur) they have access to such jobs only via their male family members. In the regular submarket, as discussed earlier, females are also excluded from the submarket for plowmen and herdsmen. (Only one woman was observed watching crops.) The women are restricted to the few domestic servant jobs available.

Males, of course, cannot generally move into women's jobs either, except for some elderly men or young children who participate in hand weeding, or boys who work as inside servants. But males would hardly desire to participate in the female submarkets. Male wages (adjusted for hours worked) in the irregular markets of these villages are roughly 80 percent higher than female wages. Male probabilities of employment are much higher as well (see Ryan, Ghodake, and Sarin, table 3). Segmentation clearly works in favor of the males and at the expense of the females.

Ideological support for this segmentation is strong. A taboo prevents women from touching the plow and, as in other societies, males who do domestic chores or other female-specific tasks are ridiculed. Low wages for women are attributed—by both males and females—to the lack of physical strength and stamina of women. One need only see the loads carried by them and the discipline evident in the paddy transplanting lines to realize that the large observed wage differentials can hardly be explained in this way.

Tied Transactions

Tied transactions as a means by which the more powerful extract favorable terms for themselves in transactions with poorer partners have become a topic of speculation (Bharadwaj 1974*a*; Bhaduri 1973) and have more recently become the focus of empirical investigation (Rudra 1975*a*, *b*; Bardhan and Rudra 1978).

In all villages, labor-credit links are restricted to RFS contracts. They provide poor people with an opportunity to raise credit that would often be totally lacking. In Akola they are of such short duration that they are probably to be interpreted as being of mutual benefit in most cases. Although the contracts are of longer duration in Sholapur, their terms do not appear to be substantially below those available in other submarkets. Only in Aurepalle are terms of credit-linked RFS contracts clearly inferior. But we believe that it is not primarily the tying that puts the laborers at a disadvantage, but the effective collusion of farmers in the absence of alternative sources of labor demand. Without collusion or other forms of monopsony or monopoly power, the terms of tied transactions may thus reflect "competitive" market conditions of supply and demand without an additional extraction of "rents" to the "stronger" partner. In this paper we have found little evidence that tied transactions in a submarket cannot be understood by a supply and demand framework for this type of transaction. Traditional analysis of market imperfections such as monopsony, monopoly, collusion, and restrictions to mobility can then be used to explain unequal or exploitative terms in regions or villages where the imperfections can be documented empirically.

9

Labor Market Behavior in Rural Villages in South India: Effects of Season, Sex, and Socioeconomic Status

James G. Ryan and R. D. Ghodake

Most developing countries of the semiarid tropics (SAT), particularly in Asia, have a relative abundance of labor resources in proportion to capital and land. Statistics on this apparent abundance are usually only available (if at all) in terms of national or regional annual aggregates, as pointed out recently by McDiarmid (1977), Bardhan (1977), and Brannon and Jessee (1977). Even these statistics are often not reliable, particularly for the rural areas. Problems of seasonal unemployment are most acute in rural areas, as revealed in the comprehensive study of Rudra and Biswas (1973). It is imperative to derive more accurate measures and a better understanding of the demand and supply parameters of labor markets, particularly in India, where 70 percent of the labor force is classified as agricultural workers.

This paper represents an attempt to bridge some of the gaps in our knowledge. It is an analysis of the labor market behavior of 240 labor and cultivator households in six semiarid tropical villages in the Maharashtra and Andhra Pradesh states of south India, a region that has largely been neglected in this field of research. The data for this study were drawn from six villages in the SAT of peninsular India, where intensive socioeconomic studies have been conducted continuously since May 1975 as part of the ICRISAT economics program.[1] Details of the labor utilization of each family member and of hired personnel were obtained. These data related to both on-farm and off-farm activities as well as to household use.[2]

The authors are grateful to T. Balaramaiah, S. S. Badhe, V. Bhaskar Rao, M. J. Bhende, N. B. Dudhane, and K. G. Kshirsagar, the investigators who were responsible for the data collection in the six villages that were the subject of this study. They also thank Mita Ṣandilya and M. Asokan for computational assistance and M. von Oppen, D. Jha, and Mark R. Rosenzweig for their critical comments on earlier drafts.

1. For a detailed description of the methodology, the villages, and the complete range of information obtained, see Jodha (chapter 5).

2. The on- and off-farm activities were collected on a two- to four-week full recall basis. Household time allocation of each household member was collected only for the day immediately preceding each interview.

The major crops grown in the Mahbubnagar villages are paddy, sorghum, groundnuts, pigeon peas, pearl millet, and castor. The Alfisol soils in these villages have a low moisture-holding capacity; this means that all nonirrigated crops are grown in the rainy season. As a result, about two-thirds of total labor use on farmers' fields occurs in the rainy season. The Sholapur villages have medium-deep and deep Vertisol soils, which have a high moisture-holding capacity; thus most nonirrigated cropping occurs in the postrainy season on residual soil moisture. More than half of the total labor use in Sholapur is concentrated in the postrainy season of September to March. The predominant crops here are sorghum, chick-peas, and safflower. Some pearl millet and pigeon peas are sown on the shallow Vertisols in the rainy season. Cotton is the primary crop of the Akola villages, being sown in rows on the medium-deep Vertisols in the rainy season, mixed with sorghum and pigeon peas. More than 90 percent of total crop labor use occurs in the rainy season in the Akola villages.

In Aurepalle and Kalman, total male labor used on crops was slightly more than total female labor used; in Dokur, Shirapur, Kanzara, and Kinkheda, however, the total female labor used on crops exceeded total male labor. Increasing amounts of cotton and irrigation seem to imply increasing employment potentials for women in these villages. These high proportions of female labor used on agricultural land far exceed the 20 percent figure cited for Asia by Boserup (1970). Little work on crops is done by children. In all six villages the proportion of female labor hired was much greater than the proportion of male labor hired: 80 to 90 percent of the labor hired in the Mahbubnagar and Akola villages and 60 to 70 percent of the labor hired in the Sholapur villages was female.[3]

Of the total hired labor used in Aurepalle, Dokur, and Shirapur, 63 to 88 percent consisted of females. In the Akola villages and in Kalman, the share of males and females in total hired labor use was almost equal. Males always represented the larger proportion (64 to 90 percent) of the total family labor utilization, especially in the Mahbubnagar villages.

In this paper we will discuss the functioning of the rural daily hired labor markets in the six villages. Particular attention will be given to the extent to which able-bodied people attempt to participate in the daily hired labor market throughout the year, the probability that they will obtain employment, and the wages they will receive, if successful. These questions will be examined separately for males and for females from the four household categories of labor, as well as small, medium, and large farms, using

---

3. Due to space limitations, all of the tables and analyses on which this paper is based could not be included. The interested reader is referred to the papers by Ghodake, Ryan, and Sarin (1978) and Ryan, Ghodake, and Sarin (1979) for details.

data collected on a two- to four-week recall basis in 1975–76. The data have been smoothed into two-week periods for the subsequent analysis.[4]

PARTICIPATION RATES

The participation rate in the rural daily hired labor market was calculated as the number of person-days of wage work plus work-seeking (involuntary unemployment) in a period, expressed as a proportion of the total number of person-days where participation could have occurred. Work on own farms was excluded. The denominator was calculated using the number of able-bodied people residing in the households at the beginning of the study. We excluded family members who were disabled, regularly at school, less than twelve years old, living permanently outside the village, or employed in regular or professional jobs. Also excluded were permanent servants in the household.

The labor force participation rate was calculated in the same manner as the labor market participation rate, except that person-days of work on own farms were also added to the numerator.[5]

Labor market participation rates for males were significantly lowest in the two Mahbubnagar villages and generally significantly highest in the two Akola villages (table 9.1). Labor market participation rates were all significantly different between pairs of districts for both the adult males and the adult females. For only 7 percent of the time did males in Aurepalle endeavor to find a job in the daily hired labor market. In Kanzara, on the other hand, males participated almost 50 percent of the time. The labor market participation rates for all villages were reduced by the meager participation by members of large-farm households and, to a lesser extent, of medium-farm households. Participation by labor and small-farm households was generally much higher. For males, the highest average labor market participation rate in 1975–76 for the labor and small-farm groups was in Kanzara—0.87 and 0.70, respectively; the lowest was in Aurepalle—0.18 and 0.14, respectively.

Females participated in the labor market substantially more (always significant at the 1 percent level) than males in Mahbubnagar villages and in Kinkheda, whereas in other villages males participated significantly more

4. For details see Subrahmanyam and Ryan (1976, pp. 11–16). Most estimates reported here are annual averages. However, the comparisons across farm-size groups, villages, and sexes were also made separately for peak and slack labor seasons. In almost all cases, results for the seasons were consistent with the annual average.

5. Farm work includes all operations involved in producing crops, such as plowing, sowing, weeding, harvesting, and threshing. It excludes labor involved in livestock rearing, building repairs and construction, trade, marketing, transport, handicrafts, and domestic work.

TABLE 9.1. Employment Conditions of Male and Female Adults in Rural Daily Hired
Labor Markets in Six SAT Villages of South India, 1975–76

District/ Village/Sex	Market Participation Rate		Probability of Market Employment		Daily Opportunity Cost		Daily Wage Rate	
	Mean	CV (percent)	Mean	CV (percent)	Mean (Rs)	CV (percent)	Mean (Rs)	CV (percent)
Mahbubnagar Aurepalle								
Male	0.07***	48	0.71	23	1.77***	25	2.50***	33
Female	0.27	61	0.69	20	1.03	26	1.49	16
Dokur								
Male	0.25***	14	0.76***	30	1.97***	35	2.59***	17
Female	0.61	10	0.82	20	1.58	30	1.93	15
Sholapur Shirapur								
Male	0.38***	29	0.70***	12	1.80***	12	2.57***	13
Female	0.25	22	0.49	37	0.68	47	1.39	18
Kalman								
Male	0.29***	19	0.92***	11	2.50***	31	2.72***	19
Female	0.22	17	0.77	18	1.08	28	1.40	14
Akola Kanzara								
Male	0.48***	14	0.82***	12	2.05***	15	3.72***	11
Female	0.39	22	0.77	30	1.41	35	1.83	12
Kinkheda								
Male	0.30***	22	0.88***	12	2.52***	19	2.86***	11
Female	0.36	20	0.91	7	1.41	22	1.55	19

Note: Work on own farms has been excluded from participation rate and employment
probability calculations. Asterisks indicate significant differences between figures for male and
female labor of the same village.

***Significant at 1 percent level.

than females. Dokur, where irrigated paddy is grown, registered the highest
average market participation for females at 0.61. In this village even females
from large farms participated 36 percent of the time, and females from labor
and small-farm households participated 82 percent of the time, the highest
rate of all villages. This indicates that the influence of paddy irrigation on
demand for female labor led to substantial participation by females, even
those from the large-farm group.

The lowest female participation rate, approximately 0.25, came in the
drought-prone, predominantly food grain–growing Sholapur villages. The

range in these two villages was from approximately 0.47 for females from labor households to 0.08 for those from the large-farm group.

There was a significant amount of seasonal variation in labor market participation of males and females, particularly in Aurepalle (table 9.1). The coefficient of variation (CV) of fortnightly male participation ranged from a high of 48 percent in Aurepalle to a low of 14 percent in Dokur and Kanzara. For females the range was from 61 percent in Aurepalle to 10 percent in Dokur. Again, the effect of extensive paddy irrigation in Dokur was reflected in much more steady market participation throughout the year.

The mean fortnightly market participation rates of males and females from labor households were always greater than those from the small-farm households. The differences were significant at the 1 percent level in paired *t* tests in five out of six villages for males, and in two out of six villages for females. The labor group also had higher market participation rates than medium-farm households for both males and females. These differences were statistically significant at the 1 percent level in five of six villages for males and in all villages for females. Except for Shirapur, males and females from small-farm households participated significantly more than those from medium-farm households.

The simple correlation between the market participation rates of males from labor and from small-farm households was positive and significant in four of the six villages. Aurepalle and Kalman had negative correlations, the latter being not statistically significant. In five of six villages there was no correlation between participation of the male members of the labor households in the market and participation of males from medium-farm households. Correlations between labor market participation of females from the labor and small-farm categories were significantly positive in three villages. Correlations for the other three villages were not significant. Labor participation rates of females from labor households were not as closely correlated with those from medium-farm households. Only two *CV*s were significantly positive, one was significantly negative, and the remaining three were not significant.

As expected, these results suggest that males and females from labor households participate more in the rural daily hired labor market than do those from cultivator households. Those from the labor group and from the small-farm group tend to enter the labor market at approximately the same time. However, there does not seem to be as much competition between participants from the labor group and from medium-sized farms, especially among males.

These participation rates were calculated excluding agricultural work on the participants' own farms; they reflect the supply of labor to the daily hired labor market as a proportion of total available labor. The rates indicate, on an average over these six villages, that 30 and 37 percent of

TABLE 9.2. Rates of Labor Force Participation and Involuntary Unemployment in
Six SAT Villages of South India, 1975–76

District/Village/Sex	Labor Force Participation Rate	Involuntary Unemployment Rate*
Mahbubnagar		
Aurepalle		
Male	0.30	0.07
Female	0.29	0.28
Dokur		
Male	0.43	0.14
Female	0.64	0.17
Sholapur		
Shirapur		
Male	0.46	0.25
Female	0.30	0.43
Kalman		
Male	0.38	0.06
Female	0.26	0.19
Akola		
Kanzara		
Male	0.55	0.16
Female	0.42	0.21
Kinkheda		
Male	0.35	0.10
Female	0.38	0.09

*Farm and labor market work is included in both the numerator and denominator to calculate probability of labor employment (*PE*), from which involuntary unemployment is calculated as $(1 - PE)$.

available male and female labor, respectively, participated in work outside their own farms, households, and businesses in 1975–76. When we include own-farm work—as is usually done when measuring labor force participation, as opposed to the labor market participation shown in table 9.1—there is a substantial increase in the rate for males in the Mahbubnagar and Sholapur villages (table 9.2). Males in these villages devote considerable time to agricultural farm work. This is not so in the Akola villages or for females generally. Very little own-farm labor is contributed by family females from the cultivator households, even though on average they participate a lot in the hired labor market. To illustrate: the average labor market participation rate for males in the six villages was 0.30, whereas the average labor force participation rate was 0.42, indicating that approximately 12 percent of the time of available male labor was devoted to agricultural work on own farms in 1975–76. Although this seems a small fraction of the time, it is larger than that of females, who spent only 3 percent of their available labor time in own-farm agricultural work. Their average labor market participation rate was 0.37; their average labor force participation rate was 0.40.[6]

All these participation rates seem quite low and suggest either that work other than farm and market work is being done in these households or that there is considerable leisure time. The latter explanation is more likely in the large-farm households; these families are generally larger and have much lower participation rates than other households. This group would tend to lower the overall village averages considerably. The large numbers of landless households in the sample with no own-farm work also keep the labor force participation rates low.

PROBABILITIES OF EMPOLYMENT

The probability of employment in the rural daily hired labor market (PME) is calculated as the number of days a person was successful in obtaining wage employment as a proportion of the number of days in the period he tried.[7] The probability of involuntary unemployment in the market ($PMU = 1 - PME$) is not equivalent to the usual measures of unemployment, which are based on stock concepts and data from one-time census or sample surveys.[8] PME is a flow concept that can be used to weight wage rates properly to indicate opportunity costs of leisure and farm or household work in the context of the new household economics framework. These opportunity costs are discussed later in this paper. For comparison with stock measures of unemployment in India, we also calculate the probability of unemployment (PU) with person-days of own-farm work included in both the numerator and the denominator to first calculate probability of labor employment (PE); PU is then calculated as $(1 - PE)$.

In the two drought-prone, predominantly food grain-producing villages of the Sholapur region and in the village of Kanzara, males have a significantly better chance of obtaining daily market wage employment than females. In Aurepalle, with its light red soils and with sorghum and castor as

6. Recall that calculation of all these rates is based on the assumption that 365 days are available for work each year. When this number is reduced to allow 1.5 days of leisure per week, the labor market participation rates are 0.39 for males and 0.47 for females, whereas the labor force participation rates rise to 0.53 and 0.51, respectively. Own-farm work then occupies 15 and 4 percent of the available labor time of all males and females, respectively.

7. In calculating the probability of employment, we have not differentiated between employment on other farms, employment in nearby urban areas, and employment for private or government employers.

8. See, for example, Krishna (1973) and Bardhan (1977). Such stock measures generally include farm- and self-employed people in the labor force.

the major crops, there is no significant difference. On the other hand, in Dokur and Kinkheda, females have a significantly higher probability of employment than males (table 9.1).

In Shirapur, females can only find market employment on half the occasions when they wish to. Males are successful 70 percent of the time. In Shirapur not only are average probabilities of female employment low but their fluctuation throughout the season is particularly high; the CV for females is 37 percent, whereas for males it is much less (12 percent). In Kalman, a village in the same region, average employment probabilities for both males and females were substantially better (0.92 and 0.77, respectively) than in nearby Shirapur. Seasonal variations were also smaller. This illustrates the difficulties of generalizing results from individual villages and applying them to the region as a whole. The fact that Shirapur is more drought-prone and has a higher proportion of postrainy season cropping/rainy season fallow than Kalman probably accounts for its meager employment potential. Postrainy season crops require much less hand weeding and interculturing than rainy season crops, and these operations are usually done by hired labor.

The most buoyant daily labor markets appear to be in the two cotton-growing Akola villages. In Kanzara, both males and females succeed about eight times out of ten in finding a job, whereas in Kinkheda they succeed nine times out of ten. Seasonal fluctuations are not substantial, except for Kanzara females ($CV = 30$ percent).

Males in Mahbubnagar are successful in finding off-farm employment in three out of four attempts. Dokur females are successful eight times out of ten but in Aurepalle females succeed only seven times out of ten. The seasonal variation in job probabilities also seems higher for males compared with females in these two villages, where irrigated paddy is important. The periods of the year when the probabilities of employment are lowest vary from village to village, even within the same region.

Paired t tests showed that for males there was a mixed picture with respect to the relationship between probabilities of market employment for the labor group and for the small- and medium-farm groups. In three villages there was no significant difference between the mean probabilities of employment of the labor and small-farm groups. In two villages the probability for small-farm males was significantly greater than for males from the labor group. In one village the reverse was true. In three villages the probability of employment for males from the medium-sized category was significantly less than that for males from the labor group, and in the other three there was no significant difference. In four villages the small-farm males had a significantly better chance of finding a job than medium-farm males. In the other two villages there was no significant difference.

Females from small farms in three of the villages had significantly better employment probabilities than those from labor households. In one village the reverse was true, but in the other two there was no significant difference. Females from the medium-farm group in three villages also had significantly better chances of finding a job than those from the labor households. There were no significant differences in the other three villages. Females from the small- and medium-farm groups did not differ statistically in their employment probabilities in four out of the six villages. In Dokur the latter group had a better chance, whereas in Shirapur the former did.

What this pattern suggests is that in general, males from labor households have a better chance of successfully finding daily wage employment—compared with their counterparts in the cultivator households—than do their spouses. Hence it is true not only that females generally are no better off and are often worse off than males in terms of daily labor market employment opportunities but that, in addition, females from the poorest households (the labor group) are often the most disadvantaged.

It seems that fluctuations in probabilities of market employment in 1975–76 for females from the labor and small- and medium-farm groups in each village were more positively related than those for males. This is suggested by the fact that all correlations were positive and significant for females, whereas for males only half were. A possible conclusion is that females from the different socioeconomic groups in these villages tended to be competing for similar jobs more frequently than males.

The overall probability of involuntary market unemployment (*PMU*) for males in these six villages in 1975–76 averaged 0.19; for females the average was approximately 0.23.[9] Because of the relatively small amount of time devoted to own-farm work in most of these villages, the probability of unemployment (*PU*) does not fall a great deal when we include farm work in the numerator and the denominator (table 9.2). The exceptions are for males in the two Mahbubnagar villages and for females in Shirapur, where own-farm work was more significant. On average across the six villages, the *PU* for males was 0.14 and for females 0.21. These estimates of the extent of unemployment are far in excess of the rates derived in the 1961 census in India, 0.005 and 0.001 for males and females, respectively. They are also much higher than those obtained in the twenty-first round of the National Sample Survey in 1966–67, of 0.018 for rural males and 0.045 for rural females, as reported in Sen (1975). However, there are many deficiencies in the aggregate statistics on unemployment in India, and these are described in detail by Sen. Our average *PU*s compare with Mehra's figure for disguised

9. The average *PMU*s for males were 0.12 and 0.39 during peak and slack periods, respectively; for females the corresponding figures were 0.11 and 0.50. These averages indicate that during peak periods the probabilities of involuntary market unemployment for males and females become almost equal, whereas during slack periods the difference increases, affecting female labor employment more adversely.

unemployment in the total agricultural labor force in India of 0.17, as reported in Sen (1975), but they are about double those derived by Krishna (1973), using National Sample Survey data on rural workers who are idle but are willing to work more. Krishna points out that his figures are minimum estimates. They are also much higher than the 0.13 derived by P. K. Bardhan (1979b) for West Bengal, using the rural subsample of the 1972–73 National Sample Survey of that state.

A number of models of rural–urban migration, such as those by Harris and Todaro (1970) and McDiarmid (1977), assume the probability of employment in rural areas to be one. Lal (1974) reports a value of one as the ratio of the market rate to the "social wage rate" in a number of states in India. These values are often used as implicit weights in the social benefit-cost analysis of projects. The results from these six villages suggest that opportunity costs of rural labor based on probabilities of employment of one may be considerably overestimated. This may explain the paradox of models that predict increasing rural–urban migration in India in spite of an apparently increasing amount of urban unemployment. Ignoring rural unemployment may be the problem in such models.

WAGE RATES

Average female daily wage rates in these six villages in 1975–76 were approximately 56 percent of those for males and also were significantly different at the 1 percent level.[10] Male wages averaged Rs 2.83 per day; daily female wages averaged Rs 1.60 (table 9.1). Male wages were generally highest in the two Akola villages. Kanzara had the highest (Rs 3.72) and the lowest was in Aurepalle (Rs 2.50).[11] Of the females, those from Dokur had the highest average wage rate, Rs 1.93 per day. This seems to be explained by the importance of the paddy crop in Dokur, which requires a large amount of female labor for transplanting and weeding. The lowest female wages were in the drought-prone Sholapur villages; they averaged only Rs 1.40 per day. The much-reduced demand for weeding labor because of the postrainy season cropping pattern in the Sholapur villages no doubt helps explain the lower female wages there.

Employed women tended to work approximately 5 to 12 percent fewer hours per day on the job than employed men (table 9.3, columns 4 and 5). Hence on an hourly basis women's wages were approximately 60 percent of men's in these villages.[12] However, women worked 10 to 30 percent more

10. This percentage is much lower than the 80 percent for thirteen states in India in 1960–61 derived by Rosenzweig (1978).

11. These wages are expressed in nominal terms only. Deflating by a food grain price index in the two states would, no doubt, bring the wages closer together.

12. Hourly wages for children are approximately 55 percent of the wages of adult males.

TABLE 9.3. Average Hours Worked per Day by Adult Males and Females and by Children in Six SAT Villages of South India, 1975–76 (percent)

District/Village	When All Activities Are for Own Farm/Household and/or for Others			When Working for Others for Wages		
	Adult Males	Adult Females	Children	Adult Males	Adult Females	Children
Mahbubnagar						
Aurepalle	6.90	8.05	6.49	7.58	6.83	7.02
	(0.91)	(1.17)	(1.80)	(1.15)	(0.94)	(0.76)
Dokur	7.19	9.34	4.56	7.50	7.13	6.94
	(1.35)	(0.94)	(1.19)	(0.87)	(0.23)	(0.29)
Sholapur						
Shirapur	8.62	9.87	7.02	8.26	7.74	8.05
	(1.25)	(1.89)	(1.16)	(0.57)	(0.95)	(0.52)
Kalman	6.65	7.23	5.54	7.71	6.80	6.70
	(0.63)	(1.03)	(0.72)	(0.95)	(0.57)	(0.90)
Akola						
Kanzara	6.81	7.42	4.17	7.42	7.01	6.73
	(0.58)	(1.50)	(1.16)	(0.55)	(0.66)	(0.76)
Kinkheda	7.76	9.54	5.85	7.70	7.31	7.53
	(1.00)	(0.68)	(0.89)	(0.45)	(0.51)	(0.48)

Note: Unlike other data on labor use in this paper, the data in this table pertain to labor used in the following: crop production, animal husbandry, building and construction repairs and maintenance, trade, marketing, transport, domestic work, food and fuel gathering/processing, and handicrafts. Time spent traveling is also included. These data are based on averages of one-day recalls made more than 20 times from mid-1975 to the end of 1976 by all respondents. Standard deviations appear in parentheses.

hours per day than men on those days when activities were performed by both for their own farms/households and/or for someone else for wages (table 9.3, columns 1 and 2). This is no doubt a reflection of the dominant role of women in domestic work, food and fuel gathering/processing, and handicrafts, which are done in addition to their participation in agricultural activities.

Table 9.3 shows that generally, the daily hours of work when done for wages did not fluctuate a great deal seasonally. As one would expect, there was a larger seasonal variation in daily hours of work when it was performed on one's own farm or in one's own household. The higher *CV* for hours of children's work was primarily a result of their lower mean hours of work (50 to 80 percent of adult females). When women and children worked for wages, they tended to work approximately the same number of hours.

There did not appear to be consistent differences in hours of work of household members across the four categories (labor and small, medium, and large farms) within each village. However, workers from large farms, particularly women, often worked fewer hours per day than those from the other households.

In support of the contention of Rodgers (1975) that the degree of seasonal wage variability is less than that of seasonal employment variability, we found more evidence for females than we did for males. Rodgers contends that wages are more "sticky" than employment, due to provision of meals by employers and interseasonal "guarantees." We found that in five of the six villages, the *CV*s of wages were less than the *CV*s of the employment probabilities for females. For males this was true in only three of the six villages. Contrary to Raj (1959), we found a general tendency for lower average employment probabilities to be associated with higher *CV*s of wages for males. Like Sethuraman (1972) and McDiarmid (1977), we found that whenever there was a statistically significant correlation between fortnightly daily wages and probabilities of employment for the labor and small-farm households, it was usually positive. However, this was true in only one of the twelve cases for males and in four of the twelve cases for females. On the other hand, there was at least one case of small-farm males in Aurepalle in which the correlation coefficient value was significant and negative, which is in line with the Rodgers (1975) hypothesis. Hence the evidence concerning this relationship is still quite weak.[13]

It seems that for males there is no tendency for the members of the labor group, who generally participate more in the rural daily hired labor market, to receive higher wages as a result of their being more continuously available throughout the year. In fact, there is evidence from these villages to the contrary. Small-farm males in these villages apparently can hire daily workers from labor households at the same time that they hire themselves out and be better off for it. The same is not true for females. This no doubt helps explain the relatively high levels of labor hiring observed on the small farms by Ghodake, Ryan, and Sarin (1978). It may also help explain the predominance of hired females in the female labor force.

There were significant positive correlations between male participation rates and probabilities of employment in four of the six villages. For females this was true in only two villages, and in two others the correlation was significantly negative. This suggests that, for males, the more the participation the better the chance of obtaining a job. This is not so true for females, implying that there may be stronger "discouraged worker" effects operating for males than for females in these villages. There are fewer hired agricultural tasks that women perform exclusively—they are mainly restricted to nursery bed raising, transplanting, planting, weeding, and thinning. This task segmentation appears to so limit effective demand for female labor that in-

---

13. Kalpana Bardhan (1977) presents an excellent review of the available Indian literature on the relationships between labor supply, labor demand, and wage determination.

creased female labor market supply (participation), combined with such a restricted demand, leads to excessive unemployment.

SUBJECTIVE OPPORTUNITY COST AND LABOR MARKET DUALISM

Opportunity cost is defined here as the expected wage forgone by a prospective labor market participant when that person works instead on the farm or in the household, or chooses leisure. Opportunity cost is measured here as OC_t where

$$OC_t = W_t(PMU)_t$$

and W_t is the market wage rate in period t. It is therefore the subjective value of time considered by individual agents in the economy. This should be contrasted with the concept of social opportunity cost used in social benefit-cost analysis, which adjusts for distortion of domestic prices relative to international markets.

Often, data can be obtained on seasonal rural market wage rates, but there is no way of knowing how close these rates are to the seasonal opportunity costs of labor. Such costs are at the heart of questions related to labor supply analysis and the value of household production and time. McDiarmid (1977) refers to the necessity of obtaining local or regional measures of seasonal opportunity costs (as opposed to the countrywide single measures he derives) in areas where religious and language constraints prevent labor mobility. These circumstances generally prevail in the parts of the Indian SAT studied here.

The opportunity cost of labor for males averaged Rs 2.26 per day in 1975–76, which was 90 percent higher than that for females (Rs 1.20). In spite of the fact that there was a mixed picture concerning the probability of employment in these villages, males consistently had significantly higher opportunity wages than females (table 9.1). The *CV*s of opportunity costs were in general higher than those of daily wages or of probabilities of employment. There would therefore seem to be considerable scope for designing technologies that specifically aim at capitalizing on periods when labor opportunity costs are low. To do so would both enhance the profitability of the technology and create employment in slack/unremunerative periods with consequent redistributive benefits.[14]

To test the labor market dualism hypothesis of Sen (1966)—that the

14. Hired labor may benefit relatively more than family labor from the creation of employment if the generally positive correlations between fortnightly total labor use and percentage of hired labor found by Ghodake, Ryan, and Sarin (1978, p. 57) are any indication. Also, large farmers have lower *CV*s of fortnightly labor use than small farmers and hire more labor (Ghodake, Ryan, and Sarin 1978, pp. 17, 24). This further suggests that the smoothing of labor peaks may benefit hired labor proportionately more.

imputed price of labor to small farmers is lower than the actual price of labor to large farmers—paired t tests were performed on the fortnightly wage rates of the labor category (by sex) compared with the fortnightly market opportunity costs of labor from the small, medium, and large farms. The hypothesis contends that because large farmers are excess demanders of labor, their labor cost is the full agricultural wage. Small farmers are excess suppliers of labor and their relevant labor "price" is their opportunity wage.

In three of the six villages, the differences between wage rates of males from labor households and small-farm male opportunity labor costs were significantly positive. In two, the differences were not significant, and in one the difference was significantly negative. In all six villages the wage rates of females from the labor group significantly exceeded the market opportunity costs of family female labor from the small-farm households. Ghodake, Ryan, and Sarin (1978) observed that the proportion of family female labor used on farms in these villages is inversely related to farm size. This was not observed to be true for family males.

In the three villages where wages of males from labor households were significantly greater than small-farm market opportunity labor costs, family male labor use per hectare was significantly greater on small farms than on large farms, as predicted by the dualism hypothesis. This was also true in all six villages for females. On the basis of this evidence the labor market dualism hypothesis receives stronger support for females than for males. A major reason is the higher involuntary unemployment probability for females (particularly those in the drought-prone regions), which creates larger divergence between their wage rates and opportunity costs. This divergence in turn leads to the more substantial differences we observed between family female labor use per hectare on small farms and on large farms.

A paradox remains, however, with regard to large farms where there was some labor market participation. In three out of six villages, the fortnightly wage rates of male labor from the labor category were significantly higher than the market opportunity labor costs of males from large farms. Five out of six villages showed positive significant differences between fortnightly labor wage rates and opportunity labor costs of females from large farms. Hence for those large farms whose members enter the labor market, the "dual labor market" hypothesis holds equally well.[15] Many large farmers are also faced with wage rates for hired labor that are higher than the market opportunity costs of their own family labor. It thus seems clear that the hypothesis is an oversimplification of the operations of the labor market in these villages.

Judging by the generally low and/or nonsignificant correlations of wage

15. It is recognized that OC_t may not be a good measure of the value of time for farmers who do not participate in the labor market. For them, OC_t is less than their "reservation wage." This selectivity bias is more important for large-farm families, where market participation is generally less than that by small-farm families.

rates of males and females, there would appear to be considerable segmentation in the male and female labor markets in five of the six villages studied here. The notable exception is Dokur, where paddy is grown under irrigation. A detailed analysis of the relative contribution of males and females to the various field activities in these villages showed there were only two "joint" operations—harvesting and threshing. Women concentrated almost exclusively on five tasks—nursery bed raising, transplanting, planting, weeding, and thinning. Men focused on nine major operations, four of them involving bullock power.

Males and females tended to participate in the daily labor market at similar times, particularly in Aurepalle and in the Sholapur villages. They also had similar chances of obtaining a job throughout the year. In theory then, one would expect wage rates of males and females also to move together if females were able to shift in and out of tasks similar to those done by males as their respective wage rates began to diverge. However, the extent to which this trend is absent in five of these six villages is an indication of the degree of apparent segregation of their male and female labor markets.

CONCLUSION

If these six villages are representative of the SAT regions of south India, it appears that women have a role equal to men in the agricultural labor force. Furthermore, it is clear that women, especially landless women, have less chance than men of finding daily wage employment, particularly in the slack agricultural seasons. If this situation is to be improved and not aggravated, new agricultural technologies for these regions must be designed to enhance demand for the tasks generally reserved for females. A large untapped reserve of female labor appears to be able and willing to engage in more market-oriented activities in slack seasons, and it may even exceed the sizable male reserves. There would thus seem to be excellent scope for designing technologies that would capitalize on this reserve.

However, there is a need for closer study of how these villagers allocate the time that presently is not devoted to own-farm or paid market work. This amounts to more than 50 percent of their total time. It is imperative to understand the reason for this surprisingly high figure in order to assess whether the large *apparent* labor reserve just mentioned is indeed a potential market supply. The work of Bardhan (chapter 12) and Rosenzweig (chapter 11) suggests that labor supply elasticities for adults in north India are less than unity. We propose to test this hypothesis on a seasonal basis, using our panel data on more than 1,500 individuals in south India, collected over several years. The new household economics models developed by Heckman (1974), MaCurdy (1979), and others would seem the appropriate ones to quantify the determinants of the individual labor supply.

10

Work Patterns and Social Differentiation: Rural Women of West Bengal

Kalpana Bardhan

Divisions of labor within the corporate family, the community, and the multicommunity village are structured largely "by the intersection of economy, demography and family."[1] Rural variations in female work patterns reflect the complex interplay of given economic choices and constraints, of the labor allocation behavior of household units that combine production and wage-earning and consumption decisions, and of the demographic structure of the household and the village. In a context with entrenched combinations of social stratification and economic inequality, one must consider another major explanatory factor: the stratificatory significance of the type of work. Occupations are differentiated by their economic return and by their appropriateness to the family status ranking. The relative weights of economic incentives and the extraeconomic significance of types of women's jobs (the significance for intrafamily power structure, for family position in the social hierarchy, and for marital and reproductive role requisites) do not remain static, particularly as the traditional modes of village life become modified to various degrees by state-initiated and growth-induced change processes, as some occupations decline in importance and others become more prominent, and as individual families move up or down the economic scale.

To analyze rural women's work patterns and the variations in them, one can use three distinct, though related, approaches. First, one can try to explain the pattern of allocation or utilization of female time in terms of selected economic and extraeconomic determinants. Even the economic explanation has to go beyond the urban-oriented frame of choice between paid work and homemaking, decided by levels of market wages on the one hand and of family income on the other. Female time is allocated not just

In revising an earlier draft, I benefited from comments made by Swapan Adnani, Kanta Ahuja, Mark R. Rosenzweig, and Ashok Rudra.

1. Tilly and Scott (1978), which is about the history of women's work patterns in France and Great Britain since 1700.

between these two, but also to the family (farming or artisanal) enterprise; to domestic work that can vary widely in range and labor intensity, depending upon available substitution possibilities between home-processed and market-processed consumption goods (clothes made at home or purchased, rice hand pounded or milled) and depending upon the degree of cultivated lavishness of homemaking (diets and cooking times vary widely across social groups and rural regions in India); and, by the very poor, also to various gathering, gleaning, and foraging activities that range from hauling water, to collecting such items as fuel, fodder, thatch, or edibles from the forest or the village commons, to scrounging for reusable scraps and discards. The relative amounts of time that rural women spend on these categories of market and nonmarket work depend upon the level of household production, the level of male earnings (from production or wages), the availability of amenities (potable water, grain mill, electricity) and the degree of commercialization affecting the time women must spend gathering and processing food and other "home" goods, apart from being a function of the family's taste for allocating female time for domestic work rather than for earning and for one form of earning over another. Interpretation of homemaking labor is complicated not only by its wide variability with local amenities and commercialization, but by the fact that in many of its income-stretching and income-supplementing forms, it makes a distinction from earning and production-generating labor difficult. For the peasant woman, running the household often includes making clothes, tending the kitchen garden and animals, processing crops and fodder, procuring wood for fuel, and cooking for the field hands. Cross-sectionally, increases in household income or in asset level correlate directly with shifts from field labor to domestic labor, and from there to supervision of servants. For a given income or land size, the allocation of female labor also appears to be sensitive to the family's caste/ethnic rank. Female workers from the lowest castes and tribes in West Bengal are concentrated in farm wage labor, whereas working women from other groups (caste Hindu and Muslim) are to be found mainly in the crafts, cottage industries, and rural white-collar work. In the first section of this paper, rural women's time allocation and occupational divisions are analyzed on the co-ordinates of economic level (landholding size) and social (caste/ethnic) rank—that is, using mainly this first approach.

From this point, one might follow a second approach and try to identify the forms of occupational and wage differentiation, which may be called discrimination, market imperfection, or exploitation, depending upon the frame of analysis. Apart from the cumulative effect of limited access to job alternatives and to education, skills, and training, occupational discrimination is evident when a certain group is blocked off (by employers and/or other groups of employees) from many alternatives and funneled or crowded into a set of low-wage jobs. Wage discrimination is evident when wage differentials are unrelated to productivity differentials. In the oligopsonistic labor market of the village, the employers are aware of the differences in economic opportunities facing different sections of employees and often use their market power to pay different wages or to allocate employees differentially, acting profitably upon differences in labor supply conditions.

A third approach is to examine the link between work participation and the other conditions that affect the status of women. Higher levels of work participation among the land-poor, low-caste, and tribal women correlate with more severe economic distress. Besides, working and earning do not amount to control over one's earnings when the wages are handed to the male "head of household," or when women working as subordinate "helpers" in the family enterprise carry vast work loads devoid of training effect or management responsibility. Parish and Whyte (1978) observe that in the villages of the Kwangtung province of China, although women's vastly increased role in argicultural labor has resulted in roughly proportional increases in their earnings, and although there is not much evidence of wage discrimination, there is still "the failure of earning power to translate into control over earnings—characteristic of most peasant cultures." Team payments are handed over to the family head;[2] "women work in the team fields as individual members of the labor force, rather than under family supervision, but when we consider the consumption and use of the income they earn, the corporate family unit still reigns supreme" (p. 238). Parish and Whyte also observe that rural women's political role and influence in decision-making in the wider community are seriously hindered, in spite of the central directives, by their double burden of an equal amount of field labor and a larger amount of domestic labor. It leaves them with little time for community leadership posts or cadre duties, or sometimes even for the evening's team meeting. Equality of employment and remuneration is obviously necessary, but not sufficient, for general equality and emancipation. Important among other necessary conditions, Parish and Whyte rightly conclude, is the ability to organize to pursue women's goals: investment of communal or village resources in facilities that will lighten the burden of their domestic labor and achieve qualitatively equal work allocation (that is, equal access to the kinds of work that are more rewarding in terms of the skills generated and the leadership or management responsibilities involved).

When pressed to achieve the massive mobilization of female labor for production, disparate societies (the United States in 1942–44 and China from the mid-1950s to the late 1960s) accomplished it not by propaganda alone, but by actively initiating two categories of concrete measures: (1) reorganizing such tasks as child care, food preparation, and laundry, and (2) readjusting "male" features of jobs (hours, shifts) and establishing training programs for

---

2. The head of the family and the fund manager may not always be the same person, but they are generally male even in families where there is a larger female contribution to earning. In the urban and educated families the fund manager is often the woman, even when she is not an earner.

the traditionally excluded (women, blacks). Correspondingly, demobilization was secured by withdrawing or reducing the facilities. In an economically unequal society, affluent women are able to secure these facilities commerically, to hire help, and to use the resources within the extended family. Poorer women, who must work for subsistence, live bent under the enormous double burden and/or forgo schooling for their daughters, who undertake the vast amount of gathering-maintenance-domestic labor. In rural West Bengal, the participation of poorer women in directly income-generating work is basically restricted by two factors. One is the ethos of signaling social distinction from the castes below by observing "propriety" in women's work. The other is the sheer enormity of domestic labor (including the survival tasks of gathering) that is a function partly of the customary intrafamily division of labor and partly of the unavailability of even the barest minimum of amenities in most villages.

In this paper, I analyze the patterns of time disposition of rural women, using mainly the first two approaches defined above, namely, to explain those patterns, and to identify the forms of labor market segmentation by wages and by occupations.

Rural West Bengal is characterized by a resource base (land-irrigation-livestock) that is both meager relative to the size of population and rather unequally distributed. If the entire cultivated area were distributed equally among all the rural households, there would be less than 1.9 acres per household, with approximately 0.5 acres receiving any kind of irrigation. Under the actual distribution, one-quarter of the households operated, in 1972, three-quarters of the cultivated area in farms of 2.5 acres or more, two-fifths of the households operated one-quarter of the cultivated area in farms smaller than 2.5 acres, and one-third worked as farm laborers.[3] For the land-poor households in rural West Bengal, unlike those in north and west India, livestock ownership is near zero. The existence of a large land-poor population has meant an abundance of labor for hire at very low wages, and this has reinforced the status-differentiating value of not having to do manual labor in the fields.

Rural West Bengal is also characterized by a rather high proportion of labor-caste and tribal households.[4] Boserup (1970) advances the hypothesis

3. National Sample Survey of Landholdings, 1971–72 (twenty-sixth round).

4. Orissa and Madhya Pradesh are the only other states in India with as high a proportion of rural households belonging to low (scheduled) castes and tribes. Low-caste/tribal labor households constitute one-quarter of all rural households in West Bengal, as compared with the Indian average of 14 percent. The phenomenon in Bengal is partly linked historically to the shifts, during the nineteenth century, in the locus of landownership from traditional peasant castes to professional and merchant groups. These noncultivating landowners often encouraged the settlement of labor castes and tribals in their villages (Basu 1962). It can also be traced to the dispossession of tribals by moneylenders and, more recently, to waves of tenant eviction that have followed upon the tenancy reform legislation.

that when the women working as farm laborers are almost entirely from a community, ethnic group, or caste level different from that of the farmers, it becomes more important for the women of landholding families to distinguish themselves from the "despised and hardworking female laborers." With three-quarters of rural female laborers from the lowest castes and tribes, and very low rates of farm work participation among the other women, rural West Bengal is clearly consistent with this hypothesis. The correlation of low social status with agricultural wage labor is stronger for women than for men and may be explained in terms of two related processes. One is what Srinivas (1966, 1978) calls "Sanskritization": observance of female immurement and propriety in women's work as instruments for hierarchical status differentiation from the castes below and emulation of those above. Peasants are normally less averse to manual labor than the upper-caste landed. Still, as they experience income increases, women are withdrawn from work in the field into home processing activities and cottage industries, and then occasionally into education for transition to white-collar jobs, the supply of which has been increasing even in rural areas. The second process, Boserup noted, is that the very presence of the laboring poor supports the status-differentiating value of eschewing manual field labor and makes it inexpensive for even the not-so-rich to have this form of conspicuous consumption.

Differentiation from the castes below is often signaled by differences in the type of work—not just the dichotomy between manual and nonmanual or home-based work, but also that between farm and nonfarm work. For a similar low level of income or landholding, a tribal or low-caste woman works in the paddy field, whereas the upper-caste or Muslim woman works as a cook or a tailor. This occupational differentiation by social status is accompanied by a wage difference, and the combination works as a form of discrimination that generally cumulates over time.

In the first two sections of this paper I analyze the overall rates and patterns of female work participation for two broad social categories. The data come from a fairly comprehensive sample survey (National Sample Survey, twenty-seventh round) covering nearly 4,900 households from 500 villages in the state, for the year from October 1972 to September 1973. Since the data do not specify caste/ethnic status beyond whether or not a household belongs to a scheduled[5] caste or tribe, I was able to study only the differences between the lowest-caste and tribal households on the one hand and the middle- and upper-caste and Muslim households on the other.

---

5. Scheduled castes and scheduled tribes include those officially listed as the most disadvantaged, both economically and socially. Although the list was carefully prepared, it is possible that some of these individuals have moved up. In addition, not all the scheduled castes are labor castes. These qualifications do not seriously affect the usability of the list for indicating roughly a low cut-off point in rural socioeconomic ranking.

These two sets include 44 percent and 56 percent, respectively, of all women aged 15–59 years in the sample. I further classified each of the two sets of households into three farm-size groups: the landless or the noncultivators (with 0–0.1 acre), the small cultivators (with 0.1–2.5 acres), and the prosperous farmers (with more than 2.5 acres). These three landholding groups comprise 31 percent, 37 percent, and 32 percent, respectively, of the sample women of prime working age (15–59 years). Table 10.1 gives the cross-classification of their work and employment data, by social status category and by farm-size group. Work participation is defined in terms of *usual activity*, that is, what a person was primarily engaged in over the reference year (columns 1–6 are based on usual activity status), and also in terms of *current activity* or time disposition during the seven days preceding the date on which a household responded to the investigator's questions (columns 7–16 are based on current weekly activities).

The third section is concerned with the core of rural working women, the casual farm laborers. Demand for female wage labor for farm operations is substantial in West Bengal, but highly seasonal. Unlike the male farm laborers, and unlike other categories of female workers, these laborers do not manage to make up for the seasonal drop in their farm employment with other kinds of work; they get both less employment and lower wages. They are thus isolated and exploited because of a combination of sex and caste/ethnic discrimination and landholding barriers, especially in agriculturally stagnating regions. Wage and employment gaps by sex among the farm laborers tend to be significantly responsive to cross-sectional differences in agricultural growth factors (such as the degree of irrigation and multiple-cropping), in closeness to urban-industrial centers (which offer alternative employment opportunities to the rural land-poor), and in the size of landholding as a generator of on-farm self-employment. The labor markets in economically advanced districts are less segmented by sex and caste/ethnic barriers. They are at the same time also characterized by a much more class-polarized agrarian structure, that is, by a sharper dichotomy between capitalist farmer-employers and wage laborers, with a diminishing buffer class of peasants. Both processes—leveling and enlarging the labor market—are derivative of the changing forces of production and growth in labor demand.

DOMESTIC WORK

Nearly three-quarters of the women of prime working age (15–59 years) in rural West Bengal were, during an agriculturally normal year like 1972–73, primarily engaged in domestic work. This is a catchall residual category that covers the many kinds of work involved in transforming, stretching, and augmenting a predominantly male income so that it becomes a living for the family.

TABLE 10.1. Participation of Women in Work Force, Wage Labor Force, and Domestic Work, by Caste/Ethnic Group and Landholding, Rural West Bengal, 1972–73.

Caste/Ethnic Group and Operational Land Holding	Percentage Distribution of Women (1)	Percentage as Domestic Workers* (2)	Domestic Work per Woman in Work Force (days/wk.) (2a)	Percentage of Women in Work Force* (3)	Percentage Distribution of All Working Women (4)	Percentage Working as Wage Laborers* (5)	Percentage Distribution of Women as Laborers (6)	Total Employment per worker (days/wk.) (7)
0–0.1 acre	31	60	0.90	32	42	25	55	4.59
Scheduled castes and tribes	17	52	0.84	44	31	36	43	4.53
Others	14	70	1.06	19	11	12	12	4.77
0.1–2.5 acres	37	70	1.34	26	41	14	36	4.37
Scheduled castes and tribes	16	59	1.29	38	26	23	26	4.23
Others	21	79	1.43	16	15	7	10	4.60
Over 2.5 acres	32	83	1.94	13	17	4	9	4.38
Scheduled castes and tribes	12	75	1.93	22	11	6	5	4.17
Others	20	87	1.95	7	6	4	4	4.76
Σ Scheduled castes and tribes	44	60	1.19	36	68	23	74	4.36
Σ Others	56	79	1.40	14	32	7	26	4.69
Σ	100	71	1.26	24	100	14	100	4.46

Source: National Sample Survey, twenty-seventh round.

*Percentages of these women primarily engaged in (according to National Sample Survey definition of "usual activity" status) domestic work (col. 2), employment of any kind (for wages, in own or family enterprise, in farm or nonfarm operations) (col. 3), and wage employment on farm or nonfarm work (col. 5). The difference between cols. 3 and 5 is the percentage of women in the group self-employed or helping in family farm or nonfarm enterprise.

Caste/Ethnic Group and Operational Land Holding	Wage employment per laborer (days/wk.)		Average Wage (Rs/day)		Employment per Laborer (days/wk.)†	Unemployment per Laborer (days/wk.)‡	Total Wage Earned per Laborer (Rs/wk.)	Percentage of Total Employment from All Farm Work§	Percentage of Total Employment from Farm Wage Labor§
	Farm work (8)	All Kinds (9)	Farm (10)	Nonfarm (11)	(12)	(13)	(14)	(15)	(16)
0–0.1 acre	2.55	4.29	2.51	2.45	4.44	1.16	10.58	47	43
Scheduled castes and tribes	2.73	4.15	2.53	2.11	4.32	1.29	9.77	53	50
Others	1.91	4.80	2.43	3.02	4.87	0.70	13.43	30	25
0.1–2.5 acres	2.66	3.78	2.19	2.00	4.60	1.29	8.87	59	37
Scheduled castes and tribes	2.56	3.77	2.18	1.95	4.36	1.49	8.09	66	41
Others	2.93	3.80	2.22	2.18	5.22	0.79	10.86	49	30
Over 2.5 acres	1.78	4.63	2.01	2.68	5.13	1.16	10.95	72	12
Scheduled castes and tribes	2.27	3.53	1.89	2.07	4.09	1.84	7.13	85	14
Others	1.17	5.98	2.31	2.88	6.41	0.33	15.61	49	9
Σ Scheduled castes and tribes	2.64	3.98	2.36	2.05	4.32	1.40	9.01	63	41
Σ Others	2.21	4.97	2.31	2.75	5.24	0.67	12.73	12	24
Σ	2.53	4.24	2.35	2.35	4.56	1.21	9.98	56	35

† Person-days of total employment (for wages, on own account, or for family enterprise) during a week for a woman primarily engaged in wage-paid work.

‡ Average time in a week for which a woman who is usually active as a wage laborer is without work and is seeking or available for more work.

§ Composition of total employment (person-days) for these women in a week. Column 15 is wage-paid and self (family)-employment in farm work. Column 16 is wage employment in farm work as a percentage of total employment. Subtraction of the figures in col. 15 from 100 gives the percentage of total employment derived from nonfarm work (for wages or in the family enterprise). Subtraction of the figures in col. 16 from 100 gives the percentage derived from self-employment of all kinds and wage employment in nonfarm work.

To study the mobilization of underused or unproductively used labor, it is obviously important to analyze domestic work and the socioeconomic composition of those primarily engaged in it. The reasons for and policy implications of the low labor force participation rates of the poorest women and the most affluent women are totally different. Essentially, two questions should be asked here. First, to what extent is the preoccupation with domestic work a form of deliberate seclusion from outside employment, a device for signifying the family's social and economic status? Second, how much of the large amount of time spent in domestic work is really unemployment—a result of the discouragement effect of a depressed economic environment, of the sheer lack of employment opportunities? Anthropologists stress the sex/caste/ethnic patterns of division of labor in a hierarchally stratified society. Economists tend to stress the effects of the growth or stagnation of the forces of production. The two aspects are, as we will observe here, actually interactive.

Dube (1959) characterized the division of labor and the permitted forms and locations of female work in an Andhra village as follows. The richest and/or high-caste women take no part in outdoor work. Women of the middle, peasant castes generally help their men in the fields and in marketing; they work mainly within the family enterprise but are not averse to occasional high-wage employment. The poorest, low-caste women regularly seek paid work to support themselves and their children. Although this structure might be generally accurate, certain other factors modify the extent to which status determines women's allocation between domestic labor and outside labor. Poverty, and the pressure to earn, does to some extent cut across the social hierarchy. In addition, the changing production and employment conditions widen the opportunity for face-saving, even status-enhancing, differentiation by type of employment rather than by sheer seclusion from outside work. Despite the blurring effects of these two factors, there remains a correlation—imperfect, but still significant—between occupation with domestic work and caste/ethnic rank as well as economic level (roughly indicated here by farm size).

The proportion of women primarily engaged in domestic work (table 10.1, column 2) increases from 52 percent in landless households belonging to the scheduled castes and tribes to 87 percent in households other than those in the scheduled castes and tribes and with more than 2.5 acres. Within *each* farm-size group, the proportion differs significantly between the two caste/ethnic sets: women in both landless and small-farm households in the "other" category are far more occupied with domestic work and withdrawn from directly income-generating activities (column 3), most of all from employment as wage laborers (column 5).

The heavy claim that domestic work places on female energy cannot be totally attributed to a hierarchical stratification design. Even among the tribal and low-caste women, who are least averse to earning by means of manual labor and who are economically under the most pressure to do so, the incidence of domestic work as the "usual activity" is quite high. How much of it is really disguised unemployment, and how much is low-productivity self-employment, both of which really reflect a depressed economic environment?

Some of the domestic workers, and some of the usually employed who spend part of their time in domestic work, may very well be discouraged laborers, who readily enter the active labor force when the scope for employment increases, such as in the agricultural peak seasons, who can therefore be utilized by the establishment of work programs that are specific as to season, location, and skills. Given the fact that for each working woman in the 15–59 age range there were nearly three women engaged in domestic work more or less regularly (aside from the younger girls and older women who were also doing it), and considering the large degree of counterseasonal variation in the time spent in domestic work (P. K. Bardhan 1978c), it is rather likely that part of the time devoted to domestic work represents involuntary unemployment, particularly on the part of the land-poor farm laborers.[6] Part of the seasonal rise in time spent on domestic work may, on the other hand, be unrecognized employment: home processing and maintenance activities phased for the lean season, especially in the landholding households; home production of consumption goods for the family, and various gathering activities. A later National Sample Survey (1977–78) sought specifically to determine the labor time engaged in such activities as gathering and weaving and sewing for household use, in combination with other domestic chores. The hours spent by rural women in West Bengal on such combined work was in the ratio of 1 : 1.8 to the time spent on "domestic work only," and in the ratio of 1 : 0.5 to the time spent in employment (for wages and/or in the household enterprise).

For the poorest households, the pressure to seek outside employment, and the enormous amount of labor that has to be allocated to gathering and scrounging activities, can interfere with schooling for girls, who often must take over the working mother's domestic chores. Landless labor families, being generally nuclear, lack the mutual help available in the extended farm households. Being generally poorer, they also have to undertake more gathering and scrounging activities for subsistence. On the other hand, their domestic chores do not include many of the crop-processing activities that peasant women have to do. There cannot be any doubt that the social reorganization of domestic work, in the forms of pooled child care and community kitchens, the provision of labor-saving public amenities (drinking-

---

6. About two-fifths of the women laborers (or two-fifths of an average laborer's weekly fifty-six hours) were fully employed. For another two-fifths the amount of unemployed time (available for more work), plus the amount of time spent in domestic work, was at least as great as the amount of time during which they were actually employed. In response to the probing questions of the National Sample Survey, most of these women, laborers by occupation, indicated their willingness to assume more regular employment inside or outside the village.

water wells and transportation), and the support of inexpensive commerical-ization of standard chores like grain processing, can be productive in the same way as the consolidation of fragmented landholdings is. More adult time can thereby be released for extra production or earning, without impeding children's schooling.[7]

The working poor often have to recruit their children to release adult labor from collection activities and domestic chores, or to earn. Table 10.2 gives a breakdown by sex of the "usual activity" of all children 8–14 years old in the sample, according to the household's landholding size and caste/ethnic level. In the landless low-caste/tribal households, 23 percent of the girls were primarily domestic workers, 8 percent were employed workers, and only 10 percent were going to school on a more or less regular basis. In upper-caste households with more than 2.5 acres, only 11 percent were domestic workers and 55 percent attended school. In between these two categories, the proportion going to school varied directly, and the proportion occupied with domestic work varied negatively, with social level and land-holding size. Within each group, the girls attending school were from families less poor than those hiring them as domestic workers.[8] At the lower social *and* economic level, the appalling lack of schooling for girls is thus partly linked with the mothers' low-wage work load; it is not just the result of hierarchical social exclusion at the school level and pessimistic parental view of the benefit of education for daughters.[9]

---

7. Ironically, severe unemployment among the adult agricultural laborers in Kerala has contributed to the high rate of school enrollment of their children.

8. Similarly, the proportion of boys attending school increases with the caste/ethnic and landholding position of household; and within each group, those who attend school come from families with a higher per capita consumption.

9. The data confirm that at any one of the social and economic levels, the boy's education is valued more than the girl's. At the same caste and farm-size level, fewer girls were released for school, and more girls were regularly occupied in domestic work than boys in employment.

I ran a multiple regression to isolate the effect of each of the determinants of children's schooling, controlling for the effects of the others. With Y as the number of days attending school per week (0 for nonattendance), X_1 as per capita household consumption, X_2 as the child's age, D_1 as the child's sex (0 for a male, 1 for a female), D_2 for caste/ethnic level (0 for scheduled castes and tribes, 1 for others), and D_3–D_6 as the seasons, referring to the quarter to which the reference week for the child's time disposition data belong, the estimated regression equation is:

$$Y = 1.48^* + 0.04^* X_1 - 1.02^* D_1 + 1.20^* D_2 - 0.53^* D_3 - 0.10 D_4 + 0.13 D_6 - 0.02 X_2,$$

$$R^2 = .17^*$$

(asterisk indicates significance at 1 percent level, for a sample of nearly 10,000 children). The extent of a child's school attendance is significantly greater for a boy ($D_1 = 0$), and for children from families *not* belonging to scheduled castes or tribes ($D_2 = 1$). It increases with a rise in the per capita consumption level of the family and decreases during the agricultural peak season in the area ($D_3 = 1$: October–December).

TABLE 10.2. "Usual Activity" of Children, by Caste/Ethnic Group and Operational Landholding, West Bengal, 1972–73

Caste/Ethnic Group and Operational Landholding	Female Children						Male Children				
	Percentage Working	Percentage Working as Domestic Workers	Percentage Attending School	Total Employment per Worker (days/wk.)	Per Capita Family Consumption (Rs/mo.) if Attending School	Per Capita Family Consumption (Rs/mo.) if Engaged in Domestic Duties	Percentage Working	Percentage Attending School	Total Employment per Worker (days/wk.)	Per Capita Family Consumption (Rs/mo.) if Attending School	Per Capita Family Consumption (Rs/mo.) if Engaged in Domestic Duties
0–0.1 acre											
Scheduled castes and tribes	8	23	10	5.5	35.00	23.43	18	19	6.1	32.12	26.96
Other	5	15	25	5.7	38.91	27.86	10	43	6.3	34.70	25.46
0.1–2.5 acres											
Scheduled castes and tribes	7	22	18	5.5	36.81	26.31	17	34	5.8	33.89	26.90
Other	2	18	40	5.2	38.49	32.67	11	55	6.2	38.68	33.29
Over 2.5 acres											
Scheduled castes and tribes	3	15	33	5.1	50.76	40.98	19	49	6.3	46.48	35.29
Other	1	11	55	6.0	62.82	45.94	13	68	6.9	59.24	58.16
Σ	4	17	32		48.27	35.79	15	46		44.61	35.49

Source: National Sample Survey, twenty-seventh round.

Notes: The remaining children aged 8–14 years (47 percent of girls, 37 percent of boys, including the 2 percent engaged in domestic duties) were reported as too young to work, to perform domestic duties on a regular basis, or to go to school, or as having unidentified "usual activities." Most of them might occassionally be helping the adults in gainful employment and/or domestic work. The same would be true of the school children.

Rural employment programs for women, in which the workplace would be used for organizing child care and canteens would be set up as a cooperative effort to produce take-home staple food, would in such a context generate enormous social as well as private gains, increasing adult work participation and girls' school enrollment at the same time. So would public investment in basic facilities to reduce the vast amounts of energy currently being used by poorer women and children for collecting water, cooking fuel, and fodder. Increased employment by itself may induce increased female work participation. But labor-saving reorganization of domestic work or commercialization of home processing may not immediately follow the increased work participation. Poorer women are often obliged to carry the double burden of employment and undiminished domestic labor, or are forced to have their female children forgo education even if it is otherwise accessible. Public investment in basic facilities and reorganization of domestic labor by pooling can be powerful tools for achieving efficient labor utilization and growth.[10] This point holds also for the simple mechanization of household processing of grain (from mortar and pestle to pedal-operated rice huller, for example), yarn spinning, and so on.[11]

OCCUPATIONAL DIVISIONS

Given the available employment opportunities, a family's social position and economic level decide a woman's minimum wages and the type of work she deems consistent with customs concerning the propriety of employment and with her skills, below which level she would rather give time to domestic labor, to processing a living out of the male income. Differentiation from the castes below is maintained by observing the customs regarding the propriety of employment. The poorer she is, or the less the male income in the household, the more likely she is to lower the mimimum supply price of her labor and to work overtime on, or shift to her daughter, her domestic duties and laborious gathering tasks.

When we look at the structure of women's time disposition patterns across households grouped by landholding size and by caste/ethnic status, we see clear patterns of differentiation in terms of (1) participation in income-

10. During the late 1950s and the 1960s, one of the officially initiated institutional changes in China, which was intended to free rural women from an excessive burden of domestic work, was the provision of nursery schools, sewing co-ops, and communal kitchens. The change resulted in a vastly increased role of women in agricultural labor and rural construction. Later, in the period following the Cultural Revolution, responsibility for both child care and meal preparation was returned to the family in many areas. See Parish and Whyte (1978).

11. Rural electrification in China radically changed the pattern of women's employment. Mechanization of rice hulling and yarn spinning released billions of hours of female work time for more productive work in agriculture and other occupations (Rawski 1979).

producing work rather than in domestic work, and (2) types of employment —a market-nonmarket dichotomy and a farm-nonfarm dichotomy.

The category of low-caste and tribal women includes 44 percent of all women aged 15–59 years in rural West Bengal, but it includes 68 percent of the regularly working women and as much as 74 percent of those working as wage laborers. The differentiation is much less for men: 46 percent of all workers and 54 percent of the laborers are from lower castes and tribes. The difference between the two social categories, in terms of women's overall work participation, and especially their labor market participation, is much larger than the differences across the farm-size groups within each category.[12] One-third of the rural women, but nearly three-quarters of the female laborers, are from low-caste and tribal households with less than 2.5 acres.

The second form of differentiation is between farm and nonfarm work. The low-caste and tribal women do proportionally more farm work, and farm wage labor in particular, whereas upper-caste and Muslim women do proportionally more nonfarm work. Associated with this occupational differentiation is a significant wage difference. The farm wage for female labor is similar between the two sets. But there is a substantial wage difference between the kinds of nonfarm employment that women from the two caste/ethnic sets have access to.[13] Women in the upper set, often having more education and marketable skills and certainly able to demand higher "acceptable" price for outside employment, manage to participate more in the types of nonfarm work that offer higher wages.

For nonfarm work, low-caste and tribal women are hired less, on a more casual basis,[14] and at lower wages. For farm labor, the category in which they are concentrated, they receive lower wages than men and yet are unemployed more of the time (table 10.1, column 13). Both employers and male laborers rationalize lower female wage in terms of alleged efficiency differences. But the fact is that their wage is lower even in operations like transplanting, in which they are recognized to be more skilled and specialized. The combination of occupational and wage differentiation and operational

12. Caste and farm size are partially, not perfectly, correlated in the state. Approximately one-quarter of the scheduled caste/tribe households cultivate farms of more than 2.5 acres.

13. A similar segmentation of nonfarm labor market by caste/ethnic status is observed for men, but the degree of differentiation—by wage and employment—is much less than for women.

14. Low-caste and tribal women participate much more in directly productive work and in the labor market, and yet they are unable to obtain as much regular employment as the fewer upper-caste women workers do. The reason is that they are funneled into a limited number of seasonal farm operations and thus denied access to many regular nonfarm jobs. This separation is related to their educational and resource disadvantage because of their backgrounds, a barrier that amounts to formidable cumulative discrimination. The supply of clerical and white-collar jobs is increasing in rural areas, but rarely are these jobs available to the low-caste or tribal landless, who have not the barest minimum of human capital or money.

and seasonal isolation from the rest of the rural labor market, means lower earnings and increased (time rate of) unemployment for women from scheduled castes and tribes. These women's poverty and the stronger pressure exerted on them to earn interact with and reinforce the prevalent segmentation of the village labor market to their disadvantage.

Migration to urban areas, though costly to the migrant in some respects, might have reduced what Francis Edgeworth calls the "crowding effect" of poverty and occupational stratification. But the rate of long-term urban migration, because of its contact-structured selectivity and initial expense, has been systematically lower for the low-caste and tribal groups, particularly the landless labor families among them.[15] Agricultural growth does tend to reduce the unemployment of women in these groups by increasing labor demand for the traditionally female farm operations (see the next section). Seasonally complementary public works programs also relieve the crowding effect. Female employment and wage levels relative to those of male laborers, in the generally low-income occupation of agricultural labor, tend to improve when the intensity of cropping is increasing or when a construction project is in progress. But the virtual exclusion of low-caste women from other types (both new and traditional) of rural nonagricultural jobs persists, largely because of the cumulative discrimination that is related to their educational and resource disadvantage and their lack of assets and skill-acquisition opportunities.

In the large, prosperous, and diversified village,[16] the correlation between caste and occupation and in particular, the concentration of farm laborers in low-caste and tribal populations, tends to be lower than in small and remote villages but continues to exist in spite of the more plentiful nonagricultural employment opportunities in large villages. The business-linked opportunities are predicated upon access to capital and information, and access to the salaried jobs depends upon education and skill level. Men and women from the artisan and farm families have been found to be in a better position to move into the business and salaried occupations than individuals from the labor castes and tribes (Rao 1981). Even in the prosperous, diversified villages, tribal and low-caste persons are mostly found doing construction labor or coolie work, or holding the lowest-paid positions in the mushrooming rural small industries. They are found more in plastic and soap factories than in textile and machine parts factories, for example (Streefkerk 1981). According to the 1977–78 National Sample Survey, over half a million women in rural India held clerical and white-collar jobs (in

15. Semipermanent migrants to urban areas are predominantly educated males from artisan and farm families belonging to the middle and upper castes, whereas short-term, intra-rural migrants are mostly low-caste and tribal farm laborers.

16. Over one-third of India's rural population lived in villages with more than 2,000 inhabitants in 1971.

public administration, schools, health services, banks, post offices, and the railways), but few of them were from landless low-caste and tribal backgrounds. However, there were half a million construction laborers, mostly from those backgrounds. The number of female farm laborers was 22 million, again mostly from the very same set.

THE FEMALE FARM LABORER

A paradox about women's work in rural West Bengal, and also in India as a whole, is that although the overall rate of work participation is low (even declining to some extent), the proportion of wage laborers among those working is high and has been rising in the recent past.[17] The proportion of women in the rural "proletariat", particularly the casual farm laborers, is much larger than their proportion of the total rural work force. More female than male farm laborers also tend to belong to the scheduled castes and tribes. The core of rural working women thus consists of tribal and low-caste farm laborers.

Poverty in rural Bengal is highly correlated with wage labor, and the correlation is more obvious with respect to women (table 10.3). Of the working women in the poorest households, nearly two-thirds were laborers in 1972–73, the year under consideration. This phenomenon of female workers being more impoverished and more market-dependent for employment results from the combined effect of the landlessness, the status-differentiating value of female seclusion from outside work, and the occupational-*cum*-wage stratification that I discussed in the preceding sections. Their deprived educational background (table 10.4) leaves them with very little scope for exercising private initiative to obtain more gainful employment in the occupationally stratified village labor market, or beyond the village. As previously mentioned, their poverty-compelled, low-wage labor supply is mostly funneled into a segmented market for farm labor, to be exploited and yet to remain underutilized. Will unionization, if and when it spreads, replicate in bargaining processes the prevailing sexual and operational divisions, or will it instead allow female labor to move substantially into the "male" farm operations? Will it be supportive of women's farm labor participation, rather than carrying over the image of female labor as a demeaning response to poverty? Will faster agricultural growth weaken the operational and wage differences by sex? Will it induce increased labor force participation? In this section, I will attempt to answer the last two

17. In India as a whole, according to the census data for the "usual status" work force, the proportion of agricultural laborers among rural working women increased from 25 percent in 1961 to 48 percent in 1971. The proportion of men agricultural laborers increased from 16 percent to 25 percent. In the National Sample Survey West Bengal sample for 1972–73, 60 percent of women workers and 50 percent of men workers were laborers.

TABLE 10.3. Percentage Distribution of Workers by Level of Living and Main Occupation, Rural West Bengal, 1972–73

Per Capita Consumption (Rs/mo.)*	Percentage Distribution of Female Population	Females by Usual Activity					Males		Highly Employed Households†
		Family Farm Workers	Family Nonfarm Workers	Farm Laborers	Nonfarm Laborers	All Female Workers	Laborers	All Male Workers	
Less than 30	44	9	11	24	11	55	26	40	57
30–50	36	8	8	11	6	33	15	37	65
More than 50	20	4	2	2	4	12	8	23	68
Σ	100	21	20	38	21	100	49	100	62

Source: National Sample Survey, twenty-seventh round.

Note: Figures in last column are for men and women aged 15–59 years. Figures in other columns are for all age-groups.

*Those with per capita household consumption expenditure not more than Rs 30 ($4.00) per month, which, at 1972–73 prices, may be regarded roughly as the minimum poverty line.

†Percentage of households, within the expenditure group, with currently active men and women (15–59 years) employed for at least 75 percent of the time per week (for at least 5.25 days out of 7 days per currently active person).

TABLE 10.4. Percentage Distribution of Employment, Unemployment, Education, and Labor Mobility by Level of Living, Rural West Bengal, 1972–73 (all age-groups)

Per Capita Consumption (Rs/mo.)	Workers' Total Unemployment (thousand days/wk.)*		Person-days per Week per Woman Casual Agricultural Laborer†		Percentage of Working Women Wanting Alternative Paid Employment‡	Percentage of Persons with at Least a Secondary Education	
	Female	Male	Total Employment	Total Unemployment		Female	Male
Less than 30	1,342 (72)	2,874 (62)	3.79	1.95	42	0.14	0.47
30–50	414 (22)	1,389 (30)	4.59	1.40	27	0.48	2.76
More than 50	105 (6)	361 (8)	4.40	1.19	18	1.77	10.59
Σ	1,861 (100)	4,604 (100)	4.04	1.76	35	0.60	3.57

Source: National Sample Survey, twenty-seventh round.

*Figures are thousands of person-days (estimated) on an average per week. Figures in parentheses are the percentages of the total in each expenditure group. Time for which the "usual status" workers were openly unemployed (seeking and/or available for work).

†Category includes all women from agricultural labor households who usually work as casual laborers.

‡Percentage of all working (usually active) women in each expenditure group who were willing to take alternative wage- or salary-paid employment inside or outside the village.

questions by referring to the National Sample Survey cross-sectional data set and will make some overall intertemporal comparisons, based on Rural Labor Enquiries data.

Between the mid-1960s and the mid-1970s, the rural work force in West Bengal became more proletarianized;[18] the proportion of women among farm laborers increased[19] and their absolute number tripled. Although the number of laborers increased greatly, the average per capita employment hardly increased at all. The average amount of time expended per week in agricultural-wage employment by a female laborer remained practically unchanged at the low level of about twenty-eight hours (as against about forty hours by a male laborer). The seasonal fluctuations in employment and wages were also much more acute for a female laborer (specifically, the seasonal drop in both employment and wage rate) (table 10.5). Correspondingly, the duration of unemployment for her was longer and was concentrated in the slack season from April to June. The reported (self-recognized) unemployment figure for a woman laborer between April and June 1973 was twenty-one hours per week; if we regard the "usual" laborer's seasonal increase in time spent on domestic work as a form of hidden unemployment, then her unemployment figure appears to be twenty-four hours a week during that quarter. The male-female wage gap also widened during the slack quarter. The combined result was that women's weekly earnings suffered a much larger decline than men's: they fell by 80 percent from the weekly earnings in the busiest season of sowing and transplantation (July–September), as opposed to a 30 percent drop for a male farm laborer.

The growth in wage labor participation at low employment intensity and for a low wage is characteristic of a situation where the poverty-driven female labor supply is crowded into a limited number of outlets. Apart from offering a cheap supply of labor for female-specialized operations like paddy transplanting, the reserve of impoverished female labor is drawn at the margin to hold back the rise in the male farm wage. Discrimination is not just an attitudinal matter; it is also a profitable strategy for the employers with market power. However, using the cheaper female unemployed for "male" operations might risk a local drop in total labor supply through excessive out-migration induced by male unemployment and thus make it harder for

18. According to the Rural Labor Enquiries for 1964–65 and 1974–75, the proportion of rural households in West Bengal with agricultural wage labor as the primary occupation increased from 25 percent to 31 percent between the two years. The absolute number of these farm labor households increased from 1.2 to 1.8 million. The rise is explained by three factors: large population increase on a marginally increasing land and irrigation base; low agricultural growth rate in the state; and increased concentration of farm size distribution.

19. The proportion of women among agricultural laborers in West Bengal increased from a stable 14–15 percent in 1956–57 and in 1964–65 to 20 percent in 1974–75. Among agricultural and nonagricultural rural laborers combined, the female proportion increased from 20 percent to 24 percent (Rural Labor Enquiries data).

TABLE 10.5. Seasonal Fluctuations in Employment and Wages of Casual Agricultural Laborers (15–59 years)

| | Females | | | | | Males | | | | |
| | Casual Farm Employment (days/wk.) | All Employment (days/wk.) | Unemployment (days/wk.) | Casual Farm Wage | | Casual Farm Employment (days/wk.) | All Employment (days/wk.) | Unemployment (days/wk.) | Casual Farm Wage | |
Quarter	(1)	(2)	(3)	Rs/day (4)	Rs/wk. (5)	(6)	(7)	(8)	Rs/day (9)	Rs/wk. (10)
Oct.–Dec.	3.93 (93)	4.49 (92)	1.12	2.29	8.99	5.28 (100)	6.08 (100)	0.53	2.76	14.59
Jan.–Mar.	2.21 (52)	3.23 (66)	2.50	2.09	4.62	4.12 (78)	5.15 (85)	1.47	2.46	10.16
Apr.–June	1.91 (45)	3.05 (63)	2.57	1.76	3.36	4.44 (84)	5.15 (85)	1.57	2.56	11.38
July–Sept.	4.24 (100)	4.86 (100)	1.28	2.64	11.18	4.90 (73)	5.67 (93)	0.86	3.11	15.23
Oct. 1972– Sept. 1973	3.15	3.97	1.83	2.33	7.33	4.69	5.52	1.11	2.75	12.91

Source: National Sample Survey, twenty-seventh round.
Notes: A casual agricultural laborer is one who usually works as a casual laborer and who belongs to a household in which agricultural labor is the principal occupation. Figures in parentheses in the first and the second columns are percentages of the highest quarterly figure.

the village landed to hold onto enough landless labor families at low wages without resorting to a great deal of overt labor-tying.[20]

The male-female gaps in the wages and employment of farm laborers seem to be negatively correlated with the level of agricultural development and the intensity of cultivation. A more stagnant agriculture evidently sustains operational segmentation of the labor market; higher agricultural intensity tends to favor female wages and employment relative to those of males. This tendency is evident from intertemporal, interseasonal, and interregional comparisons. Let me summarize these three sets of evidence.

Between 1964–65 and 1974–75, although most of the farm wage increase in West Bengal was canceled out by a rise in the food price (or in the farm laborers' cost of living index), there was still a narrowing of the male-female wage gap. This, together with the increased proportion of women among farm laborers, indicates the effect of even a moderate agricultural growth on labor demand for the traditionally female operations. It may also indicate some marginal substitution in the traditionally male-dominated operations.

Across seasons and districts in the 1972–73 data set, a similar tendency is observed. The gaps become narrower (1) during the agricultural peak season compared with the slack season, and (2) in the agriculturally and industrially more developed regions in the state compared with the less developed regions. During the busy season (July–September), the female farm laborer earned 27 percent less than the male farm laborer; during the slack season (April–June), she earned 70 percent less than the male farm laborer.

Comparison of the districts (table 10.6) shows that some of the lowest, and seasonally most fluctuating, employment levels for women and some of their highest time-rates of unemployment occur in the less developed districts: Midnapore and Purulia in the eastern part of the state, Murshidabad and West Dinajpur in the north. The rate of women's employment is higher and seasonally more stable in the agriculturally prosperous districts, Birbhum and Burdwan, and in Hooghly, where the development level for agriculture *and* industry taken together is relatively high. The advanced districts have less labor market segmentation, but they also have a much more class-polarized agrarian structure, with a proportionally small family labor–based peasant class in between the semilandless laborers and the labor-hiring affluent farmers, compared with the districts that have the lowest agricultural productivity in the state (P. K. Bardhan 1982). Agricultural growth, to the extent it has occurred, has tended to undermine the social-hierarchical segmentation of rural labor markets and also to proletarianize the agricul-

---

20. Not surprisingly, farm labor is mainly casual in West Bengal; bonded laborers and permanent farm servants are uncommon here. But in the agriculturally growing regions, which have a tightening labor market, there is evidence of a narrowing male-female gaps and an increasing incidence of various forms of contractual labor-tying.

TABLE 10.6. Employment and Unemployment of Rural Women (15–44 years) usually in Labor Force, in Relation to District Development

District	District Development Index*	Percentage of Cultivated Area Irrigated†	Fertilizer Use per Acre (lbs. N)‡	Days/Week per Woman — Employed	Days/Week per Woman — Unemployed	Min./Max. of Quarterly Averages of Days per Week§ — Employed	Min./Max. of Quarterly Averages of Days per Week§ — Unemployed
Darjeeling	99.4	2 }	1	5.04	0.45	0.84	0.87
Jalpaiguri	100.8			4.33	0.79	0.51	0.78
Cooch Bihar	84.8			4.40	1.73	0.33	0.95
West Dinajpur	71.3			3.63	1.16	0.56	0.88
Malda	87.8	10 }	8 }	5.74	0.44	0.65	0.91
Murshidabad	74.3			3.84	1.66	0.46	0.83
Nadia	65.9			4.16	0.43	0.68	0.94
24 Parganas	100.0	4 }	13 }	4.50	0.62	0.78	0.94
Howrah	82.8		20 }	2.88	1.19	0.32	0.64
Hooghly	111.1	37	33	4.26	0.63	0.76	0.94
Burdwan	117.3	59	20	4.37	1.26	0.72	0.82
Birbhum	124.5	53	26	5.63	0.74	0.72	0.93
Bankura	97.9	22	15	3.18	2.54	0.55	0.79
Midnapur	93.3	10	10	4.23	1.27	0.69	0.90
Purulia	77.3	11	2	3.73	0.88	0.58	0.82

*The Reserve Bank of India Bulletin (October 1969) included a composite index of agricultural development for most districts in India in the mid-1960s. This index is a weighted average of a number of agroclimatic and commercialization indexes relating to (1) percentage of gross cropped area irrigated, (2) multiple-cropping intensity, (3) average rainfall, (4) soil rating, (5) percentage of area under cash crops, and (6) surplus of cereals over consumption in the district. I have used the composite index for the year 1964–65 for the districts in West Bengal.

†Figures are for 1972–73 and refer to irrigated and total operated area for the sample households covered by the National Sample Survey, twenty-seventh round.

‡Chemical fertilizer use figures for 1974–75, from West Bengal State Statistical Board bulletins, have been divided by cropped acreage figures.

§Total employment per week for a woman aged 15–44 who is usually in labor force (employed and/or seeking employment) was calculated for each quarter. The lowest quarterly average is expressed here as a proportion of the highest quarterly average. Same for days unemployed. Data from National Sample Survey, twenty-seventh round.

tural work force. The high-growth areas have a higher incidence of politicized movements and encounters that might be indicative of the incipient unionization of farm labor.

The experience of India is that neither rapid agricultural growth (as in Punjab and Haryana) nor unionization (as in Kerala) is quite sufficient to eliminate rural poverty, rooted as it is in cumulative discrimination and the resource handicap of certain population groups. The poverty-targeted programs adopted in India so far are oriented mainly to the poor as producers rather than to the poor as laborers. Training and work programs specifically targeted on the asset-poorest rural laborers might improve their bargaining position by widening the range of employment choices. Since young girls, in the usually nuclear households of landless laborers, often have to take over the collection, maintenance, and housekeeping activities and thus miss education even if it is made available, there is also a very urgent need for organizing —at the group-specific level, and at the workplace—facilities that will reduce the time landless rural labor families need to spend on these activities.

SUMMARY

In this paper I have studied the patterns of work participation and occupational differentiation among rural women and the condition of the female laborers at the bottom of the occupational scale with respect to both social hierarchy and segmentation of the farm labor market by sex and caste/ethnic position.

The patterns of work participation, withdrawal, and division of labor are explained by hierarchy and by income and landholding structures, as well as by the production environment of the rural economy. I have focused on three aspects of female time disposition and earning power: (1) domestic work, (2) effects of landholding and caste/ethnic position, and (3) male-female gaps in wages and employment among farm laborers.

For women in the relatively affluent middle and upper social strata, domestic work is largely a status-oriented preference. Part of the time spent in domestic work by poorer women from low-caste or tribal families is disguised unemployment resulting from a seasonally or generally slack market. Such time is allocated to the labor market during peak seasons and when there is agricultural growth. A large part of the domestic work done by the rural poor includes many gathering activities as well. In nuclear labor households, poverty and low status impose a double burden on the working women and mean loss of education for girls.

Landholding and caste/ethnic position are the two major socioeconomic correlates of female work participation and occupational division. The land-poor, lowest caste, and tribal women have a higher participation rate and are concentrated in farm labor. Employment is less common among the others and is concentrated in nonfarm occupations. There is a significant degree of, though not complete, stratification because of a double dichotomy between farm and nonfarm work and between wage employment and family employment. The degree of this kind of stratification is much less in evidence in the male work pattern. Male time is concentrated in farm work and particularly in farm self-employment, both across caste/ethnic groups and across farm-size groups.

Among farm laborers, female wage and employment levels are generally lower and seasonally more unstable than are those of males. The main economic explanation for the operationally segmented farm labor market, though its rationalization is often couched in terms of custom and alleged efficiency differences, is that the employers thus insure against the excessive out-migration of landless labor families and against the labor supply uncertainty of peak seasons by giving priority to male laborers during the slack seasons, in spite of the cheaper availability of female labor. Such an arrangement serves informally to tie in the male laborers, who are often the prime movers in the migration of landless families. Employers gain from this segmentation that depresses wages in two ways: by inhibiting the male unemployment–induced outflow of entire labor families, and by maintaining a reserve of cheaper female labor to hold down wage increases at the margin.

The female laborers' higher unemployment rate (even at the lower wages), and their responsiveness to increases in labor demand, make it very likely that agricultural growth will tend to increase the female laborers' share of farm wage employment and their relative wage. This conclusion is consistent with intertemporal, cross-seasonal, and interdistrict data relating to rural West Bengal. Thus, in areas with a large proportion of landless labor households, female employment and wages will remain relatively more depressed unless increased measures are taken to initiate the process of agricultural growth. Because agricultural growth by itself is not reducing poverty as much as it is reducing rural labor market segmentation, the need for poverty-targeted programs will remain strong even in the high-growth regions.

III

Econometric Models of Labor Supply and Demand

11

Determinants of Wage Rates and Labor Supply Behavior in the Rural Sector of a Developing Country

Mark R. Rosenzweig

This paper is concerned with the determination of wages and family labor supply in the agricultural sector of a developing country. The available literature assumes but does not test that (1) rural labor markets in less developed countries (LDCs) are noncompetitive, with rigid, institutionally set exogenous wages (Bardhan and Srinivasan 1971); (2) significant underemployment or unemployment exists (Lewis 1954; Ranis and Fei 1961); (3) "special" models of rural households differentiated by size of landholding and/or access to labor markets, are appropriate (Sen 1966); and (4) rural labor is homogeneous (Bardhan and Srinivasan 1971; Sen 1966). Recent developments in the study of labor supply and the availability of both household and aggregate data (from India) appear to facilitate rigorous tests of the implications of alternative assumptions—that rural wage rates for different age/sex groups are endogenous and are affected by relative supplies of labor and that the supply of labor from all rural households to the market is determined by a neoclassical optimization process similar to that characterizing family labor supply decisions in developed countries.

Although the implict assumption of most of the development literature is that the neoclassical competitive framework is inappropriate for the study of LDCs, many characteristics of the rural areas of developing nations may make the application of the neoclassical labor supply model more appealing when applied to the labor markets in those countries than to the developed-country labor markets; for example, labor within age/sex groups is less heterogenous (but wage rates within narrowly defined occupations vary greatly because of geographical immobility), nonpecuniary differences in wage-paying jobs are likely to be fewer, taxation of earnings may be ignored, and the amount of time worked may be more flexible. Unfortunately, the standard neoclassical family labor supply model, designed to explain behavior in developed-country labor markets (Kosters 1966; Ashenfelter and Heckman 1974), yields few predictions that are testable without high-quality data on nonearnings income, which are particularly difficult to obtain in developing countries. It is shown here, however, that the extension of the theory to households owning land (a major part of the rural households in India), and the comparison of landless and landholding household market supply relationships, yield an array of refutable predictions that do not require the estimation of compensated effects and do not appear to be readily derived from the surplus labor hypothesis. In order to both derive predictions and test them, however, it is additionally assumed that the market for land is imperfect—with landownership exogenously fixed—and that geographical mobility is insignificant, such that India is composed of a large number of geographically distinct, competitive rural labor markets. This latter assumption is also tested. The model is thus neither "perfectly" competitive nor fully general.

In the first section I show that there is a spatial distribution of agricultural wages and wage differentials for males, females, and children across Indian districts, which does not appear to be consistent with a simple institutional wage hypothesis or with the assumption that labor is homogenous. I also present descriptive data on the labor force characteristics of rural Indian households by access to land and land size that indicate that almost all households in Indian agriculture participate as buyers or sellers, or both, in the wage labor market. In the second section, a competitive, three-sector general equilibrium model of an agricultural labor market with two kinds of labor, based on neoclassical labor supply assumptions and consistent with the features of Indian agriculture discussed in the earlier section, is formulated and the stability and other properties of the equilibrium are described. In the third section I utilize district-level Indian data to examine the simultaneous determination of rural wages and labor supply for men, women, and children across labor markets and test the implications of the neoclassical model of male and female labor supply in both landed and landless families using household-level Indian data.

The empirical results do not support the institutional or exogenous wage hypotheses, indicating that rural wages are influenced by shifts in demand and supply within the agricultural sector, and appear to be consistent with the implication of the neoclassical framework that the annual number of days of wage employment observed for individuals is mainly supply determined. Geographical immobility, however, appears to be a marked characteristic of rural labor markets, particularly for males in landholding households and for all females.

CHARACTERISTICS OF THE RURAL LABOR MARKET

Two salient but neglected features of the Indian agricultural labor market are (1) the heterogeneity of the labor force and (2) the pervasiveness of some form of labor market participation by all rural households. With respect to labor

TABLE 11.1. Distribution of Districts in India by Age/Sex Group and by Daily Wages, 1960–61 (annual averages)

Rupees per Day	Men		Women		Children	
	Number	*Percentage*	*Number*	*Percentage*	*Number*	*Percentage*
0.25–0.50	—	—	—	—	16	9.0
0.50–0.75	—	—	24	12.9	68	38.4
0.75–1.00	8	4.1	67	36.0	51	28.8
1.00–1.25	55	28.4	34	18.3	21	11.9
1.25–1.50	46	23.8	25	13.7	14	7.9
1.50–1.75	28	14.5	20	10.8	4	2.3
1.75–2.00	14	7.3	9	4.8	1	0.6
2.00–2.25	13	6.7	5	2.7	1	0.6
2.25–2.50	18	9.3	2	1.1	1	0.6
2.50–2.75	5	2.6	—	—	—	—
2.75–3.00	3	1.6	—	—	—	—
3.00–3.25	2	1.0	—	—	—	—
3.25–3.50	—	—	—	—	—	—
3.50–3.75	1	0.5	—	—	—	—
Total districts	193		186		177	
Mean wage	1.54		1.13		0.86	

Source: Directorate of Economics and Statistics, *Agricultural Wages in India, 1960–61,* Delhi, 1965.

force composition, there are at least three distinct groups—male, female, child—that appear to perform different agricultural tasks and that receive different wage rates even for the same category of work. The distribution of annual average daily agricultural wage levels and wage differentials by age and sex for up to 193 Indian districts in thirteen states in 1960–61 for which such data are available is shown in tables 11.1 and 11.2. Whereas the inter-district variance in wage levels might be explained by the differences in con-sumer prices, the variation in intergroup wage ratios cannot. Wage levels for each age/sex group do not appear to be "pushed up" against some minimum subsistence level, although the number of observations does not allow mak-ing the standard Kolmogorov–Smirnov test to discriminate among different hypothesized distributions. Thus, there does not appear to be either one institutional wage or a "law of institutional wage differences" (Hansen 1969) in India. However, it is possible that these wage data are inaccurate, with all observed differences representing "noise." A stronger test, based on predic-tions from the competitive framework, is performed below.

Table 11.3 shows the extent of labor market participation by rural households in India in 1970–71, stratified by gross cropped area, computed from an all-India survey of 5,115 rural households collected by the National Council of Applied Economic Research (NCAER) for the periods 1968–69, 1969–70, and 1970–71. The table is based on households that supplied in-

TABLE 11.2. Distribution of Districts in India by Wage Differentials for Women and
Children, 1960–61 (annual averages)

Percentage of	Women		Children	
Men's Wages	Number	Percentage	Number	Percentage
10–15	5	3.1	2	1.2
15–20	—	—	—	—
20–25	—	—	1	0.6
25–30	—	—	1	0.6
30–35	—	—	6	3.8
35–40	—	—	7	4.4
40–45	3	1.9	26	16.4
45–50	6	3.8	23	14.5
50–55	5	3.1	26	16.4
55–60	13	8.2	22	13.8
60–65	14	8.8	12	7.5
65–70	15	9.4	10	6.3
70–75	38	23.9	12	7.5
75–80	24	15.1	4	2.5
80–85	15	9.4	3	1.9
85–90	8	5.0	1	0.6
90–95	7	4.4	—	—
95–100	6	3.8	3	1.9
Total districts		159		159
Mean		79.6		55.9

Source: Same as for table 11.1.

formation on all of the charácteristics shown—approximately two-thirds of
the total number of cultivators sampled. One advantage of this data set is that
because higher income households were oversampled, more statistically reliable information on large landowners was provided than in most sample
surveys.

Columns of 1 and 3 of table 11.3 indicate that almost all cultivator
households, large and small, participated actively in the labor market as
either buyers or sellers of labor services; almost 88 percent of the households
that cultivated a gross cropped area of less than 1.5 hectares utilized some
hired labor. Of these small-farm households, 79 percent had some family
members who participated in the labor market (column 5), and 55.1 percent
reported household members who were earning agricultural wages. Although
column 4 suggests that the purchase of hired labor by the smallest farms was
evidently only a seasonal phenomenon, column 2 indicates that the total
number of days in the year spent in agricultural market (off-farm) employment by all members of households with a gross cropped area of less than
1.5 hectares, given an average daily agricultural wage (for all workers) in
1970–71 of about Rs 2, was about 240 or an average of 100 days for each
household member over ten years of age. Average days of off-farm agricul-

TABLE 11.3. Labor Force Characteristics of Indian Rural Households by Land Size, 1970–71

Gross Cropped Area (ha)	Percentage Reporting Agricultural Wage Income (1)	Mean Agricultural Wage Income (2)	Percentage Reporting Payments to Labor (3)	Mean Payments to Labor (4)	Percentage Reporting Wages or Salary Earnings (5)	Mean Wage and Salary Earnings (6)	Percentage Reporting Family Workers* (7)	Number of Households (sample Weight 10^{-3}) (8)
Less than <1.5	55.1	485.3	87.7	64.5	79.0	1,397.26	19.9	3.4
		(551.3)		(83.2)		(1,562)		(20.1)
1.5–3.0	70.5	522.7	83.7	101.4	83.6	925.0	33.3	281
		(555.7)		(139.5)		(1,040)		(16.0)
3.0–4.5	54.3	389.9	78.3	138.7	71.4	812.5	42.7	199
		(500.1)		(214.1)		(1,171)		(15.2)
4.5–6.0	52.7	355.2	82.7	213.8	72.0	843.2	45.0	207
		(460.2)		(413.2)		(1,074)		(14.8)
6.0–8.0	37.2	236.6	85.8	269.8	58.0	792.8	53.4	188
		(394.7)		(381.1)		(1,276)		(10.7)
8.0–10.0	30.0	216.3	85.8	367.3	56.4	923.4	63.6	140
		(414.8)		(506.3)		(1,430)		(9.6)
10.0–15.0	19.7	163.3	90.3	429.4	39.3	714.7	69.4	223
		(428.0)		(589.5)		(1,585)		(6.7)
15.0–20.0	14.6	92.5	94.5	501.5	31.0	417.2	73.2	151
		(285.4)		(657.1)		(881)		(5.1)
20.0–25.0	12.8	108.6	91.9	639.0	35.1	579.9	69.4	94
		(314.6)		(837.9)		(1,002)		(5.6)
25.0–30.0	6.9	87.8	96.0	884.7	32.8	754.6	73.0	58
		(360.8)		(1,100.8)		(1,509)		(4.5)
more than 30.0	3.4	25.3	96.0	1,316.7	21.6	431.3	79.6	88
		(148.3)		(1,609.8)		(995)		(3.4)
Total	40.4	294.3	87.0	418.7	59.3	794.6	48.7	1943

Source: NCAER, Additional Rural Income Survey (ARIS), third round.

Note: Standard errors are in parentheses in cols. 1–7.

*Excludes household work.

tural work per potential household earner drops, as expected, with (effective) land size, with only 3.4 percent of the households with gross cropped area exceeding 30.0 hectares reporting agricultural wage income. Thus these data, although not inconsistent with the existence of seasonal or even year-round underemployment, do not appear to support the assumption that agriculture in India is dualistic in the sense that family members on small farms cannot find substantial amounts of market work as hired agricultural laborers.

Moreover, whereas 96 percent of the largest farms hired labor, 80 percent also utilized family workers. (A family worker was defined in the survey as an individual over ten years of age who spends the major part of the year working his or her own land.) The proportion of farms reporting family laborers declines, as expected, with farm size, with less than 20 percent of the smallest farms reporting family workers. These data thus indicate the purchase of labor by almost all farms regardless of size and the extensive use of family labor by the largest farms. They suggest that the usual "dichotomization" of cultivating households by objective function (small-farm households maximizing utility, large-farm owners maximizing profits and using only hired labor) would appear to be not only counterfactual but less useful than merely distinguishing large and small farms according to whether they are net importers or exporters of labor services.

These "gross" data do not appear to support many of the characterizations of rural labor markets founded on noncompetitive assumptions. However, to more accurately assess the ability of a neoclassical framework to "explain" the data, it is necessary to formulate a more rigorous model that can be systematically tested.

THE COMPETITIVE MARKET MODEL AND PROPERTIES OF EQUILIBRIUM

The Model

To capture the essential features of rural agriculture highlighted in the preceding section and to maintain tractability, I assume a labor market composed of two types of labor, "male" and "female," and three agricultural households—a landless household and two households with different-size plots (small and large) of quality-standardized land producing a homogeneous agricultural commodity. The market is initially assumed to be competitive so that all households are price-takers, but wage rates are determined endogenously. There are, however, fixed costs per unit of labor time spent on the land owned by other households, which are assumed to be borne entirely by workers. Each household includes two persons, one of each labor type, each owning a unit of labor time. The two types of labor are imperfect substitutes in agricultural production but labor of each type from different households is perfectly substitutable.

The landless household supplies $\ell_{fM}^N = 1 - \ell_M^N$ and $\ell_{fW}^N = 1 - \ell_W^N$ amounts of labor to the market, where ℓ_M^N and ℓ_W^N are the quantities of leisure time of the "husband" and "wife" in the landless household. Total consumption of the landless family, assuming no saving and a unit price for the composite consumption commodity, is thus

$$X^N = \ell_{fM}^N \Pi_M^N + \ell_{fW}^N \Pi_W^N, \tag{11.1}$$

where $\Pi_K^N = W_K - \rho_K$ ($K = M, W$), W_K are the market wages paid to (hired) male and female labor and ρ_K is the fixed cost per unit of labor time supplied to the market.

The small-farm household owns A^S units of land and is by definition a net exporter of the labor services of both the husband and the wife. The large-farm household owns θA^S units of land, where θ is a scalar chosen such that the household is an importer of labor. If we denote L_M^i and L_W^i, $i = S, L$, as the total amounts of male and female labor utilized on the land owned by each landowning household, then the quantities of male and female labor supplied (exported) to the market by the small household, λ_M^S and λ_W^S, and the amounts of labor hired (imported) by the large landowning family, λ_M^L and λ_W^L, are given by

$$\lambda_K^S = \ell_{fK}^S - L_K^S > 0 \tag{11.2}$$

and

$$\lambda_K^L = L_K^L - \ell_{fK}^L > 0, \qquad K = M, W, \tag{11.3}$$

where ℓ_{fK}^i is the total work time of family member K on the farm of size i.

The quantities consumed by the landowning households, X^S and X^L, are thus

$$X^i = F(L_M^i, L_W^i, \theta^j A^S) + \lambda_M^i \Pi_M^i + \lambda_W^i \Pi_W^i, \qquad i = S, L, \qquad j = \begin{matrix} 0 \text{ for } i = S \\ 1 \text{ for } i = L \end{matrix}, \tag{11.4}$$

where $\Pi_K^L = W_K$, $\Pi_K^S = W_K - \rho_K$, and F is a twice, continuously differentiable, strictly concave production function with positive cross-partials.

Each of the three households maximizes an identical, twice differentiable family utility function, given by equation (11.5), with respect to the consumption commodity X^i and the leisure of the two household members, each of which is assumed to be noninferior, subject to the relevant budget constraints in equations (11.1) and (11.4):

$$U = U(X^i, \ell_M^i, \ell_W^i), \qquad i = N, S, L. \tag{11.5}$$

If only interior solutions are considered, the necessary conditions for each household, in addition to those implied by the budget constraints, are given by equations (11.6) through (11.8):

$$U_X^i - \Psi^i = 0, \qquad i = N, S, L, \tag{11.6}$$

$$U_{\ell_k}^i - \Psi^i \Pi_K^i = 0, \qquad i = N, S, L, \tag{11.7}$$

and

$$F_{L_K}^i - \Pi_K^i = 0, \qquad i = S, L, \tag{11.8}$$

where Ψ^i is the Lagrangian multiplier for household i.

Equations (11.7) and (11.8) give the standard utility and profit-maximizing results describing the optimal quantities of leisure and total labor use, if any, for each household. With $\rho_K > 0$, the market is dualistic in the sense that small landowning households utilize more labor per acre than large landowners because of the differential shadow prices of labor: $F_{L_K}^S < W_K$, $F_{L_K}^L = W_K$. Each member of the small landowning household allocates his (her) labor on the family's land up to the point where the value of his (her) marginal product just equals the net wage he (she) receives in the market, $W_K - \rho_K$. Members of the large landowning households devote all their work time to their own land and hire each type of labor up to the point at which the marginal value product of that labor type is equal to the appropriate market wage, W_K.

Comparative Statics

To derive the partial equilibrium comparative static properties for the three households, we first write the following matrix:

$$\beta^i = \begin{bmatrix} U_{XX}^i & U_{X\ell_M}^i & U_{X\ell_W}^i & -1 \\ U_{X\ell_M}^i & U_{\ell_M\ell_M}^i & U_{\ell_W\ell_M}^i & -\Pi_M^i \\ U_{X\ell_W}^i & U_{\ell_M\ell_W}^i & U_{\ell_W\ell_W}^i & -\Pi_W^i \\ -1 & -\Pi_M^i & -\Pi_W^i & 0 \end{bmatrix}, \qquad i = N, S, L.$$

Differentiating equations (11.1), (11.6), and (11.7) for $i = N$, we get

$$[\beta^N] \begin{bmatrix} dX \\ d\ell_M \\ d\ell_W \\ d\Psi^N \end{bmatrix} = \begin{bmatrix} \Psi^N dW_M - \Psi^N d\rho_M \\ \Psi^N dW_W - \Psi^N d\rho_W \\ -\ell_{fM}^N dW_M - \ell_{fW}^N dW_w \ell_{fM}^N d\rho_M \ell_{fW}^N d\rho_W \end{bmatrix}. \tag{11.9}$$

β^N is thus the bordered Hessian matrix for the landless household. Denoting the determinant of β^i as ϕ^i and the cofactor of row r and column c of β^i as ϕ_{rc}^i, we obtain the standard Slutsky equations for the landless household's labor supply:

$$\frac{d\ell_{fK}^N}{dW_K} = -\psi^N \frac{\phi_{nn}^N}{\phi^N} + \ell_{fK}^N \frac{\phi_{4n}^N}{\phi^N} = \sigma_{KK}^N - \ell_{fK}^N \sigma_K^N, \qquad \begin{array}{l} K = M, n = 2, \\ K = W, n = 3, \end{array} \quad (11.10)$$

and

$$\frac{d\ell_{fK}^N}{dW_h} = -\psi^N \frac{\phi_{23}^N}{\phi^N} - \ell_{fh}^N \frac{\phi_{4n}^N}{\phi^N} = \sigma_{Kh}^N - \ell_{fh}^N \sigma_K^N. \qquad K \neq h. \quad (11.11)$$

Second-order conditions constrain the first term in equation (11.10), the compensated substitution effect, to be positive, since $\phi^N < 0$ and $\phi_{nn}^N > 0$. The normality assumption, however, implies that the income effect on work time, σ_K^N, is negative so that equation (11.10) is consistent with either a backward-bending or a positively sloped supply curve for landless laborers of either sex. The sign of equation (11.11) depends on whether the leisure times of the husband and wife are complements or substitutes, being unambiguously negative if the leisure times of the spouses are substitutes. Total differentiation of equations (11.4) and (11.6) through (11.8) for $i = S, L$ yields:

$$\begin{bmatrix} U_{XX}^i & U_{X\ell_M}^i & U_{X\ell_W}^i & 0 & 0 & -1 \\ U_{X\ell_M}^i & U_{\ell_M\ell_M}^i & U_{\ell_M\ell_W}^i & 0 & 0 & -\Pi_M^i \\ U_{X\ell_W}^i & U_{\ell_M\ell_W}^i & U_{\ell_W\ell_W}^i & 0 & 0 & -\Pi_W^i \\ 0 & 0 & 0 & F_{L_M L_M}^i & F_{L_M L_W}^i & 0 \\ 0 & 0 & 0 & F_{L_M L_W}^i & F_{L_W L_W}^i & 0 \\ -1 & -\Pi_M^i & -\Pi_W^i & 0 & 0 & 0 \end{bmatrix} \begin{bmatrix} dX^i \\ d\ell_M^i \\ d\ell_W^i \\ dI_M^i \\ dL_W^i \\ d\Psi^i \end{bmatrix}$$

$$= \begin{bmatrix} -\Psi^i dW_M \\ -\Psi^i dW_W \\ -dW_M - F_{L_M A^i} dA^i \\ -dW_W - F_{L_W A^i} dA^i \\ (L_M^i - \ell_{fM}^i) dW_M (L_W^i - \ell_{fW}^i) dW_W - F_{A^i} dA^i \end{bmatrix} . \quad (11.12)$$

Noting that β^i is the second bordered principal minor of the bordered Hessian matrix in equation (11.12) and must be negative, we obtain the following results for the two landowning households, employing Cramer's rule:

$$\frac{d\ell_{fK}^i}{dW_K} = -\psi^i \frac{\phi_{nn}^i}{\phi^i} + (L_K^i - \ell_{fK}^i) \frac{\phi_{4n}^i}{\phi^i} = \sigma_{KK}^i - (L_K^i - \ell_{fK}^i)\sigma_K^i, \qquad n = 2, 3, \quad (11.13)$$

$$\frac{d\ell_{fK}^i}{dw_h} = -\psi^i \frac{\phi_{23}^i}{\phi^i} + (L_n^i - \ell_{fK}^i) \frac{\phi_{4n}^i}{\phi^i} = \sigma_{Kh}^i - (L_h^i - \ell_{fh}^i)\sigma_K^i, \quad (11.14)$$

$$\frac{dL_k^i}{dW_h} = \frac{F_{\ell_K \ell_h}^i}{\Delta^i} \begin{array}{l} < 0 \text{ for } k = h \\ > 0 \text{ for } k \neq h \end{array}, \tag{11.15}$$

$$\frac{d\ell_{fK}^i}{dA^i} = F_A^i \frac{\phi_{4n}^i}{\phi^i} = -F_{A^i}\sigma_K^i < 0, \tag{11.16}$$

and

$$\frac{dL_K^i}{dA^i} = \frac{F_{L_h A}^i F_{L_M L_W}^i - F_{L_K A}^i F_{L_h L_h}^i}{\Delta^i}, \tag{11.17}$$

where $\Delta^i = F_{L_W L_W}^i F_{L_M L_M}^i - (F_{L_M L_W}^i)^2 > 0$.

Equations (11.13) and (11.14), which give the own and cross wage effects on the total supply of work time for each household member in the landowning households, indicate that the substitution and income effects in those households are qualitatively similar to those in the landless households and are identical if the labor market is nondualistic and competitive ($\Pi_K^N = \Pi_K^S = W_K$) and if the utility function in equation (11.5) is homothetic. However, the uncompensated own wage effect on total (family) labor supply in labor-importing farms, in contrast to landless laborers and small landowners (labor exporters), is unambigiously positive, since a wage rise must lower net income for these households.

An important implication of equations (11.15) and (11.17), giving the (own and cross) effects of a rise in wage rates and landholdings on total labor usage on the landowning farms, is that the "production" and "consumption" sectors of the farms are independent, as equations (11.15) and (11.17) depend only on the properties of the production function. Thus if competitive conditions prevail, the partial equilibrium changes in the allocation of production resources will be identical whether or not (some) households maximize utility or profits. However, as will be shown below, the assumption that large landowners maximize utility and utilize family labor has consequences for the allocation of market (nonfamily) labor and thus for the levels of the equilibrium wage rates and the stability of the rural labor markets, which are functions of market supply and demand curves only.

The relationship between the supply of off-farm labor of type K from small farms and changes in wage rates, from equations (11.13), (11.14), and (11.15), is expressed in equation (11.18):

$$\frac{d\lambda_K^S}{dW_h} = \left[\sigma_{Kh}^S - \frac{F_{L_K L_h}^S}{\Delta^S} \right] - \lambda_h^S \sigma_K^S. \tag{11.18}$$

Whereas for $K = h$, the terms in brackets (the own compensated substitution effect and the negative of the labor usage effect) must be greater than zero, expression (11.18) may be of either sign because of the positive income effect on leisure. We note, however, that a comparison of equation (11.18) with equation (11.10), giving the own uncompensated wage effect on the labor supplied to the market by members of landless households, suggests that the wage effect on the market supply of (small) landowners will exceed that on the labor supply of the landless, given identical income effects (homotheticity), because of the allocation of labor to own farm production. This prediction, based on the land status distinction under neoclassical assumptions, is tested in the last section.

For the labor-importing, utility-maximizing farms, the own and cross wage effects on the quantity of labor of sex K hired, λ_K^L, is given by:

$$\frac{d\lambda_K^L}{dW_h} = \left[\frac{F_{L_K L_h}}{\Delta^L} - \sigma_{Kh}^L\right] - \lambda_h^L \sigma_K^L. \tag{11.19}$$

Since the demand for all labor of sex K to be used in agricultural production decreases and the quantity of labor supplied by family members of sex K increases when W_K rises, a priori, the demand for hired labor must decline in response to a wage rise. Because of this family labor supply effect, equation (11.19) implies that (1) utility-maximizing large farms will display more elastic demand curves for hired labor than farms using only hired labor, and (2) the demand for hired labor is a function of unearned income or wealth.

The effects of an exogenous increase in household landholdings on the off-farm labor supply (small farms) and on the demand for hired labor of sex K (large farms), given by equations (11.20) and (11.21), depend also on both production and income-leisure effects but are of unambiguous signs. An increase in the size

$$\frac{d\lambda_K^S}{dA} = -F_A^S \sigma_K^S - \left(\frac{F_{L_h A}^S F_{L_K L_h}^S - F_{L_K A}^S F_{L_h L_h}^S}{\Delta^S}\right) < 0 \tag{11.20}$$

$$\frac{d\lambda_K^L}{dA} = F_A^L \sigma_K^L + \left(\frac{F_{L_h A}^L F_{L_K L_h}^L - F_{L_K A}^L F_{L_h L_h}^L}{\Delta^L}\right) > 0 \tag{11.21}$$

of labor-exporting farms will reduce their supply of labor to other farms; an increase in the holdings of labor-exporting households will increase the demand for hired labor because of reinforcing production and income-leisure effects.

Labor Market Equilibrium

Labor market equilibrium is characterized by equations (11.1), (11.4), and (11.6) through (11.8), as well as the equilibrium conditions in equation (11.22):

$$\ell_{fK}^N + \lambda_K^S = \lambda_K^L, \qquad K = M, W. \tag{11.22}$$

A necessary condition for (Hicksian) multimarket static stability in the market for hired agricultural labor, from equations (11.13), (11.18), and (11.19), is that

$$\frac{d(\lambda_K^L - \lambda_K^S - \ell_{fK}^N)}{dW_K} = \sum_{i=S,L} \frac{F_{L_K L_K}^i}{\Delta^i} - \sum_{i=S,L,N} \sigma_{KK}^i - \lambda_K^L \sigma_K^L + \ell_{fk}^N \sigma_K^N + \lambda_k^s \sigma^s < 0.$$

(11.23)

The assumptions imposed in the analysis so far do not ensure that the condition in equation (11.23) will be met; it is thus possible that with sufficiently negatively sloped market supply curves of agricultural labor, the market equilibrium will not be stable. However, the likelihood that static instability is the major reason for the existence of institutional (nonmarket determined) wages is low. Positive income-leisure effects in small-landowner and landless households must be extremely large—not only exceeding the income effects in labor-importing households, but greater than the sum of the production and consumption substitution effects in all households and the income–labor supply effect in the large households, each of which is negative, for equation (11.23) to be violated. Indeed, the existence of labor-hiring institutions (large landowners) that maximize utility and employ family labor, as in India (table 11.3), as well as of labor-supplying households whose members both work their own land and offer labor services to the market, makes the fulfillment of the static stability conditions more likely in Indian agriculture than in developed-country (modern sector) labor markets. In the latter, employers of hired labor are profit maximizers and household members who supply labor do not participate in household income production, so three negative terms tending toward stability, $F_{L_K L_K}^S/\Delta^S$, $-\sigma_{KK}^S$, and $-\lambda^L \sigma_K^L$, will not appear in equation (11.23). Moreover, because of the participation of family members in agricultural production on labor-importing farms, the stability condition must be satisfied if the utility function is homothetic (and $\rho = 0$), since the last three terms in equation (11.23) vanish ($\sigma_K^L = \sigma_K^N = \sigma_K^S$).

General Equilibrium Comparative Statics

Assuming a unique, stable equilibrium, we can ascertain the effects of a change in landholdings A^i, or in any other exogenous variable hypothesized to influence supply behavior, on the wage rates of the two types of labor by totally differentiating equations (11.1), (11.4), (11.6) through (11.8), and (11.22) and solving for dW_M and dW_W. First, let us briefly consider the effects of an increase in nonagricultural factors that might draw labor from all agricultural households. Let Z represent one of these factors employed outside the farm sector such that $d\ell_{fK}^i/dZ < 0$, $i = N, S, L$, so that $d\lambda_K^L/dZ > 0$, $d\lambda_K^S/dZ < 0$. Then for a small change in Z around equilibrium, the effect on male and female agricultural wage rates can be written in terms of the partial equilibrium comparative static results where $\varepsilon_{KX}^i = d\lambda_K^i/dX$:

$$\frac{dW_K}{dZ} = \left[\frac{(d\ell_{fK}^N/dZ + \varepsilon_{KZ}^S - \varepsilon_{KZ}^L)}{(\varepsilon_{KW_K}^L - \varepsilon_{KW_K}^S - \varepsilon_{KW_K}^N)} - \frac{(\varepsilon_{hZ}^S + d\ell_{fh}^N/dZ - \varepsilon_{hZ}^L)}{(\varepsilon_{hW_h}^L - \varepsilon_{hW_h}^S - \varepsilon_{hW_h}^N)}\right.$$
$$\left.\cdot \frac{(\varepsilon_{KW_h}^L - \varepsilon_{KW_h}^S - \varepsilon_{KW_h}^N)}{(\varepsilon_{KW_K}^L - \varepsilon_{KW_K}^S - \varepsilon_{KW_K}^N)}\right]\Omega^{-1}, \tag{11.24}$$

where

$$\Omega = 1 - \frac{(\varepsilon_{KW_h}^L - \varepsilon_{KW_h}^S - \varepsilon_{KW_h}^N)(\varepsilon_{hW_K}^L - \varepsilon_{hW_K}^S - \varepsilon_{hW_K}^N)}{(\varepsilon_{KW_K}^L - \varepsilon_{KW_K}^S - \varepsilon_{KW_K}^N)(\varepsilon_{hW_h}^L - \varepsilon_{hW_h}^S - \varepsilon_{hW_h}^N)}.$$

To sign equation (11.24), we note that the assumption of strict concavity in production and second-order conditions require that $\Omega > 0$ and that if the equilibrium is dynamically stable, from equation (11.23), $(\varepsilon_{KW_K}^L - \varepsilon_{KW_K}^S - \varepsilon_{KW_K}^N) < 0$ and $(\varepsilon_{KW_h}^L - \varepsilon_{KW_h}^S - \varepsilon_{KW_h}^N) > 0$. The first term in brackets (the own wage effect) must therefore be positive and own and cross wage effects are reinforcing so that an increase in nonagricultural capital will increase both male and female wage rates, the magnitude of the effect being positively related to the sensitivity of labor supply to changes in Z and negatively related to the sensitivity of market agricultural demand and supply curves to changes in agricultural wages. This "prediction" of the competitive wage model, that increases in nonagricultural labor demand will raise agricultural wage levels, is one of the few that directly contradict one of the implications drawn from the nutritional wage model by Rodgers (1975), who suggests that increases in slack-season nonagricultural employment may lower all agricultural wages.

The competitive general equilibrium model can also be used to demonstrate that the attenuation of factors inhibiting only female participation in market work, such as religious or cultural attitudes, will not necessarily result in wider male-female wage differentials but will most probably lower agricultural wage rates generally, consistent with Rodgers's (1975) observations. To demonstrate this, let R be an environmental characteristic such that $d\ell_{fW}^N/dR, d\lambda_W^S/dR < 0$; $d\ell_{fM}^N/dR, d\lambda_M^S/dR$, and $d\lambda_K^L/dR = 0$. Then

$$\frac{dW_W}{dR} = \left[\frac{d\ell_{fW}^N/dR + d\lambda_W^S/dR}{(\varepsilon_{WW_W}^L - \varepsilon_{WW_W}^S - \varepsilon_{WW_W}^N)}\right]\Omega^{-1} > 0, \tag{11.25}$$

$$\frac{dW_M}{dR} = \left[\frac{d\ell_{fW}^N/dR + d\lambda_W^S/dR}{(\varepsilon_{WW_W}^L - \varepsilon_{WW_W}^S - \varepsilon_{WW_W}^N)}\right]\left[\frac{(\varepsilon_{WW_M}^L - \varepsilon_{WW_M}^S - \varepsilon_{WW_M}^N)}{(\varepsilon_{MW_M}^L - \varepsilon_{MW_M}^S - \varepsilon_{MW_M}^N)}\right]\Omega^{-1} > 0. \tag{11.26}$$

Equations (11.25) and (11.26) must be greater than zero, so an increase in female market participation must reduce female wage rates and male wage rates as well. However, the change in the wage rate differential, given by equation (11.27), cannot be predicted:

$$\frac{d(W_M - W_W)}{dR} = \left[\frac{d\ell_{fW}^N/dR + d\lambda_W^S/dR}{(\varepsilon_{WW_W}^L - \varepsilon_{WW_W}^S - \varepsilon_{WW_W}^N)} \right]$$
$$\cdot \left[\frac{(\varepsilon_{WW_M}^L - \varepsilon_{WW_M}^S - \varepsilon_{WW_M}^N)}{(\varepsilon_{MW_M}^L - \varepsilon_{MW_M}^S - \varepsilon_{MW_M}^N)} - 1 \right] \Omega^{-1}. \tag{11.27}$$

EMPIRICAL APPLICATIONS

Rural Wage Determination across Indian Districts

In this section data from 159 Indian districts for 1960–61 are used to determine whether the differential levels in annual agricultural wage rates across Indian districts, as presented in table 11.1, are importantly influenced by the variation in factors in the agricultural sector (in contrast to the view expressed by Bardhan and Srinivasan 1971) and, more specifically, whether interdistrict differences in the quantities of rural aggregate market labor supplied to agriculture influence wage levels, in contrast to the institutional wage hypothesis.

The six structural demand and supply equations for hired labor in agriculture to be estimated are given by equations (11.28) and (11.29):

$$W_j = \alpha_L L_j + \alpha_D X_j^D + \alpha_R X_j^R + \alpha_P X_j^P + \alpha_E X_j^E + u_{1j}, \qquad j = 1, \ldots, 159, \tag{11.28}$$

$$L_j = \beta_W W_j + \beta_D X_j^D + \beta_Z X_j^Z + \beta_M X_j^M + \beta_E X_j^E + u_{2j}, \tag{11.29}$$

where W = WAGEM, WAGEF, WAGEC; L = LABM, LABF, LABC; X^D = NOLAND, AVLAND, DIST; X^R = RAIN, IRR; X^Z = URB, FACTRY, FUEL, SCALE; X^M = MUSLIM; X^P = PLANTN; X^E = PRIMM, PRIMF, MATM, MATF, CASTE, and α_L, β_W are 3×3 coefficient matrices. The variables used are defined and their means and standard deviations given in table 11.4.

Each of the six structural equations satisfies the rank and order conditions for identifiability. The four assumptions underlying the coefficient restrictions imposed are as follows.

1. Nonagricultural demand factors X^Z influence only the off-farm labor supply of landless and small-landowning households; they do not significantly attract members of large-farm families away from family agricultural employment and thus do not affect the demand for hired agricultural labor.

TABLE 11.4. Variable Definitions, Means, and Standard Deviations, 159 Indian Districts, 1960–61

Variable	Definition	Mean	Standard Deviation
WAGEM	Daily wage in rupees for male field laborers (sowers, reapers, weeders, plowers)	1.52	0.43
WAGEF	Daily wage in rupees for female field laborers (sowers, reapers, weeders, plowers)	1.11	0.37
WAGEC	Daily wage in rupees for child field laborers and herders	0.85	0.37
LABM	Percentage of males per household aged 15–59 working at least one hour per day as hired agricultural laborers	23.4	11.2
LABF	Percentage of females per household aged 15–59 working at least one hour per day as hired agricultural laborers	22.0	14.4
LABC	Percentage of children per household aged 5–14 working at least one hour per day as hired agricultural laborers	5.75	3.98
PRIMM	Percentage of males aged 15–59 with primary education	12.7	9.27
PRIMF	Percentage of females aged 15–59 with primary education	3.34	4.11
MATM	Percentage of males aged 15–59 with secondary education	2.44	2.50
MATF	Percentage of females aged 15–59 with secondary education	0.27	0.68
RAIN	Average normal rainfall per year in cm	302.2	584.2
IRR	Percentage of cultivated acres irrigated	12.8	17.4
DIST	Kuznets ratio of landholding inequality	81.7	16.3
AVLAND	Average land owned per landowning household	12.4	10.3
NOLAND	Percentage of households without land	34.9	13.1
MUSLIM	Percentage of population Muslim	33.2	66.6
CASTE	Percentage of population in scheduled tribes	12.8	6.32
URB	Proportion of population living in urban areas	0.17	0.11
PLANTN	Dummy = 1 if at least one plantation in district	0.10	
FACTRY	Factories and workshops per household	0.17	0.18
FUEL	Percentage of factories and workshops using power	20.5	19.2
SCALE	Percentage of factories and workshops employing 5 or more persons	3.9	4.0

Source: Rosenzweig (1978).

Note: States covered: Andhra Pradesh, Assam, Bihar, Gujurat, Kerala, Madhya Pradesh, Madras (Tamil Nadu), Maharashtra, Mysore, Orissa, Punjab (and Haryana), Uttar Pradesh.

2. The X^R variables influence only the demand for hired agricultural labor since land-augmenting factors do not directly affect the quantity of labor supplied by landless households.

3. Plantation agriculture, pertaining only to large farms, influences wages directly, and/or the demand for hired laborers, but not the supply of wage labor.

4. The Muslim religion does not affect the demand for hired labor since it would only have a deterrent effect on female off-farm labor supply and thus should not influence the supply of family labor on labor-importing farms. In addition, because of multicollinearity, I set the off-diagonal elements of the β_W matrix equal to zero, thus abstracting from cross-wage effects on household labor supply to the market. I also include only the own education variables in the demand equations.

I have chosen to specify the demand equations in equation (11.28) with the wage rate as the dependent variable so that the direct influence of labor supply changes on wage rates can be more easily tested. If wage rates are influenced by shifts in supply and demand, as assumed in the theoretical analysis, the diagonal elements in the α_L matrix should display negative signs since, from equation (11.25), an increase in the quantity of labor of sex K must have a negative "own" wage effect in equilibrium. The cross-effects are likely, from equation (11.26), to be negative as well.

The uncompensated wage rate effects on market labor supply, in equation (11.27), are theoretically ambiguous, as was shown. However, rigorous tests of neoclassical labor supply behavior, based on the distinction between landed and landless households, are performed using household data in the next section. For purposes of brevity, I also omit discussion of the predicted and actual effects of other variables on wages and wage labor supply; they are discussed in Rosenzweig (1978).

Because of omitted or nonmeasurable variables, the error terms in the six equations are likely to be correlated, especially those within the sets of demand and supply equations, as is confirmed by inspection of the residual correlation matrix (not reported) obtained from the estimation of equations (11.28) and (11.29) by three-stage least squares. Accordingly, I estimate the system of market demand and supply equations using full information maximum likelihood (FIML) to capture the potential efficiency gains indicated by the residual correlations. As a check on the robustness of the results to estimation technique and as insurance against a likelihood function with undesirable properties, I also employ three-stage least squares. The parameter estimates obtained, which have the same asymptotic properties, are indeed quite close. I discuss the FIML estimates rather than those obtained using three-stage least squares because of the additional invariance property of FIML, which may be of importance because of the placement of wages on the left-hand side of the demand equations.

The structural coefficient estimates are shown in table 11.5. Coefficient signs are generally consistent with the expectations generated by the market model of rural agriculture. In particular, the matrix of supply variable coefficient signs in the demand equations is supportive of the market hypothesis, as wages appear to be sensitive to shifts in the supply of laborers for hire—increases in the number of people participating in the agricultural

TABLE 11.5. FIML Coefficient Estimates, 159 Indian Districts, 1960–61

Independent Variable	Dependent Variable					
	WAGEM	*WAGEF*	*WAGEC*	*LABM*	*LABF*	*LABC*
LABM	−0.0055	−0.0342	−0.0501	—	—	—
	(0.39)	(0.24)	(0.31)			
LABF	−0.0285	−0.0321	−0.0325	—	—	—
	(2.49)	(2.78)	(2.30)			
LABC	−0.0295	−0.0440	−0.0395	—	—	—
	(0.79)	(1.30)	(0.98)			
WAGEM	—	—	—	6.82	—	—
				(0.96)		
WAGEF	—	—	—	—	18.94	—
					(1.37)	
WAGEC	—	—	—	—	—	8.68
						(1.07)
AVLAND	0.0170	0.0131	0.0058	−0.173	−0.328	−0.0441
	(3.69)	(3.65)	(1.39)	(1.24)	(1.53)	(0.70)
NOLAND	0.0058	0.0031	−0.0013	0.368	0.390	0.0765
	(1.20)	(0.62)	(0.23)	(4.66)	(3.47)	(2.09)
DIST	−0.0064	−0.0028	−0.0050	0.430	0.606	0.173
	(1.32)	(0.54)	(0.89)	(4.63)	(4.38)	(3.30)
IRR	0.0060	0.0022	0.0002	—	—	—
	(3.41)	(1.23)	(0.10)			
RAIN	0.0003	0.0002	0.0001	—	—	—
	(4.41)	(3.44)	(1.54)			
PRIMM	0.0149	—	—	0.153	0.0092	−0.136
	(4.51)			(1.01)	(0.04)	(1.35)
PRIMF	—	0.0122	—	−0.217	−0.474	−0.0057
		(2.47)		(0.61)	(0.81)	(0.03)
MATM	0.0065	—	—	−0.328	−0.441	−0.158
	(0.65)			(0.89)	(0.80)	(1.02)
MATF	—	−0.117	—	−3.54	−6.59	−2.58
		(0.26)		(2.05)	(2.78)	(2.46)
FACTRY	—	—	—	−4.52	−8.52	−3.32
				(1.09)	(1.31)	(1.80)
SCALE	—	—	—	−0.211	−0.248	−0.102
				(0.84)	(0.65)	(0.97)
FUEL	—	—	—	−0.0382	−0.284	−0.0694
				(0.79)	(2.98)	(1.39)
PLANTN	−0.278	−0.353	−0.277	—	—	—
	(2.21)	(2.88)	(1.95)			
URB	—	—	—	−12.49	−18.11	−4.74
				(1.61)	(1.65)	(1.52)
CASTE	−0.0015	−0.0004	−0.0057	−0.296	−0.838	−0.281
	(0.25)	(0.07)	(0.83)	(1.92)	(2.82)	(1.79)
MUSLIM	—	—	—	0.0411	−0.0092	−0.0229
				(2.32)	(0.33)	(1.38)
Constant	1.64	1.16	0.92	−37.30	−49.74	−12.59
	(7.37)	(5.13)	(3.55)	(2.50)	(2.51)	(2.01)
S.E.E.	0.302	0.302	0.377	8.60	12.43	4.04

Note: Asymptotic *t* values are in parentheses.

labor market, from any age/sex group, reduce all agricultural wage rates. The negative supply effects of males and children on their respective wage rates are not statistically significant, however. The strongest supply impact on wages appears to come from shifts in female participation—a 10 percent increase in the number of women working as hired laborers reduces their own wage rate and those of males and children by 4, 6, and 8 percent, respectively. Contrary to Boserup's (1970) observation, however, we cannot reject the null hypothesis that an increase in female labor supply has equal negative effects on male and female wages; differences in female market participation are therefore not a proximate cause of the variation in male-female wage differentials across Indian districts, although they do significantly affect wage levels. The results also reject the Bardhan–Srinivasan (1971) hypothesis that the set of within-agriculture variables (such as land distribution and schooling) does not significantly affect rural wages directly.

The supply equation structural estimates suggest that the relationship between the quantity of laborers in each age/sex group supplying labor to the agricultural labor market and the level of wage rates is positive, although none of the wage coefficients are statistically significant by conventional standards. The labor supply results, however, support the hypothesis that where alternative employment is available, the amount of labor supplied to agriculture is decreased. This finding implies that wages in agriculture are higher in more "industrialized" rural areas, because of the decreased availability of workers in agriculture, as is evident in the reduced form parameters derived from the structural estimates (not reported).

These aggregate results thus appear to be supportive of a world of geographically distinct, internally competitive rural labor markets with endogenous wages. To examine more closely the theoretical foundations of the labor supply relationships, only crudely analyzed here because the data do not allow separation of landed and landless households as deemed necessary by the theoretical analysis and do not permit distinct estimates of own and cross wage effects on labor supply, I exploit household-level data in the next section.

Labor Supply Behavior: Analysis of Household Data

Data and estimation techniques. In this section the labor supply predictions derived from the landless and landholding household models formulated under the assumption of competitive labor markets are tested using data from the Additional Rural Incomes Survey (ARIS), a national sample survey of rural households in India, collected in three rounds (1968–69, 1969–70, and 1970–71) and coded by the National Council of Applied Economic Research (NCAER). This survey provides information on a wide variety of household and farm characteristics, including the number of days worked annually for pay in agricultural and nonagricultural activities and the earnings from those activities for each household member. The sample used, stratified into landless and landholding households, is based on information collected in the third round of the survey, 1970–71. Households in which either the head or the spouse was absent or was a government employee and/or salaried worker were excluded, so that the data are restricted to cultivators and "casual" workers employed on a monthly or daily basis.

The market (for pay) labor supply equations to be estimated for heads of households and their wives in the two subsamples are given by equations 11.30 and 11.31:

$$\lambda_K^N = \alpha_K^N + \beta_{1K}^N W_M + \beta_{2K}^N W_F + \beta_{3K}^N I^N + \beta_{4K}^N E_M^N + \beta_{5K}^N E_F^N + \beta_{6K}^N e_M^N$$
$$+ \beta_{7K}^N e_F^N + \beta_{ZK}^N Z_K^N + u_K^N, \quad K = M, F, \tag{11.30}$$

and

$$\lambda_K^L = \alpha_K^L + \beta_{1K}^L W_M + \beta_{2K}^L W_F + \beta_{3K}^L I^L + \beta_{4K}^L E_M^L + \beta_{5K}^L E_K^L + \beta_{6K}^L e_M^L$$
$$+ \beta_{7K}^L e_F^L + \sum_{i=8}^{11} \beta_{ik}^L \kappa_i + \beta_{ZK}^L Z_K^L + u_K^L, \tag{11.31}$$

where β_{jK}^N, β_{jK}^L are the relevant coefficients for the landless and landholding households, Z^N, Z^L are vectors of control variables, to be discussed below, and u_K^N, u_K^L are stochastic error terms. The theoretical analysis implies the following coefficient or coefficient differential signs:

1. $\beta_{1M}^L - \beta_{1M}^N > 0$ 6. $\beta_{5K}^L - \beta_{5K}^N < 0$

2. $\beta_{2F}^L - \beta_{2F}^N > 0$ 7. $\beta_{6K}^L - \beta_{6K}^N < 0$

3. $\beta_{3K}^N < 0$ 8. $\beta_{7K}^L - \beta_{7K}^N < 0$

4. $\beta_{3K}^L < 0$ 9. $\beta_{iK}^L < 0$,

5. $\beta_{4K}^L - \beta_{4K}^N < 0$ $i = 8, \ldots, 11, \quad K = M, F.$

Sign relations 1 and 2 reflect the differential own gross wage effects in landless and landholding households for the two sexes, from equations (11.10) and (11.18); sign relations 3 and 4 are consistent with the assumption that leisure is a normal good (I^N, I^L = unearned income); coefficient restrictions 5 through 8 embody the hypothesis that schooling (E_K^N, E_K^L) and experience (e_K^N, e_K^L) augment the managerial ability of the husband and wife in agricultural production; and the four sign predictions in 9 correspond to the predicted farm production asset effects on net labor supply, from equation (11.20).

TABLE 11.6. Mean Household Characteristics of Rural Household Sample by Sex, Market Participation, and Landownership, 1971

	Males			Females		
	Nonmarket	*Market*	*Total*	*Nonmarket*	*Market*	*Total*
Landless						
Sample size	0	309	309	82	227	309
Days worked annually	—	247.7	247.7	0	195	143.4
Landholding						
Sample size	510	352	862	611	251	862
Days worked annually	—	166	68.0	—	171	49.9
Land size (acres)	13.22	4.66	9.72	11.87	4.49	9.72

Source: NCAER ARIS Survey.

Because the NCAER data do not indicate the amount of family labor used on the land held by landholding households, net labor supply—the difference between sex-specific total labor supply $(1 - l_K)$ and total farm labor usage (L_K)—is observed only for households in which the head or wife worked off the farm; the variable is subject to censoring. Table 11.6, which gives household characteristics (days worked annually by sex and landownership) for the total sample, indicates that whereas all the heads of landless households and 73.5 percent of their wives worked at least one day for pay, only 40.8 percent of the household heads with land and 29.1 percent of their wives supplied any market labor. The dependent variable used to represent net labor supply, days worked for pay, D_K^L, is thus bounded at zero and concentrated at that bound in the landholding subsample:

$$D_K^L = 0, \qquad \lambda_K^L - u_K^L \leq 0,$$

$$D_K^L = \lambda_K^L - u_K^L, \qquad \lambda_K^L - u_K^L \geq 0.$$

The properties of the D_K^L dependent variable imply that if u_K^L is distributed $N(o, \sigma)$, the tobit estimation procedure would be more appropriate than classical least squares (see Tobin 1958) in the estimation of the equations given by expression (11.31), where λ_K^L would represent the tobit index (and the theoretical variable of interest) and D_K^L would represent the observed days worked off the farm. However, in contrast to the usual "corner solution" application of tobit in United States studies of female labor supply (Rosen 1976; Schultz 1975), all males in the landholding subsample are earners and the "true" index λ_M^L may take on negative values (for net hirers of labor). The tobit index, or net supply, coefficients for males are thus appropriately compared to the least squares landless male coefficients, estimated from equation (11.29), for which censoring is not a problem $(D_M^N = \lambda_M^N)$, in verifying the restrictions of the neoclassical framework. Only for purposes of predicting the relationships between observed off-farm work and the independent variables are the elasticities of the "expected value" or off-farm days worked relevant. A proportion of women in both types of households devote all their time to household activities; thus for the females in the landholding subsample, the number of days worked (for pay) variable, D_F^L, is not only subject to censoring (we do not observe λ_F^L if the wife only works on the farm) but also may be zero-valued because the wife does not participate in any earning activities.

A second consequence of the lack of information on labor use in landholding households is that the rates of daily wages paid to laborers by households holding land but supplying no labor to the market, and thus the value of the time of family labor, are not available. The usual procedure employed in United States studies of (female) labor supply, both to solve the missing wage problem and to eliminate the definitional relationship between the labor supply variable and the computed wage, is to impute a wage rate based on the personal characteristics of the relevant household member. In Indian rural labor markets, however, the chief source of wage rate variability appears to be geographical rather than personal, once sex has been taken into account—annual averages of sex-specific adult daily agricultural wages, as shown in table 11.1 and even computed within sharply defined categories such as weeding, reaping, and plowing, vary significantly across Indian districts. Because of the geographical immobility of rural households, as indicated by the econometric results in table 11.5, individual wage rates are determined by the interaction of aggregate labor demand and supply in individual labor markets, which is in turn a function of such factors as the distribution of landholdings, the availability of water, and the existence of rural industry.

Table 11.7 displays for heads and wives alternative specifications of household-level wage equations in which the dependent variable is the natural logarithim of the computed (sex-specific) daily wage, based on a combined sample of landless and landholding households, in which either the head or the wife worked in the market. In specification 1, which corresponds to a human capital earnings function, schooling attainment and the two age variables explain less than 3 percent of the variation in male wages and none of the variance in the female wage rate [the critical F value $(500, 3) = 3.86$ (5 percent level)], although the coefficient of the schooling of the male head is statistically significant. Specification 2 includes characteristics of the local labor market reported in the sample survey data that may affect daily wage rates—dummy variables taking on the value of one if crops are not adversely affected by weather conditions (WEATHER), if a factory is present in the village (FACTRY), or if there is any small-scale industry (SSIND), and variables indicating the size of the village (SIZEVLG), the distance, in kilometers, between the household's residence

TABLE 11.7. Sex-Specific ln Wage Equations, Unsalaried Market Workers

Independent Variable	Males				Females			
	(1)	(2)	(3)	(4)	(1)	(2)	(3)	(4)
ED	0.060	0.039	0.009	0.010	0.007	0.022	0.021	0.020
	(4.12)	(2.45)	(0.75)	(0.83)	(0.61)	(1.44)	(1.40)	(1.30)
AGE	-0.007	0.009	0.008	0.008	-0.023	-0.016	-0.016	-0.016
	(0.57)	(1.00)	(1.00)	(0.01)	(1.55)	(1.10)	(1.07)	(1.10)
AGESQ	0.0001	-0.0001	-0.0001	-0.0001	-0.0003	0.0003	0.0003	0.0003
	(0.60)	(0.71)	(0.70)	(0.72)	(1.45)	(1.71)	(1.58)	(1.69)
WEATHER	—	0.166	0.166	0.168	—	0.091	0.099	0.095
		(3.46)	(3.70)	(3.73)		(1.75)	(1.90)	(1.79)
FACTRY	—	0.503	0.440	0.443	—	0.231	0.218	0.217
		(5.43)	(5.06)	(5.05)		(2.12)	(1.98)	(1.97)
SSIND	—	0.087	0.033	0.032	—	0.118	0.117	0.118
		(1.37)	(0.56)	(0.53)		(1.55)	(1.54)	(1.55)
SIZEVLG($\times 10^{-3}$)	—	0.062	0.042	0.043	—	0.076	0.069	0.068
		(9.98)	(6.56)	(8.17)		(7.67)	(6.27)	(6.18)
DSTANCE	—	0.224	0.256	0.250	—	1.274	1.338	1.322
		(0.34)	(0.42)	(0.41)		(2.00)	(2.10)	(2.08)
IADP	—	0.006	0.050	0.049	—	0.007	0.012	0.030
		(0.12)	(1.07)	(1.04)		(0.12)	(0.02)	(0.51)
LWAGE	—	—	0.419	0.423	—	—	0.119	0.116
			(7.75)	(7.69)			(2.37)	(2.05)
LAND	—	—	—	0.002	—	—	—	-0.003
				(0.55)				(0.61)
Constant	1.075	0.364	0.057	0.051	0.127	0.299	0.252	0.256
$\overline{R}^2$	0.029	0.246	0.338	0.337	-0.001	0.263	0.265	0.263
F	5.73	16.72	23.09	20.96	0.98	11.26	10.32	9.39
n	900	900	900	900	522	522	522	522

Note: t values are in parentheses.

and the village (DSTANCE), and whether the household resides in an agricultural development district subject to governmental technical assistance and credit programs (IADP). These variables, although they add significantly to the explanatory power of the wage equations for both males and females, do not completely capture all the important characteristics of local labor markets that might influence wage levels. As a proxy for aggregative market conditions, therefore, the natural logarithim of the sex-specific district-level daily wage pertaining to the district in which the household resides (LWAGE) is added in specification 3. The inclusion of this variable not only further improves the explanatory power of the wage equations but reduces the male schooling coefficient to insignificance; thus none of the human capital characteristics of the individual are significantly correlated with the wage received. The lack of significance of the schooling variables in the more fully specified household-level equations explaining the wage rates of nonsalaried and nongovernment workers of both sexes should not, however, be interpreted as evidence that schooling does not increase earnings in India. Aside from the managerial efficiency effect for heads and wives in farm households, which is discussed below, schooling attainment appears to be positively correlated with the likelihood of being in a salaried or government job; computed mean wage rates in such occupations are higher than those observed in the sample of workers used.

The results in specification 3 are consistent with the hypotheses that labor is not perfectly mobile geographically in rural India and that wage rates are not importantly affected by human capital attributes in the nonsalaried, private-sector occupations that make up the rural labor market. It is possible, however, that if the wage labor market is noncompetitive, jobs may be rationed according to the status of the worker, with discrimination in wage offers related to size of landholdings, for example. In specification 4 the amount of land owned (LAND) by the worker is entered as an additional regressor. The insignificance of this variable in the two wage equations, however, indicates that large landowners are not able to exert market power to obtain higher wages. Moreover, stratification of the worker samples by landholding status (not reported) and application of the Chow test indicate that the hypothesis that the sets of coefficients (excluding LAND) in the wage equations for the two land status groups are identical cannot be rejected. The hypothesis that all farm workers in the same geographical labor market and of the same sex face the same wage thus appears to be supported by the data.

The relative unimportance of personal attributes in determining the wages received by market workers suggests that (1) *an individual's* wage is not significantly affected by the number of days worked (which is a function of the personal characteristics of the individual worker), and (2) selectivity bias, inherent in a wage imputation procedure, based on specification 3 of table 11.7, may not be significant. The error components in the wage equations, based on market conditions, are likely to be minimally correlated with the error terms in the individual supply (shadow wage) equations, consisting solely of household variables.

The male and female wage rates used in equations (11.29) and (11.30) are thus estimated using the quasi-instrumental variables approach, based on a wage-predicting equation including the variables of specification 3 of Table 11.7 but without schooling and age. Of the other regressors in equations (11.29) and (11.30) requiring comment, the household's combined income from interest, dividends, and other personal (nonfarm) property income is used to represent unearned income (NEARN), and the age of the head and spouse (AGEM, AGEF) are included to capture life cycle and cohort effects in the landless sample and to serve, in addition, as proxies for farm-specific work experience in landholding households. The variables representing nonlabor farm assets, κ_8, κ_9, κ_{10}, and κ_{11}, consist of a three-year average of gross cropped area, in acres (LAND), and dummy variables indicating farm irrigation (IRR = 1 if irrigated, 0 otherwise), weather conditions, and whether the farm household resides in an agricultural development district (IADP) and thus is exposed to governmental credit programs (increasing access to credit) and to the introduction of high-yielding grain varieties. Each of these farm assets variables should be positively correlated with farm labor productivity and thus negatively related to market (off-farm) labor supply.

Included in the Z vector are variables representing proximity to sources of nonagricultural employment—FACTRY, SSIND, DSTNCE—which will be significant determinants of days worked annually for geographically immobile laborers.

The number of children less than 5 years of age (KIDS) is also added to the market supply equations to test whether the presence of young children is importantly related to work decisions in rural areas of a developing country. However, because this demographic variable is likely to be endogenous (see Rosenzweig and Evenson 1977), two specifications are used, one with the children variable omitted.

Male and female market supply function parameter estimates. Tables 11.8 and 11.9 report the coefficient estimates obtained for the market labor supply functions of males and females in landless and landholding households using ordinary least squares and tobit instrumental variables (OLS-IV TOBIT-IV). The overall results (which are not qualitatively altered by further stratification of the subsamples according to the wife's participation in earning activities) are generally supportive of the neoclassical framework —of the 22 possible refutable sign restrictions, only one (the differential

TABLE 11.8. OLS-IV and TOBIT-IV Market Supply Equations: Days Worked Annually for Pay by Unsalaried Males

Independent Variable	Landless		Landholding			
	OLS-IV		OLS-IV		TOBIT-IV	
	(1)	(2)	(1)	(2)	(1)	(2)
PWAGEM*	−16.29	−17.35	−11.52	−11.27	−7.10	−7.12
	(1.43)	(1.51)	(1.29)	(1.26)	(3.43)	(3.44)
PWAGEF*	11.66	13.91	4.68	3.62	62.03	61.02
	(0.69)	(0.82)	(0.29)	(0.22)	(1.72)	(1.69)
EDM	2.77	2.94	−4.18	−4.19	−9.04	−9.18
	(0.78)	(0.84)	(2.03)	(2.03)	(1.97)	(2.00)
EDF	−0.971	−0.968	−4.18	−4.27	−8.55	−8.77
	(0.43)	(0.43)	(2.00)	(2.04)	(1.82)	(1.86)
NEARN	−0.038	−0.041	−0.005	−0.005	−0.045	−0.045
	(1.19)	(1.27)	(0.64)	(0.65)	(1.48)	(1.47)
LAND	—	—	−2.20	−2.14	−12.58	−12.39
			(8.00)	(7.66)	(10.46)	(10.17)
IRR	—	—	−22.20	−22.58	−36.14	−36.63
			(3.70)	(3.76)	(2.70)	(2.74)
WEATHER	—	—	−1.83	−1.93	−15.14	−15.52
			(0.26)	(0.27)	(0.95)	(0.97)
IADP	—	—	−36.59	−36.70	−79.57	−79.66
			(5.43)	(5.45)	(5.82)	(5.83)
FACTRY	7.74	7.21	24.72	24.48	93.67	92.60
	(0.55)	(0.51)	(1.88)	(1.86)	(2.97)	(2.94)
SSIND	4.45	3.68	23.91	22.88	53.72	51.73
	(0.33)	(0.27)	(2.26)	(4.63)	(2.28)	(2.19)
DSTNCE ($\times 10^{-3}$)	−40.43	−39.48	−68.90	−67.46	−485.96	−482.26
	(0.35)	(0.34)	(1.24)	(1.21)	(2.02)	(2.01)
AGEM	−1.10	−0.990	−0.327	−0.363	−1.24	−1.30
	(1.19)	(1.07)	(0.61)	(0.68)	(1.07)	(1.13)
AGEF	−0.499	−0.485	−1.44	−1.42	−2.34	−2.34
	(0.50)	(0.49)	(2.59)	(2.58)	(1.91)	(1.91)
KIDS	—	6.54	—	−3.06	—	−6.38
		(1.09)		(1.09)		(0.96)
Constant	332.29	321.70	212.33	216.58	374.87	384.49
					(8.15)	(8.16)
$\bar{R}^2$	0.054	0.054	0.257	0.257	—	—
F/χ^2	2.75	2.60	22.21	20.82	459	459
n	309	309	862	862	862	862

Note: Asymptotic t values are in parentheses.

*Instrumental variable.

TABLE 11.9. OLS-IV and TOBIT-IV Market Supply Equations: Days Worked Annually for Pay by Unsalaried Females

Independent Variable	Landless				Landholding			
	OLS-IV		TOBIT-IV		OLS-IV		TOBIT-IV	
	(1)	(2)	(1)	(2)	(1)	(2)	(1)	(2)
PWAGEF*	50.78 (2.23)	50.77 (2.20)	50.95 (1.46)	49.93 (1.42)	3.54 (0.22)	3.85 (0.24)	58.18 (1.82)	58.53 (1.69)
PWAGEM*	−61.73 (3.99)	−61.73 (3.97)	−79.95 (3.62)	−79.51 (3.59)	−10.39 (1.18)	−10.46 (1.18)	−82.96 (2.78)	−82.64 (2.77)
EDF	2.27 (0.75)	2.27 (0.75)	2.94 (0.75)	2.94 (0.75)	−2.87 (1.39)	−2.83 (1.37)	−7.90 (1.21)	−7.79 (1.18)
EDM	3.17 (0.67)	3.17 (0.66)	2.50 (0.40)	2.40 (0.38)	−4.25 (2.09)	−4.25 (2.09)	−13.46 (2.04)	−13.32 (2.02)
NEARN	−0.061 (1.41)	−0.061 (1.41)	−0.166 (1.79)	−0.165 (1.78)	−0.006 (0.75)	−0.006 (0.74)	−0.094 (1.48)	−0.094 (1.48)
LAND	—	—	—	—	−1.42 (5.23)	−1.43 (5.20)	−12.20 (7.38)	−12.36 (7.28)
IRR	—	—	—	—	−18.35 (3.14)	−18.24 (3.12)	−42.21 (2.28)	−42.01 (2.22)
WEATHER	—	—	—	—	−13.49 (1.96)	−13.51 (1.97)	−29.28 (1.33)	−29.44 (1.34)
IADP	—	—	—	—	−28.78 (4.36)	−28.74 (4.35)	−94.83 (4.97)	−94.61 (4.96)
FACTRY	27.40 (1.43)	27.40 (1.43)	34.7 (1.37)	34.91 (1.38)	16.40 (1.28)	16.47 (1.28)	74.33 (1.63)	74.81 (1.64)
SSIND	39.49 (2.17)	39.49 (2.16)	48.12 (2.02)	48.52 (2.03)	21.36 (2.05)	21.66 (2.07)	68.68 (2.04)	69.86 (2.06)
DSTNCE ($\times 10^{-3}$)	−149.74 (0.95)	−149.74 (0.95)	−210.58 (1.04)	−210.88 (1.04)	−28.21 (0.53)	−28.62 (0.54)	−354.67 (1.31)	−356.86 (1.32)

	(1)	(2)	(3)	(4)	(5)	(6)	(7)	(8)
AGEF	-0.577	-0.577	-0.727	-0.733	-1.56	-1.56	-4.07	-4.05
	(0.43)	(0.43)	(0.41)	(0.41)	(2.83)	(2.83)	(2.27)	(2.26)
AGEM	-1.08	-1.08	-1.55	-1.59	0.203	0.213	-0.590	-0.556
	(0.86)	(0.86)	(0.95)	(0.97)	(0.39)	(0.40)	(0.35)	(0.34)
KIDS	—	-0.015	—	-3.00	—	0.895	—	4.02
		(0.01)		(0.28)		(0.33)		(0.42)
Constant	270.80	270.83	324.53	329.38	156.46	155.22	359.82	353.54
			(7.67)	(7.20)			(5.46)	(5.25)
$\bar{R}^2$	0.144	0.141	—	—	0.166	0.165	—	—
F/χ^2	6.19	5.61	3.05	3.05	13.26	12.37	422	422
n	309	309	309	309	862	862	862	862

Note: Asymptotic t values are in parentheses.
*Instrumental variable.

in the male age coefficients in the female supply equations, table 11.9) is wrong, although it is not statistically significant. Of the 21 correct coefficient signs, 14 are statistically significant at (at least) the 10 percent level.

As discussed already, the estimates from the landless supply equations cannot be used by themselves as a test of neoclassical labor supply theory. Although the results for landless male workers (but not for landless females), are particularly weak in terms of the statistical significance of the individual coefficients, the hypothesis that the number of days worked by landless males is randomly determined, one possible job allocation mechanism in a surplus labor economy, is rejected at the 1 percent level [critical $F(15,200+)$ $= 2.05$]. Moreover, although the 11 independent variables only explain 5 percent of the variation in days worked by landless males, similar (landless) male supply equations estimated with micro data from the United States also suffer from low explanatory power (Kniesner 1976). The landless male results may thus indicate the limitations of the neoclassical theory of labor supply more than the existence of a "surplus labor" economy. Interestingly, the own landless male supply elasticity estimate of -0.16 is consistent with estimated male supply elasticities obtained by Kneisner (1976) (dependent variable = weeks worked) and Finegan (1962) based on cross-sectional household and aggregate data from the United States. The negative signs of the unearned income coefficients in all equations are, moreover, in accordance with the expectation that leisure is a normal good and thus are consistent with negative own wage effects on labor supply, but the estimates only approach statistical significance.

The tobit estimates for landholding households indicate that the net labor supply of farm males—the difference between total male labor usage on the farm and the total labor supplied by the farm male—is also backward bending, with the own-wage coefficient significantly less than zero at the 1 percent level; the own wage elasticity for off-farm days worked is -0.18. Consistent with the theoretical framework, the coefficient of NEARN is negative, significant at the 10 percent level, and the male wage coefficient estimate is algebraically greater in the landholding than in the landless households, although the difference is not statistically significant. However, the negative differential in the male education coefficients between the two households is significant at the 5 percent level and supports the hypothesis that the schooling of male farm managers improves managerial efficiency. Thus higher schooling levels of male heads of landholding households are associated with lower levels of (male) net labor supply, despite the small positive association between male schooling and male market work indicated in the landless equations. The more negative coefficient for female schooling in the landholding male equations, significant at the 10 percent level, additionally supports the hypothesis that the formal education of farm wives enhances the productivity of all farm inputs, including the husband's time in farm production. However, the coefficients of the age variables in the two households suggest that farming experience has only a minimal productivity effect; the age coefficient differentials have correct signs but are not statistically significant.

Another difference between the two subsamples is that the proximity of a factory or the existence of a small-scale industry near the household are significantly and positively associated only with the market days worked of farm males, suggesting that males from farm households are significantly less geographically mobile than landless males. Such a result is consistent with the notion that there are strong imperfections in land and capital markets in India, as suggested by P. K. Bardhan (1973) and Sen (1966).

Of the farm production asset variables, all the coefficients also display the theoretically correct (negative) signs, with those of LAND, IRR, and LADP statistically significant at the 1 percent level. The coefficient estimates suggest that a 10 percent increase in gross cropped area is associated with a 12 percent decline in the number of days worked off the farm by heads of landholding households and that the net supply of male labor on farms with irrigation facilities or in IADP districts is approximately 36 and 50 man-days less than that on nonirrigated farms or on farms in non-IADP areas.

In the equations for females (table 11.9), the qualitative results are similar to those obtained for males except that the market supply curves of women appear to be positively sloped, consistent with United States studies of female labor supply (Rosen 1976; Rosen and Welch 1971; Schultz 1975). The TOBIT and OLS estimates of the female supply coefficients in the landless subsample are not significantly different, owing to the high proportion of landless women participating in the market, except that the negative coefficients of NEARN increase in absolute value in the tobit equation. However, as expected, the OLS and TOBIT net female supply coefficients in the landholding subsample diverge significantly, with all coefficients increasing in absolute value in the tobit equation. The tobit estimates indicate that the wage elasticity of observed days worked by women from landless households is 0.67, the wage elasticity of observed female off-farm work is 0.72, and the elasticity of the net supply farm women is 2.0.

The estimated gross male wage effects on female market labor supply in both landless and landholding households are negative and significant, consistent with the United States results cited above. Indeed, female market labor supply appears quite sensitive to movements in the male wage —a 10 percent rise in the wage rate of males is associated with a 14 percent reduction in the number of days worked by landless females and a 20 percent decrease in the number of days worked off the farm by wives of landholders, the latter due in part to the substitution of the wife's time for male labor in farm production, as suggested in equation (11.23) of the theoretical analysis.

Of the "predicted" coefficients, all but one conform to the implications of the neoclassical framework—the differential in the male age effect on female market labor supply between the two households. All the theoretically correct (tobit) coefficient signs or sign differentials, except for the differential own gross wage effect, are statistically significant (10 percent level). Thus, as indicated by the theory and as found for rural males, less market work is supplied by women in households with higher levels of unearned income, greater landholdings, and irrigated land that are located in agricultural development districts and in areas experiencing good weather. Moreover, the schooling attainment of both household heads and their wives is associated significantly more negatively with the number of market days worked by wives in landholding than in landless households.

The presence of children less than 5 years of age appears to have no significant effect on the market labor supply of women in India, a result that contrasts with findings based on United States data (Kniesner 1976; Leibowitz 1972; Rosen 1976; Schultz, 1975), suggesting that *market* work and child-rearing are not competitive activities in rural areas of developing countries. Thus even if a part of fertility is "excess," in the sense that the number of children born to a family exceeds the number that would have been born if parents had had more access to birth control information, the results suggest that the intensification of family planning programs in India may not have a significant impact on the quantities of labor supplied to the market by rural women (or rural men).

Finally, the results for females, in contrast to those for males, indicate that the proximity of small-scale industry and, to a lesser extent, of factories, is associated with higher amounts of market work on the part of females in landless as well as landholding households, suggesting that females are significantly less geographically mobile than males in rural India, although female labor supply is not less responsive than male labor supply to changes in economic variables.

CONCLUSION

Little empirical evidence exists on labor supply behavior and wage determination in rural areas of developing countries. Yet such information is crucial to any model of economic development formulated to serve as a useful policy-prescribing apparatus. In this paper refutable predictions were derived from a model of the rural labor market incorporating neoclassical labor supply behavior by landless and landholding households to establish a test of the applicability of the competitive framework to rural labor markets in less developed countries. Empirical results, based on both district-level and household data, were generally consistent with this framework; they indicated a high degree of responsiveness of rural wages to aggregate changes in the quantities of labor supplied to agriculture and wage-supply relationships consistent with the neoclassical approach. The data also suggested the importance of sex differences in the labor market and the importance of labor supply as a family decision.

The estimates presented here thus suggest that adjustment mechanisms pertaining to wages and labor supply are quite flexible in the rural Indian labor market, although geographical mobility appears to be somewhat limited. The evidence thus appears to call into question the implications of development models that assume a rural sector characterized by rigidities, an undifferentiated labor force, strong barriers to competition and mobility within geographical areas, or household behavior distinct from that found in developed societies.

12

Determinants of Supply and Demand for Labor in a Poor Agrarian Economy: An Analysis of Household Survey Data from Rural West Bengal

Pranab K. Bardhan

The analytical literature on employment, unemployment, and wage determination in poor agrarian economies is extensive, albeit inconclusive. Empirical work in this area is comparatively scanty. The latter mostly relates either to the question of "surplus" labor in peasant agriculture (and in other unorganized activities) or, in studies of production functions fitted to farm management data, to .the question of labor use and productivity. There has hardly been any systematic empirical study of labor supply and of the labor market participation behavior of peasant households. The usual farm management data are not adequate for this purpose, particularly because they exclude the substantial class of landless laborers who do not have a farm. In this paper I have used detailed data collected from nearly 4,900 rural households (including landless laborers, farmers, and non-agricultural workers) in West Bengal in what may be one of the first econometric attempts to estimate labor supply functions[1] in peasant agriculture.

I am grateful to Bent Hansen, Lyn Squire, T. N. Srinivasan, and S. D. Tendulkar for comments on an earlier draft: to Nikhilesh Bhattacharyya and Sudhir Bhattacharyya for help and guidance at the stage of data collection; and to Dan Kirshner and Karen Olsen for research assistance. The Indian Council of Social Science Research financed the data collection and collation and the Ford Foundation financed research analysis and computer costs. All errors, needless to say, are mine alone.

1. Yotopoulos and Lau (1974) have estimated labor supply functions on the basis of Indian farm management data as part of the micro foundations for their general equilibrium model of the agricultural sector. But farm management data exclude the landless households, which contribute a substantial part of the agricultural labor supply. Also, it seems they have run regressions over cross sections of data that include the group averages presented in Indian government publications of farm management surveys of eight districts in different parts of India. Given the heterogeneity of these widely scattered agroclimatic regions and the facts that the *districts* for the purpose of the surveys were chosen purposively and not on a random sample basis and that the data were already aggregated over size classes of farms in the published reports, I would regard this as a rather unsatisfactory basis on which to estimate labor supply functions. Yotopoulos and Lau (1974) take care to emphasize the merely illustrative purpose of their exercise.

The data set is part of a very large-scale employment and unemployment survey of households carried out by the National Sample Survey Organization in India for the one-year period October 1972 to September 1973. In the first two sections I describe the nature of the data and present the results on labor supply behavior. My evidence seems to be against the standard horizontal supply curve of labor assumed in a large part of the development literature. In the third and fourth sections I use the same data set to estimate labor demand functions in agriculture and then present a simultaneous equations system of labor demand and supply in agriculture. In the next section I analyze the wage rates quoted as "acceptable" by different groups of respondents in the survey in response to hypothetical questions on wage employment to obtain some idea of the supply prices of labor. I end the paper with a brief summary of my conclusions and comment on the limitations of the framework of this empirical exercise.

THE DATA AND THE SPECIFICATIONS

West Bengal is a densely populated (second highest density of the major Indian states), poor (44 percent of the rural population had less than Rs 30—about $4—per capita per month expenditure in 1972–73 at current prices) region with paddy-jute agriculture, heavy rainfall, and little irrigation. Pockets of advanced industrialization and commercialization exist in the megalopolis of Calcutta and its hinterland.

The sampling design of the survey for rural West Bengal was stratified in two stages, villages and households. The survey period of one year was divided into four subrounds of three months each. One-fourth of the sample villages were surveyed in each subround and each sample village was visited only once during the year. The sample units were so staggered over the four subrounds that valid estimates could be built up for each subround separately. (I shall later compare the subrounds to capture the seasonality effects of agriculture.) In all, there are data for approximately 8,500 rural workers belonging to nearly 4,900 sample households drawn from about 500 sample villages. For 38 percent of the households, cultivation of a farm (either owned by themselves or leased in) is the principal occupation (the single most important source of income); for 32 percent, agricultural wage labor (on someone else's farm) is the principal occupation. Cultivation is the secondary occupation (the second most important source of income) of 17 percent of the households; agricultural wage labor is the secondary occupation of 9 percent. The data that we have for each household may be classified in three groups:

1.   Data relating to characteristics of the household as a whole and also to those of each individual member of the household, whether a worker or not.

2. Day-to-day time disposition particulars for *each* of the seven days preceding the date of the survey (along with wage and salary earnings reported for the week) for those currently in the labor force. (A *current* laborer is defined as one who worked for at least one hour during the reference week or who sought work or was available for work.[2]) Intensity of work in any activity on each day was measured in binary codes of "full" and "half" days (so that what in the judgment of the respondent was a half day's work was counted as half a day worked).[3]

3. Responses to various probing (and sometimes hypothetical) questions about the long-term work pattern, job search, and minimum acceptable wage/salary rates from members of the household belonging to the usual labor force. (A *usual* laborer is one whose "enduring status"—the status that has prevailed over, say, the last year and that is also likely to continue in the future—is that of work or looking for work or being available for work.)

In estimating labor supply functions the first serious problem is to find an appropriate wage as an independent variable. If the daily wage rate is derived as wage earnings divided by days worked and if the days worked also appear as the dependent variable, there is the well-known measurement error problem (if the number of days worked is too high, the wage rate definitionally will be too low, giving rise to a negative bias); there is also a "simultaneity" problem because both the amount of labor supplied and the wage may be jointly determined by other variables. On top of this, we have the practical problem that those who did not work at all (in the reference week) did not have a wage to report even though the wage rate in the market may have been positive. One solution is to estimate the wage rate as determined by other independent variables for the workers who reported work at some wage rate W for casual farm work, and from this equation obtain a predicted wage rate for everybody, including the individuals who did not have an actual wage to report.[4] Let us call this wage variable $\hat{W}$.

I have also found another predicted wage variable quite useful. We have data for the hypothetical minimum acceptable wage rate at which casual agricultural laborers report willingness to do outside work (within the village). We have estimated this hypothetical minimum acceptable wage rate as a proportion of the actual wage rate, the proportion being determined by other independent variables for the workers who reported both wage rates, and from this equation a predictable wage ratio can be estimated for every-

2. The standard definition of work or "gainful" work excludes purely domestic work.

3. Since work in agriculture cannot easily be reduced to a standard hourly pattern and since the rural respondents found it rather difficult to report the hourly disposition of their time, intensity of work by "full" or "half" days has been adopted as a better measure.

4. Hall (1973) uses this procedure in his estimates of labor supply in the United States. But as Gronau (1973) and Heckman (1974) have pointed out, under certain circumstances this procedure may lead to a bias in the estimation of labor supply parameters.

body. Let us call this predicted wage ratio variable $\hat{\omega}$. This variable indicates the predicted ratio of the minimum acceptable wage rate to the current wage rate for casual farm labor.

In some cases I have used even another alternative wage variable. On the basis of the data on wage earnings and days of wage employment for each worker in a village, I have worked out an aggregate[5] weighted average wage rate for agricultural work for the village as a whole in the current week. Let us call this village wage variable VW. Presumably, to the individual worker the VW variable is more exogenous and less amenable to individual control than the actual individual wage rate as derived from the individual's reported wage earnings. Also, VW is quite often positive even though an individual may not have reported any wage work.

A fourth alternative wage variable I have used is a variation on VW. Even if we accept VW as an accurate approximation of the prevailing market wage rate in the village, it may not represent the *expected* wage rate relevant for labor supply decisions, since in a situation of widespread unemployment and underemployment, the probability of getting a job at the market wage rate is less than unity. I have therefore calculated an aggregate weighted average unemployment rate (denoted as VUR)[6] for each village. Using that to indicate the probability of getting a job, I have computed an expected wage rate as being equal to $VW(1 - VUR)$. Let us call this expected wage rate in the village VEW. For our sample, VEW is roughly 87 percent of VW.

Let us now turn to changes in the dependent variable, agricultural labor days supplied in the reference week.[7] First, the number of days in the week when the laborer did not work but either was seeking work or reported being available for work (presumably at the going market wage rate)[8] should obviously be added to the number of days actually worked to constitute the labor supply from the point of view of the supplier. In the rest of this section, except when otherwise stated, the labor supply variable should be taken in this more general sense. Second, since many laborers also have some family (or leased-in) land to cultivate, and since the wage response and other deter-

5. Since the agricultural work done on different farms by the workers in one village during a fortnight when the village is surveyed is not likely to be different in kind, such aggregation may be legitimate.

6. The unemployment rate is measured as the number of days in the reference week the respondents in a village reported seeking work or being available for work as a proportion of the total number of days in the reference week they worked or reported seeking work or being available for work.

7. Only 4 percent of the total days worked by those who were cultivators by usual status was spent in nonfarm work; only 5 percent of the total days hired out by casual agricultural laborers was spent in nonfarm work.

8. I have assumed that when cultivators or agricultural laborers reported that they were seeking work or were available for work in the reference week, it was agricultural work they were after. This is not necessarily so, but it is likely to be so in most cases.

minants of hired out labor and self-employed labor may be different, I have
adopted two alternate kinds of supply variables, one to represent the hiring
out behavior and the other to represent the *total* supply of labor days
including both labor offered in the agricultural wage market and labor
applied on the family farm. Third, since the decisions concerning labor supply
in rural families are quite often made at the household level rather than by
each individual, I have also computed total household labor supply variables
(by aggregating the labor supply of all the working members of the household). For the corresponding wage rates I have used the village wage variables, VW or VEW. Fourth, since social and economic constraints on labor
supply are different for men and women, I have tried to distinguish between
their labor supply functions. In particular, I have made some separate
estimates in order to analyze the factors influencing the female rate of
participation in the labor force.

As for independent variables other than the wage variable, I shall
comment on them as I present the estimated functions.

LABOR SUPPLY

Let us first take the set of casual agricultural laborers who constitute 29
percent of the usual labor force. In the reference week each worker supplied
approximately 5.6 days of agricultural wage labor (including days looking for
or being available for work) on an average. (Approximately 19 percent of the
casual agricultural laborers did not have any agricultural wage work to
report in the reference week.) Let us call this individual supply of days of
farm wage labor H_1. Our estimated linear equation for this is as follows:

$$H_1 = 8.2882 - 0.9017\hat{\omega} - 1.0050X_1 - 0.0117X_2 + 0.1075X_3$$
$$\quad (0.1088) \quad (0.0180) \quad (0.2036) \quad (0.0023) \quad (0.0218)$$

$$+ 0.2195DS2 + 0.3791DS3 + 0.3005DR1 - 0.2201DR3,$$
$$\quad (0.0779) \quad\quad (0.0751) \quad\quad (0.1516) \quad\quad (0.0692)$$

$$(12.1)$$

$$R^2 = 0.455, \qquad F = 349.5.$$

In equation (12.1), $\hat{\omega}$ is, as defined earlier, the *predicted* ratio[9] of the minimum
acceptable wage (for work inside the village) to the current wage rate for
casual farm labor; X_1 is the per capita amount of land cultivated (in acres) by
the household; X_2 is the age (in years) of the individual; X_3 is the number of
dependents per earner in the household; $DS2$ and $DS3$ are dummy variables
representing subrounds 2 (January–March quarter) and 3 (April–June
quarter), respectively; $DR1$ and $DR3$ are dummy variables representing

9. The independent variables taken for the estimated equation of $\hat{\omega}$ are W, X_2, X_3,
X_8, X_{13}, $D2$, and $D6$; in this equation $R^2 = 0.207$ and $F = 52.4$.

region 1 (the Himalayan region of West Bengal) and region 3 (the Central Plains), respectively.[10]

Equation (12.1) shows that the supply of labor for hiring out is larger, the higher is the current wage rate relative to the individual's minimum acceptable wage rate and the lower is the per capita amount of land cultivated by the household, as expected.[11] Age tends to decrease hiring out and a larger number of dependents per earner seems to necessitate more hiring out. The January–March and April–June quarters are relatively slack seasons in West Bengal agriculture and laborers seem willing to hire out more in these seasons. All the variables in the equation are significant at less than the 5 percent level and the F value for the estimated equation is extremely high.

Let us now analyze labor supply decisions at the household level and also include some of the small cultivators along with the landless laborers. For this purpose we take out of the whole sample the set of households with less than 2.5 acres of cultivated land per household and for which agriculture is the single most important source of household income. Clearly, these households are the major suppliers of labor (particularly wage labor) in agriculture. They constitute about half of the total rural households. Let us use H_2 to denote the aggregate supply of farm wage labor for all adults[12] in such a household in the reference week. (On an average H_2 was 6.3 days in the reference week.) Our estimated equation for H_2 is as follows:

$$H_2 = 0.5993 + 1.6071VW - 0.3411(VW)^2 + 0.2104X_3 + 3.7293X_4$$
$$\quad (0.3852) \quad (0.2619) \quad (0.0563) \qquad (0.0400) \quad (0.0813)$$

$$\quad - 3.3574X_5 - 0.4438DS2 - 0.6292DR1 - 0.4111DR2, \qquad (12.2)$$
$$\quad (0.0988) \quad (0.1830) \qquad (0.3099) \qquad (0.1923)$$

$$R^2 = 0.508, \qquad F = 406.4.$$

---

10. The four subrounds in which the year 1972–73 was divided are: October–December (subround 1), January–March (subround 2), April–June (subround 3), and July–September (subround 4). Of these subrounds, 1 and 4 are the relatively busy seasons; the latter in most areas includes sowing and transplantation of the main crop of winter paddy and harvesting of autumn paddy and jute, and the former includes harvesting of autumn and winter paddy. Subrounds 2 and 3 are relatively slack seasons when some of the minor crops (including summer paddy) are sown or harvested. The whole state of West Bengal has also been subdivided into four regions: region 1 is the Himalayan region (districts of Darjeeling, Jalpaiguri, and Cooch Behar), region 2 is the Eastern Plains (districts of West Dinajpur, Malda, Murshidabad, Nadia, and Birbhum), region 3 is the Central Plains (districts of 24 Parganas, Howrah, Hooghly, and Burdwan), and region 4 is the Western Plains (districts of Bankura, Purulia, and Midnapur).

11. A larger farm (per capita) reduces the supply of labor in two ways, partly through the income effect of larger nonwage income and partly through a status effect of making a person more reluctant to work for others.

12. In this paper adults have been defined as those belonging to the 15–60 age-group.

In equation (12.2), VW is, as defined earlier, the aggregate weighted average farm wage rate in the village in the current week (for the household as a whole, the general village wage rate seems more appropriate than any individual wage rate received); X_3 is, as before, the number of dependents per earner in the household; X_4 is the number of adults in the household who are in the farm labor force by *usual* status; X_5 is the amount of land cultivated by the household; $DS2$ is the dummy variable for subround 2 (January–March); $DR1$ and $DR2$ are dummy variables representing region 1 (the Himalayan region) and region 2 (the Eastern Plains), respectively.

Equation (12.2) shows that H_2 responds positively to VW, but the coefficient for the quadratic term—$(VW)^2$—is negative. As in equation (12.1), hiring out seems to decrease with land cultivated and increase with the number of dependents per earner in the household. The larger the number of working adults in the households, obviously, the more labor days are available for hiring out. In contrast to equation (12.1), there is *less* willingness to hire out in the relatively slack season (the income effect is possibly outweighed by the general job search discouragement effect) of January–March and in the Himalayan region of West Bengal. All the variables in equation (12.2) are significant at less than the 5 percent level and the F value for the estimated equation is extremely high.

In equation (12.2), H_2 refers to the supply of farm wage labor for the adults in the household as a whole. Let us see how the estimates differ for only the male adult members in the household. We define H_{2m} as the total supply of adult male farm wage labor for each household belonging to the set of agricultural labor and small-cultivator (with less than 2.5 acres) households. (On an average, H_{2m} was 5.1 days in the reference week.) Our estimated equation for H_{2m} is as follows:

$$H_{2m} = 0.7038 + 1.1826VWM - 0.2317(VWM)^2 - 2.7754X_5$$
$$(0.2535) \quad (0.1843) \qquad\quad (0.0403) \qquad\qquad\quad (0.0780)$$

$$+\ 4.2763X_6 - 1.9208X_7 - 0.2362DS2, \qquad\qquad (12.3)$$
$$(0.0809) \qquad (0.1525) \qquad (0.1425)$$

$$R^2 = 0.559, \qquad F = 666.2.$$

In equation (12.3), VWM is the aggregate weighted average farm wage rate for adult male laborers in the village, X_6 is the number of adult males in the household, and X_7 is the number of adult males in the household having more than primary education. The response of the wage rate, the quadratic term, of land cultivated, and of the dummy variable for subround 2 are of the same sign as in equation (12.2). The larger the number of adult males in the household, obviously, the more labor days are available for hiring out. It is interesting to note that education discourages hiring out of agricultural wage labor: the larger is X_7, the lower is H_{2m}. X_3, the number of dependents per earner in the household, and all the region dummy variables turn out to be insignificant; their F value is so low that their omission from equation (12.3) has improved the value of $\bar{R}^2$. All the variables in equation (12.3) are significant at less than the 1 percent level except $DS2$, which is significant at the 10 percent level; the F value for the estimated equation is extremely high.

I ran an equation similar to equation (12.3) for landless wage labor and small-cultivator households (less than 2.5 acre) separately. The results were very similar to those in equation (12.3), except that VWM was positive and significant for males in wage labor households and positive but statistically not very significant for small-cultivator households and the latter, for obvious reasons, hire out *less* in the busy quarter of October–December.

Let us now see how the results change if, in equation (12.3), we substitute for VWM the variable $VEWM$, the expected village wage rate for male agricultural laborers, calculated as VWM in the current week multiplied by the difference of the estimated village unemployment rate in the current week from unity. Our estimated equation is now:

$$H_{2m} = 0.8925 + 1.2979VEWM - 0.3007(VEWM)^2 - 2.7834X_5$$
$$(0.2490) \quad (0.2024) \qquad\qquad (0.0474) \qquad\qquad\qquad (0.7789)$$

$$+ 4.2714X_6 - 1.9067X_7 - 0.2838DS2, \qquad\qquad (12.4)$$
$$(0.8095) \quad\;\; (0.1523) \quad\;\; (0.1432)$$

$$R^2 = 0.559, \qquad F = 666.3.$$

Equation (12.4) is very similar to equation (12.3). As VWM of equation (12.3) was replaced by $VEWM$ in equation (12.4), VW of equation (12.2) may be replaced by VEW without much change.

In equation (12.1)–(12.4) we have analyzed the hiring out behavior of agricultural laborers and small cultivators. What about the hiring out behavior of all cultivators taken together? Let us take the set of households cultivating more than 0.1 acre of land and having cultivation as the principal occupation. We shall use H_{3m} to denote the aggregate supply of farm wage labor for all male adults in such a household. (On an average, H_{3m} was only 1.6 days in the reference week.) Our estimated equation for H_{3m} is as follows:

$$H_{3m} = 1.3809 - 0.4327VWM - 0.2641X_3 + 1.5667X_6$$
$$(0.3346) \quad (0.0991) \qquad\quad (0.0297) \qquad (0.0712)$$

$$- 0.4256DR2 + 0.3308DS3, \qquad\qquad (12.5)$$
$$(0.1584) \qquad\;\; (0.1573)$$

$$R^2 = 0.180, \qquad F = 101.7.$$

Not only does equation (12.5) explain a much smaller proportion of the variation in hiring out than does, say, equation (12.3), but the wage response is now significantly negative. This is in contrast to all the earlier equations relating to agricultural laborers and small cultivators. $DS3$ is the dummy variable for subround 3 (April–June), which is a relatively slack season when presumably the cultivator households have less work on their own farms and are more willing to hire out labor, contrary to the situation described by equation (12.2) for less landed households. As in equation (12.2), there is less hiring out in region 2 (the Eastern Plains). As expected, the supply of hired out male labor is positively associated with the number of adult males in the household; it is not, however, clear why it is negatively associated with X_3. (It is possible that males burdened with a larger number of dependents in primarily cultivator households work more intensively on their own farms and have less time for hiring out.) The coefficients X_5, the amount of land cultivated, and X_7, the number of adult males having more than primary education, are appropriately negative, but they turn out to be insignificant and their F value is so low that their omission from equation (12.5) improves the value of $\bar{R}^2$.

For approximately 77 percent of this set of cultivating households, H_{3m} is zero. I therefore also tried a *logit* model of predicting the binary choice behavior of these households in terms of H_{3m}, taking zero and positive values. Without going into detail, I will merely note that, consistent with the regression equation (12.5), the logit maximum likelihood estimates suggest that a smaller number of adult males in the household, a higher village average wage rate, a larger amount of land cultivated, and a larger number of dependents all increase the likelihood that H_{3m} will take the value zero (the likelihood ratio is 0.309).

In all the equations so far we have looked at the supply of farm wage labor in the market. For the set of cultivator households that we have taken for equation (12.5), the predominant component of labor supply is that of work on the family farm. Let S be the total supply of adult farm labor days (including work on family farm, hiring out, and seeking or being available for work) for the cultivating household as a whole. (On an average, S was 11.2 days in the reference week.) Our estimated equation for S is now as follows:

$$S = 0.1882 + 0.1883X_3 + 5.3620X_4 + 0.1522X_5 - 0.8743DS2, \qquad (12.6)$$
$$(0.2094) \quad (0.0342) \qquad (0.0793) \qquad (0.0312) \qquad (0.1849)$$

$$R^2 = 0.701, \qquad F = 1354.3.$$

The wage rate variable does not appear in equation (12.6) since it turned out to be extremely insignificant. (It is possible that for cultivating households, the relevant wage variable is not the wage rate in the reference week, but the *annual* wage income as the opportunity cost of working on one's own farm—for which we do not have data.) The number of working adults as well as the size of the household farm is obviously positively associated with total labor supply and so is the number of dependents per earner necessitating more work. $DS2$, the dummy variable for subround 2 (January– March), implies a smaller total labor supply in a slack season. All the independent variables are significant at less than the 1 percent level and the F value for the equation is extremely high.

In equation (12.6), S refers to the total supply of adult farm labor days for the cultivating household. Let us now consider the estimate for only the adult male farm labor days. Let S_m be the total supply of adult male farm labor days for the cultivating household. (On an average, S_m was 9.1 days in the reference week.) The following loglinear equation for S_m gives a better fit than the linear equation:

$$\log S_m = -0.6164 + 0.0884 \log VWM + 0.0406 \log X_3 + 0.2156 \log X_5$$
$$ (0.1327) \quad (0.1795) (0.0235) (0.0704)$$

$$+ 1.1349 \log X_6 - 0.0955 \log X_7 + 0.3140 DS1 + 0.3304 D1,$$
$$ (0.0204) (0.0104) (0.1085) (0.0949)$$

$$\tag{12.7}$$

$$R^2 = 0.615, \qquad F = 615.6.$$

In equation (12.7) the variables are as defined before except $D1$, which is a dummy variable indicating whether the village is predominantly a multiple-crop producer. Note that VWM has a positive but statistically insignificant response. As expected, S_m is positively associated with the number of dependents per earner, the number of adult males in the household, the size of the family farm, the dummy variable indicating village multiple-cropping, and $DS1$, the dummy for subround 1 (October–December), which, as we noted earlier, is a relatively busy season. As before, education seems to discourage agricultural work: S_m is negatively associated with the number of adult males in the household having more than primary education. Except for VWM, the coefficients for all the other variables in equation (12.7) are statistically significant (at less than the 5 percent level for X_5, X_6, X_7, $DS1$, and $D1$ and at less than the 10 percent level for X_3) and the F value for the equation is extremely high.

To briefly summarize our results in this section, the wage response of labor supply seems to be significantly positive for the set of agricultural laborers and small cultivators. The wage response is not significant for *total* labor supply for the set of cultivators of all size groups taken together. There seems to be some evidence for at least a locally backward-bending supply curve of hired out farm labor for the set of cultivators of all size groups taken together.

Even when the wage response of hiring out farm labor is positive, as it is for agricultural laborers and small cultivators, it is not very large.

According to our estimates, the elasticity of H_2 with respect to VW is 0.29 and that of H_2 with respect to VEW is 0.26; the elasticity of H_{2m} with respect to either VWM or $VEWM$ is approximately 0.2. These elasticity values are drastically different from the infinite elasticity presumed in the horizontal supply curve of farm labor used in much of the development literature. (It is possible, however, that the presumed horizontal supply curve of labor in the literature is not an *ex ante* supply curve, as in our estimates, but more like a locus of equilibrium points, as is the Keynesian aggregate supply curve, suggesting constancy of the equilibrium wage rate. My comments on the latter are given in the third section.)

In general, it seems that labor supply is not highly responsive to the wage rate but is primarily determined by other economic, social, and demographic constraints. Some, though certainly not all, of these constraints are reflected in the relationship with some of the independent variables other than wage in our regression equations. Hiring out behavior is usually positively related to the number of adult workers in the family and the number of dependents per earner; it is negatively related to the amount of land cultivated by the household, the level of living, and the educational level of adults in the household. Total labor supply (including supply on family farms) of cultivators behaves similarly, except that in this case, understandably, it is positively associated with the amount of land cultivated by the household, the village multiple-cropping index, and the busy season and negatively associated with the slack season.

LABOR DEMAND

Let us now turn to the demand for farm labor on the part of households cultivating land. Suppose that L denotes the demand for labor days hired on the farm by a cultivating household in the reference week. Our estimated equation for L is as follows:

$$L = -4.3010 - 0.1075 VWL - 0.8808 X_4 + 2.2699 X_5 + 2.2979 X_{11}$$
$$\quad\;\; (0.7576)\; (0.0891) \qquad\;\; (0.2720) \quad\;\; (0.1096) \quad\;\; (0.9193)$$

$$+\; 3.0523 X_{12} + 1.0283 D1 + 1.9158 DS4 + 3.6044 DS4, \qquad (12.8)$$
$$\quad (0.3187) \qquad (0.6064) \qquad (0.7076) \qquad (0.7515)$$

$$R^2 = 0.237, \qquad F = 119.2.$$

In equation (12.8) the new variables are VWL, the aggregate weighted average village wage rate for adult farm labor hired in; X_{11}, the percentage of the farm's cultivated area under irrigation; and X_{12}, the total number of adults in the household having more than primary education. The wage response of labor demand is negative but statistically insignificant. As expected, the demand for hired labor is positively associated with the size of the farm, the irrigated proportion of land, the dummy variable indicating village multiple-cropping intensity, and the busy seasons. The larger the number of farm workers in the family, clearly, the smaller is its demand for hired labor; but the larger is the number of more educated adults in the family, the larger is the demand for hired farm labor. Except for VWL and $D1$, all the independent variables are significant at the 1 percent level; $D1$ is significant at less than the 10 percent level.

Equation (12.8) pertains to the demand for hired labor; let us now analyze the total demand for farm labor (including self-employment on the family farm) on the part of the cultivating households. Let N denote this total demand for labor days used on the farm by a cultivating household in the reference week. Our estimated equation for N is as follows:

$$N = 5.5274 - 0.0932VWL + 2.0584X_4 + 3.3376X_5 + 0.0504X_9$$
$$\quad (2.0318) \ (0.0935) \qquad (0.2865) \quad (0.1072) \quad (0.0206)$$

$$+ 2.0169X_{11} - 3.7248DS2 - 2.1730DS3 + 1.1519D1, \qquad (12.9)$$
$$\quad (1.0759) \qquad (0.8571) \qquad (0.8897) \qquad (0.6451)$$

$$R^2 = 0.328, \qquad F = 130.8.$$

As in equation (12.8), the wage response to demand for labor is insignificant in equation (12.9). Not unexpectedly, total labor use on the farm is positively associated with the size of the farm, the number of adult workers in the household, the proportion of irrigated land, the village multiple-cropping dummy variable, and X_9, the agricultural development (composite) index of the district where the farm is located,[13] and negatively associated with the slack seasons. Except for VWL, $D1$, and X_{11}, all the independent variables are significant at the 2 percent level; $D1$ and X_{11} are significant at less than the 10 percent level.

SIMULTANEITY OF LABOR DEMAND AND SUPPLY

In the preceding sections we have estimated farm labor hiring *out* functions for labor-selling households and farm labor hiring *in* functions for labor-buying households. We should be able to use our data set to estimate simultaneous equations system for the demand for and supply of agricultural

13. *The Reserve Bank of India Bulletin* (October 1969) included a composite index of agricultural development for most districts in India in the mid-1960s. This index is a weighted average index of a number of agroclimatic and commercialization indexes related to (1) the percentage of gross cropped area irrigated, (2) multiple-cropping intensity, (3) average rainfall, (4) soil rating, (5) percentage of area under cash crops, and (6) surplus of cereals over consumption in the district. I have used the composite index for the different districts in West Bengal, 1964–65, to distinguish households in our sample located in areas with different agroclimatic environments.

wage labor in the labor market. One major problem is to choose the appropriate geographical unit for which such a simultaneous system for the labor market may be feasible as well as meaningful. In many ways the village may be regarded as such a unit for the present sample, but quite often households resident in one village sell labor to households in other villages or buy labor from households in other villages and the total hiring in of labor by households in a village may not be equal to the total hiring out by households in the same village.[14] As long as the excess or deficit for a particular village is determined by factors exogenous to the village economy, this should not be a problem for our estimation of the simultaneous equations system. But such an assumption may not always be tenable. (A net export of labor supply from our village to the adjacent village may be as much a result of depressed agricultural conditions in our village as of attractive job opportunities in the adjacent village.) Our estimation of a simultaneous equations system for the village labor market is, therefore, extremely crude and subject to this restrictive assumption that the net export from the village labor market (or import into it) is determined by conditions outside the village.

We shall confine our exercise to the male wage labor market in the village. Suppose we let VHM denote the total male farm labor days hired out by all the households in the village (per acre of cultivated land in the village[15]); VLM denotes the total male farm labor days hired in by all the households in the village (per acre of cultivated land in the village). Using two-stage least squares, we get the following estimate of a simultaneous equations system in the village labor market:

$$VHM = 9.1216 + 4.8428VWM - 0.0111VX3 + 2.3863VX6 - 6.8806VX7$$
$$\quad (2.7832) \ (1.1664) \qquad (0.0055) \qquad (0.0336) \qquad (1.1366)$$

$$\quad - 0.0359VX8 - 1.0942D5 - 2.4801DS4, \qquad\qquad (12.10)$$
$$\quad (0.0128) \qquad (0.3176) \quad (0.6664)$$

$$R^2 = 0.940, \qquad F = 799.3;$$

and

$$VLM = 1.9508 - 0.5076VWM + 0.0019VX3 + 0.0064VX5 + 2.1949VX7$$
$$\quad (1.4817) \ (0.4880) \qquad (0.0028) \qquad (0.0041) \qquad (0.4723)$$

$$\quad - 0.8315DS2 - 0.6073DS3 + 0.0947D1 + 0.1563D7, \qquad (12.11)$$
$$\quad (0.3103) \qquad (0.2702) \qquad (0.1325) \qquad (0.1522)$$

$$R^2 = 0.130, \qquad F = 6.7.$$

14. It would have been better if we could have carried out the exercise for a set of adjacent villages, but the villages in our sample were randomly chosen and we do not have any data concerning adjacent villages.

15. We normalize the variables on a per acre basis to abstract from the effects of village size differences.

In equation (12.10) and (12.11), VWM is, as before, the weighted average village wage rate for male farm labor, $VX3$ is the average number of dependents per earner in the village, $VX5$ is the amount of land cultivated per household, $VX6$ is the total number of adult males per cultivated acre in the village, $VX7$ is the number of adult males in the village having more than primary education, $VX8$ is the average standard of living in terms of per capita consumer expenditure in the village, $D1$ is the dummy variable indicating multiple-cropping in the village, $D5$ is a dummy variable indicating the importance of nonfram employment in the village, $D7$ is a dummy variable indicating village irrigation, and $DS2$, $DS3$, and $DS4$ are the subrounds 2 (January–March), 3 (April–June) and 4 (July–September), respectively.

It seems that the wage response of supply is significantly positive, but the negative wage response of labor demand is insignificant. This is consistent with our results for the household-level supply and demand functions.

Supply of hired out farm labor is positively associated with the number of adult males and negatively associated with the percentage of more educated males, the number of dependents per earner, the average standard of living, the importance of nonfarm work in the village (which reduces the supply of farm labor), and the relatively busy season of subround 4 (which keeps more workers busy on their own farms). Demand for hiring in labor on a farm is positively associated with the percentage of more educated males in the village and negatively associated with the relatively slack seasons of subrounds 2 and 3; the other independent variables in the demand equation do not have statistically significant coefficients. The F value for both of the equations is significant at less than the 1 percent level. Equation (12.10) explains a very high proportion of the variance in VHM, but the explanatory power of equation (12.11) is much weaker.

The simultaneous equations system, with all its limitations, seems to point to a demand-supply theory of wages. The wage equation in the first stage of the two-stage least squares simultaneous equations system is:

$$VWM = 2.0631 + 0.5780VX7 + 0.0036VX8 + 0.0047VX9$$
$$\quad\ (0.1937)\ \ (0.1987)\qquad (0.0026)\qquad (0.0019)$$

$$\qquad + 0.2332DS1 + 0.4875DS4 - 0.7117VURM, \qquad (12.12)$$
$$\qquad\ \ (0.0941)\qquad (0.0933)\qquad (0.2787)$$

$$R^2 = 0.1500 \qquad F = 7.11,$$

where $VX9$ is the agricultural development index for the district where the village is located and $VURM$ is the weighted average village unemployment rate for male workers. As expected, the wage rate is positively associated with the district agricultural development index, the busy seasons, and the more educated proportion of adult males; it is negatively associated with the village unemployment rate. This is in contrast to the implications of the rather popular "subsistence theory" of wage (or the more nebulous and frequently undefined idea of the "institutional" determination of wages) concerning a constant level of real wages that is invariant to changes in demand or in productivity conditions. For more on this topic, see P. K. Bardhan (1979c).

ACCEPTABLE WAGE RATES

Apart from reporting wage and salary earnings actually received in the reference week, the respondents in our data set also answered hypothetical questions about an acceptable wage rate (should they be looking for wage employment) inside and outside the village. It is interesting to analyze this information on what might be considered the *ex ante* supply prices of workers. Approximately 30 percent of the casual agricultural laborers said they were willing to accept wage employment inside or outside the village. (About 22 percent were willing to accept wage employment inside but not outside the village.) For the laborers who reported both a current farm wage received and an acceptable wage for a hypothetical wage employment inside the village that they were prepared to take, the value of the ratio of the acceptable wage to the actual wage is estimated to be approximately 1.6; 60 percent thus seems to be, on an average, the desired margin of wage on a hypothetical job inside the village over their current wage.[16] Similarly, 87 percent is estimated to be the desired margin of wage on a hypothetical job outside the village over the current wage for those who reported preparedness to accept jobs outside the village.[17]

Let us denote as A_c the acceptable wage rate reported by casual agricultural laborers for hypothetical wage employment inside the village. For those who report it, the mean value of A_c is Rs 3.73 with a standard deviation of 1.61. Let us now try to determine the factors that may influence the level of A_c. The estimated equation for A_c that follows leaves unexplained most of the variations in A_c, but it is at least able to identify some of the factors bearing on it:

$$A_c = 3.1170 + 0.1810W + 0.0687X_3 + 0.3515X_{13} - 0.4401D6$$
$$\quad\ (0.1464)\ \ (0.0444)\quad (0.0337)\quad (0.1771)\quad\ (0.1256)$$

$$+ 0.2176D2, \tag{12.13}$$
$$\ (0.1036)$$

$$R^2 = 0.041, \qquad F = 12.1.$$

16. Forty-one percent of the males among these laborers quoted an acceptable wage of Rs 3.5 or less and the rest quoted a figure higher than Rs 3.5.

17. In the survey neither the nature of the job (such as agricultural, factory work, public works) nor its location (which determined whether shifting from current residence was necessary) was specified.

In equation (12.13) the new variables are X_{13}, which is a measure of the rate of underemployment for casual agricultural laborers, $D2$, which is a dummy variable indicating households *not* belonging to scheduled castes or tribes; and $D6$, which is a dummy variable intended to separate women. All the independent variables are significant at the 5 percent level, and although the R^2 is very low, the F value for the equation is significant at less than the 1 percent level. Predictably, the acceptable wage rate is higher the higher is the current wage rate received, the larger is the number of dependents per earner in the household (indicating greater need), and the higher is the caste status the individual enjoys (presumably implying more bargaining power); It is lower for women. But what is not so clear is why A_c is positively associated with the measure of current underemployment for the individual. (It is possible that those who have been severely underemployed for some time have become adjusted to the rhythms of various kinds of domestic work or collection activities to obtain "free" goods (such as roots and firewood) from common property in the village, so that a higher than usual wage is required to bring them back to the wage labor market.)

We can also try to explain variations in a similar reportedly acceptable wage rate inside village for the self-employed farmers and family helpers— let us denote this wage rate as A_s. For those who reported it, the mean value of A_s is Rs 4.27, which is higher than the mean of A_c for casual agricultural laborers. Our estimated equation for A_s, again, leaves unexplained most of the variations in it, but it is at least able to identify some of the factors affecting it:

$$A_s = 3.3395 + 0.0769X_3 + 0.2201VW + 1.6057VUR - 1.4306D6$$
$$ (0.2095) \quad (0.0288) \quad\;\; (0.0677) \qquad (0.4572) \qquad\;\; (0.2898)$$

$$ + 1.2624D8, \tag{12.14}$$
$$ (0.4084)$$

$$R^2 = 0.118, \qquad F = 13.6.$$

The new variables in equation (12.14) are $D8$, which is a dummy variable intended to distinguish those having more than primary education, and VUR, which is the weight average unemployment rate for the village. In equation (12.11) all the independent variables are significant at less than the 1 percent level and, although the R^2 is low, the F value is significant at less than the 1 percent level.

As expected, A_s is positively associated with the number of dependents per earner in the household, with the village wage rate, and with the level of education of the respondent; it is negatively associated with women. Again, as in equation (12.13), the positive response of VUR, the village unemployment rate, is not entirely clear and may have a similar explanation.

CONCLUSION

In this paper I have analyzed a very large set of cross-sectional data for agricultural workers in rural West Bengal in estimating farm labor demand and supply functions. I find hardly any evidence of the standard horizontal supply curve of labor frequently assumed in the theoretical literature on development. The wage elasticity of supply turns out to be rather small. It seems that labor supply (as well as the reported supply price for extra work) is primarily determined by the social and demographic conditions of the labor-supplying household and its asset situation (as reflected by the size of the household farm). There is hardly any wage response of the labor demand functions, possibly indicating some rigidity in the labor requirements of agricultural operations in a given season. As expected, labor demand[18] depends on such variables as the demographic composition of the labor-buying household, the size of the farm, the extent of irrigation, and the multiple-cropping pattern, and the demand shifts with busy or slack agricultural seasons. After estimating labor supply and demand functions at the household (and the individual) level, we also estimated a simultaneous equations system of labor supply and demand at the village level, which yielded similar results. There is a considerable degree of variation in the wage rates, which is partially explainable in terms of demand or productivity factors, and also in the social and demographic characteristics of laborers. This is in striking contrast to the implied constancy of the real wage in theories of subsistence wage or nutrition-determined efficiency wage.

Although the evidence significantly points to the responsiveness of the wage rates to shifting parameters in the labor demand and supply functions, it is inadequate to support any further elaboration of the actual wage determination mechanism. A competitive wage theory, for example, is not necessarily confirmed by the evidence presented here in favor of a demand-supply framework. As I have suggested, the labor demand functions possibly indicate certain rigidities in labor requirements. We may also note that the wage rate, even though it is sensitive to demand pressures, does not adjust sufficiently to fully clear the labor market; even in the relatively busy seasons in our survey, subrounds 1 (October–December) and 4 (July–September), there was a significant rate of underemployment among agricultural laborers.[19] No doubt, a subround of three months is too long to coincide with the

18. It should be noted, however, that this survey did not seek any detailed input or output information relevant to estimating labor demand functions, as farm management surveys usually do, and also that the labor demand data for each farm refer only to one week.

19. Underemployment, measured in the way specified in footnote 6, is estimated for male casual agricultural laborers to be 8 and 14 percent in the relatively busy subrounds 1 and 4, respectively, and 22 and 24 percent in the relatively slack subrounds 2 and 3, respectively; for female casual agricultural laborers it is estimated to be 19 and 21 percent in the relatively

duration of the busy season in any particular locality and the underemployment even in the busiest quarter partially reflects that area's occasional periods of slackness. But the persistence of some hard-core unemployment, in spite of some flexibility in wages, even for extremely poor households, which are unlikely to be voluntarily idle, and the fact that our estimated equations for the wage rate leave a large part of the variations unexplained, suggest that the theories of wage determination have to go beyond the simple demand-supply framework and investigate the adjustment mechanisms and the nature of lags and inflexibilities in the process. The data base for the household survey we have used is not detailed enough to support such an investigation. For this purpose what we need are not only more intensive, possibly small-scale, micro surveys of the employment and social or demographic characteristics of laborers, but also an integrated picture of the various terms and conditions of contracts in the labor and related markets (land, credit, and commodity markets, in particular) in which labor households participate, and some general background information on the asset and power distribution in the village. The survey investigators visited a household only once during the year and asked questions on time disposition and wage-earning particulars for the preceding week as well as some more general questions concerning the preceding year. For a better understanding of the wage adjustment mechanism, we need data obtained in frequent visits to the same household over the agricultural crop cycle. The present survey also has not given us sufficient information about the nature of the various "pull" factors that might have been operating on the village labor market (such as the distance of the village from, and the conditions in, nearby urban or nonagricultural production and market centers, other prosperous villages, and public works project sites).

---

busy subrounds 1 and 4, respectively, and 44 and 43 percent in the relatively slack subrounds 2 and 3, respectively. The percentage of villages where the village average male underemployment rate was more than 5 percent and yet the village average male wage rate, VWM, was more than Rs 3 (whereas the mean for the whole sample was Rs 2.76) is 12.5 in subround 1, 9.3 in subround 2, 17.0 in subround 3, and 22.6 in subround 4. I should also mention that the estimates of underemployment rates just given do not take into account the discouraged (in view of bleak job prospects) dropouts from the labor force, particularly women. For an analysis of the underemployment data in the survey and for a somewhat better measure of the rate of underemployment (taking into consideration this dropout rate), see P. K. Bardhan (1978*b*).

APPENDIX 12.1

Variables Used in This Chapter

W Wage rate received by casual agricultural laborers in farm work in the reference week.

$\hat{W}$ Predicted farm labor wage rate.

VW Aggregate weighted average wage rate received by adult farm laborers in the village in the current week.

VWM Aggregate weighted average wage rate received by adult male farm laborers in the village.

VEW Expected wage rate for farm laborers in the village.

$VEWM$ Expected wage rate for male farm laborers in the village.

VWL Aggregate weighted average wage rate for adult farm labor hired in the village.

ω Ratio of the minimum acceptable wage rate at which casual agricultural laborers report willingness to do wage work within the village to the current wage rate received by them.

$\hat{\omega}$ Predicted value of ω.

A_c Acceptable wage rate at which casual agricultural laborers report willingness to do wage work within the village.

A_s Acceptable wage rate at which self-employed farmers and family helpers report willingness to do wage work within the village.

H_1 Individual supply (including days seeking or being available for work) of farm wage labor for each casual agricultural laborer.

H_2 Total supply (including days seeking or being available for work) of farm wage labor for all adults in agricultural labor and small-cultivator households.

H_{2m} Total supply (including days seeking or being available for work) of adult male farm wage labor for all adults in agricultural labor and small-cultivator households.

H_{3m} Total supply (including days seeking or being available for work) of adult male farm wage labor from households cultivating more than 0.1 acre and having cultivation as the principal occupation.

S	Total supply (including work on family farm, hiring out, and seeking or being available for work) of adult farm labor days for cultivating households.
S_m	Total supply (including days seeking or being available for work) of adult male farm labor days in cultivating households.
L	Demand for labor days hired on the farm by a cultivating household in the reference week.
N	Demand for labor days used on the farm by a cultivating household in the reference week.
VHM	Total male farm labor days hired out by all households in a village (per acre of cultivated land in the village).
VLM	Total male farm labor days hired in by all households in a village (per acre of cultivated land in the village).
X_1	Per capita amount of land (in acres) cultivated by the household.
X_2	Age (in years) of the individual.
X_3	Number of dependents per earner in the household.
X_4	Number of adults in the household who are in the farm labor force by usual status.
X_5	Amount of land (in acres) cultivated by the household.
X_6	Number of adult males in the household.
X_7	Number of adult males in the household having more than primary education.
X_8	Per capita consumer expenditure in the household.
X_9	District agricultural development (composite) index.
X_{11}	Percentage of the farm's cultivated area under irrigation.
X_{12}	Total number of adults in the household having more than primary education.
X_{13}	Rate of underemployment for casual agricultural laborers.
$D1$	Dummy variable taking the value of 1 when more than one crop is grown in the village; otherwise, it is 0.
$D2$	Dummy variable taking the value of 0 when the household members belong to a scheduled caste or a scheduled tribe; otherwise, it is 1.
$D5$	Dummy variable taking the value of 0 when the proportion of total labor days spent on nonfarm employment in the village is 25 percent or less and the value of 1 when the proportion is more than 25 percent.
$D6$	Dummy variable taking the value of 1 for females; otherwise, it is 0.
$D7$	Dummy variable taking the value of 1 when most of the cultivated land in the village is irrigated; otherwise, it is 0.
$D8$	Dummy variable indicating individuals having more than primary education.

$DS1$ Dummy variable for subround 1, October–December.
$DS2$ Dummy variable for subround 2, January–March.
$DS3$ Dummy variable for subround 3, April–June.
$DS4$ Dummy variable for subround 4, July–September.
$DR1$ Dummy variable for region 1 (the Himalayan region).
$DR2$ Dummy variable for region 2 (the Eastern Plains).
$DR3$ Dummy variable for region 3 (the Central Plains).
$DR4$ Dummy variable for region 4 (the Western Plains).
$VX3$ Aggregate village-level value of X_3.
$VX5$ Aggregate village-level value of X_5.
$VX6$ Aggregate village-level value of X_6.
$VX7$ Aggregate village-level value of X_7.
$VX8$ Aggregate village-level value of X_8.
$VX9$ Aggregate village-level value of X_9.
VUR Weighted average unemployment rate for all village laborers.
$VURM$ Weighted average unemployment rate for all male laborers in the village.

13

Estimating Labor Demand Functions for
Indian Agriculture

Robert E. Evenson and Hans P. Binswanger

The level of employment and of wage rates in the agricultural sector of developing countries in Asia is clearly of importance to policymaking. It is unlikely that substantial reductions in poverty or improvements in relative income distribution can be achieved in the absence of rapidly rising real wages for rural unskilled labor since the incomes of not only the landless but also of small farmers depend to a considerable extent on agricultural wage levels and employment opportunities. This is particularly true in areas where labor supply growth rates are high and where nonagricultural employment opportunities are not expanding rapidly.

A primary objective of studying labor markets is to acquire a capacity to analyze quantitatively the impact of shifts in labor demand or labor supply on the level of employment and of wage rates in rural areas either *ex post* or in projection analysis. Shifts in demand for agricultural labor can come from changes in output market conditions or from technical change. A rich literature exists on the subject of the direct labor demand impact of the green revolution and of investments in irrigation or in agricultural mechanization. (For recent summaries of such studies with regard to India, see International Labor Office 1978; Bartsch 1977; and Binswanger 1978*a*.) Shifts in agricultural labor supply arising from population growth or intersectoral or interregional migration have also been extensively analyzed (Indian Government Planning Commission 1978).

Much of the analysis of the employment and wage effects of such shifts is based on an implicit or explicit assumption of constant wages, or at least fixed technological coefficients of the alternatives considered. This is partly a legacy of the economic development literature of the 1950s, which stressed institutionally determined wages and shared poverty mechanisms in the rural sector. The papers presented earlier in this volume show that wages cannot be considered fixed even if they appear to be determined by institutional arrangements; both the choice of institutional arrangements and their evolution are responsive to changes in supply and demand. Thus a quantitative analysis of the impact of shifts in supply and demand on employment, wages, and earnings requires knowledge of labor supply and labor demand elasticities.

Unfortunately, very few attempts have yet been made to estimate labor supply and demand relations empirically in the Asian context—again a reflection of the emphasis on institutional determinism. The papers by P. K. Bardhan and Rosenzweig in this volume focus primarily on the labor supply side; our effort complements theirs by focusing on labor demand.

Our effort starts from the recognition—one now well supported by empirical studies—that farmers' output supply is responsive to prices and to opportunities for technological innovation. These studies strongly support the hypothesis that Indian farmers are cost and profit conscious. This does not mean that all farmers are equally efficient or that they do not make technical and economic errors. Change is always costly, takes time, and usually is accompanied by experimentation. The cost consciousness of farmers, however, can be expected to make their labor demand decisions responsive to wage rates and to output prices.

In our judgment, therefore, the most appropriate methodological approach to the estimation of a labor demand function is to treat the demand for labor as part of a system of output supply and factor demand equations that takes full account of the interdependent nature of output and input decisions by farmers. The model that we employ in developing our empirical specification is based on the maximization of variable profits by farmers. We do, however, perform statistical tests regarding the imposition of profit-maximizing constraints or restrictions on our specification. We utilize data from several sets of Indian *Studies of the Economics of Farm Management.*

SYSTEMS OF OUTPUT SUPPLY AND FACTOR DEMAND

Systems of output supply and factor demand equations can be derived from a profit function. It should be noted that such systems can exist independently of the behavioral mechanisms of profit maximization, as long as the behavior of individual agents is suffcently stable over time and can be agregated for all farmers. Therefore, the estimated equations are useful for economic analysis whether the theory restrictions of profit maximization hold or not. However, if the restrictions of profit maximization do not hold, we cannot make inferences from the supply and demand equations about the production function underlying them, since behavioral and technological relationships are then confounded in those equations.

We now adopt the following convention. There are n commodities, Y_i, of which the first m are outputs and those indexed $m + 1, \ldots, n$ are variable inputs under the control of the individual agent; that is, we have an $(n \times 1)$ vector of commodities Y such that

$$Y_i \geq 0 \text{ for } i = 1, \ldots, m \quad \text{and} \quad Y_i \leq 0 \text{ for } i = m + 1, \ldots, n. \quad (13.1)$$

These commodities have prices $P_i \geq 0$ for all i. Π is variable profits or return to fixed factors of production and $\Pi = Y'P$ where P is an $(n \times 1)$ vector. Since inputs are defined as negative quantities, they subtract from revenues of the positive outputs. There are also k fixed factors of production, Z_k, $k = 1, \ldots, k$, such as fixed capital or land quality. Let t stand for time or a technology index. If a sufficiently "well-behaved" transformation function[1] exists, $g(Y, Z, t) = 0$, and agents maximize variable profits Π, then a profit function exists that relates maximized profits Π^* to the price of the variable commodities, the fixed factors, and time:

$$\Pi^* = \Pi^*(P, Z, t). \quad (13.2)$$

This profit function has the following properties (where Π_i^* and Π_{ij}^* are derivatives of the function with respect to the ith price or the ith and jth prices).

1. It is monotonically increasing in P if i is an output price and monotonically decreasing in P if i is an input price. The output supply and factor demand curves are:

$$Y_i = \Pi_p^*(P, Z, t) \begin{matrix} \geq 0, \\ \leq 0, \end{matrix} \quad \begin{matrix} i = 1, \ldots, m, \\ i = m + 1, \ldots, n. \end{matrix} \quad (13.3)$$

2. It is symmetric, that is,

$$\Pi_{ij}^* = \Pi_{ji}^*. \quad (13.4)$$

3. It is convex, that is, the (singular) matrix of its cross-derivatives Π_{ij}^* is *positive semidefinite* or all its characteristic roots are positive or zero.

4. It is homogeneous of degree one and the supply and demand equations are homogeneous of degree zero. The matrix

$$[\eta_{ij}] = \left[\frac{\partial Y_i}{\partial P_j} \frac{P_j}{Y_i} \right]$$

defines the output supply and factor demand elasticities, and the following constraint on these elasticities holds:

$$\sum_{j=1}^{n} \eta_{ij} = 0. \quad (13.5)$$

We will consider two alternative functional forms for equation (13.2) in our empirical work. The first, the Generalized Leontief, is written as

$$\Pi^* = \sum_i \sum_j b_{ij} P_i^{\frac{1}{2}} P_j^{\frac{1}{2}} + \sum_i \sum_k b_{ik} P_i Z_k + \sum_i b_{it} P_i t. \quad (13.6)$$

1. For the conditions that must be imposed on the transformation function, see Diewert (1978).

TABLE 13.1. Output Supply and Factor Demand Equations

Functional Form	*Generalized Leontief*	*Normalized Quadratic*
Form of output supply and factor demand equations	$Y_i = b_{ii} + \sum\limits_{j \neq i} b_{ij} \left(\dfrac{P_j}{P_i}\right)^{\frac{1}{2}}$ $+ \sum\limits_{k} b_{ik} Z_k + b_{it} t$ for $i = 1, \ldots, n.$	$Y_i = a_i + \sum\limits_{j=1}^{n-1} b_{ij} \dfrac{P_j}{P_n}$ $+ \sum\limits_{k} b_{ik} Z_k + b_{it} t$ for $i = 1, \ldots, n-1.$ $Y_n = a_o - \dfrac{1}{2} \sum\limits_{i=1}^{n-1} \sum\limits_{j=1}^{n-1} b_{ij} \dfrac{P_i}{P_n} \dfrac{P_j}{P_n}.$
Homogeneity constraint	Imposed not testable.	Imposed, not testable.
Symmetry constraint	$b_{ij} = b_{ji}, i \neq j.$	$b_{ij} = b_{ji}, i, j \neq n,$ and including the b_{ij} of equation $n.$
Elasticities		
Cross-price	$\eta_{ij} = \dfrac{b_{ij}}{2Y_i} \left(\dfrac{P_j}{P_i}\right)^{\frac{1}{2}}.$	$\eta_{ij} = b_{ij} \dfrac{P_j}{Y_i P_n}, i \neq n.$ $\eta_{nj} = \dfrac{P_j}{P_n 2 Y_n} \sum\limits_{i=1}^{n-1} b_{ij} P_i,$ $j = 1, \ldots, n-1.$
Own-price	$\eta_{ii} = \sum\limits_{j \neq i} \dfrac{b_{ij}}{2Y_i} \left(\dfrac{P_j}{P_i}\right)^{\frac{1}{2}}.$	$\eta_{ii} = b_{ii} \dfrac{P_i}{Y_i P_n}, i \neq j, n.$ $\eta_{nn} = -\sum\limits_{j=1}^{n-1} \eta_{nj}.$

The corresponding output supply and factor demand system is given in the first column of table 13.1. All n equations can be estimated jointly but the profit function (13.6) is not linearly independent since it is the linear combination $\sum_{i=1}^{n} Y_i P_i$ of the individual equations. Note that in this system homogeneity is not testable because for each equation, η_{ii} is estimated residually and we have no other independent estimates of it. This characteristic is a serious liability when data sets are not complete.

The second functional form is derived from the Normalized Quadratic profit function. (For a discussion of normalized profit functions, see Lau 1976.) A normalized profit function is derived by stating the initial profit-maximizing problem in terms of normalized prices $q_i = P_i/P_n$, where all prices and profits are divided by the price of the nth commodity. Normalized profits then are written as

$$\tilde{\Pi} = \frac{\Pi}{P_n} = \sum_{i=1}^{n-1} Y_i q_i + Y_n. \tag{13.7}$$

Shephard's Lemma then states that $\partial \tilde{\Pi} / \partial q_i = Y_i$. The Normalized Quadratic profit function is written as

$$\tilde{\Pi} = a_o + \sum_{i=1}^{n-1} a_i q_i + \frac{1}{2} \sum_{i=1}^{n-1} \sum_{j=1}^{n-1} b_{ij} q_i q_j + \sum_{i=1}^{n-1} \sum_k b_{ik} q_i Z_k + \sum_{i=1}^{n-1} b_{ik} q_{it}. \quad (13.8)$$

The output supply and factor demand curves for the first $n-1$ outputs and factors are given in column 2 of table 13.1, in terms of the original prices. Homogeneity of degree zero is imposed on the equations and cannot be tested. Symmetry is tested in the usual way. Note that in this system we do not have the nth commodity equation, which has to be derived from equation (13.8) and the commodity equations

$$Y_i = a_i + \sum_{j=1}^{n-1} b_{ij} q_j + \sum_k b_{ik} Z_k + b_{it}. \quad (13.9)$$

From equation (13.7) we can compute $Y_n = \tilde{\Pi} - \sum_{i=1}^{n-1} Y_i q_i$, and substituting into this equation (13.8) and the commodity equations we have

$$Y_n = a_o - \frac{1}{2} \sum_{i=1}^{n-1} \sum_{j=1}^{n-1} b_{ij} q_i q_j. \quad (13.10)$$

The derivatives of this equation with respect to individual prices are

$$\frac{\partial Y_n}{\partial P_j} - -\sum_{i=1}^{n-1} b_{ij} \frac{P_i}{P_n^2}, \quad j < n, \quad (13.11)$$

from which we can compute the elasticities for the nth equation as

$$\eta_{nj} = \frac{\partial Y_n}{\partial P_j} \cdot \frac{P_j}{Y_n} = -\frac{P_j}{P_n^2 Y_n} \sum_{i=1}^{n-1} b_{ij} P_i. \quad (13.12)$$

Finally, η_{nn} can be determined residually, using equation (13.5), as $\eta_{nn} = -\sum_{j=1}^{n-1} \eta_{nj}$. Note that we could include equation (13.6) in the estimation process or leave it out and estimate the elasticities of the nth equation residually.

All equations reported in this study are estimated jointly by generalized least squares, taking account of error interdependence across equations (Zellner 1962). Dummy variables for region effects are included in the equations. Restrictions across equations are then tested by means of F tests. Elasticities are computed using the equations in table 13.1 and the predicted values of those dependent variables that appear in the equations. The standard errors of the elasticities reported are approximations since they only take account of the variance of the coefficients in the equations and not the variance of the predicted values.

DATA AND DEFINITIONS OF VARIABLES

The Indian Farm Management Studies have provided a valuable data base for a number of studies of Indian agriculture. They were conducted in selected districts throughout India from 1954–55 to 1971–72, when they were discontinued. Summary reports have now been published for 26 or more studies conducted in 22 different districts in 14 states. These studies utilized relatively standardized statistical designs and data collection methods and concepts. The typical statistical design of the studies was first to randomly select 10 or 15 sample villages in the district. Then a random sample of 10 to 15 farms stratified by acreage farmed was selected in each village. Data on production, inputs, prices, and costs were carefully collected from the 150 sample farms for three consecutive years.

Several districts conducted studies in the 1950s and again in the 1960s. The study reports include data for the average farm in an aggregated group. A typical report provides all of the relevant data for farms in five to seven size groups and two or three regions. We have utilized the average farm characteristics of these groups of farms as observations. District studies were divided into four major geoclimatic regions: Northern Wheat, Eastern Rice, Coastal Rice, and the Semiarid Tropics. Table 13.2 gives definitions of the variables and indicates the allocation of Farm Management Studies by region. The dependent variables reflect the structure of the systems of equations estimated. Equations were estimated for output, bullock labor, human labor, and, using the Northern Wheat data, for tractors.

We have treated operated area, irrigation intensity, and fragmentation as fixed factors. We have also treated buildings and minor implements as a fixed capital stock. This treatment may not be fully consistent with reality, but because some quantity rationing takes place in the market for credit and for major implements, we believe this treatment to be justified.

We do not have consistent data on farm operator characteristics such as experience and schooling and thus were unable to include these as fixed factors. Our output price variables are based on district average prices received by farmers rather than on prices actually reported by farmers since the latter reflected decisions as to when to sell the crop. Price of human labor is the average village-level wage for each region.

TESTS OF RESTRICTIONS

We first estimated the equations systems for each data set in unrestricted and restricted form for each functional form and performed a test of the compatibility of the restrictions imposed by variable profit-maximizing behavior with the data. This is a test comparing the weighted mean square error for the system with and without restrictions. The test results are reported in table 13.3. The value of computed F's for which one would reject the hypothesis that mean square errors are not significantly higher in the presence of restrictions is roughly 2.1 or greater at the 5 percent probability level and 2.9 at the 1 percent level.

TABLE 13.2. Definitions and Means of Variables by Geoclimatic Region

Variable/Definition	Northern Wheat	Eastern Rice	Coastal Rice	Semiarid Tropics
Dependent variables				
Output (value in constant prices of main product plus by-product)	15,038.22	10,199.95	4,240.85	1,706.76
Bullock labor (days used, hired, and owned)	469.89	147.78	164.60	229.49
Human labor (days worked by family, permanent, casual workers)	610.66	343.03	1,392.65	598.65
Tractors (days used)	15.103	—	—	—
Independent variables				
Land (operated area, in ha)	8.39	3.31	4.88	7.13
High-yielding varieties (proportion of land planted to high-yielding varieties of wheat, rice, and sorghum)	3.06	0.15	9.47	—
Irrigation intensity (gross irrigated area/gross cropped area)	0.74	0.125	0.569	0.202
Fragmentation (number of fragments/operated area)	1.59	4.46	3.55	1.17
Buildings and equipment (value in Rs)	3,465.97	650.23	3,270.52	2,249.52
Minor implements (value in Rs)	1,127.97	—	—	—
Price of output (value in Rs)	1.12	1.03	1.03	1.10
Price of bullock labor (value in Rs)	6.24	2.13	5.79	4.36
Price of human labor (value in Rs)	2.076	2.068	1.73	1.18
Price of tractors (value in Rs)	64.74	—	—	—

Sources: Indian *Studies of the Economics of Farm Management* (by year), arranged by region:

Northern Wheat. Uttar Pradesh: Meerut (54, 55, 56), Muzaffarnagar (66, 67, 68). Punjab: Amritsar and Ferozepur (55, 56, 57); Ferozepur (67, 68, 69); Karnal, Rohtak, Jind (61, 62, 63).
Eastern Rice. Assam: Nowgong (68, 69). Bihar: Shahabad (60, 61, 62). Orissa: Samabalpur (57, 58, 59). West Bengal: Hooghly (54, 55, 56).
Coastal Rice. Andhra Pradesh: West Godavari (57, 58, 59). Kerala: Aleppy and Quilon (62, 63, 64). Orissa: Cuttack (67, 68, 69). Tamil Nadu: Thanjavur (67, 68, 69).
Semiarid Tropics. Madhya Pradesh: Akola and Amraoti (55, 56). Maharashtra: Ahmednagar and Nasik (54, 55, 56). Rajasthan: Pali (62, 63, 64). Uttar Pradesh: Deoria (66, 67, 68). Andhra Pradesh: Cuddapah (67, 68, 69). Karnataka: Bangalore (60, 61). Gujarat: Bulsar and Surat (66, 67, 68). Tamil Nadu: Coimbatore and Salem (55, 55, 56, 70, 71). Madhya Pradesh: Raipur (62, 63, 64).

TABLE 13.3. Summary of Restriction Tests

Region	Generalized Leontief	Normalized Quadratic
Northern Wheat	4.78	8.06
Eastern Rice	1.26	5.77
Coastal Rice	1.85	0.62
Semiarid Tropics	3.54	2.79

Table 13.3 indicates that the symmetry restrictions are rejected in the Northern Wheat and Semiarid Tropics regions for the Generalized Leontief form and in all regions except Coastal Rice for the Normalized Quadratic form. It should be noted also that the own price elasticities are computed residually for the Generalized Leontief form and they are thus subject to error form left-out variable biases. We believe, however, that in the interest of comparability, we should report both restricted and unrestricted estimates for both functional forms. The elasticity estimates are very similar for both functional forms and for the restricted and unrestricted forms.[2] The issue of the "preferred" estimates depends on one's willingness to impose theory on data.

Tables 13.4 and 13.5 report estimates of the labor demand elasticities for the Normalized Quadratic and the Generalized Leontief forms. When the symmetry test was not met, unrestricted estimates are reported. The elasticities are computed with sample means. The t ratios are reported in parentheses. The appendix at the end of this chapter gives full system estimates for the restricted Normalized Quadratic equations to enable the reader to judge the consistency of the full model.

DISCUSSION OF ESTIMATES

We would first point out that the estimates obtained are generally consistent with a priori expectations. All estimates of the elasticity of the demand for labor with respect to the wage rate are negative. Most estimates of the elasticity with regard to crop price are positive as expected. We also expect human and bullock labor to be substitutes in production and this is borne out by the data. The key elasticity estimated, the wage elasticity, is remarkably robust to the data and to the estimation procedure. In general, the full systems are also well estimated; most of the estimates in the appendix have the expected signs. We now turn to a discussion of each elasticity estimated.

Wage Elasticities

This elasticity is of obvious importance from a policy perspective. Our estimates are generally highly significant and fall within a range of -0.2 to -0.7 (except for Coastal Rice in the restricted Generalized Leontief form), indicating that the demand for labor in Indian agriculture is wage inelastic.

---

2. A statistical approach would call for rejecting restricted estimates when the test was not met. On the other hand, a more theoretical approach might imply that even when the test is not met, restricted estimates may be superior because they are estimated subject to restrictions consistent with a priori theorizing. One could, for example, explain variance in a spurious fashion by including endogenous variables in an equation.

TABLE 13.4. Estimated Labor Demand Elasticities: Normalized Quadratic Form

Variable	Northern Wheat			Eastern Rice		Coastal Rice	Semiarid Tropics	
	Unrestricted	Restricted	Restricted	Unrestricted	Restricted	Restricted	Unrestricted	Restricted
Wage rate	−0.3472	−0.4141	−0.5886	−0.6065	−0.5347	−0.2938	−0.3106	−0.3555
	(4.016)	(4.966)	(7.527)	(6.669)	(6.193)	(1.576)	(4.599)	(5.134)
Bullock labor price	0.0853	0.2141	−0.0898	0.2384	0.1028	0.1855	−0.1170	0.0615
	(0.7558)	(2.056)	(0.8299)	(3.371)	(2.238)	(3.208)	(0.9285)	(0.7832)
Crop price	0.2619	0.2000	−0.4237	0.3682	0.4319	0.1083	0.4276	0.2940
	(2.041)	(1.5805)	(2.764)	(3.405)	(4.118)	(0.5632)	(3.462)	(3.147)
Tractor price	—	—	1.1021	—	—	—	—	—
	—	—	(8.164)	—	—	—	—	—
Operated area	0.4125	0.4134	0.4834	0.8824	0.8969	0.4046	0.5065	0.5081
	(11.455)	(11.483)	(14.628)	(17.080)	(17.477)	(4.413)	(16.095)	(16.152)
Irrigation intensity	0.0018	−0.0149	0.0821	0.0772	0.0824	−0.6386	0.0541	0.0548
	(0.0238)	(0.2006)	(1.061)	(3.716)	(3.992)	(2.509)	(1.281)	(1.297)
Capital	0.0797	0.0903	0.0458	0.0780	0.0609	−0.0808	0.1333	0.1311
	(2.785)	(3.182)	(2.145)	(2.224)	(1.773)	(0.7520)	(9.091)	(8.977)
Fragmentation intensity	−0.3196	−0.3109	−0.2616	0.0041	0.0077	−0.4853	−0.2050	−0.2040
	(6.015)	(5.862)	(4.900)	(0.0540)	(0.1010)	(2.866)	(5.089)	(5.065)
High-yielding varieties	−0.0059	−0.0038	−0.0056	−0.0110	−0.0126	0.0512	—	—
	(0.5963)	(0.3824)	(0.5586)	(1.866)	(2.147)	(0.1104)	—	—

TABLE 13.5. Estimated Labor Demand Elasticities: Generalized Leontief Form

	Northern Wheat		Eastern Rice	Coastal Rice	Semiarid Tropics	
Variable	Restricted	Unrestricted	Restricted	Restricted	Restricted	Unrestricted
Wage rate	−0.1547	−0.1994	−0.6610	−1.2672	−0.3460	−0.3541
	(2.3883)	(2.7853)	(5.9253)	(4.3263)	(4.5477)	(4.6368)
Bullock labor price	0.1096	−0.0058	0.0809	0.3221	0.2127	0.2194
	(1.1773)	(0.0594)	(1.8055)	(2.4543)	(3.2191)	(2.5052)
Crop price	0.0451	0.2052	0.5801	0.9451	0.1333	0.1347
	(0.4130)	(1.7122)	(4.8047)	(2.8064)	(1.4471)	(1.2785)
Operated area	0.3967	0.3945	0.9251	0.4328	0.5014	0.5010
	(10.805)	(10.744)	(16.628)	(4.931)	(15.901)	(15.879)
Irrigation intensity	0.0585	0.0534	0.0850	−0.5941	0.0523	0.0523
	(0.7997)	(0.7254)	(4.056)	(2.437)	(1.237)	(1.237)
Capital	0.0472	0.0464	0.0585	−0.1392	0.1428	0.1436
	(1.746)	(1.705)	(1.681)	(1.410)	(9.340)	(9.269)
Fragmentation intensity	−0.3632	−0.3682	0.0220	−0.5694	−0.2099	−0.2099
	(6.843)	(6.933)	(0.2854)	(3.465)	(5.212)	(5.212)
High-yielding varieties	−0.0124	−0.0131	−0.0101	0.1160	—	—
	(1.247)	(1.308)	(1.744)	(0.2624)	—	—

These estimates are consistent across data sets and fairly robust to estimation procedures.

Output Price Elasticities

The response of labor demand to output price is also clearly of importance. The estimates range from 0.04 to 0.9 and are quite stable (except for Northern Wheat, when tractor prices are also included, and Coastal Rice). We conclude that farmers respond to output prices by hiring more labor. Again, this is relatively inelastic.

Bullock Labor Price Elasticities

Our estimates of this elasticity range from 0.06 to 0.32 in the restricted estimates indicating that human and bullock labor are moderately good substitutes for each other. Negative values occurring in three cases are not statistically significant. Therefore, when bullock labor prices rise, farmers tend to hire more labor.

Land and Irrigation Elasticities

Our operated area elasticities range from 0.4 to 0.9, showing that large farms generally employ fewer workers per hectare. The irrigation elasticities are generally quite low and are actually negative in the Coastal Rice region. It appears that an expansion of irrigated acreage per se will not produce a substantial increase in the demand for labor.

Fragmentation Elasticities

We find substantial evidence that fragmentation reduces the demand for labor. Land consolidation would presumably increase the demand for labor.

Capital Elasticities

In general, we find that expanded use of conventional farm implements (such as carts), has a very small impact on the demand for labor. In the Northern Wheat estimates we are able to define a tractor price variable. Here we find that when tractors are treated as a variable factor, they show up as a strong substitute for labor (but not for bullocks). A 10 percent decrease in the price of tractors will result in an 11 percent decrease in labor employment by our estimate.

High-yielding Varieties

Our findings with respect to this variable are inconclusive and inconsistent with micro evidence. It appears that the use of high-yielding varieties does not increase the demand for labor.

SUMMARY

The systems approach used in the estimation specification described in this paper is quite demanding of data. Farmer behavior must be observed in relation to substantial price variation for all the factors of production used. This generally requires observations that are spread over several years. There are alternative procedures for estimating labor demand functions that are less demanding of data. With linear programming, for example, a minimum of data over time is required. One could also estimate a production function from quantity data and proceed to infer, or calculate, a labor demand function by supposing the existence of profit-maximizing behavior. Our approach has been to estimate the labor demand function directly from observed behavior.

We believe that our estimates are of sufficient quality to be the subject of policy-related discussion. Our major findings are:

1. The elasticity of demand for labor with respect to the wage rate facing farm employers is low, in the -0.2 to -0.7 range.

2. The elasticity of demand for labor with respect to output prices is positive and generally in the 0.1 to 0.4 range.

3. Bullock power appears to be a good substitute for labor.

4. Irrigation investment does not appear to have a large employment effect.

5. The adoption of high-yielding varieties does not appear to have a large employment effect.

6. Fragmentation reduces the demand for labor.

7. Growth in fixed capital stock is associated with small increases in employment.

8. Tractors are good substitutes for labor.

The picture that emerges is thus one of a labor market that is relatively inelastic to wage changes. A rightward shift in the supply function of labor to the agricultural sector will not be absorbed with only a small decrease in wages. Conversely, a leftward shift could result in a significant increase in wage rates. Migration policies, for example, that were designed to reduce migration out of a rural area would be likely to have severe wage effects for those remaining in rural areas. And, of course, policies inducing more migration would have the reverse effects. Policymakers should not presume that the agricultural system is flexible enough to absorb labor easily. Nor can policy be based on an assumption that output prices have little effect on the demand for labor. Our estimates show an inelastic, but statistically significant, response of labor demand to output prices.

Our data do not suggest that investment in fixed capital or irrigation infrastructure has high employment effects. We find some evidence that a decrease in tractor prices has a large negative employment effect.

The findings of Rosenzweig and P. K. Bardhan reported in the preceding chapters imply low supply elasticities of labor with regard to workers resident in a particular village or region. Inelastic supply and demand for agricultural labor together imply a substantial sensitivity of rural wage rates to shifts in labor demand or supply or to the policies that induce them. This is in sharp contrast to the earlier theoretical literature on rural labor markets, which stressed institutional wage fixities and income-sharing mechanisms that would jointly imply a capacity of agriculture to absorb additional labor, without substantial deterioration of rural wages or standards of living.

TABLE A13.1. Regression Estimates of Models by Region

	Bullocks	Northern Wheat (including tractors)		
		Labor	Tractor	Output
Intercept	−110.698	45.237	9.521	15,019,620
	(−0.73)	(0.34)	(0.82)	(2.29)*
Price ratios				
Bullocks/output	16.651	9.719	−1.532	280.703
	(1.15)	(0.79)	(−1.51)	(0.44)
Labor/output	9.719	191.396	−11.493*	17.994
	(0.79)	(7.17)*	(−7.78)	(0.01)
Tractor/output	−1.532	−11.493	0.335*	−270.854
	(−1.51)	(−7.78)*	(2.19)	(−3.08)*
Operated area	−36.300*	−35.146	−1.786	529.048
	(−13.69)	(−14.63)*	(−9.37)*	(4.73)*
Irrigation	22.170	−66.984	4.615	15,640.140
	(0.31)	(−1.06)	(0.89)	(5.27)*
Fragmentation	−25.683	99.922	−4.311	−3,837.410
	(−1.12)	(4.90)*	(−2.64)*	(−4.04)*
High-yielding varieties	16.738*	1.114	−0.191	140.527
	(7.39)	(0.56)	(−1.18)	(1.51)
Capital	5.006E-3	−1.197E-2	−2.574E-4	2.538
	(0.78)	(−2.15)*	(−0.57)	(9.73)*
Regional dummies				
1	103.545	−34.174	9.387	−12,549.700
	(0.91)	(−0.35)	(1.19)	(−2.63)*
2	−2,275.780	−677.230	−5.657	−501.522
	(−15.33)*	(−5.19)*	(−0.55)	(−0.08)
3	314.915	74.519	12.194	−3,241.500
	(3.39)*	(0.91)	(1.82)	(−0.82)
4	147.805	−327.372	5.144	7,208.342
	(1.47)	(−3.72)*	(0.73)	(1.75)

TABLE A13.1—(continued)

	Northern Wheat (excluding tractors)			Eastern Rice		
	Bullocks	Labor	Output	Bullocks	Labor	Output
Intercept	−103.004 (−0.72)	−358.055 (−2.98)*	11,051.57 (1.98)*	−67.340 (−1.27)	−254.074 (−3.16)*	28,908.380 (6.04)*
Price ratios						
Bullocks/output	14.360 (0.98)	−23.743 (−1.97)*	−702.601 (−1.20)	36.312 (4.60)*	−17.221 (−2.13)*	−251.832 (−0.36)
Labor/output	−23.743 (−1.97)*	138.054 (4.75)*	−3,745.31 (−2.76)*	−17.221 (−2.13)*	92.124 (5.91)*	847.443 (0.90)
Operated area	−32.617 (−10.815)*	−30.060 (−11.48)*	160.082 (1.35)	−39.430 (−10.30)*	−98.866 (−17.48)*	1,355.103 (4.13)*
Irrigation	95.690 (1.44)	12.116 (0.20)	16,720.34 (6.09)*	−30.242 (−0.79)	−225.728 (−3.99)*	922.200 (0.28)
Fragmentation	−19.211 (−0.84)	118.749 (5.86)*	−4,838.54 (−5.26)*	−0.877 (−0.22)	−0.588 (−0.10)	347.225 (1.03)
High-yielding varieties	16.894 (7.48)*	0.759 (0.38)	76.539 (0.85)	11.766 (1.27)	29.354 (2.15)*	2,532.046 (3.19)*
Capital	−5.935E-3 (−1.11)	−1.591E-2 (−3.18)*	2.579 (11.29)*	9.119E-3 (0.74)	−0.032 (−1.77)	−1.008 (−0.95)
Regional dummies						
1	1.756 (0.02)	−162.260 (−1.59)	−10,335.3 (−2.13)*	56.620 (1.44)	116.056 (2.04)*	−34,960.900 (−10.19)*
2	−2,317.29 (−16.10)*	−643.101 (−4.91)*	419.611 (0.07)	−7.325 (−0.17)	200.736 (3.05)*	−33,974.700 (−8.61)*
3	244.399 (2.63)*	−75.442 (−0.89)	−1,474.4 (−0.37)	−122.112 (−3.22)*	376.505 (6.10)*	−32,976.400 (−9.28)*
4	26.868 (0.27)	−438.921 (−5.05)*	9,126.81 (2.30)*			

TABLE A13.1—(continued)

	Coastal Rice			Semiarid Tropics		
	Bullocks	Labor	Output	Bullocks	Labor	Output
Intercept	-104.508 (-0.26)	-2,714.520 (-0.63)	-8,934.630 (-0.73)	-65.427 (-2.68)*	-232.948 (-3.36)*	581.842 (1.20)
Price ratios						
Bullocks/output	3.456 (0.37)	-46.028 (-3.02)*	133.955 (0.50)	-2.724 (-0.33)	-10.296 (-0.76)	-541.828 (-3.38)*
Labor/output	-46.028 (-3.02)*	242.738 (1.49)	-889.372 (-1.93)	-10.296 (-0.76)	219.248 (5.00)*	1,010.912 (3.24)*
Operated area	-27.328 (-11.10)*	-115.384 (-4.41)*	1,386.214 (18.82)*	-33.889 (-34.88)*	-42.650 (-16.15)*	38.571 (2.09)*
Irrigation	-86.085 (-1.46)	1,562.022 (2.51)*	6,418.777 (3.64)*	10.426 (0.23)	-162.219 (-1.30)	870.806 (1.00)
Fragmentation	-3.846 (-0.62)	190.112 (2.87)*	184.484 (0.99)	-14.918 (-1.97)*	104.263 (5.06)*	-1,471.270 (-10.22)*
High-yielding varieties	3.342 (0.52)	-7.524 (-0.11)	104.735 (0.55)	—	—	
Capital	-8.632E-3 (-2.00)*	0.034 (0.75)	-0.547 (-4.24)*	6.129E-3 (4.31)*	-3.489E-2 (-8.98)*	2.789E-2 (1.02)

TABLE A13.1—(continued)

Regional dummies

1	186.351 (0.45)	−78.022 (−0.02)	819.869 (0.07)	211.473 (4.81)*	−463.367 (−4.33)*	5,534.089 (6.58)*
2	295.237 (0.73)	552.438 (0.13)	10,706.390 (0.88)	58.188 (0.84)	−301.260 (−1.59)	2,976.600 (2.25)*
3	260.826 (0.64)	259.614 (0.06)	6,631.349 (0.55)	231.050 (2.27)*	−831.191 (−4.83)*	9,943.236 (5.08)*
4				−20.685 (−0.90)	64.229 (1.02)	130.912 (0.30)
5				230.863 (2.99)*	−641.063 (−4.10)*	3,878.475 (6.09)*
6				139.699 (4.14)*	−284.381 (−3.15)*	3,799.108 (5.89)*
7				184.175 (4.89)*	76.723 (0.74)	144.150 (0.19)
8				(168.425) (6.11)*	−205.561 (−3.32)*	1,157.463 (2.22)*
9				197.678 (2.88)*	−916.838 (−5.67)*	21,411.160 (16.43)*
10				−33.822 (−1.72)	−92.554 (−1.73)	−200.187 (−0.53)

*Significant at 5 percent level.

14

Interstate and Within-State Migration in India

Sanjay Dhar

In this paper I analyze the response of migrants in India to economic incentives and disincentives from the late 1960s to 1971. The data for analysis were limited to males, since a large proportion of female migration in India is for noneconomic reasons such as marriage. The period covered is of particular interest because it coincides with the initial adoption of the new agricultural technology in India. It is by now well documented that agricultural growth during that period (and subsequently) has been very uneven. Although the potential for the spread of the new techniques is present in many regions where the productivity of agriculture is low, it is clear that there are wide differences in the potential for development among these regions, caused mainly by disparities in irrigation resources and rainfall. Thus, any long-term plan aiming at an increase in labor productivity and rural employment opportunities should consider the possibility of the migration of a relatively large proportion of the population away from areas of low agroeconomic potential. In this context it becomes important to calculate migration responses to changes in economic variables that have already occurred.

The plan of this paper is as follows. The first section describes the empirical model to be used in the estimation of the migration functions. The next two sections give estimates of interstate and within-state migration, respectively. In the last section I state some conclusions arising from the results that I have presented.

I would like to thank Hans P. Binswanger, Robert E. Evenson, Mark R. Rosenzweig, and T. Paul Schultz for helpful comments, Sidney Feit and Kurt Kaboth for advice on programming issues, and the Indian census authorities for permission to use unpublished migration data. Errors, if any, in reporting or interpreting data are my own. Partial funding for this paper was provided by a grant from USAID Project AID/DSAN-C-0020. This paper consists of parts of my dissertation entitled "An Analysis of Internal Migration in India," Yale University, 1980.

THEORETICAL SPECIFICATION AND THE CHOICE OF ECONOMETRIC
TECHNIQUE

The Gravity Model of Migration

Explanatory variables in migration functions typically include origin and destination wage rates or income levels, unemployment or employment rates, education or literacy rates, and urbanization and population levels, as well as measures of the distance between regions of origin and destination. Although there seems to be a consensus as to the type of economic variables that affect migration, there is no uniformity concerning the manner in which demographic variables are entered into the migration function. A variety of dependent variables are used, even in ordinary least squares (OLS) estimation; for example, M_{ij}/P_i, $M_{ij}/(P_i \cdot P_j)$, M_{ij}, where M_{ij} is the gross flow of migrants from region i to region j, P_i is the population of region i, and P_j is the population of region j.

The origin of most empirical research of this type is the "gravity" model of migration, in which gross flows of migrants are assumed to be directly proportional to origin and destination populations and inversely proportional to the distance between origin and destination, in addition to being dependent on a number of other origin and destination variables:

$$M_{ij} = P_i^\alpha P_j^\beta D_{ij}^\gamma f(x_i, x_j), \qquad i, j = 1, \ldots, n, \tag{14.1}$$

where D_{ij} is the distance between region i and region j, and x_i, x_j are vectors of origin and destination variables, respectively. Estimation of equation (14.1) is usually done in double logarithmic form.

The normalization most frequently adopted in actual estimation is to divide migration flows by the origin population. Strict adherence to the gravity model would require including both origin and destination populations on the right-hand side of the equation as, for example, suggested by Levy and Wadycki (1972):

$$M_{ij}/P_i = P_i^{\alpha-1} P_j^\beta D_{ij}^\gamma f(x_i, x_j). \tag{14.2}$$

However, population variables included on the right-hand side often tend to be highly correlated with other explanatory variables, and the method of their inclusion may vary with the problems encountered when using different data sets. Other authors have omitted both population variables from the right-hand side or imposed a "constant returns to scale" property with respect to origin and destination populations (Mundlak 1979)—the rationale being that doubling the origin and destination populations should double the flow of migration, other factors remaining constant. Imposing homogeneity ($\alpha = 1 - \beta$) in equation (14.1) implies that

$$M_{ij}/P_i = (P_j/P_i)^\beta D_{ij}^\gamma f(x_i, x_j). \tag{14.3}$$

Another normalization is $M_{ij}/(P_i \cdot P_j)$, which was used by Greenwood (1971b) and Huntington (1974). It imposes the restriction of $\beta = 1$ (in addition to $\alpha = 1$) if P_i, P_j are left out of the right-hand side. The unnormalized dependent variable, M_{ij}, is difficult to interpret in economic terms and also suffers from other statistical problems. For a discussion of the economic and statistical problems associated with various formulations of the gravity model, see Schultz (1977, 1978), who recommends the polytomous logit model. The reasons why this statistically preferable model was not used here are discussed in my dissertation.

In the present study the dependent variable for all the migration equations is the gross migration flow divided by the relevant (rural or urban) origin population. The origin population has been excluded from the right-hand side of the function to avoid the problem of a high correlation with other explanatory variables; its inclusion always produced a negative coefficient, implying that $\alpha < 1$ in equation (14.2), and the coefficient was often found to be not significant. The constant returns to scale property of origin and destination populations assumed by Mundlak (1979) was tested for the interstate flows using equation (14.1) and was rejected in each case. Destination population was therefore included in unrestricted form on the right-hand side and its coefficient was consistently found to be positive and highly significant. This variable was, of course, also correlated with a number of other explanatory variables, but comparison of parameter coefficients of equations with and without its inclusion indicated a reasonably high level of stability of the parameter estimates.

Simultaneity

Estimation of the determinants of migration using single-equation methods has been the practice in nearly all previous work, reflecting the fact that models of intersectoral mobility have not been developed sufficiently to satisfactorily handle the endogenous relationship of migration, wages, employment, and so on. However, the likelihood of serious simultaneous equation biases will depend on the scope of the study; for example, lifetime flows are more likely to suffer from this problem than migration measured over shorter periods. In this study, the ratio of migration flows to origin and destination populations is very low, and the use of single-equation techniques is justifiable. The main emphasis here is therefore on OLS estimation. However, sufficient data for the separate estimation of rural wage equations were available, and it was also possible to estimate the migration relationship in a simultaneous equation framework in which the rate of migration as well as rural wages were taken to be endogenous.

INTERSTATE MIGRATION

Characteristics of the Data

Any migration study is to a large extent dependent on the type of information that is available. In some aspects the 1971 census of India's migration data is the best source available for less developed countries. Not only are migration flows disaggregated by rural and urban sectors but information is also provided on the duration of residence of migrants in their place of destination. However, useful classifications of migration by age, occupation, and education are only available for the big cities and the place of origin of these migrants is not given. A complete matrix with information on place of origin as well as place of destination could therefore only be compiled on the basis of migration flows disaggregated by rural and urban sectors and by the duration of residence. Interstate flows for rural to urban, urban to rural, and rural to rural migration were examined separately for migrants who resided in their destinations for a period of 1–4 years and for a period of less than 1 year; the results for 1–4 years are presented first for each type of flow. Data from 15 major states were used, with each state serving as both origin and destination. This procedure resulted in observations on 210 (15 × 14) migration flows for each of the above categories.

The fact that 1970–71 explanatory data are used for 1966–70 as well as for 1970–71 migration may be questioned. There are several points to note here. First, a complete set of time series data for all the explanatory variables does not exist, thus precluding the systematic use of a model with lagged independent variables. Second, previous work, such as Greenwood's (1971a) analysis of Indian migration using the 1961 census, has obtained very similar results for *lifetime* as compared with annual migration using 1961 explanatory data only, suggesting that the ranking of states in terms of different economic variables has remained stable over long periods. During a 4-year period, one can expect a sizable quantity of return migration as well as migration into a state other than that of planned destination. Therefore, the use of data pertaining to the end of the migration period will facilitate a more accurate estimation of the relatively permanent flows that occured over this period, since all the people sampled in the census will have had the benefit of observing later-period economic variables. A comparison of the results of using this estimation procedure with the results of introducing earlier wage data is made in my dissertation.

The rationale for choosing economic variables for migration functions has traditionally come from an investment theory approach in which the individual migrant from state *i* to state *j* takes into consideration the net expected returns from migration. Where states are separated into rural and urban sectors, the migrant may be influenced not only by economic variables in the sector/state of origin and destination, but also by conditions in the other sector of origin and/or destination states. This effect was found to be particularly significant in migration to the rural sector; such migrants were often found to be influenced by economic variables in the urban sector of the destination state, suggesting that the aim of eventual residence in urban areas was an important factor.

On the basis of the hypothesis that the individual balances the costs of and returns to migration, inclusion of a variety of variables can be justified. Variables such as origin wage, destination unemployment, distance, and differences in origin and destination language can enter into a cost function represented both by pecuniary benefits and by nonpecuniary deterrent effects, whereas returns, also broadly defined, may be a function of destination wage, origin unemployment, and destination literacy. The combined migration function is thus specified in terms of both costs and returns, and that stategy is followed here. However, given the aggregate nature of the data, it seems preferable not to base our expectations about the results on a single hypothesized response. We should be aware that different economic sections of the population will respond differently to changes in economic variables and also that individuals in the same migration stream may have widely different reasons for moving. Accordingly, an attempt is made in this paper to offer, where necessary, competing explanations of particular results.

Appendix 14.1 gives the definitions of the variables used in the discussion of interstate migration. All the variables (except for the language dummy) are in the form of logarithms, and since the equations were estimated in double logarithmic form, parameter estimates represent elasticities. The T statistics are presented in parentheses below the coefficient values.

Rural–Urban Migration

Tables 14.1 and 14.2 give estimates for rural–urban migration. Ordinary least squares estimates are presented in column 1. I reestimated the migration relationship (column 2) using two-stage least squares (2SLS) with rural wages (column 3) as the other endogenous variable. Since the results of the equations (columns 1 and 2) are very similar in both tables, I will initially limit the discussion to the OLS equations.

The coefficient of the origin rural wage is negative, as expected, in column 1 of both tables and significant in table 14.1. This result is in marked contrast to the results described in Greenwood (1971*b*)—where 1961 rural average incomes instead of wages are used—as well as to my own preliminary results. In both cases the coefficient of origin rural wage (or income) is found to be significantly positive. The change from the puzzling positive to the expected negative coefficients is basically a result of the introduction into the equations of variables describing the levels of education and distribution

TABLE 14.1. Rural–Urban Migration, 1–4 Years

Variable	(1) OLS $M_{ij}/RPOP_i$	(2) 2SLS $M_{ij}/RPOP_i$		(3) 2SLS $RWAGE_i$
$M_{ij}/RPOP_i$				0.0136
				(2.51)
$RWAGE_i$	−1.35	−1.15		
	(2.62)	(2.06)		
$UWAGE_j$	2.69	2.69	TFP_i	0.463
	(6.42)	(6.42)		(6.25)
$UWAGE_i$	−3.68	−3.49	$IRRIG_i$	0.280
	(5.69)	(5.15)		(9.65)
$RUNEMPL_i$	0.0393	0.0383		−0.0845
	(0.22)	(0.22)		(3.99)
$UUNEMPL_j$	−0.592	−0.592		
	(3.20)	(3.20)		
$REDUCI_i$	−4.20	−3.96		−1.08
	(4.37)	(3.98)		(7.42)
$REDUCP_i$	−1.34	−1.28		−0.108
	(4.05)	(3.80)		(2.20)
$REDUCA_i$	1.22	1.14		0.0825
	(4.37)	(3.96)		(1.89)
$ULIT_j$	1.37	1.37	AGE_i	0.220
	(1.37)	(1.37)		(0.54)
$CULT_i$	0.861	0.757	$AGLAB_i$	0.224
	(1.27)	(1.10)		(5.96)
$LAOWN_i$	0.0985	0.0907	$SMOWN_i$	−2.98
	(1.51)	(1.38)		(9.17)
LD_{ij}	−0.634	−0.625		
	(3.60)	(3.54)		
$DISTB_{ij}$	−1.57	−1.57		
	(12.22)	(12.23)		
$UPOP_j$	1.04	1.04		
	(8.76)	(8.75)		
Constant	18.12	17.11		15.41
	(3.06)	(2.84)		(6.40)
R^2	0.774	0.773		0.846
F	47.44	47.21		108.48

Note: A blank in col. 3 indicates it was not appropriate to include this variable (e.g., UUNEMPL$_j$) in the estimation of RWAGE$_i$. The variables *between* columns 2 and 3 are included *only* in the estimation of RWAGE$_i$ (col. 3).

TABLE 14.2. Rural–Urban Migration, <1 Year

Variable	(1) OLS $M_{ij}/RPOP_i$	(2) 2SLS $M_{ij}/RPOP_i$		(3) 2SLS $RWAGE_i$
$M_{ij}/RPOP_i$				0.0184 (2.70)
$RWAGE_i$	−0.846 (1.53)	−0.781 (1.31)		
$UWAGE_j$	1.38 (3.09)	1.38 (3.09)	TFP_i	0.401 (6.20)
$UWAGE_i$	−3.50 (5.05)	−3.44 (4.74)	$IRRIG_i$	0.270 (9.08)
$RUNEMPL_i$	0.506 (2.68)	0.506 (2.68)		−0.0908 (4.24)
$UUNEMPL_j$	−0.901 (4.57)	−0.901 (4.57)		
$REDUCI_i$	−3.14 (3.05)	−3.06 (2.88)		−1.07 (7.36)
$REDUCP_i$	−0.830 (2.33)	−0.811 (2.24)		−0.111 (2.27)
$REDUCA_i$	1.25 (4.13)	1.22 (3.91)		0.0836 (1.88)
$ULIT_j$	2.68 (2.51)	2.68 (2.50)	AGE_i	0.277 (0.67)
$CULT_i$	1.91 (2.64)	1.88 (2.56)	$AGLAB_i$	0.228 (6.04)
$LAOWN_i$	0.188 (2.69)	0.186 (2.63)	$SMOWN_i$	−2.88 (8.76)
LD_{ij}	−0.212 (1.12)	−0.209 (1.10)		
$DISTB_{ij}$	−1.37 (9.93)	−1.37 (9.93)		
$UPOP_j$	0.990 (7.72)	0.990 (7.72)		
Constant	2.49 (0.39)	2.17 (0.34)		14.75 (6.04)
R^2	0.689	0.689		0.846
F	30.58	30.54		107.82

Note: See note to table 14.1.

of wealth in the origin rural sector, suggesting that the exclusion of such variables can lead to serious biases in the remaining coefficient values.

The breakdown of rural education by the level of education attained (column 1 of both tables) is particularly revealing. In both equations an increasing propensity to migrate with increasing education can be observed. The percentage of males who were illiterate is negatively related to the rate of rural out-migration; it is only for the above-matriculation category (REDUCA) that the education coefficient becomes positive. (The category of literate but not educated was left out to avoid linear dependence among the education variables.)

Both $CULT_i$, the percentage of cultivators in the rural labor force (those who owned any land at all), and $LAOWN_i$, the percentage of land-owners owning more than 10 ha of land, are positively related to the rate of rural–urban migration, suggesting that the probability of this type of migration increases for the relatively wealthier sections of the rural population. There are a number of reasons to expect such a result. The levels of both wealth and education are likely to be positively related to the opportunities for urban employment, as well as to the access to information about such opportunities. Also, the results for interdistrict migration indicate that poorer (presumably landless) people migrate shorter distances, so a lot of their mobility is not picked up in the interstate flow analyzed here.

The coefficient of urban wage of the destination state is positive and significant (column 1 of both tables). The drop in significance of this variable (table 14.2, column 1) suggests that a substantial proportion of migrants who have resided in their destinations for less than a year may be moving on to other towns, possibly in a third state, so that the destination wage variable is not capturing the total intended effect. The urban wage rate of the origin state, $UWAGE_i$, might be of potential importance for this type of migrant, since before migrating to the urban area of another state it seems logical that he would consider the option of moving to his own urban area. The coefficient of $UWAGE_i$ is negative as expected and highly significant (column 1 of both tables), suggesting that higher urban wages in the origin state tend to stem the flow of interstate rural–urban migration.

Rural origin unemployment has a positive coefficient in both equations as expected but is significant only in table 14.2 (column 1). Note that the figures for rural unemployment do not incorporate any estimate of under-employment and therefore represent only a partial measure of the under-utilization of rural labor. The unemployment rate of the urban destination is negative and significant in both tables (column 1), suggesting that high unemployment in urban areas does dampen rural–urban migration.

The coefficient of urban literacy rate in the destination state is positive in column 1 of both tables, though more significant in table 14.2. There are two effects to note here: (1) literacy rates are positively related to educational and employment opportunities, and (2) high literacy rates result in more competition from the local population for such opportunities. The positive coefficient of $ULIT_j$ suggests that, at least in the short run, the former effect is stronger.

The coefficient of the language dummy (LD_{ij}) is negative as expected in both tables (column 1) but significant only in table 14.1. Since the longer term (1–4 years) stream of migration in general has proved a more stable indicator of parameter effects, we can conclude that language is a strong barrier in this type of migration.

The distance between origin and destination state is the most significant (negative) variable for each category of interstate migration. The population coefficient of the destination is also consistently highly significant (positive). Given the constancy of economic factors, we can expect the flow of migration to be proportional to both origin and destination populations. In addition, we can expect that the size of the labor market and the number of job opportunities will be correlated with population size, suggesting that economic factors may also affect the coefficient of the variable.

Two-stage least squares estimates of the rate of rural–urban migration and the rural wage are given in columns 2 and 3 of both tables. It can be seen that the necessary and sufficient identification conditions are satisfied for both equations. A detailed description of rural wage determination is included in my dissertation. For present purposes it is sufficient to note that the value of the migration coefficient in column 3 of both tables is small (but significant and of the expected sign). Variables such as rural total factor productivity and the percentage of cultivated area irrigated have strong positive effects on wages. Both the percentage of illiterates and the percentage of landowners owning less than 10 ha have strong negative effects.

In both tables, the relatively low migration coefficients in column 3 suggest that the problem of simultaneous equation bias in the estimation of $RWAGE_i$ in column 1 should not be serious. This is verified by a comparison of column 2 with the OLS estimates in column 1. The rural wage coefficients are very similar in the two columns (in fact they are slightly less negative in column 2), and there are no significant differences to report among the rest of the coefficients estimated under the separate procedures.

Urban–Rural Migration

A large proportion of urban–rural migration is likely to be composed of discouraged urban workers or work seekers, possibly recent rural–urban migrants, who are returning to their own villages or to other rural or (eventually) urban areas where the prospects of gaining employment seem brighter. It is for this reason that the significance of the unemployment rates in sectors other than those of origin and destination has been explored more fully for

TABLE 14.3. Urban–Rural Interstate Migration, 1–4 Years

Variable	(1) $M_{ij}/UPOP_i$	(2) $M_{ij}/UPOP_i$	(3) $M_{ij}/UPOP_i$
$UWAGE_i$	−0.942 (2.37)	−0.912 (2.27)	−0.806 (2.10)
$RWAGE_j$	−0.0342 (0.13)	−0.0764 (0.29)	−0.0108 (0.04)
$UUNEMPL_i$	0.187 (1.11)	0.358 (2.46)	
$RUNEMPL_j$	−0.407 (2.53)	−0.342 (2.71)	
$RUNEMPL_i$	0.225 (2.11)		0.294 (3.15)
$UUNEMPL_j$	0.195 (0.80)		0.199 (1.03)
$RLIT_j$	1.40 (3.58)	1.55 (4.28)	1.20 (3.08)
LD_{ij}	−0.287 (1.74)	−0.307 (1.87)	−0.201 (1.23)
$DISTB_{ij}$	−1.68 (13.28)	−1.67 (13.14)	−1.69 (13.32)
$RPOP_j$	0.474 (4.73)	0.534 (7.41)	0.611 (7.35)
Constant	4.76 (2.63)	3.75 (2.27)	4.97 (2.71)
R^2	0.640	0.631	0.626
F	35.01	42.45	41.71

Note: A blank in col. 2 indicates it was not appropriate to include this variable (e.g., $RUNEMPL_i$) in the estimation of $M_{ij}/UPOP_i$. The same principle applies to the blanks in col. 3.

this type of migration. In tables 14.3 and 14.4, estimates of urban–rural migration with all variables included are given in column 1. However, the high correlation between rural and urban state unemployment rates means that separate estimation (as in column 2 for $UUNEMPL_i$ and $RUNEMPL_j$ and in column 3 for $RUNEMPL_i$ and $UUNEMPL_j$) may do more justice to the individual effects of these unemployment variables. Since column 2 in both tables includes the immediately relevant unemployment variables, the discussion of variables other than unemployment will be based on these equations.

The origin state urban wage rate is negative in column 2 of both tables but significant only in table 14.3, implying that over the longer run, an increase in urban wages can definitely be expected to deter this type of return migration. Destination rural wages are not particularly significant

TABLE 14.4. Urban–Rural Interstate Migration, <1 Year

Variable	(1) $M_{ij}/UPOP_i$	(2) $M_{ij}/UPOP_i$	(3) $M_{ij}/UPOP_i$
UWAGE$_i$	−0.493	−0.460	−0.434
	(1.04)	(0.97)	(0.95)
RWAGE$_j$	0.284	0.287	0.325
	(0.91)	(0.92)	(1.02)
UUNEMPL$_i$	0.0809	0.263	
	(0.41)	(1.53)	
RUNEMPL$_j$	−0.532	−0.563	
	(2.76)	(3.71)	
RUNEMPL$_i$	0.232		0.271
	(1.82)		(2.44)
UNEMPL$_j$	−0.0480		−0.546
	(0.17)		(2.36)
RLIT$_j$	1.16	1.14	0.887
	(2.47)	(2.64)	(1.91)
LD$_{ij}$	−0.276	−0.312	−0.175
	(1.40)	(1.59)	(0.896)
DISTB$_{ij}$	−1.54	−1.52	−1.57
	(10.26)	(10.15)	(10.41)
RPOP$_j$	0.564	0.555	0.748
	(4.83)	(6.66)	(7.71)
Constant	3.35	3.07	3.72
	(1.56)	(1.57)	(1.71)
R^2	0.568	0.561	0.551
F	25.68	31.48	30.26

Note: See note to table 14.3.

for the urban–rural migrant, suggesting that the attraction of higher rural wages was not of primary importance here. If a large proportion of these migrants eventually move on to other urban areas, we need not necessarily expect rural wages to be of much significance. For the shorter period (table 14.4), a positive coefficient of the destination wage is more significant. This result could be picking up the effect of seasonal migrants who cross state barriers for short periods when labor demand is temporarily higher in the villages.

From column 2 of both tables we can observe that unemployment in the state of origin encourages out-migration whereas rural unemployment in the destination state serves as a significant deterrent. Column 3 indicates that a significant proportion of urban–rural migrants take into consideration the unemployment rates in sectors other than those of origin and destination.

As expected, high rural unemployment in the individual's own state encourages migration to rural areas of other states, whereas high urban unemployment in the destination state reduces this type of flow, implying that the goal of eventual urban residence is important for this type of migrant.

The rural literacy rate in the destination state has a positive and significant coefficient, suggesting that the migrant, whose previous residence was in an urban area, seems to show a preference for rural states with higher levels of literacy. The language dummy is again negative for each equation and slightly more significant in table 14.3.

Distance is again the most significant variable, whereas destination population, though still highly significant, produces a lower coefficient value. This suggests that the economic interpretation of destination population in terms of size of labor markets is more valid when the destination is urban.

Rural–Rural Migration

The first thing to notice in table 14.5 is that the significance of the strictly economic variables is low: in column 1 only LD, DISTA, and RPOP are statistically significant. Possible reasons for this result may be that (1) economic factors are not very relevant in the decision-making process for this category of migrant, or (2) the data do not permit a sufficient level of disaggregation for a more revealing analysis. On the basis of a more detailed examination of the coefficients of these variables, and of the results available concerning interdistrict rural–rural migration (presented in the following section), my own presumption is that the latter explanation is more likely.

Origin and destination rural wages are not significant in either column of table 14.5. Two-stage least squares estimates (included in my dissertation), with both origin and destination rural wages taken to be endogenous, suggest that the problem of simultaneous equation bias is not the principal cause of the rather low wage coefficients. One reason for the possible downward bias of the rural destination wage coefficients (in both rural–rural and urban–rural migration) is the following. There is a tendency for the smaller states in India (Punjab, Haryana, Delhi, Kerala) to have the highest rural wages (the correlation coefficient between RWAGE and RPOP $= -0.461$). Therefore, given that the coefficient of the destination population is positive and significant, normalization of the dependent variable by origin population may lead to a bias against the smaller states. The alternative of dividing the gross migration flow by the population of both origin and destination regions is not satisfactory (1) for an economic interpretation of the rate of migration, and (2) since the value of the population coefficients in table 14.5 is well below unity. The high negative correlation between RWAGE and RPOP does lead me to conclude, however, that the estimates of $RWAGE_j$ are

TABLE 14.5. Rural–Rural Migration

Variable	(1) 1–4 Years $M_{ij}/RPOP_i$	(2) <1 Year $M_{ij}/RPOP_i$
$RWAGE_i$	0.276 (0.46)	−0.190 (0.32)
$RWAGE_j$	−0.196 (0.38)	0.0925 (0.18)
$UWAGE_j$	0.208 (0.28)	0.813 (1.13)
$RUNEMPL_i$	−0.147 (0.60)	−0.132 (0.53)
$RUNEMPL_j$	0.144 (0.79)	−0.376 (2.11)
$REDUCI_i$	−1.51 (1.17)	−1.94 (1.51)
$REDUCP_i$	−0.351 (0.77)	−0.670 (1.43)
$REDUCA_i$	0.692 (1.62)	1.03 (2.42)
$RLIT_j$	0.331 (0.62)	0.146 (0.27)
$CULT_i$	0.346 (0.35)	1.12 (1.18)
AGE_i	2.93 (0.64)	3.81 (0.84)
LD_{ij}	−0.631 (2.44)	−0.296 (1.15)
$DISTA_{ij}$	−2.70 (13.23)	−2.57 (12.69)
$RPOP_j$	0.650 (6.41)	0.472 (4.73)
Constant	7.28 (0.39)	3.38 (0.18)
R^2	0.689	0.670
F	29.25	26.37

biased downward. In any case, the conclusion of relatively little response at the aggregate level seems to be valid.

There are many possible reasons for this result. The poorest segments of the population, who might be expected to be prominent among those attracted by higher wages, are also the category for whom the risks of long-distance migration are the greatest in terms of the consequences of not obtaining employment in their destination. Alternatively, higher wages may be the result of a variety of factors such as unionization and effective minimum wage legislation. Such factors would tend to lead employers to use labor-saving technology, and the resulting unemployment created would have a negative effect on migration flows.

Another reason for regarding the coefficients of rural wages with caution is the inadequacy of the rural wage rate as a proxy for total income received. (RWAGE was calculated using National Sample Survey data for the wages of hired labor.) For landless laborers, earnings from wages may be the sole source of income (though even for this category there is a great deal of variation in the percentage of total income composed of wages—see P. K. Bardhan 1979c, for example), whereas for small farmers the proportion of income earned in the form of wages is a decreasing function of the amount of the land owned. Wage increases often mean that other changes such as the introduction of larger scale technology are taking place. One of the effects of this may be the increased willingness of large landowners to buy smaller plots, a consideration that may be important in the small farmer's decision to migrate. The coefficient of $CULT_i$, the percentage of workers owning some land, is positive in both equations but the significance of this variable is lower than that of the variable for rural–urban migration, suggesting perhaps that cultivators who migrate are more likely to have an urban destination.

As in rural–urban migration, the coefficient of the origin rural wage was significantly positive before the inclusion of rural education variables, broken down by categories of education. The education coefficients show the same increasing trend observed in rural–urban migration, indicating that the probability that an individual will undertake long-distance rural–rural migration increases with his level of education. The significance levels of these variables are, however, lower than the parallel cases for rural–urban migration. The fact that inclusion of these education categories does reduce the coefficient of the origin rural wage suggests again that the level of educational attainment is an important determinant of how the population responds to wage differentials. Educational factors alone are not the only determinants of this response, but since the level of educational attainment is likely to be highly correlated with levels of wealth and land ownership, it serves in part as a proxy for these variables.

The rural sector can also be usefully thought of as being divided into net sellers and net buyers of labor (see Rosenzweig 1978). Obviously, the two categories will respond very differently to changes in agricultural wages. (The distribution of land among landowners was found to have an important effect on wages—see column 3, tables 14.1 and 14.2—but not on this category of migration.)

The coefficient of the urban wage of the destination state, thought to be a possible cause of interstate migration of this type, is positive but not significant. Except for the expected negative coefficient of rural unemployment in the destination state in column 2, the rural unemployment coefficients are insignificant. Some of the problems with using this measure have already been described. A comparison with coefficient values of the corresponding variable at the district level (below) is also helpful.

The language dummy is again negative and statistically significant in column 1, whereas the variable DISTA, used here for the distance between geographical centers of states, is slightly more significant than DISTB, the rail distance between capital cities (used for the other flows). Distance is again highly significant and the absolute value of the coefficient is highest for this type of migration, indicating that distance is more of a restraining factor for rural–rural migrants (use of DISTB produced coefficients of the order of -2.35).

We know from the above results of rural–rural and rural–urban migration that relatively wealthy and more educated persons, who are likely to be the net buyers of labor, have a higher propensity to migrate. However, the poorer individuals, who can be expected to respond to agricultural wages in a positive manner, form a much larger proportion of the rural population. My hypothesis therefore is that the interstate rural–rural flow is relatively evenly divided between net buyers and net sellers of labor, thus negating any significant wage response at the aggregate level.

Lipton (1976) also observed a bimodal distribution of migrants from rural Indian villages, with the poor migrating short distances in response to agricultural changes whereas the longer distance migrants consisted of wealthier youths sent out to acquire education and better jobs. (In table 14.5, the percentage of males between the ages of 15 and 29 in the origin state is positive but not significant. However, there is not much variation in this variable so a high degree of confidence should not be placed in the coefficient value.)

WITHIN-STATE MIGRATION

Data

This section presents estimates of urban–rural (tables 14.6 and 14.7) and rural–rural (tables 14.8 and 14.9) interdistrict or within-state migration. (The variables used in this discussion are defined in appendix 14.2.) For this category of migration, a complete matrix of migration flows by origin and destination district is not available. For any district j in state i, we know the figure for the sum of the migrants whose origin was other districts of state i and whose destination was district j, but we cannot identify the individual district of origin. Therefore, the district-level variables that appear in the regressions below all refer to the district of destination only. A total

TABLE 14.6. Urban–Rural Within-State Migration, 1–4 Years

Variable	(1) OLS $M_{ij}/PODU$	(2) 2SLS $M_{ij}/PODU$	(3) 2SLS DWAGE		(4) OLS $M_{ij}/PODU$
M_{ij}			−0.336 (1.96)		
DWAGE	1.08 (3.18)	1.34 (2.15)		URW	4.81 (2.09)
DFP			0.185 (1.36)		
DUN	−0.438 (1.88)	−0.397 (1.60)	−0.240 (2.07)	URU	−0.372 (1.79)
DLIT	0.586 (2.04)	0.577 (2.00)		URL	3.78 (2.43)
DIRR			0.263 (3.30)		
PDR	0.609 (3.93)	0.623 (3.95)			0.0250 (3.71)
D1	−3.42 (2.76)	−3.78 (2.61)	2.17 (1.92)		−0.194 (0.12)
D2	−3.12 (2.53)	−3.44 (2.46)	2.19 (1.89)		1.68 (1.18)
D3	−4.16 (3.09)	−4.68 (2.72)	2.27 (2.42)		0.346 (0.17)
D4	−4.24 (3.14)	−4.78 (2.73)	2.41 (2.48)		−0.743 (0.31)
D5	−5.65 (4.71)	−5.98 (4.35)	1.38 (1.54)		−4.73 (3.31)
R^2	0.795	0.792	0.946		0.845
F	40.90	40.06	183.57		57.61

Note: A blank in col. 1 indicates it was not appropriate to include this variable (e.g., DFP) in the estimation of M_{ij}. The same principle applies to the blanks in cols 2, 3, and 4. The variables *between* cols. 3 and 4 are included *only* in the estimation of M_{ij}/PODU in col. 4.

of 111 districts from the states of Andhra Pradesh, Karnataka, Haryana, Punjab, and Utter Pradesh were used in the estimation. Since data from only 5 states were used, individual state variables to represent the origin were not included, as their coefficient values could not be interpreted with a high degree of confidence. Given the variability of the states, geographically and in terms of size and cultural attributes, a better estimation strategy proved to be the use of dummy variables to take into account differences in individual state characteristics. Finally, rural–urban migration was not estimated because of the lack of urban data at the district level.

The format of tables 14.6 through 14.9 is identical. Column 1 gives

TABLE 14.7. Urban–Rural Within-State Migration, <1 Year

Variable	*(1)* OLS $M_{ij}/PODU$	*(2)* 2SLS $M_{ij}/PODU$	*(3)* 2SLS DWAGE		*(4)* OLS $M_{ij}/PODU$
M_{ij}			-0.282 (1.88)		
DWAGE	0.935 (2.22)	1.71 (2.18)		URW	1.69 (1.29)
DFP			0.214 (1.54)		
DUN	-0.0749 (0.26)	0.0487 (0.16)	-0.089 (0.88)	URU	-0.109 (0.92)
DLIT	0.967 (2.73)	0.941 (2.61)		URL	2.48 (2.80)
DIRR			0.267 (3.24)		
PDR	0.547 (2.86)	0.588 (2.98)			0.0134 (3.49)
$D1$	-5.58 (3.65)	-6.68 (3.68)	1.14 (1.52)		-0.136 (0.15)
$D2$	-5.64 (3.70)	-6.61 (3.76)	1.11 (1.47)		-0.0254 (0.03)
$D3$	-5.29 (3.18)	-6.86 (3.18)	1.63 (2.23)		3.34 (2.95)
$D4$	-6.29 (3.78)	-7.93 (3.61)	1.48 (2.16)		-0.578 (0.42)
$D5$	-7.46 (5.04)	-8.44 (4.90)	0.572 (0.86)		-2.33 (3.10)
R^2	0.680	0.673	0.949		0.872
F	22.43	21.68	197.96		71.70

Note: See note to table 14.6.

the OLS estimate of district in-migration. In column 2 the relationship is reestimated using two-stage least squares, with destination wage also taken to be endogenous and estimated in column 3. Column 4 indicates how the relative position of a district in a state affects migration into that district from the rest of the state. Coefficients are estimated for the ratios of the destination district to the origin state with regard to wages, unemployment, and literacy. Except for the dummy variables, the data in columns 1–3 are in the form of logarithms so that coefficient values again represent migration elasticities (or wage elasticities, in column 3). However, the coefficients in column 4 were estimated in linear form because taking the logarithm of ratios would involve linear dependencies between the origin and dummy variables.

TABLE 14.8. Rural–Rural Migration, 1–4 Years

Variable	(1) OLS $M_{ij}/PODR$	(2) 2SLS $M_{ij}/PODR$	(3) 2SLS DWAGE		(4) OLS $M_{ij}/PODR$
M_{ij}			−1.10 (0.77)		
DWAGE	0.817 (2.35)	0.861 (1.36)		RRW	1.13 (2.38)
DFP			0.927 (0.82)		
DUN	−0.268 (1.13)	−0.261 (1.03)	−0.539 (0.92)	RRU	−2.13 (2.77)
DLIT	0.0421 (0.14)	0.0406 (0.14)		RRL	1.27 (1.34)
DIRR			0.299 (1.24)		
PDR	0.253 (1.60)	0.256 (1.59)			0.0148 (1.96)
D1	−0.304 (0.24)	−0.369 (0.59)	6.32 (0.80)		1.35 (0.73)
D2	−0.0217 (0.02)	−0.0771 (0.05)	5.84 (0.80)		2.26 (1.33)
D3	0.705 (0.51)	0.795 (0.45)	5.07 (0.91)		0.997 (0.46)
D4	−0.580 (0.42)	−0.674 (0.38)	5.62 (0.91)		3.24 (1.92)
D5	−2.26 (1.84)	−2.32 (1.65)	4.55 (0.77)		−1.87 (1.20)
R^2	0.766	0.764	0.733		0.806
F	34.62	34.21	28.95		43.85

Note: A blank in col. 1 indicates it was not appropriate to include this variable (e.g., DFP) in the estimation of M_{ij}. The same principle applies to the blanks in cols. 2, 3, and 4. The variables *between* cols. 3 and 4 are included *only* in the estimation of M_{ij} in col. 4.

Results

The most important result that emerges from the district-level regressions is that the coefficients of rural wages as well as their ratios are always of the expected sign (positive for destination), are practically always significant, and are usually among the most significant of explanatory variables in the migration equations. In three out of four cases the wage coefficient increases in the 2SLS estimates whereas the expected negative migration coefficient in column 3 certainly is not negligible. These results indicate that, for this shorter distance migration, rural wages are (1) more important in migration

TABLE 14.9. Rural–Rural Migration, <1 Year

Variable	(1) OLS $M_{ij}/PODR$	(2) 2SLS $M_{ij}/PODR$	(3) 2SLS DWAGE		(4) OLS $M_{ij}/PODR$
M_{ij}			−0.423 (1.19)		
DWAGE	0.870 (1.98)	0.630 (0.78)		RRW	0.702 (2.17)
DFP			0.486 (1.29)		
DUN	−0.303 (1.01)	−0.342 (1.07)	−0.286 (1.52)	RRU	−0.880 (1.68)
DLIT	0.336 (0.91)	0.344 (0.93)		RRL	0.724 (1.12)
DIRR			0.199 (2.41)		
PDR	0.244 (1.22)	0.231 (1.13)			0.0103 (2.00)
D1	−1.81 (1.13)	−1.46 (0.78)	2.03 (1.23)		0.203 (0.16)
D2	−1.85 (1.16)	−1.54 (0.86)	1.71 (1.17)		0.149 (0.13)
D3	−1.78 (1.03)	−1.29 (0.58)	2.15 (1.62)		2.28 (1.55)
D4	−2.44 (1.40)	−1.93 (0.85)	2.07 (1.64)		0.593 (0.52)
D5	−3.66 (2.37)	−3.35 (1.89)	1.29 (1.00)		−1.56 (1.47)
R^2	0.593	0.586	0.906		0.769
F	15.35	14.93	101.15		35.04

Note: See note to table 14.9.

decisions and (2) more likely to be affected by migration flows than they are in interstate migration. Given the stronger wage response, it also seems likely that the composition of the interdistrict flows is relatively more homogeneous—of the wage earner type—than the corresponding categories at the interstate level.

In general, rural unemployment in the destination district produces negative coefficients, indicating a deterrent effect on in-migration. Both destination literacy rates and population levels consistently have positive coefficients, in each case more significant for the urban–rural flows. In each migration equation D5, the dummy variable for the state of Uttar Pradesh, produces the lowest coefficient among all dummy variables. This is again to be expected since Uttar Pradesh is the largest state. The dependent variable is normalized by the entire population (sectoral) of the rest of the state, whereas the bulk of migration into a district is likely to originate from the immediately neighboring districts. Therefore, rates of migration as measured here should, a priori, be lower for larger states.

Finally, in the rural wage equations, rural total factor productivity and the percentage of cultivated area irrigated produce the expected positive coefficients, whereas the rural unemployment coefficient is negative in each case.

CONCLUDING OBSERVATIONS

Distance

The distance variable—included to serve as a proxy for the monetary, opportunity, and psychic costs of migration—turned out consistently to be the most significant variable in every regression in which it was included. The results indicate that the deterrent effects of distance on migration are very strong in India even when compared with other less developed countries. See, for example, Todaro (1976) for a report on the effect of distance on migration in certain other less developed countries.

Language

The coefficient of the language variable was always negative as expected. In addition, two trends are distinguishable from the results. The variable was more significant for the longer term (1–4 years) migrant group, suggesting that in the longer run, migrants prefer to reside in states having languages similar to their own. Also, the variable was more significant for migrants of rural origin, suggesting that language is more of a barrier to this type of migrant, who, on average, is less educated.

Education and Literacy

For migrants of rural origin the probability of migration increased with the level of educational attainment. This trend was particularly strong in rural–urban migration. Destination literacy levels were also found to be positively related to the rate of in-migration, suggesting that migration for education purposes was of major importance, especially when the destination was urban.

Unemployment

The urban unemployment rate was always of the expected sign. The limitations of using a rural unemployment figure have already been discussed.

Nevertheless, we observe a positive origin coefficient for interstate rural–urban migration, a negative destination coefficient for interstate and within-state urban–rural migration, and a negative destination coefficient for within-state rural–rural migration. These observations indicate the importance of this variable in determining labor mobility. In addition, unemployment rates in sectors and states that could be regarded as alternatives to the actual destination were often found to significantly influence the rate of migration. Such results suggest that unemployment rates are an important consideration in the decision to undertake migration, and their exclusion from previous studies of Indian migration does not appear to be justified.

Wages

In every type of migration flow, the coefficient of the urban wage was always of the expected sign and was practically always significant. Rural wages for within-state urban–rural and rural–rural migration were also of the expected signs. This suggests that the somewhat insignificant coefficents obtained for this variable at the interstate level for these flows were mainly the result of the aggregation of groups with different motivations for migrating.

Variables Used in Analysis of Interstate Migration

M_{ij} — Number of males whose previous place of residence was state i and whose present place of residence (March 1971) was state j, disaggregated by rural and urban sectors for origin and destination, and by duration of residence in the destination state.

RWAGE — Rural real wage—male wage rate divided by a consumer price index for agricultural laborers (1970–71).

UWAGE — Urban real wage—factory wage rate divided by an urban consumer price index (1970).

TFP — Index of total factor productivity in agriculture (1971).

RUNEMPL — Rural unemployment rate—percentage of rural nonworkers reported to be seeking work (1970–71).

UUNEMPL — Urban unemployment rate—percentage of urban non-workers reported to be seeking work (1970–71).

RLIT — Percentage of rural literate males (1971).

ULIT — Percentage of urban literate males (1971).

LD_{ij} — Language dummy variable (0 for same or similar language, 1 for different language).

$DISTA_{ij}$ — Distance between state centers.

$DISTB_{ij}$ — Rail distance between capital cities.

RPOP — Rural population (1971).

UPOP — Urban population (1971).

REDUCI — Percentage of rural males who were illiterate (1971).

REDUCP — Percentage of rural males with primary and middle education (1971).

REDUCA — Percentage of rural males with above-matriculation education (1971).

AGLAB — Agricultural laborers as a percentage of total workers (1971).

NOTE: Subscript i refers to origin state; subscript j refers to destination state.

CULT	Cultivators as a percentage of total workers (1971).
SMOWN	Percentage of landowners owning less than 10 ha (1971).
LAOWN	Percentage of landowners owning more than 10 ha (1971).
IRRIG	Percentage of cultivated area irrigated (1971).
AGE	Percentage of rural males between the ages of 15 and 29 (1971).

Variables Used in Analysis of Within-State Migration

M_{ij}	Number of males whose previous place of residence was state i, district other than j, and whose present place of residence (March 1971) was state i, in a rural area of district j, disaggregated by urban and rural sectors for origin, and by duration of residence in the destination district.
PSU	State urban population.
PSR	State rural population.
PDU	District urban population.
PDR	District rural population.
PODU	Urban population of origin: PSU − PDU.
PODR	Rural population of origin: PSR − PDR.
DWAGE	District wage (rural).
DFP	District total factor productivity (rural).
DUN	District unemployment (rural).
DLIT	District literacy percentage (rural).
DIRR	District irrigated area percentage.
URW	Ratio of rural district wage to urban state wage.
RRW	Ratio of rural district wage to rural state wage.
URU	Ratio of rural district unemployment to urban state unemployment.
RRU	Ratio of rural district unemployment to rural state unemployment.
URL	Ratio of rural district literacy to urban state literacy.
RRL	Ratio of rural district literacy to rural state literacy.
$D1$	Dummy variable taking the value of 1 if district is in Andhra Pradesh, 0 otherwise.
$D2$	Dummy variable taking the value of 1 if district is in Karnataka, 0 otherwise.
$D3$	Dummy variable taking the value of 1 if district is in Haryana, 0 otherwise.

*D*4   Dummy variable taking the value of 1 if district is in Punjab, 0 otherwise.

*D*5   Dummy variable taking the value of 1 if district is in Uttar Pradesh, 0 otherwise.

References

Ahmed, Iqbal. 1981. Wage determination in Bangladesh agriculture. *Oxford Economic Papers* 33.

Alexander, K. C. 1978. *Agricultural labor unions: A study in three South Indian States*. Hyderabad: National Institute of Rural Development.

Ali, M. 1979. Share tenancy arrangements in Bangladesh. M. A. thesis, School of Economics, University of the Philippines, Diliman.

Allen, R. G. D. 1964. *Mathematical analysis for economists*. New York: St. Martin's Press.

Arrow, K. J. 1963. Uncertainty and the welfare economics of medical care. *American Economic Review* 53.

———. 1971. The theory of risk aversion. In *Essays in the theory of risk bearing*. Chicago: Markham.

Ashenfelter, Orley, and Heckman, James J. 1974. The estimation of income and substitution effects in a model of family labor supply. *Econometrica* 42.

Asian Development Bank. 1977. *Rural Asia: Challenge and opportunity*. Hong Kong: Federal Publications.

Bagi, F. S. 1979. Relationship between farm size, tenancy, productivity, and returns to scale in Haryana (India) agriculture. Manuscript, Tennessee State University.

Bandyopadhyaya, N. 1975. Tenancy in West Bengal. *Economic and Political Weekly* 10.

Bangladesh Rice Research Institute. 1977. *Sharecropping survey*.

Bardhan, Kalpana. 1973. Factors affecting wage rates for agricultural labor. *Economic and Political Weekly* 8.

———. 1977. Rural employment, wages, and labor markets in India: A survey of research. Pts. I, II, and III. *Economic and Political Weekly* 12.

Bardhan, P. K. 1973. Size, productivity, and returns to scale: An analysis of farm-level data in Indian agriculture. *Journal of Political Economy* 81.

———. 1976a. *Determinants of supply and demand for labor in a poor agrarian economy: An analysis of household survey data in West Bengal*. Berkeley: University of California, Department of Economics, Working Paper no. 83.

―――. 1976*b*. Variations in extent and forms of agricultural tenancy: An analysis of Indian data across regions and over time. *Economic and Political Weekly* 11.

―――. 1978*a*. Interlinked factor markets and agrarian development: A review. Paper presented at the Yale Labor and Population Workshop, Yale University, New Haven, Conn. (November).

―――. 1978*b*. On measuring rural unemployment. *Journal of Development Studies* 14.

―――. 1978*c*. Some employment and unemployment characteristics of rural women: An analysis of NSS data for West Bengal, 1972–73. *Economic and Political Weekly* 13 (March 25).

―――. 1979*a*. Agricultural development and land tenancy in a peasant economy: A theoretical and empirical analysis. *American Journal of Agricultural Economics* 61.

―――. 1979*b*. Labor supply functions in a poor agrarian economy. *American Economic Review* 69 (March).

―――. 1979*c*. Wages and unemployment in a poor agrarian economy: A theoretical and empirical analysis. *Journal of Political Economy* 87.

―――. 1980. Interlocking factor markets and agrarian development: A review of issues. *Oxford Economic Papers* 32.

―――. 1981. Labor tying in a poor agrarian economy: A theoretical and empirical analysis. Manuscript, University of California at Berkeley.

―――. 1982. *land, labor, and rural poverty: Essays in development economics*. New York: Columbia University Press.

Bardhan, Pranab K., and Rudra, Ashok. 1980. Interlinkage of land, labour, and credit relations: An analysis of village survey data in East India. *Economic and Political Weekly* 13.

―――. 1980. Terms and conditions of sharecropping contracts: An analysis of village data in India. *Journal of Development Studies* 16.

―――. 1981. Terms and conditions of labor contracts in agriculture, 1979. *Oxford Bulletin of Economics and Statistics* 43.

Bardhan, Pranab K., and Srinivasan, T. N. 1971. Cropsharing tenancy in agriculture: A theoretical and empirical analysis. *American Economic Review* 51.

Bardhan, Pranab K., and Srinivasan, T. N., eds. 1974. *Poverty and income distribution in India*. Calcutta: Calcutta Statistical Publishing Society.

Barnum, Howard, and Squire, Lyn. 1979. An econometric application of the theory of the farm household. *Journal of Development Economics* 6.

Bartsch, W. H. 1977. *Employment and technology choice in Asian agriculture*. New York: Praeger.

Basu, T. K. 1962. The Bengal peasant from time to time, chapter 4.

Behrman, Jere, and Wolfe, Barbara. 1980. *Women and fertility in a developing country*. Madison: University of Wisconsin, Institute for Research in Poverty, Discussion Paper DP 610-80.

Bell, Clive. 1977. Alternative theories of sharecropping: Some tests using evidence from Northeast India. *Journal of Development Studies* 13.

Bell, Clive, and Braverman, Avishay. 1980. On the nonexistence of "Marshallian" sharecropping contracts. *Indian Economic Review*.

Bell, Clive, and Zusman, Pinhas. 1976. A bargaining theoretic approach to cropsharing contracts. *American Economic Review* 66.

————. 1979. New approaches to the theory of rental contracts in agriculture. Paper presented at 17th International Conference of Agricultural Economists, Banff, Canada (July).

————. 1980*a*. Towards a general bargaining theory of equilibrium sets of contracts: The case of agricultural rental contracts. Paper presented at World Congress of the Econometric Society, Aix-en-Provence, France.

————. 1980*b*. *On the interrelationship of credit and tenancy contracts*. Washingtons D.C.: The World Bank, Development Research Center.

Ben-Porath, Y. 1980. The F-connection: Families, friends and firms and the organization of exchange. *Population and Development* 6: 1–30.

Beteille, André. 1965. *Class, caste, and power*. Berkeley and Los Angeles: University of California Press.

————. 1972. Agrarian relations in Tanjore District, South India. *Sociological Bulletin* 21.

Bhaduri, Amit. 1973. Agricultural backwardness under semifeudalism. *Economic Journal* 83.

————. 1977. On the formation of usurious interest rates in backward agriculture. *Cambridge Journal of Economics*.

————. 1979. A rejoinder to Srinivasan's comment. *Economic Journal* 89.

Bhalla, Sheila. 1976. New relations of production in Haryana agriculture. *Economic and Political Weekly* 11.

Bharadwaj, Krishna. 1974*a*. *Production conditions in Indian agriculture*. Cambridge: At the University Press.

————. 1974*b*. *Production relations in Indian agriculture: A study based on farm management surveys*. Cambridge, England: Cambridge University, Department of Economics, Occasional Paper no. 33.

Bhattacharya, Durgaprasad, and Roy, Rama Deb. 1976. A note on agricultural wages in India. *Social Scientist* no. 1961.

Binswanger, Hans P. 1978*a*. *The economics of tractors in South Asia: An analytical review*. New York: Agricultural Development Council.

————. 1978*b*. Issues in modeling-induced technical change. In H. P. Binswanger and V. W. Ruttan, eds., *Induced innovation: Technology, institutions, and development*. Baltimore: Johns Hopkins University Press.

————. 1980. Attitudes toward risk: Experimental measurement in rural

India. *American Journal of Agricultural Economics* 62.
Binswanger, Hans P., and Jodha, N. S. 1978. *Manual of instructions for economic investigators in ICRISAT's village-level studies.* Hyderabad: International Crops Research Institute for the Semi-Arid Tropics, Village-Level Studies Series, vol. 11.
Binswanger, Hans P.; Jodha, N. S.; Ryan, J. G.; and von Oppen, M. 1977. *Approach and hypotheses for the village-level studies of the ICRISAT.* Hyderabad: International Crops Research Institute for the Semi-Arid Tropics, Economics Program, Occasional Paper no. 15.
Binswanger, Hans P., and Ruttan, Vernon W., eds. 1978. *Induced innovation: Technology, institutions, and development.* Baltimore: Johns Hopkins University Press.
Bliss, Christopher J. 1976. Risk bearing in Indian agriculture. Agricultural Development Council Seminar on Risk and Uncertainty in Agricultural Development, CIMMYT, El Baton, Mexico.
Bliss, Christopher J., and Stern, N. H. 1978. Productivity, wages, and nutrition. Pts. I and II. *Journal of Development Economics* 5.
―――. 1981. *Palanpur: The economy of an Indian village.* Oxford: Oxford University Press.
Boserup, Ester. 1965. *The conditions of agricultural growth: The economics of agrarian change under population pressure.* Chicago: Aldine.
―――. 1970. *Women's role in economic development.* London: Allen & Unwin.
Brannon, R. H., and Jessee, D. L. 1977. *Unemployment and underemployment in the rural sectors of the less developed countries.* Occasional Paper, Series no. 4, Economics and Sector Planning Division, Office of Agriculture, Technical Assistance Bureau, United States Agency for International Development. Washington, D.C.: USAID.
Braverman, Avishay, and Guasch, J. L. 1984. Capital requirements, screening and interlinked sharecropping and credit contracts. *Journal of Development Economics* (forthcoming).
Braverman, Avishay, and Srinivasan, T. N. 1981. Credit and sharecropping in agrarian societies. *Journal of Development Economics* 9.
Braverman, Avishay, and Stiglitz, Joseph E. 1981*a. Landlords, tenants, and technological innovations.* Washington, D.C.: The World Bank.
―――. 1981*b. Moral hazard, incentive flexibility and risk: cost sharing arrangements under sharecropping.* Washington, D.C.: The World Bank.
―――. 1982. Sharecropping and the interlinking of agrarian markets. *American Economic Review* 72.
Breman, Jan C. 1978. Seasonal migration and cooperative capitalism: The crushing of cane and labor in the sugar factories of Bardoli. *Journal of Peasant Studies* 6 (October).
Cain, Mead T. 1977. The economic activities of children in a village in

Bangladesh. *Population and Development Review* 3.

Cain, Mead T.; Khanam, Syeda Rokeya; and Nahar, Shamsun. 1979. Class, patriarchy, and women's work in Bangladesh. Paper presented at the ADC-ICRISAT Conference on Adjustment Mechanisms of Rural Labor Markets in Developing Countries, Hyderabad (August).

Cañete, C. C. 1971. An economic analysis of corn production in Bukidnon. M. S. thesis, Department of Agricultural Economics, University of the Philippines, Los Banos.

Castillo, Gelia T. 1975. *All in a grain of rice: A review of Philippine studies of the new rice technology.* Laguna, Philippines: South East Asian Regional Center for Graduate Study and Research in Agriculture.

Chakravarty, A., and Rudra, A. 1973. Economic effects of tenancy: Some negative results. *Economic and Political Weekly* 8.

Chattopadhyay, M. 1979. Relative efficiency of owner and tenant cultivation: A case study. *Economic and Political Weekly* 14.

Chayanov, A. K. 1966. *The theory of the peasant economy.* Homewood, Ill. Irwin Press.

Cheung, S. N. S. 1968. Private property rights and sharecropping. *Journal of Political Economy* 76.

—————. 1969. *The theory of share tenancy.* Chicago: University of Chicago Press.

Clay, Edward C. 1976. Institutional change and agricultural wages in Bangladesh. *Bangladesh Development Studies* 4.

Collier, William L.; Wiradi, Gunawan; and Soentoro. 1973. Recent changes in rice harvesting methods. *Bulletin of Indonesian Economic Studies* 9.

Collier, William L.; Wiradi, Gunawan; Soentoro; and Makali. 1976. Agricultural technology and institutional change in Java. *Food Research Institute Studies* 13.

Darity, William A. 1980. The Boserup theory of agricultural growth: A model for anthropological economics. *Journal of Development Economics* 7.

Demsetz, H. 1967. Toward a theory of property rights. *American Economic Review* 57.

Dhar, Sanjay. 1980. An analysis of internal migration in India. Ph.D. dissertation, Yale University, New Haven, Conn.

Diewert, W. E. 1978. *Duality approaches to micro-economic theory.* Vancouver: University of British Columbia, Department of Economics, Discussion Paper 78-09.

Directorate of Economics and Statistics. 1976. *Agricultural wages in India, 1970–71.* Delhi: Publications Office.

Dixon, R. 1978. *Rural Women at Work: Strategies for Development in South Asia.* Baltimore: Johns Hopkins University Press.

Dube, S. C. 1959. *Indian village.* London: Routledge & Kegan Paul, chapter 6.

Eder, J. 1974. The origin, maintenance, and perpetuation of social inequality in a Philippine community. Ph.D. dissertation, University of California, Santa Barbara.

Evenson, R. E. 1972. *Labor in the Indian agriculture sector. A report to the Agency for International Development.* New Haven, Conn.: Yale University, Economic Growth Center.

Finegan, T. A. 1962. Hours of work in the United States: A cross-sectional analysis. *Journal of Political Economy* 70.

Geertz, Clifford. 1965. *The social history of an Indonesian town.* Cambridge, Mass.: MIT Press.

Ghodake, R. D.; Ryan, J. G.; and Sarin, R. 1978. *Human labor use with existing and prospective technologies in the semi-arid tropics of peninsular India.* ICRISAT, Economics Program, Progress Report no. 1, Patancheru, A.P. 502324, India.

Green, Jerry, and Sheshinski, Eytan. 1975. Competitive inefficiencies in the presence of constrained transactions. *Journal of Economic Theory.*

Greenwood, Michael J. 1971*a*. An analysis of the determinants of internal labor mobility in India. *Annals of Regional Science* 5.

———. 1971*b*. A regression analysis of migration to urban areas of a less-developed country: The case of India. *Journal of Regional Science* 2.

Griffin, Keith. 1974. *The political economy of agrarian change.* London: Macmillan.

Gronau, Reuben. 1973. The intra-family allocation of time: The value of the housewife's time. *American Economic Review* 63.

Gulati, L. 1976. Unemployment among female agricultural laborers. *Economic and Political Weekly* 11.

Hahn, Frank H. 1971. Equilibrium with transactions costs. *Econometrica* 39.

Hall, Robert E. 1973. Wages, income, and hours of work in the U.S. labor force. In G. Cain and H. Watts, eds, *Income maintenance and labor supply.* Chicago: Rand McNally.

Hallagan, W. 1978. Self-selection by contractual choice and the theory of sharecropping. *Bell Journal of Economics* 9.

Hammond, Peter J. 1977. *On the irrelevance of share contracts.* University of Essex, Department of Economics, Discussion Paper 100.

Hansen, Bent. 1969. Employment and wages in rural Egypt. *American Economic Review* 59.

Hanumantha Rao, C. H. 1971. Uncertainty, entrepreneurship, and sharecropping in India. *Journal of Political Economy* 79.

———. 1975. *Technological change and distribution of gains in Indian agriculture.* New Delhi: Institute of Economic Growth.

Harberger, Arnold. 1964. The measurement of waste. *American Economic Review. Papers and Proceedings* 54.

Harris, J., and Todaro, M. 1970. Migration, unemployment, and development: A two-sector analysis. *American Economic Review* 60.

Harris, Marvin. 1971. *Culture, man, and nature: Introduction to general anthropology*. New York: Thomas Y. Crowell.

Harris, Milton, and Raviv, Artur. 1978. Some results on incentive contracts with application to education and employment, health insurance, and law enforcement. *American Economic Review* 68.

Hart, Oliver. 1975. On the optimality of equilibrium when markets are incomplete. *Journal of Economic Theory*.

Hayami, Yujiro, and Hafid, Anwar. 1979. Rice harvesting and welfare in rural Java. *Bulletin of Indonesian Economic Studies* 15.

Hayami, Yujiro, and Kikuchi, Masao. 1981. *Asian village economy at the crossroads*. Tokyo and Baltimore: University of Tokyo Press and Johns Hopkins University Press (1982).

Heckman, James J. 1974. Shadow prices, market wages, and labor supply. *Econometrica* 42.

Higgs, R. 1974. Patterns of farm rental in the Georgia cotton belt, 1890–1900. *Journal of Economic History* 33.

Holmstrom, Bert. 1979. Moral hazard and observability. *Bell Journal of Economics* 10.

Hossain, Mahbub. 1977. Farm size, tenancy, and land productivity: An analysis of farm-level data in Bangladesh agriculture. *Bangladesh Development Studies* 5.

Huntington, H. 1974. An empirical study of ethnic linkages in Kenyan rural–urban migration. Ph.D. dissertation, State University of New York, Binghamton.

Immink, Maarten D. C., and Viteri, Fernando E. 1981. Energy intake and productivity of Guatemalan sugarcane cutters: An empirical test of the efficiency wage hypothesis. Pts. I and II. *Journal of Development Economics* 9.

Imperial Gazetteer of India, vols. 5, 7, 12, 13, 14, 18, 22, 1907–09. Reprinted by Today and Tomorrow Publications, New Delhi.

Indian Government. 1978. *Draft five-year plan, 1978–83*. New Delhi: Government of India, Planning Commission.

International Labor Office, Asian Regional Program for Employment Promotion. 1978. *Labor absorption in Indian agriculture: Some exploratory investigations*. Bangkok: ILO.

James, W. T. 1979. An economic analysis of public land settlement alternatives in the Philippines. Ph.D. dissertation, University of Hawaii, Honolulu.

Jaynes, Gerald D. 1979. *Production and distribution in agrarian economies*. New Haven, Conn.: Yale University, Economic Growth Center, Discussion Paper 309.

———. 1982. Production and distribution in agrarian economies. *Oxford*

Economic Papers 34, no. 2 (July).

Jha, Dayanath. 1980. *Fertilizer use and its determinants: A review with special reference to semi-arid tropical India.* ICRISAT, Economics Program, Progress Report no. 11, Patancheru, A. P. 502324, India.

Jodha, N. S. 1974. A case of the process of tractorisation. *Economic and Political Weekly* 9.

————. 1978. Effectiveness of farmers' adjustment of risk. *Economic and Political Weekly* 13.

Jodha, N. S.; Asokan, M.; and Ryan, J. G. 1977. *Village study methodology and resource endowments of the selected villages in ICRISAT's village-level studies.* ICRISAT, Economics Program, Occasional Paper no. 16, Pantancheru, A.P. 50234, India.

Johnson, D. Gale. 1950. Resource allocation under share contracts. *Journal of Political Economy* 58.

Jones, R. 1895. *Peasant rents.* London: Macmillan.

Jones, R. 1964. *Lectures and tracts on political economy.* New York: Sentry Press.

Jorgenson, W. Dale. 1966. Testing alternative theories of the development of a dual economy. In Irma Adelman and Eric Thorbecke, eds., *The theory and design of economic development.* Baltimore: Johns Hopkins University Press.

————. 1967. Surplus agricultural labor and the development of a dual economy. *Oxford Economic Papers* 19.

Jose, A. V. 1974. Trends in real wage rates of agricultural laborers. *Economic and Political Weekly* 9.

————. 1976. The origins of trade unions among the agricultural laborers in Kerala. *Social Scientist* 5.

Joshi, P. C. 1975. Land reforms: A trend report. *Survey of Research in Economics* 4. Agriculture, Pt. 11. Bombay: Allied Publishers.

Khusro, A. M. 1973. *The economics of land reforms and farm size in India.* Bombay: Macmillan.

Kikuchi, Masao; Cordova, V. G.; Marciano, E. G.; and Hayami, Y. 1974. *Changes in rice harvesting systems in Central Luzon and Laguna.* Manila, Philippines: International Rice Research Institute, Research Paper Series no. 31.

Kikuchi, Masao; Hafid, Anwar; Saleh, Chaerul; Hartoyo, Sri; and Hayami, Yujiro. 1980. *Class differentiation, labor employment, and income distribution in a West Java village.*

Kikuchi Masao, and Hayami, Yujiro. 1982. Inducements to institutional innovations in an agrarian community. *Economic Development and Cultural Change.* 30.

Kniesner, Thomas J. 1976. An indirect test of complementarity in a family labor supply model. *Econometrica* 44.

Kosters, Marvin. 1966. Income and substitution parameters in a family labor supply model. Ph.D. dissertation, University of Chicago.

Krishna, Raj. 1971. *Rural unemployment—A survey of concepts and estimates for India*. Washington, D.C.: The World Bank, Staff Working Paper no. 234.

———. 1973. Unemployment in India. *Economic and Political Weekly* 8.

———. 1975. *Unemployment in India*. New York: Agricultural Development Council, Reprint series.

Lal, Deepak. 1974. *Social prices for non-traded commodities*. New Delhi: Government of India, Planning Commission, Technical Paper no. 12.

———. 1976a. Agricultural growth, real wages, and the rural poor in India. *Economic and Political Weekly* 11.

———. 1976b. Supply price and surplus labor—Some Indian evidence. *World Development* 4.

Lau, L. J. 1976. A characterization of the normalized restricted profit function. *Journal of Economic Theory* 12 : 131–63.

Leibenstein, Harvey. 1957. *Economic backwardness and economic growth*. New York: John Wiley & Sons.

Leibowitz, Arleen S. 1972. Women's allocation of time to market and nonmarket activities: Differences by education. Ph.D. dissertation, Columbia University.

Levy, Michael, and Wadycki, W. 1972. A comparison of young and middle-aged migration in Venezuela. *Annals of Regional Science* 6.

Lewis, H. T. 1971. *Ilocano rice farmers: A comparative study of two Philippine barrios*. Honolulu: University of Hawaii Press.

Lewis, W. Arthur. 1954. Economic development with unlimited supplies of labour. *Manchester School of Economic and Social Studies* 22.

———. 1972. Reflections on unlimited labour. In L. Di Marco, ed., *International economics and development*. New York: Academic Press.

Lipton, Michael. 1976. Migration from rural areas of poor countries: The impact on rural productivity and income distribution. Paper presented at the World Bank Research Workshop on Rural–Urban Labor Market Interactions.

———. 1980. Migration from rural areas of poor countries: The impact on rural productivity and income distribution. *World Development* 8.

Lumayag, Eutiquio. 1979. *Contractual arrangements in abaca production in some selected villages in the Philippines*. M. S. thesis, University of the Philippines, Los Banos, Laguna.

Mabro, Robert. 1971. Employment and wages in dual agriculture. *Oxford Economic Papers* 23.

Madden, J. F. 1973. *The Economics of Sex Discrimination*. Lexington, Mass.: Lexington Press.

McDiarmid, O. J. 1977. *Unskilled labor for development: Its economic cost*.

Baltimore: Johns Hopkins University Press.

MaCurdy, Thomas E. 1979. *An empirical model of labor supply in a life cycle setting.* Stanford, Calif.: Stanford University and National Bureau of Economic Research.

Mangahas, Mahar. 1975. An economic theory of tenant and landlord based on a Philippine case. In Lloyd G. Reynolds, ed., *Agriculture in development theory.* New Haven, Conn.: Yale University Press.

Mangahas, Mahar; Miralao, V. A.; and De Los Reyes, R. P. 1976. *Tenants, lessees, and owners: Welfare implications of tenure change.* Quezon City, Philippines: Atteneo de Manila University Press.

Marshall, Alfred. 1961. *Principles of economics.* Cambridge: At the University Press.

Marx, Karl. 1856. *Das kapital* 3.

Matias, Apolonia. 1979. Contractual arrangements in corn production in selected villages in the Philippines. M.S. thesis, University of the Philippines, Los Banos, Laguna.

Mazumdar, Dipak. 1959. The marginal productivity theory of wages and disguised unemployment. *Review of Economic Studies* 26.

Mazumdar, V., and Sharma, K. 1979. Women's studies: New perceptions and challenges. *Economic and Political Weekly* 14 (January 20).

Mill, John Stuart. 1926. *Principles of political economy.* London: Longmans, Green.

Mirrlees, James A. 1975. A pure theory of underdeveloped economies. In Lloyd G. Reynolds, ed., *Agriculture in development theory.* New Haven, Conn.: Yale University Press.

Mitra, Pradeep K. 1982. A theory of interlinked rural transactions. *Journal of Public Economics* 20.

Mundlak, Yair. 1979. *Intersectoral factor mobility and agricultural growth.* Research Report no. 6. Washington, D.C.: International Food Policy Research Institute.

National Sample Survey. 1977. *Some key results from the survey on employment and unemployment.* Subround 1, July–September. NSS 27th Round. NSS 32d Round, (no. 282/1). Government of India.

Newbery, D. M. G. 1974. Cropsharing in agriculture: A comment. *American Economic Review* 64.

————. 1975a. The choice of rental contracts in peasant agriculture. In Lloyd G. Reynolds, ed., *Agriculture in development theory.* New Haven, Conn.: Yale University Press.

————. 1975b. Tenurial obstacles to innovation. *Journal of Development Studies* 11.

————. 1977. Risk sharing, sharecropping, and uncertain labor markets. *Review of Economic Studies* 44.

Newbery, D. M. G., and Stiglitz, J. E. 1979. Sharecropping, risk sharing, and the importance of imperfect information. In James A. Roumasset, Jean-Marc Boussard, and Inderjit Singh, eds., *Risk, uncertainty, and agricultural development*. New York: Southeast Asian Regional Center for Graduate Study and Research in Agriculture and Agricultural Development Council.

Paglin, Morton. 1965. Surplus agricultural labor and development: Fact and theories. *American Economic Review* 55.

Parish, W. L., and Whyte, M. K. 1978. *Village and family life in contemporary China*. Chicago: University of Chicago Press, chap. 12.

Radner, Roy. 1970. Problems in the theory of markets under uncertainty. *American Economic Review* 60.

Rahman, Atigur. 1979. Usury capital and credit relations in Bangladesh agriculture: Some implications for capital formation and capitalist growth. *Bangladesh Development Studies* 7.

Raj, K. N. 1959. Employment and unemployment in the Indian economy: Problems of classification, measurement, and policy. *Economic Development and Cultural Change* 7.

Ranade, C. 1977. Distribution of benefits from new agricultural technologies: A study at the farm level. Ph.D. dissertations, Cornell University, Ithaca, N.Y.

Ranis, Gustay, and Fei, John. 1961. A theory of economic development. *American Economic Review* 51.

Ransom, R., and Sutch, R. 1978. *One kind of freedom*. Cambridge, Mass.: Harvard University Press.

Rao, C. H. H. 1975. *Technological change and distribution of gains in Indian agriculture*. Delhi: Institute of Economic Growth.

Rao, V. M. 1972. Land transfers in rural communities: Some findings in the Ryotwari region. *Economic and Political Weekly* 7.

———. 1981. Nature of Rural Underdevelopment, *Economic and Political Weekly* (October 10, 1981).

Rawski, T. G. 1979. *Economic growth and employment in China*. New York: Oxford University Press.

Reid, Joseph D. 1973. Sharecropping as an understandable market reponse: The post-bellum South. *Journal of Economic History* 33.

———. 1976. Sharecropping and agricultural uncertainty. *Economic Development and Cultural Change* 24.

———. 1979. Sharecropping and tenancy in American history. In James A. Roumasset, Jean-Marc Boussard, and Inderjit Singh, eds., *Risk, uncertainty, and agricultural development*. New York: Southeast Asian Regional Center for Graduate Study and Research in Agriculture and Agricultural Development Council.

Reynolds, Lloyd G. 1965. Wages and employment in a surplus labor economy. *American Economic Review* 55.

————. 1975. *Agriculture in development theory*. New Haven, Conn.: Yale University Press.

Rodgers, Gerry B. 1975. Nutritionally based wage determination in the low-income labor market. *Oxford Economic Papers* 27.

Rosen, Harvey. 1976. Taxes in a labor supply model with joint wage-hour determination. *Econometrica* 44.

Rosen, Sherwin, and Welch, Finis. 1971. Labor supply and income redistribution. *Review of Economics and Statistics* 53.

Rosenzweig, Mark R. 1978. Rural wages, labor supply, and land reform: A theoretical and empirical analysis. *American Economic Review* 68.

————. 1980. Neoclassical theory and the optimizing peasant: An econometric analysis of market family labor supply in a developing country. *Quarterly Journal of Economics* 95.

Rosenzweig, Mark R., and Evenson, Robert E. 1977. Fertility, schooling, and the economic contribution of children in rural India. *Econometrica* 45.

Rosenzweig, Mark R., and James Morgan. 1976. On the correct specification of human capital models: Wage discrimination. A comment. *Journal of Human Resources* 11.

Rosenzweig Mark R., and Schultz, T. Paul. 1982. Market opportunities, genetic endowments, and the intra-family distribution of resources: Child survival in rural India. *American Economic Review* 72.

Ross, Steven A. 1973. The economic theory of agency: The principal's problem. *American Economic Review* 63.

Roumasset, James A. 1974. *Induced institutional change, welfare economics, and the science of public policy*. Davis: University of California, Department of Economics, Working Paper no. 46.

————. 1976. *Rice and risk: Decision-making among low-income farmers*. Amsterdam: Elsevier/North Holland.

————. 1978. The new institutional economics and agricultural organization *Philippine Economic Journal* 17.

————. 1979. Sharecropping, production externalities, and the theory of contracts. *American Journal of Agricultural Economics* 61.

Roumasset, James A.; Boussard, Jean-Marc; and Singh, Inderjit, eds. 1979. *Risk, uncertainty, and agricultural development*. New York: Southeast Asian Regional Center for Graduate Study and Research in Agriculture and the Agricultural Development Council.

Roumasset, James A., and James, W. T. 1979. Explaining variations in share contracts: Land quality, population pressure, and technological change. *Australian Journal of Agricultural Economics* 23.

Roumasset, James A., and Uy, M. 1980. Piece rates, time rates, and teams: Explaining patterns in the employment relation. *Journal of Economic Behavior and Organization* 1.

Rudra, Ashok. 1975*a*. Loans as part of agrarian relations: Some results from

a preliminary survey in West Bengal. *Economic and Political Weekly* 10.
———. 1975*b*. Sharecropping arrangements in West Bengal. *Economic and Political Weekly* 10.
Rudra, Ashok, and Biswas, R. 1973. Seasonality of employment in agriculture. *Economic and Political Weekly* 8.
Rudra, Ashok and Sen, Amartya. 1980. Farm size and labor use: Analysis and policy. *Economic and Political Weekly* 15.
Rural Labor Enquiry Reports, 1963–64 and 1974–75. Labor Bureau, Government of India.
Ruttan, Vernon W. 1978. Induced institutional change. In H. P. Binswanger and V. W. Ruttan, eds., *Induced innovation: Technology, institutions, and development*. Baltimore: Johns Hopkins University Press.
Ryan, James G.; Ghodake, R. D.; and Sarin, R. 1979. Labor use and labor markets in semi-arid tropical rural villages of peninsular India. Paper presented at the ICRISAT International Workshop on Socioeconomic Constraints to Development of Semi-Arid Tropical Agriculture, Hyderabad, India.
Ryan, James G., and Rathore, M. S. 1978. *Factor proportions, factor market access, and the development and transfer of technology*. ICRISAT, Journal Article no. 48, Patancheru, A.P. 50234, India.
Sabot, Richard H., ed. 1981. *Migration and the labor market in developing countries*. Boulder, Colo.: Westview Press.
Sanyal, S. K. 1978. Trends in some characteristics of land holdings: An analysis for a few states. *Sarvekshana* 1.
Sarma, J. 1960. A village in West Bengal. In M. N. Srinivas, ed., *India's villages*. New York: Asia Publishing House.
Schultz, T. Paul. 1975. *Estimating labor supply functions for married women*. R-1265-NIH/EDA. Santa Monica, Calif.: RAND Corporation.
———. 1977 *A conditional logit model of internal migration: Venezuelan lifetime migration within educational strata*. New Haven, Conn.: Yale University, Economic Growth Center, Discussion Paper no. 266.
———. 1978. *Notes on the estimation of the microeconomic determinants of migration*. New Haven, Conn.: Yale University, Economic Growth Center, Discussion Paper no. 283.
———. 1980. Estimating labor supply functions for married women. In James P. Smith, ed., *Female labor supply*. Princeton, N.J.: Princeton University Press.
Schultz, Theodore W. 1964. *Transforming traditional agriculture*. New Haven, Conn.: Yale University Press.
Sen, Amartya K. 1966. Peasants and dualism with or without surplus labor. *Journal of Political Economy* 74.
———. 1975. *Employment, technology, and development*. London: Oxford University Press.

Sethuraman, S. V. 1972. Seasonal variations in unemployment and wage rates: Implications for rural works programme. *Economic and Political Weekly* 7.

Shavell, Steven. 1979. Risk sharing and incentives in the principal and agent relationship. *Bell Journal of Economics.* 10.

Sillers, Donald A. 1980. Measuring risk preference of rice farmers in Nueva Ecija, the Philippines: An experimental approach. Ph.D. dissertation, Yale University.

Singh, Inderjit. 1981. *Small farmers and the landless.* Washington, D.C.: The World Bank.

Smith, Adam, 1977. *An inquiry into the nature and causes of the wealth of nations.* Edited by Edwin Cannan. Chicago: University of Chicago Press.

Srinivas, M. N. 1966. *Social change in modern India.* Berkeley and Los Angeles: University of California Press.

―――. 1976. *The remembered village.* Berkeley and Los Angeles: University of California Press, chapter 5.

―――. 1978. *Changing position of Indian women.* Delhi: Oxford University Press.

Srinivasan, T. N. 1978. *India: Project on the impact of agricultural development on employment and poverty. Phase 1, A Methodological Note.* Washington, D.C.: The World Bank.

―――. 1979. Agricultural backwardness under semi-feudalism: A comment. *Economic Journal* 89.

Stiglitz, Joseph E. 1974a. Alternative theories of wage determination and unemployment in LDCs: The labor turnover model. *Quarterly Journal of Economics* 88.

―――. 1974b. Incentives and risk sharing in agriculture. *Review of Economic Studies* 41.

―――. 1976. The efficiency wage hypothesis, surplus labour, and the distribution of income in LDCs. *Oxford Economic Papers* 28.

Streefkerk, H. 1981. Too little to live on, too much to die on: Employment in small-scale industries in rural Gujarat. *Economic and Political Weekly,* April 11, 18, 25.

Subrahmanyam, K. V., and Ryan, J. G. 1976. Analysis of the rural labor market in Kanzara village, Maharashtra, India. Paper presented at the Agricultural Development Council Workshop on Household Studies, Singapore.

Takahashi, A. 1969. *Land and peasants in central Luzon.* Tokyo: Institute of Developing Economies.

Tilly, L. A., and Scott, J. W. 1978. *Women, work, and family.* New York: Holt, Rinehart, and Winston.

Tobin, James. 1958. Estimation of relationships for limited dependent variables. *Econometrica* 26.

Todaro, M. P. 1976. *Internal migration in developing countries.* Geneva: International Labor Office.

Turgot, A. J. Anne Robert Jacques. 1844. *Oeuvres de Turgot,* vol. 1. Paris.

Utami, Wydia, and Ihalauw, John. 1973. Some consequences of small farm size. *Bulletin of Indonesian Economic Studies* 9.

Vyas, V. S. 1970. Tenancy in a dynamic setting. *Economic and Political Weekly* 5: A.73–A.80.

Wannacott, Paul. 1962. Disguised and overt unemployment in underdeveloped economies. *Quarterly Journal of Economics* 76.

Weiss, Andrew. 1980. Job queues and layoffs in labor markets with flexible wages. *Journal of Political Economy* 88.

White, B. 1974. Agricultural Innovation: A Critical Note. Mimeographed. Jakarta: Agricultural Economic Survey.

White, Benjamin, and Makali. 1979. Wage labor and wage relations in Javanese agriculture. Paper presented at the Conference on Adjustment Mechanisms in Rural Labor Markets in Developing Areas, Hyderabad.

Williamson, Oliver E. 1975. *Markets and Hierarchies, Analysis and Anti-trust Implications: A Study in the Economics of Internal Organization.* New York: Free Press.

Yotopoulos, P. A., and Lau, L. J. 1974. On modeling of agricultural sector in developing economies. *Journal of Development Economics* 1: 105–27.

Yotopoulos, P.; Lau, L. J.; and Somel, K. 1970. Labor intensity and relative efficiency in Indian agriculture. *Food Research Institute Studies* 9: 43–55.

Yotopoulos, P., and Nugent, J. 1976. *Economics of development.* New York: Harper & Row.

Zellner, A. 1962. An efficient method for estimating seemingly unrelated regressions and tests for aggregation bias. *Journal of the American Statistical Association* 57: 348–68.

List of Contributors

T. Balaramaiah
  ICRISAT Center

Kalpana Bardhan
  Department of Economics
  University of California, Berkeley

Pranab K. Bardhan
  Department of Economics
  University of California, Berkeley

M. J. Bhende
  ICRISAT Center

Hans P. Binswanger
  The World Bank

Avishay Braverman
  The World Bank

Jan C. Breman
  Faculty of Social Sciences
  Erasmus University

Sanjay Dhar
  New York Federal Reserve Bank

Victor S. Doherty
  ICRISAT Center

Robert E. Evenson
  Department of Economics
  Yale University

R. D. Ghodake
  ICRISAT Center

Anwar Hafid
  Agroeconomic Survey
  Bogor, Indonesia

Yujiro Hayami
  Faculty of Economics
  Tokyo Metropolitan University

Gerald D. Jaynes
  Department of Economics
  Yale University

N. S. Jodha
  ICRISAT Center

Masao Kikuchi
  National Research Institute of
  Agricultural Economics
  Tokyo

K. G. Kshirsagar
  ICRISAT Center

P. S. S. Raju
  ICRISAT Center

Mark R. Rosenzweig
  Department of Economics
  University of Minnesota

James A. Roumasset
  Economics Department
  University of Hawaii

James G. Ryan
  ICRISAT Center

T. N. Srinivasan
  Department of Economics
  Yale University

Index

Absentee landlords. *See* Landownership
Additional Rural Incomes Survey (ARIS), 228, 230
Age, 31, 239; division of labor by, 147, 150, 162, 167, 183, 213; of female workers (West Bengal), 189; and wage rates, 32, 213
Agrarian reform, 44, 56, 62, 63–81. *See also* Land reform
Agricultural Labor Enquiry, 25
Agricultural Wages in India, 1970–71 (Directorate of Economics and Statistics), 30
Arrow–Debreu security markets, 55, 56
Asian Development Bank, 82
Aurepalle. *See* ICRISAT villages

Bangladesh, 20, 24, 27–33 passim, 37, 83, 85, 117
Bangladesh Rice Research Institute, 83
Bardhan, Kalpana, 32, 37, 175n8, 180n13
Bardhan, Pranab K., 7, 13, 16n9, 17n10, 23–32 passim, 33n18, 35, 36, 37, 39n21, 61n11, 67n3, 74, 81, 96, 100, 110, 146, 168, 169, 178, 183, 193, 204, 211, 224, 228, 239, 256, 259n19, 264, 275, 293
Bardoli. *See* India
Bawon system (Java), 117–29 passim
BIMAS (Javanese government program), 122
Binswanger, Hans P., 5n6, 18, 37, 40, 99, 263; coauthor, 7, 13, 22, 24, 32, 35, 37, 97
Boserup, Ester, 40, 170, 187, 188, 228
Braverman, Avishay, 3n2, 17, 22, 26, 28, 34, 36, 61n11, 62, 68n4, 71, 75–78 passim, 81
Breman, Jan C., 34, 165
Bullock labor price elasticities, 273, 274
Bullock market. *See* Markets

Cain, Mead T., 20, 32, 33
Cannan, Edwin, 47
Capital elasticities, 273
Capitalism: cooperative (Indian sugar factories), 131–42; monetized market, 44; money rent and, 51; share contracts and, 52, 58
Capital market. *See* Markets
Caste, 14, 144, 146, 155, 156–59, 162, 164, 165–66, 167; of female workers, 33, 150, 157, 185, 186, 187–88, 189, 192, 196–99, 206; -occupation correlation, 198–99; rank, and labor market participation, 156–57. *See also* Social differentiation
Ceblokan (kedokan, ngepak-ngedok) system (Java), 118–30 passim
Chayanov, A. K., 11
Cheung, Steven N. S., 16, 17, 44–48 passim, 52, 54–57, 62, 64, 72, 80, 82
Child labor, 32, 67, 147, 150, 162, 167, 170, 179, 194, 195, 228; in sugar factories, 135; and wage differentials, 178n12, 213, 214. *See also* Labor
Children: and work decisions/labor supply, 234, 240
China: female workers in, 186, 196nn10, 11
Classical and neoclassical economy, 15–16, 37, 44, 120n2; and labor supply, 211, 216, 230, 238, 240, 241; and land tenure, 44–45, 46, 48, 51, 52, 54, 62
Clay, Edward C., 23, 24, 30, 31, 35, 117
Cobb–Douglas production function, 79
Collateral, lack of. *See* Loans
Collusion, 5, 35–36, 150, 165, 168. *See also* Monopoly
Competition, labor market, 34, 38, 94, 211–12; and competitive equilibrium, 55, 56,

Economic Growth Center Book Publications

Werner Baer, *Industrialization and Economic Development in Brazil* (1965). Out of print.

Werner Baer and Isaac Kerstenetzky, eds., *Inflation and Growth in Latin America* (1964). Out of print.

Bela A. Balassa, *Trade Prospects for Developing Countries* (1964). Out of print.

Albert Berry and Miguel Urrutia, *Income Distribution in Colombia* (1976).

Hans P. Binswanger and Mark R. Rosenzweig, eds., *Contractual Arrangements, Employment, and Wages in Rural Labor Markets in Asia* (1983).

Thomas B. Birnberg and Stephen A. Resnick, *Colonial Development: An Econometric Study* (1975).

Benjamin I. Cohen, *Multinational Firms and Asian Exports* (1975).

Carlos F. Díaz Alejandro, *Essays on the Economic History of the Argentine Republic* (1970).

Robert Evenson and Yoav Kislev, *Agricultural Research and Productivity* (1975).

John C. H. Fei and Gustav Ranis, *Development of Labor Surplus Economy: Theory and Policy* (1964). Out of print.

Gerald K. Helleiner, *Peasant Agriculture, Government, and Economic Growth in Nigeria* (1966). Out of print.

Samuel P. S. Ho, *Economic Development of Taiwan, 1860–1970* (1978).

Nurul Islam, *Foreign Trade and Economic Controls in Development: The Case of United Pakistan* (1981).

Lawrence R. Klein and Kazushi Ohkawa, eds., *Economic Growth: The Japanese Experience since the Meiji Era* (1968). Out of print.

Paul W. Kuznets, *Economic Growth and Structure in the Republic of Korea* (1977).

A. Lamfalussy, *The United Kingdom and the Six* (1963). Out of print.

Markos J. Mamalakis, *The Growth and Structure of the Chilean Economy: From Independence to Allende* (1976).

Markos J. Mamalakis and Clark W. Reynolds, *Essays on the Chilean Economy* (1965). Out of print.

Donald C. Mead, *Growth and Structural Change in the Egyptian Economy* (1967). Out of print.

Richard Moorsteen and Raymond P. Powell, *The Soviet Capital Stock* (1966). Out of print.

Kazushi Ohkawa and Miyohei Shinohara, eds. (with Larry Meissner), *Patterns of Japanese Economic Development: A Quantitative Appraisal* (1979).

Douglas S. Paauw and John C. H. Fei, *The Transition in Open Dualistic Economies: Theory and Southeast Asian Experience* (1973).

Howard Pack, *Structural Change and Economic Policy in Israel* (1971).

Frederick L. Pryor, *Public Expenditures in Communist and Capitalist Nations* (1968). Out of print.

Gustav Ranis, ed., *Government and Economic Development* (1971).

Clark W. Reynolds, *The Mexican Economy: Twentieth-Century Structure and Growth* (1970). Out of print.

Lloyd G. Reynolds, *Image and Reality in Economic Development* (1977).

Lloyd G. Reynolds, ed., *Agriculture in Development Theory* (1975).

Lloyd G. Reynolds and Peter Gregory, *Wages, Productivity, and Industrialization in Puerto Rico* (1965). Out of print.

Donald R. Snodgrass, *Ceylon: An Export Economy in Transition* (1966). Out of print.

Due